Double Double

Double Double

How Tim Hortons Became a Canadian Way of Life, One Cup at a Time

Douglas Hunter

HarperCollins Publishers Ltd

Double Double
Copyright © 2012 by Douglas Hunter.

Published by HarperCollins Publishers Ltd

First edition

HarperCollins books may be purchased for educational, business, or sales promotional use through our Special Markets Department.

HarperCollins Publishers Ltd
2 Bloor Street East, 20th Floor
Toronto, Ontario, Canada
M4W 1A8

www.harpercollins.ca

Library and Archives Canada Cataloguing in Publication information is available upon request

ISBN 978-1-44340-673-4

Printed and bound in the United States
RRD 9 8 7 6 5 4 3 2 1

In memory of Miles Gilbert Horton

Contents

Introduction

In October 2010, I received an email from a vintage paper collector. Attached was an image of a coupon. "DROP IN AT . . . Tim Horton's Restaurant," read the black type on yellow paper announcing the opening of a new outlet, at 353 Yonge Street in Toronto, in what had become a four-restaurant chain. This coupon was good for ten cents off "1 doz. delicious donuts"—sixty five cents instead of the usual seventy-five—and promised "Over 50 Varieties to choose from." The bottom of the coupon listed the three other restaurant locations: 1961 Lawrence Avenue East, at Wayne; 3092 Kingston Road, at McCowan Road; and 111 Lakeshore Boulevard, in Port Credit, to the west of Toronto. A note on the back of the coupon, the collector explained, was dated December 10, 1963.

"I am trying to research these four locations and I can't find any information about them," she wrote me. "Do you know if these are Tim Hortons locations?"

In the official capsule history of Tim Hortons, these outlets and this formative period do not exist. The Toronto era of original restaurants bearing Horton's name remains a complicating prelude that the present "quick-service" (a.k.a. "fast food") restaurant juggernaut doesn't address. Officially, the restaurant chain's start is variously given as 1964, when the first franchise opened in Hamilton, or 1965, when the company Tim Donut Ltd. (TDL), the core legal entity of today's operation, was incorporated. And yet, as this collector's marvellous find reiterated, there *were* restaurants with Tim Horton's name on them in and around Toronto in 1963, and indeed doughnuts were involved.

Despite the fact that the collector said she couldn't find any information about these four restaurants, I had discussed them in *Open Ice,* my 1994 biography of the restaurant chain's eponymous founder. I presume the book was why she contacted me in the first place. Except for Horton himself, who had been dead for twenty years, I had interviewed pretty well all of the principal figures in the earliest days of Horton's restaurant ventures for that book and knew at once that this coupon upheld my research.

The coupon was promoting one of the very first restaurants Tim Horton set up in 1963 with a partner, Jim Charade, through a company called Timanjim Ltd. The three outlets listed at the bottom were burger drive-ins (the one in Port Credit had home-delivery chicken). The new restaurant at 353 Yonge had an open grill as well as a display of doughnuts that were made at and driven down from the very first Horton-branded doughnut outlet, called Tim Horton Do-Nut, a separate business from Timanjim Ltd. that Charade operated in Scarborough, for which he licensed Horton's name. The coupon most certainly was made by a fellow named Dennis Griggs, who produced signage and promotional coupons for Charade, at one point ran two of the early doughnut outlets in Toronto and was a good friend of Horton's. Charade and Griggs were part of a milieu of small businesspeople Horton had gotten to know in Scarborough, during his glory days as a star defenceman with the Toronto Maple Leafs, as he looked for opportunities beyond the NHL even as he was in the midst of winning four Stanley Cups between 1962 and 1967.

To say the least, the Tim Hortons restaurant story had evolved considerably since Charade and Horton opened the fourth outlet in the Timanjim partnership and stuck some doughnuts from Charade's Scarborough doughnut store in the window. But the story had also evolved considerably since I published Horton's biography in 1994. The chain, then privately held by Ron Joyce—who entered the story as the third franchisee at the original Hamilton store in 1965 and became Horton's business partner in 1966—had almost doubled in size since 1990 and was approaching 1,000 outlets when *Open Ice* came out. Nine days before I heard from the vintage paper collector in 2010, Tim Hortons, a publicly traded company listed on the Toronto and New York stock exchanges since 2006, had concluded its third quarter with an operating income of $133 million on net sales of $670.5 million from almost 4,000 outlets. But those numbers represented only Tim Hortons' take as the franchisor. Systemwide, the restaurants were generating more than $5 billion in revenues annually.

I had wanted to return to the Tim Hortons story—the story of the restaurant chain—ever since *Open Ice* was published in 1994. By sheer coincidence, I had just begun working on the book you are now reading when the email from the paper collector arrived. The corporate-origins story I had previously told was buried inside a sport biography. Many of the people I had interviewed, including Tim Horton's brother, Gerry, and his widow, Lori; his original partner, Jim Charade; the first franchisee at the celebrated "first" outlet in Hamilton, Spencer Brown; and Horton's close friend on the Leafs, Billy Harris, had since died. The memories and observations they had all shared with me were precious records of the company's origins and of Tim Horton the individual. With this book, I could revisit those early days in the context of the modern company that bears Horton's name.

I was fortunate to have my interviews with many key people who were no longer alive, as well as other significant figures, including Ron Joyce. (As a note of style, I have flagged quotations from those past interviews with the phrases "recalled for me" and "told me.") As I returned to these interviews, I found new issues to explore in the early history, among them the role of Harvey's, the landscape of coffee shops in Hamilton when the first franchise opened, how this modest coffee-and-doughnut enterprise fit into the nascent quick-service restaurant (QSR) sector, and how Tim's managed to emerge from this primordial entrepreneurial soup to dominate the Canadian QSR industry.

One of the most compelling issues today is the nature of identity and brand, of where (if anywhere) Tim Horton the man can be found in his namesake chain today. I also wanted to delve into how the chain has come to be embraced as a national cultural symbol in Canada, to the point of becoming entwined in the electoral fortunes of politicians and parties shaping brand identities of their own. I now also wanted to understand how Canada collectively was supposed to have somehow become Tim Hortons as well, which had not been the case almost twenty years ago. I also hoped to make sense of what the future might hold for such an iconic Canadian institution as it pursues expansion in the United States and confronts unprecedented competition in its own backyard.

NOTWITHSTANDING the Toronto backstory captured by the promotional flyer the vintage paper collector had come upon, the essential tale of Tim Hortons is that the chain began with the single franchise outlet in Hamilton in 1964, which led to a partnership between Horton and franchisee Ron Joyce in 1966. After Horton's death in a car accident in February 1974, the parent company, or franchisor, Tim Donut Ltd., became owned half by Joyce and half by Horton's widow, Lori, albeit with a trust instrument triggered by Horton's death that gave Joyce control. Joyce bought out Lori Horton in 1975 for $1 million and a company car. In 1987, Lori filed suit against Joyce and her lawyer at the time of the sale, claiming she had been mentally incompetent at the time of the sale because of drug and alcohol abuse and had been taken advantage of by a lowball purchase. The suit failed.

In 1995, Tim Hortons—or, as Canadians like to call it, Tim's, Timmy's or Timmy Ho's—merged with the American fast-food operation Wendy's International, which made Joyce the single largest shareholder in the combined firm and Tim Hortons a Delaware company, although head office remained in Oakville, Ontario, as it operated largely independent of Wendy's. Tim's continued to grow in Canada and made a renewed push to expand in the United States. Joyce retired in 2001, and in 2006, pressured by minority shareholder Nelson Peltz, Wendy's agreed to spin off Tim Hortons to release its suppressed value within the struggling Wendy's International. Tim Hortons went public in 2006, still a Delaware company; in 2009, the company was repatriated to Canada.

Tim's at that point had surpassed 3,000 outlets in Canada and 600 in the U.S. It had also passed McDonald's in sales in Canada in 2002 to become the country's largest restaurant chain, and in 2010 became the first Canadian chain to produce domestic system sales of $5 billion. By the end of fiscal 2011, there were more than 4,000 Tim Hortons outlets on the planet—3,295 in Canada, 714 in the U.S. and 5 in the United Arab Emirates.

This is not a conventional corporate history. It does not rigorously follow a chronology, and I do not devote any time to analyzing EBITDA or the company's merits as a stock investment. My effort here is detailed, but neither encyclopedic nor definitive. There are other books people can read for insights into particular matters. To know about Tim Horton himself (and even greater detail about the founding of the chain), you can track down *Open Ice,* as well as Lori Horton's reminiscences of life with Tim, *In Loving Memory.* Ron Joyce's *Always Fresh* provides the co-founder's perspective on his life and the company he ran. Steve Penfold's *The Donut: A Canadian History* is a very good study of the domestic business overall, especially its cultural elements.

Ron Buist's *Tales from Under the Rim* recounts his career in marketing at Tim Hortons, which included creating the hugely successful Roll Up the Rim to Win campaign. If you're interested in the issue of Canadian identity, you can try John Stackhouse's *Timbit Nation*.

You quickly learn when trying to write about Tim Hortons that, like many businesses, it is an entity with incredibly short event horizons. Every day seems to bring some new development, whether it is a new menu item, a quiet test-marketing of free Wi-Fi, quarterly financial results, a restaurant design prototype or news that a man has just been arrested for appearing naked at a drive-through. When I began researching and writing this book, the chain's connection to hockey star Sidney Crosby seemed especially important. A year later, far more critical was the remarkable role of Tim Hortons as an electioneering stop and as a litmus test of a politician's Canadian authenticity, which surged to the fore in the 2011 federal and Ontario provincial elections.

It became important for me not to be sidetracked by the staccato chatter of the relentless Tim Hortons news stream, but rather to focus on the larger themes that had developed over the enterprise's life. Those themes, which began gathering momentum at the very beginning of the restaurant chain, and indeed were surfacing when the paper collector's flyer was printed in late 1963, will continue to inform the future trajectory of this company. Ultimately, these themes all come back to the issue of brand.

This is not an official history. It is neither endorsed nor approved by the company. While I received cooperation from its communications department in having certain factual questions answered and in arranging for the visit to the original Tim Horton Children's Foundation camp at Lorimer Lake, my request for a formal interview with any senior executive to address my broader questions about issues such as brand management went unfulfilled. I have been left to my own devices, and the opinions of experts I sought out, to answer those questions.

This is a more personal story than anything I ha
That is because I found myself reliving the proc
people seventeen or eighteen years ago, many of wh
with us, and also because, as someone over the age of fifty who wa
born and raised in Hamilton, the veritable ground zero of the Tim Hortons experience, I was alive before the first Tim's opened in the city and have gotten older with it, as a customer and as an observer. My own experiences in researching this story, past as well as present, inform the narrative, just as in successive chapters the past tends to inform the company's present state and future opportunities and challenges.

I have a pretty good idea where Tim Hortons came from and where it's been. I'm not entirely sure of where it's headed as an iconic Canadian brand with high expectations for conquering the problematic American market. In another eighteen years, I might want to explore the answer. Depending on how the brand is managed (and how well the company endures), those future consumers may know even less about who Tim Horton was, or they might know much more, than consumers do today. Tim Horton is, as I explain, a ghost in the machine of the chain that he founded. My persistent fascination with the idea of a flesh-and-blood individual and a commercial persona drove much of my curiosity as I travelled to disparate places in pursuit of answers, among them the site of Jim Charade's Scarborough doughnut store, the children's camp at Lorimer Lake, the original franchise outlet in Hamilton and the Tim Hortons outlets of midtown Manhattan. The research turned into a big, extended Tim's run, and I sampled a lot of product along the way, more than I probably should have. I returned slightly larger, and a lot wiser. I understand better than I did eighteen years ago how this chain got started. I hope that I can help the reader better appreciate where it's been, where it might be going and if, as Canadians, we're all going along with it.

1

Turning the Key: The Franchising Brandscape

"Eight hundred seventy thousand!" I heard the woman exclaim to her friend as they passed on my left, heading in the opposite direction. She didn't say 870,000 of *what,* but she could only have meant dollars. And as we were at The Franchise Show, in late February 2011 at Hall H of the Toronto Congress Centre, out by Pearson International Airport, those dollars could only have referred to what is known as the turnkey cost of getting up and running in some kind of franchise.

The woman and her friend apparently hadn't given up on their ownership dreams, as they were walking down Aisle 600, deeper into the show's exhibits, rather than bolting for the exit. They were running a gauntlet of restaurant and pub concepts—to their left were Select Sandwich/Urban Kitchen and Panago Pizza, and to their right, Sunnyside Grill and D'Arcy McGee's.

Many other concepts that had nothing to do with food were pitching show-goers. The would-be and actual franchise chains included a spa concept, a deck and solar energy outfit, pet supplies, children's tutoring, flooring, lighting, cut flowers, courier services, landscaping, teeth whitening and weight loss. The annual show's producer is the Canadian Franchise Association, a trade group of franchisors formed in 1967 that claims to be the "national voice of franchising" in Canada, with almost 500 corporate members. It serves as a lobby group on franchise-related legislation, a role that heated up when Ontario produced its first franchise statute, the Wishart Act of 2000, which introduced mandatory disclosure standards for information that franchisors provide to prospective franchisees.

At the time of the Wishart Act, the CFA had about 300 members, a number that increased about 40 percent over the next decade. Even so, the CFA does not represent the entirety of the Canadian franchise industry. It has no auto manufacturers as members, despite the fact that auto dealerships represent one of the most significant franchise categories. Nor are there any supermarket chains. Gas station franchisors are also few in number—Petro-Canada was a lone member from that category at the time of the Wishart Act hearings, but it no longer belongs. Shell Canada does belong, and so does Canadian Tire, which operates gas stations in addition to its retail stores and auto-service centres.

The CFA membership nevertheless contains a bewildering array of franchising concepts, gathered in its annual directory into fifty categories. The exhibitors at the February 2011 show were a mere selection of the many different concepts in the CFA membership looking for new franchisees to help them expand, or simply to begin turning a nascent business of a few outlets into a profit-spewing chain.

Franchising is a very old concept, at least as old as the ancient practice of monarchs awarding individuals the right to collect taxes as "tax farmers." In the old sense of the word, the awarding of a telecommunications licence by the Canadian Radio-television and Telecommunications Commission is a form of franchising. But for the exhibitors at the CFA show looking for franchisees (and their money), and the show-goers looking for a franchisor in which to invest, franchising involves a business system. In return for an initial franchisee fee, an ongoing royalty and an advertising fee, a franchisor allows a franchisee to operate a business, usually called a unit franchise. The franchisee can use the franchisor's trademarks and other intellectual property, sell its proprietary products or services and tap into the business expertise and experience of the head office. In return, the franchisor supports the franchisee with advice, business systems, training, advertising and marketing, new product development and often the products it sells or the ingredients and equipment it needs to make them.

Although franchising promoters routinely tout the appeal of "owning your own business," in reality a franchisee can own precious little for the capital they invest. In the restaurant business, for example, they don't always own the actual restaurant building or hold the head lease on the land on which it is built or on the commercial space being rented. They can only sell their franchise at a profit if they are assigned the intangible goodwill that accumulates in the business. A franchise agreement has a fixed term, and a franchisor can sue to terminate an agreement if it decides a franchisee isn't living up to the letter of the franchise agreement or is behaving in a way that imperils the trademarks. Franchisees also surrender a tremendous amount of authority over their operations, generally granting the franchisor the right to inspect their books and their premises. One could argue that the better the franchise system is, the more controlling it is of a franchisee's behaviour and the nosier it is about its day-to-day operations. To operate a unit franchise is to surrender to the Borg: there can be no discernible difference between the individual franchise and the franchise system overall, beyond the variations approved by the franchisor. If there could be, there would be no point to franchising, which is ultimately about replication.

For all the tribulations, franchising appeals to businesses looking to expand into a chain, as well as to people looking for a sure thing in which to invest and work. The model is praised for the way it allows small business capital to participate profitably in the economy (and with hopefully lower risks) by leveraging the expertise and economies of scale of a much larger corporation. Rather than having to come up with their own system or product, franchisees buy into that of the franchisor. They gain the right to deal in a proven product or service that has been developed and continuously fine-tuned by the franchisor's professionals, and they benefit from the ongoing innovations. They can gain from economies of scale in purchasing made by the franchisor, or in supply contracts arranged by or through it. They can reap the benefits of advertising and promotional campaigns that are produced by major ad agencies and reach national audiences in a way they could never afford if they had to pay for such promotions themselves.

From the franchisor's side of the equation, one of the most appealing aspects of the system is that it turns to these contracted operators to raise the capital (some of it of their own, much of it often through bank loans) necessary to open, run and periodically refurbish an outlet. Still, a franchisor's own needs for capital remain substantial if it wishes to follow the model adhered to by Tim Hortons* and other enterprises and acquires the property required for an outlet. And franchising carries undeniable risks for the franchisor. For all the fine print that can be crammed into a franchise agreement, the typical franchisee is still an independent operator, not an employee who can be readily hired, fired or reassigned. Many franchise systems have foundered on poor choices of franchisees, particularly when expanding into new markets.

Franchising wouldn't work if consumers didn't like it, too. Firm numbers are hard to come by for Canada, but here are a few. In 2004, there were reportedly 1,327 franchisors, with 63,642 franchisees, bringing in

* Throughout this book I have used "Tim Hortons" generically to describe the parent company that serves as franchisor of the restaurants that bear this name. The company was incorporated as Tim Hortons Inc. when it was repatriated to Canada in 2009. Its subsidiaries include TDL Group Corp., the largest Canadian subsidiary; Tim Donut Ltd., the original legal entity dating back to 1965; and the American subsidiary Tim Hortons USA Inc. For simplicity's sake, I have called all restaurants "Tim Hortons," irrespective of historic signage variants, unless the historic name is pertinent to the narrative.

some US$90 billion in sales, or about 10 percent of the country's GDP. In 2006, it was estimated that about one in five consumer dollars spent on goods and services went to franchises, which employed about a million people. At the time of the 2011 show, the CFA asserted that Canada had more than 1,200 franchise systems (of which "400 plus" were CFA members) and more than 78,000 franchise locations. A 2005 report on Canadian franchise law, prepared by Jeffrey P. Hoffman of the legal firm Gowlings, asserted that in Ontario, franchising's share of retail spending "is fast approaching 50%. It has moved from a somewhat novel alternative distribution option to one of the first distribution choices considered by a wide variety of businesses."

Modern franchising dates back to the Singer Sewing Machine Company, which began franchising distributors in the 1850s. General Motors launched dealer franchising in 1898, and in the 1930s oil companies turned to franchising to open service stations. Canadian Tire was an early retail franchisor, opening its first associate store in Hamilton, Ontario, in 1934. After the Second World War, franchising began to spread to other business sectors as a way to profit from the rise of brand-based consumer-product ubiquity, and at the same time to promote its hegemony. When the national electronic media of television came to the fore, businesses in general recognized the appeal, and the inevitability, of national brands (both products and services) because of the centralized opportunities of promotion. Advances in transportation, including commercial aircraft and highways, made it possible to deliver advertised-brand goods efficiently across large regions, nations and even hemispheres.

Although some major QSR chains, like McDonald's and Burger King, began to take shape in the 1950s, franchising as a means of creating restaurant chains came into its own in the 1960s. It took particular hold in the QSR sector, but it also spread to casual dining. Today, restaurants (including bars and specialty food and beverage retailing) may comprise the most active area of franchising.

The CFA show's exhibition hall was a simmering stew of food franchising opportunities. Casual-dining and bar/pub concepts (whose turnkey costs I suspect inspired the woman's exclamation) included sector heavyweight Boston Pizza, and Prime Restaurants' casual-dining concepts Casey's Grill/Bar and East Side Mario's, as well as its pubs Fionn MacCool's and D'Arcy McGee's. Other exhibitors in the broad spectrum of casual dining included Firkin Pubs, Il Fornello (which positions itself as a "fine dining" concept), Ricky's All Day Grill and Shoeless Joe's Sports Grill. Anyone considering a franchise investment in this sector would likely have been investigating a number of CFA members who weren't exhibiting. Cara Operations alone has Kelsey's, Montana's Cookhouse, Milestones Grill & Bar and Swiss Chalet. Other contenders in the exhibition included The Keg Steakhouse and Bar, Moxie's Classic Grill, Applebee's, Mandarin, Pizza Hut and Ponderosa Steakhouse.

A mélange of restaurants and niche products comprised the show's QSR sector. There were burger joints, chicken joints, delis, ice-cream parlours, pizza parlours, snack treats, new contenders in corporatized ethnic food, and more: Baskin-Robbins, BeaverTails, Cultures, Dairy Queen, Druxy's, Fatburger, Mary Brown's Famous Chicken & Taters!, New Orleans Pizza, OPA Souvlaki of Greece, Orange Julius, Pita Pit, Pizza Nova, Pizza Pizza, Quiznos, Smoke's Poutinerie, Sushi Shop, TacoTime, Tandori and Wok Box Fresh Asian Kitchen.

As with casual dining, not every CFA member in the QSR sector was on hand. The CFA listed forty-nine businesses in its 2011 directory just under the category "food: baked goods/coffee/donuts." Most were regional players, and many were little more than glimmerings of franchising greatness in the eyes of their concept owners. Country Style, which under previous owners had been rocked by bad publicity surrounding poor relations with franchisees, a rash of outlet closings and a 2001 filing for protection from creditors, was on hand, working hard under new ownership with free samples as it pitched its fresh concept as an upscale café/bistro, not a down-market coffee-and-doughnut shop. But the cream of the amorphous coffee/café/bakery sector of QSR otherwise was not on hand.

There was no Timothy's Coffees of the World, a Toronto-based chain acquired by Vermont's Green Mountain Coffee Roasters, Inc. in November 2009. Nor could one find Second Cup, which had gone public on the Toronto exchange in 2004 and called itself "the largest Canadian-owned specialty coffee retailer," with more than 340 Canadian outlets and another 50-plus internationally. Also absent was a chief competitor of Timothy's and Second Cup in specialty-coffee retailing, Starbucks, which had 799 Canadian outlets by October 2010.

Starbucks was missing because Starbucks is not in the franchising business—a reminder that not all of the QSR industry operates on a franchise model. Most Starbucks outlets in North America are corporate-owned; the rest are licensed outlets, a strong growth area for the chain, by which established businesses with a presence in consumer retailing (such as Indigo bookstores) are home to a Starbucks. And among crossover QSR competitors in quick meals, there was no Harvey's (another Cara property), Burger King, Subway, McDonald's or A&W Canada.

The franchisor most notably absent was Tim Hortons, a CFA member since 1993, whose outlets ring up more sales than any QSR restaurant system in Canada by a long shot. It had passed McDonald's as Canada's top QSR chain on revenues in 2002 and became the first QSR to record $5 billion in Canadian systemwide sales in fiscal 2010, building a 25 percent sales lead over the Golden Arches, its nearest rival. While absent in corporate fact, Tim's had an undeniable presence: more than a few of the show-goers were wandering the aisles holding a Tim Hortons coffee. The twenty-fifth-anniversary Roll Up the Rim contest was underway, and right next door to the Congress Centre on Airport Road was a Tim's outlet, with a separate drive-through kiosk deeper in the adjoining parking lot. Show-goers could literally taste the opportunity Tim's represented, but could not touch it. They had a better chance of winning one of the contest's forty Toyota Matrix XRS vehicles than they did of landing a Tim's franchise.

In the most recent fiscal year, 2010, which had ended on January 2, 2011, Tim's had opened 149 new Canadian outlets, using its own supply of prospective and existing franchisees as well as contracted operators. With more than 3,100 locations in the country, Tim Hortons' desire to find new Canadian franchisees has long been outstripped by the challenge of finding new territories in which to plant new outlets. Nevertheless, the company would open another 175 in fiscal 2011, and is aiming to have 4,000 before it exhausts its domestic expansion opportunities. It can open a franchise pretty well anywhere it chooses in Canada (three opened in Nunavut in 2010) and not lack for known candidates to run it. There was no shortage of people beyond the doors of the Congress Centre who yearned for the chance. At head office in Oakville, Ontario, the company maintains a list of prospective franchisees. It has more than 3,000 names on it: about one for every Canadian outlet that already exists, or about three for every single new franchise it ever hopes to open in this country.

The CFA trade show was full of people looking for restaurant opportunities, who would never find the route to a Tim Hortons outlet in the bustling aisles, made slightly desperate by intonations of large six-figure dollar sums. A few months later, I dropped in on a Tim's franchisee who had managed to wind up with six of them.

2

Greektown: At Danforth and Logan with a Tim Hortons Franchisee

I HADN'T SEEN CAM MACDONALD in at least twenty years when I heard that he and his wife, Karen, had six Tim Hortons franchises. For someone like me, born and raised in Hamilton, Ontario, learning that a fellow Hamiltonian from your youth had managed to end up with a personal suzerainty of half a dozen Tim's outlets is like learning they own the defensive backfield of the CFL's Ti-Cats. Such good fortune scarcely seems possible or logical, regardless of the individual's qualities. The fact that these franchises weren't in Hamilton, but in Toronto, only made Cam's achievement more intriguing. I called my dad, who called Cam's older brother Sandy, who gave my dad Cam's phone number.

I nearly slew-footed my overture to have Cam tell me about his odyssey into multiple Tim Hortons proprietorships by referring to his considerably older brother, Sandy, as his father. Out of touch for so long, I had badly scrambled the kinship network of Hamilton's MacDonald clan, but Cam waved it off: "I'm a younger, nicer version of Sandy." Cam and Sandy, as well as Keith, are sons of Jack MacDonald, a fixture of city politics who died in May 2010. The MacDonald boys perpetuate Jack's delight in putting people on, in testing them to see what they're made of, to figure out how they tick, to see if they'll credulously take the bait, push back or play along. It's a quality that served Jack MacDonald well in quickly measuring up people through decades of public life, and I was reminded of it when Cam related the story of his sister's funeral in 2003.

"Let me tell you a MacDonald story," he said to me at a table near the door of his main Tim Hortons outlet, at the southeast corner of Danforth and Logan avenues in Toronto's Greektown, as I nursed a coffee (cream only) and ate a ham BELT on a twelve-grain bagel.

I was confused at first, thinking Cam was trying to tell me a story about Tim Hortons' chief QSR rival, the McDonald's chain. "No, the *MacDonald family,*" he corrected me, then added, "I hear a lot of jokes about a MacDonald running a Tim Hortons," before proceeding with the story.

The family was holding a memorial service for his sister Nancy. In March 1993, Cam had been one month into running his first Tim Hortons franchise, the outlet we were sitting in, when Nancy died suddenly, at 54. His brothers introduced him to a woman who had come to pay her respects. When they told her he was a Tim's franchisee, her expression hardened.

"I need to talk to you about the Dutchie," she said, all commiseration having given way to all business, and she launched into a tirade about the controversy that had recently erupted over the chain's new parbaking system.

"Nancy is propped up at forty-five degrees across the room," Cam reminded me, as this stranger lambasted him over the legitimacy of the company's "always fresh" slogan and fretted over what the new baking system might do to her beloved Dutchie, the raisin-studded yeast doughnut that Tim Hortons invented.

The MacDonald brothers closed ranks and launched an impromptu counteroffensive, a routine in which every one of them was the straight man. They persuaded the woman that their family was so close to the

Tim Hortons chain, so deeply immersed in its history, that nothing bad could ever possibly happen to the Dutchie. Why, the Dutchie had *almost* been named the Nancy. That's right: their dear departed sister, lying in state in that very room, had come *this close* to having this woman's beloved doughnut named after her. Impressed and mollified, the woman abandoned her rant.

Their father, Jack, came over after Cam's accuser had withdrawn. "What are you boys up to?" They told him about the ruse they had just pulled off, and Jack smiled and said, "Nancy would have enjoyed that." I never knew Nancy, but Cam assured me, as he sipped a Tim Hortons coffee, "She would have."

IN A SPEECH to the Yonge Bloor Bay Business Association in January 1969, George B. Sukornyk, president of Harvey's Foods Ltd., held forth on the key ingredients to running a successful franchising business. At the time, Sukornyk was an oft-quoted authority on what was then called fast-food franchising. Harvey's Foods was a public company that had been listed on the Toronto exchange in 1967 and oversaw a growing chain of Harvey's grill outlets and a handful of Swiss Chalet barbecue chicken restaurants. Sukornyk told his audience that the ideal franchise owner was someone who worked hard, but also was a man between the age of thirty-nine and forty-five who had never made more than $8,000 a year, which was then a middle-class income.

"We've never taken a man who made more," Sukornyk told his audience with a smile. "He wouldn't take the abuse and controls we inflict upon him." His company's franchise owners, he related, included former engineers, accountants, policemen, a carpenter and his own barber. Only one had been in the restaurant business before. Their common features were age, low income and "the consequent fear of impoverished old age."

More than forty years later, the profile of the typical franchise operator defies a neat categorization, although it's certainly no longer the case that a franchisee needs to be (or is assumed to be) a man. Women are now prime candidates, and according to a 2008 survey of franchisees conducted by Research Strategy Group for the Canadian law firm Gowlings, women among them were less inclined to have considered opening an independent business—36 percent, compared to 50 percent of men who had become franchisees.

But certain truths endure about the typical franchisee, especially the aspiring ones. Recessions seem to have a way of creating demand for franchises. People lose their jobs, receive settlements and, with little hope or desire of returning to the business sector or corporate world that unceremoniously expelled them, turn to the idea of going into business for themselves. That idea quickly leads them to consider the option of a franchise rather than an independent start-up. The Gowlings survey showed 42 percent of franchisees had been an employee when they turned to their new business venture. It also found that a remarkable 46 percent of franchise owners who had not considered starting an independent business only looked at one franchise concept: something about one franchise system (they liked eating there?) caught their eye.

Hard data is elusive, but it probably remains as true today as it was when Sukornyk addressed his audience that franchisees enter the business from all walks of life. Although some restaurant franchisees have previous experience in the business, it is fairly safe to say that, like Cam MacDonald, most do not. They rely on the franchisor's system to tell them how to run a restaurant profitably.

To understand the story of Cam MacDonald's foray into Tim Hortons franchising, you need a tour of the backstory of the MacDonald clan. His dad, Jack, had first been elected to Hamilton's city council in 1949, at the age of twenty-two, and served continuously as an alderman until 1976, when he began a one-term stint as mayor. Smilin' Jack, as many constituents (admirers and otherwise) knew him, was a silver-maned civic booster and a lifelong, loyal political Conservative. He never served federally (an unsuccessful campaign in 1984, which he lost to Liberal Sheila Copps, daughter of a legendary mayor, Vic Copps, was the end of his political run), but Jack had long been a key member of the local party machinery. When John Diefenbaker, the Conservative prime minister from 1957 to 1963, died in 1979, MacDonald was an honorary pallbearer.

I got to know Jack in his retirement years, in the early 1990s, and had especially enjoyed Jack's reminiscences of elbows-out city politics. Amid all the stories Jack had told me about decades of adventures on city council was one that Cam was pleased to recount: in 1964, when a zoning change for an old Esso station on Ottawa Street in Hamilton's East End was required so that it could become the first Tim Horton coffee-and-doughnut restaurant franchise, it was the Ward 8 alderman, Jack MacDonald, who finessed the bylaw through council.

It seemed fitting, then, that a son of the politician who had helped the original Tim Hortons franchise set up shop in Hamilton would end up becoming one of the hugely successful chain's multiple franchisees—and that a grandson of Jack's, Sandy's son, Jay, would also become a franchisee, moving to the United States for the opportunity to open a restaurant in Warren, Pennsylvania.

The fact that the MacDonald household had lived and breathed municipal politics would not be inconsequential where Cam's career as a Tim Hortons franchisee is concerned. But knowing the political pedigree of the MacDonald family can tempt you to connect dots that suggest that a nepotistic Conservative cabal allowed Cam to breach the ranks of Canadian franchisees, ranks that otherwise can seem so closed that a Senate or Supreme Court appointment looks like a more reasonable ambition. The chain's co-founder, Ron Joyce, whose waterfront home in Burlington is across the harbour from Hamilton, has long been involved in Conservative party activities. While Joyce is no longer associated with the company, having retired from active duty in 2001, Mike Harris, the Conservative premier of Ontario from 1995 to 2002, sits on the board of the charitable Tim Horton Children's Foundation. As a columnist in his retirement years for *The Hamilton Spectator,* Jack MacDonald championed (with occasional reservations) Harris's Common Sense Revolution. And, as we'll see, the branding of the federal and Ontario Conservative parties became deeply intertwined with Tim Hortons, producing conjoined public images as a party and a restaurant chain of ordinary Canadians. In the fall of 2011, Tim Hudak, leader of Ontario's Progressive Conservatives, seemed to spend much of the provincial election campaign being photographed meeting and greeting in Tim Hortons outlets and sporting a takeout cup of coffee.

But where Cam MacDonald and Tim Hortons are concerned, the dots are not neatly connected with the party. They lead, instead, back into the city's industrial East End, where the Tim Hortons franchising operation got its start in 1964, with Jack MacDonald's help.

Another necessary bit of backstory: I had gotten to know the MacDonald clan of Hamilton through competitive sailing, in a three-person dinghy class called the Lightning, in which my own dad had been racing since the 1950s. In my teens and early twenties, I mainly raced against, but sometimes with, all of the sailing MacDonalds, Cam included. Like Cam's cousin Larry Jr., who became a sail maker, and Cam's brother Sandy, who opened a marina in Hamilton, I too ended up in the sailing business, in my case as a journalist, author and magazine editor. I left the boating publishing biz (after an interregnum spell as a staff writer at the *Financial Post*) in 1991, when I resigned my editorship at *Canadian Yachting*. Two years later, Cam came through the door of *Canadian Yachting* as an ad sales rep. We had passed like ships unseen over the horizon, and I had to ask Cam how he had wound up there after I left.

"I was working at Samuel Strapping, in industrial sales. I got bounced in the downturn." He responded to an ad for a sales rep for *Canadian*

Yachting, which was published in Mississauga, Ontario, and was hired. Cam was soon promoted to publisher, but recreational marine publishing in Canada made for tough slogging, and through (and with) his wife, Karen, the grand opportunity of Tim Hortons arose.

Karen's dad had been in the same sort of east-end Hamilton enterprise as Cam's dad and uncle, who had a plumbing contracting business. Karen's family had a contracting firm called Elliott Mechanical. (Cam and Karen actually met on vacation, in Athens, at the Parthenon. Cam's dad, Jack, would quip at their wedding that Cam had to travel eight thousand miles to meet a woman who lived eight minutes from him.) Buffeted by economic headwinds, Karen's dad had wound up the company, leaving her brothers, Brian and Gary, to pursue other avenues of opportunity. The Elliott brothers got their break in Barrie, a fast-growing city about an hour's drive north of Toronto that was turning into a bedroom community of the provincial capital.

"The boys started with Tim Hortons, and they worked their asses off," Cam explained. "And if you work your ass off with Tim Hortons, you get rewarded." After taking over one existing franchise and proving themselves, they expanded to five in that city.

In 1995, Tim Hortons was acquired by the U.S.–based burger chain Wendy's International in a corporate merger; there were about 1,000 Tim Hortons outlets, and the chain was rapidly expanding. In 1998, the Elliott brothers were offered a sixth outlet, closer to Toronto, in Newmarket. Brian and Gary turned to their sister and her husband and made them an offer in turn: Cam could manage the Newmarket outlet for them. If he learned the ropes, if he proved himself and did a bang-up job, he too could be rewarded.

Cam and Karen moved to Newmarket, and Cam, as the hands-on manager, began a long apprenticeship that was also an evaluation, a corporate sizing-up of what made him tick. After four years in Newmarket, Cam and Karen got their chance to join Brian and Gary Elliott as franchisees when they were offered an existing outlet, the one Cam and I were sitting in at Logan and Danforth. Tim Hortons leases the space in the building, a former Canadian Imperial Bank of Commerce branch. ("It's owned by the pool hall upstairs," Cam said, then corrected himself. "The Billiards Academy. I haven't met any graduates," he deadpanned.) It was then a corporate-owned store co-branded with an adjoining Wendy's. A TD Canada Trust branch on the northwest corner affirms that this intersection has long marked the commercial heart of Greektown.

In February 2003, Cam and Karen became newly minted franchisees of this Tim Hortons—Wendy's would withdraw from the building after the burger chain spun off Tim Hortons in 2006. Today, Cam and Karen MacDonald can vie with Brian and Gary Elliott for familial franchise bragging rights: they now have four other outlets along the Danforth, and a sixth outlet nearby, at Coxwell and O'Connor.

All of which is a bit of a roundabout way of explaining why Tim Hortons doesn't bother with a booth at The Franchise Show.

MONEY ISN'T NEARLY ENOUGH to secure a Tim Hortons franchise in Canada. In fact, money alone cannot get you through the door of a restaurant of your own. Nor will having a plot of land that you think would be ideal for an outlet. The company's real estate department is on the constant prowl for sites, both for new franchises and more advantageous locations of existing ones. While it listens to credible overtures, the company, not a prospective franchisee, generally defines local market opportunities, chooses the appropriate store configuration and creates the outlet. Then it finds the right person to run it.

The brand has long been so strong, and the opportunities for new franchises so increasingly narrow as expansion has infiltrated every nook and cranny of much of the available Canadian marketplace, that the company has had the luxury of choosing its franchisees judiciously.

The company operates "a comprehensive restaurant owner screening and recruitment process that employs multi-level interviews with our senior operations management and requires candidates to work two to three different shifts in an existing restaurant owner's restaurant," as the 2010 annual report explained. This careful grooming and selection in turn has only strengthened the brand.

Tim Hortons is not unlike other franchise operations in that, once it has an operator it likes, it prioritizes them for further expansion plans. "If you get a store and you hit the ball—you run the store properly and make the product properly and serve the customers properly—you'll get another opportunity," Cam MacDonald said.

Franchising companies in general like to have franchisees with multiple outlets. It's far better for both the franchisor and the franchisees for one franchisee to have three outlets than for three to have three. Fewer absolute numbers of franchisees mean fewer potential headaches for the company arising from the human factor. Expansion can capitalize on the experience of existing franchisees who are awarded new outlets; a single franchisee also can spread costs across multiple outlets and improve their own profitability.

Developing multiple-store franchisees means that the company can infill a particular region with the franchise industry's retail version of carpet-bombing, saturating or "intensifying" the terrain with outlets without creating turf wars between single-outlet franchisees. A multiple-outlet franchisee can tolerate some poaching or cannibalization of business from their existing stores if additional outlets allow them to net ahead.

Let's say an existing outlet is doing $100,000 in sales over a given period. Opening another outlet a few blocks away could conceivably reduce sales of the established outlet to $90,000. But if the new outlet does $90,000 in business and is also run by the same franchisee, netting $180,000 from two outlets where they were previously generating $100,000 from one can be an attractive proposition, especially if the additional outlet can relieve operating costs such as staffing borne by the single original store. That additional outlet can also discourage a rival concept from attempting to establish itself in the area.

Tim Hortons outlets traditionally have come in two forms, "standard" and "satellite." The terminology is typical of the QSR industry, and can be a little confusing. Satellite outlets are smaller, secondary stores in a given area that may not provide the full services and menu of a standard outlet. In Tim Hortons parlance, these lesser, satellite stores are also referred to as "non-standard." Standard stores have a dining area, a kitchen and, where permitted, a drive-through, and, except for urban storefronts, they are free-standing buildings. As opportunities shrink in established markets to open standard stores, Tim's has been figuring out how to make them even smaller. In its 2010 annual report, the company said a standard outlet on average was 1,400 to 3,090 square feet, but changed that to 1,000 to 3,080 square feet in 2011. Development otherwise has favoured the "non-standard" outlets found in institutional settings like offices, airports, colleges and universities, hospitals, grocery stores, gas bars and convenience stores. These non-standard formats, which range from 150 to 1,000 square feet, include smaller-scale stores that may have a full kitchen with a full menu range; drive-through-only outlets at roadside service centres; outlets that operate seasonally in sports facilities; and self-serve kiosks that are embedded in other retail businesses.

The overall range of store types, then, is considerable, and it's important to keep in mind that when Tim Hortons talks about having a certain number of stores overall or in a given territory, unless it provides distinctions, it is counting the standard store with seating and a drive-through in equal weight to an unstaffed self-serve kiosk in a supermarket. To complicate matters, Tim's separately counts self-serve kiosks, which are otherwise discussed as part of its non-standard formats (and can include carts), when listing its outlets in various states and provinces. All three formats—standard, non-standard and self-serve kiosks—are franchised by the company, and only standard and non-standard stores are ever operated as corporate outlets.

Tim Hortons' non-standard outlets include concepts comparable to the STO ("small town oil") concepts of McDonald's, in which restaurants with limited menus share space with the convenience store of a service station. Tim Hortons in the past developed non-standards with Petro-Canada, and since 2002 has been working in concert with Imperial Oil's Esso service centres and its On the Run convenience stores.

Cam MacDonald's unusual Toronto store at Danforth and Greenwood is something of a variation. Next to an Esso service station is the historic Allenby (later the Roxy) Theatre, which once screened *The Rocky Horror Picture Show* ad infinitum/nauseam. MacDonald and Tim Hortons converted the property, which is listed with the Toronto Historical Board, into a restaurant that shares the interior with an Esso On the Run. The theatre's interior is long gone, except for some elements that are true to the original lobby. The exterior has been fully restored, complete with the Allenby name and an array of LED bulbs disguised in period-appropriate housings. In lieu of a typical trademark Tim Hortons sign, the marquee reads TIM HORTONS where film titles were once displayed. In another location, this might have been a non-standard outlet, but because the compact restaurant has its own Always Fresh baking equipment and seating for thirty-two, it's pretty much a stand-alone standard outlet.

It is common for a franchisor like Tim Hortons to pursue expansion by granting a standard outlet to a franchisee, and then once this outlet is performing satisfactorily to have the franchisee open satellites. Kiosks have been awarded to franchisees as additional outlets that, with minimal servicing, can generate income by selling goods produced in one of their other stores. In this way, franchisees have come to average 3.1 outlets each. The unquestioned king of Tim's franchises is Moncton's Gary O'Neill, who secured his first one in

1974, only weeks before Tim Horton died. O'Neill is credited with pioneering the Timbits minor sports program and persuading Ron Joyce to open a second Tim Horton Camp for underprivileged children down east. He operates a true empire of thirty-four outlets in New Brunswick through his company, Corey Craig (named after his two sons), producing a per-capita density that allows Moncton to challenge Hamilton and St. Catharines in Ontario for bragging rights as the most serviced Tim Hortons community on the planet surface.

Before the switch to the Always Fresh parbaking system, which was rolled out from 2002 to 2004, a standard Tim Hortons outlet at the hub of a franchisee's personal fiefdom of stores was the central baking facility, producing doughnuts and other goods two or three times a day and distributing them to the satellite operations by delivery truck. With the switch to parbaking, on-site baking (at least, finishing-off baking) has been introduced to satellite operations as well. It remains the case that franchisees who develop mini-empires will have perhaps one standard store and two smaller satellite operations, with the standard store housing the office (as Cam and Karen MacDonald's Danforth and Logan outlet does) and staffing being managed across multiple sites. Though some franchisees have amassed a network that includes more than one standard outlet, the idea of a standard outlet with a number of smaller satellite operations in a given geographic area remains a common configuration. It has allowed Tim Hortons franchisees to expand their empires without having to invest exclusively in full stores.

Smaller satellite stores have been the means by which leading franchisors such as Tim Hortons have wrested the greatest possible revenue out of a fruitful territory without overdoing it with large outlets. Bear in mind, however, that like McDonald's, Tim Hortons generally doesn't assign exclusive territories to franchisees. If it thinks a region can support another outlet of whatever particular size and configuration, it will install one, with or without the participation of an existing franchisee. But it's fundamentally in the best interest of the company not to swamp a market, squander money, annoy valuable existing franchisees or create ugly rivalries between neighbouring franchisees. Whether Tim Hortons can avoid oversaturating markets in Canada as it continues to seek growth amid ever more limited opportunities with ever smaller outlet formats is another question.

People who get into franchising—and succeed at it—are team players by nature, as it's not a business model for lone wolves and iconoclasts. Franchisees are attracted by a proven turnkey system, and the promise of being awarded additional franchises can reinforce an already strong culture of mutual loyalty, both within the franchisee ranks and between franchisees and head office. They're all in it together. With Tim's, above and beyond their own hard work, Canadian franchisees—especially more recent ones—owe their good business fortune to a corporation that was willing to select them from an endless oversupply of candidates, and to fellow franchisees who may have recommended them or helped them get started as store managers.

As the company's outlets have approached the saturation point in many Canadian regions, Tim Hortons has become ever more in the driver's seat when it comes to franchisee relations. So long as brand value, consumer loyalty and revenues remain strong, Tim's can set the bar very high for franchisee performance. Strong franchise candidates who face interminable waits for a shot at a Canadian store (as was the case with Cam's nephew Jay) can be persuaded to relocate and set up operations in new markets. The backlog of wannabe franchisees in Canada is one of Tim Hortons' great secret weapons: they are troops in reserve, and can be called upon to go wherever the company asks as it expands.

Like other successful franchise systems, Tim Hortons has long enjoyed the upper hand in franchise agreements, able to dictate substantially the terms it wishes. Franchise agreement terms reflect the reality that the company has been able to choose carefully the people it wishes to work with, and not be unduly beholden to them. In the U.S., where the brand is far less known and a new outlet is significantly more risky than one in Canada, the company has had to offer more generous financial terms to franchisees and be willing to defer royalties and paybacks.

Not all restaurant chains use franchising, but Tim Hortons was launched with a single franchise outlet, and the company has adhered to the model ever since. More than 99 percent of Tim Hortons outlets in Canada and more than 98 percent in the U.S. are franchise operations, with only a handful run by the parent company. Its few designated corporate outlets are mainly training facilities, although these have included the one that was staffed by the Canadian armed forces in Kandahar in Afghanistan. While it has turned over franchise operations to corporations that specialize in food-service management in the case of institutional outlets in hospitals and universities, it has overwhelmingly favoured the individual, couples or members of a family.

Tim Hortons franchisees may operate their single or multiple stores through corporations, but they remain fundamentally small businesspeople, and the company expects them to live in, or at least be active in, the communities in which they operate. Cam and Karen MacDonald still live in Newmarket, where they broke into the Tim's business managing Karen's brothers' outlet. Cam says he would be gently nudged by a district manager, asking him when they were going to move to the Danforth, until Cam finally said that if someone could find him a house in the vicinity of his stores that was as nice as his home in Newmarket for the same money, they'd move. The gentle nudging stopped. Cam commutes daily to the stores down the Don Valley Parkway in a Toyota 4Runner and is a member of the local business improvement association.

The Danforth and Logan location was also one of the first Canadian stores to get a Cold Stone Creamery service counter, in 2009, as a result of the master licensing agreement Tim Hortons struck with Cold Stone's parent, Kahala Franchising, LLC, which gave Tim's exclusive rights to Cold Stone in Canada and created an agreement to pursue co-branding opportunities in the United States. Behind the counter, MacDonald showed me where the treats were prepared. Ice cream that was freshly made in a $35,000 machine in the back was mixed with toppings on a refrigerated stone slab, then served up in a waffle bowl.

MacDonald knew he had to increase brand awareness, and was doing whatever he could. "Yes," he solemnly volunteered, "I have a banana costume." During the Taste of the Danforth street festival in August, he wheeled a refrigerated cart through the crowds, serving up samples. The cart was crated up in a corner of the restaurant, waiting to go back to head office. "They sent it down for me to use, and they're picking it up again," he said as we walked past it. "It's the kind of support they give you." The vast majority of people who tried the ice cream during the street festival, he volunteered, had never heard of the brand. "It's a great product. Our job is just to get it in people's mouths."

I didn't doubt that MacDonald was grateful for landing on his feet in Tim Hortons and getting the opportunities the company had extended to him and his wife. He's a sharp, hard-working guy who executes the corporate system according to the manual and praises its culture. "It's the quality of character of the people that is very attractive about what I do. The franchisees are top-drawer people. They're very hard working. When you get together with them, they all have their war stories about their first two years in business. I'm a really, really lucky guy, because I got in."

SITTING IN THE TIM HORTONS outlet at Danforth and Logan, feasting on a BELT washed down with a trademark coffee, I had spent a good part of the morning catching up with a man I hadn't seen in decades. I was reminded that I have been frequenting Tim Hortons outlets for most of my natural life. The first franchise outlet that opened in the East End of Hamilton in 1964 with the help of Cam MacDonald's dad was a few blocks from my grandmother's house. It started serving up doughnuts and coffee about a month before my fifth birthday.

The restaurant concept had seen tremendous changes over the course of almost fifty years, in menu, interior design and outlet concepts. In looking around the interior of MacDonald's main outlet, seeking out the twenty-minute no-loitering signs that in fact no longer existed, I was reminded of what else was missing: any acknowledgment of the former existence of the man whose stylized signature formed the company logo. Tim Horton has been dead for almost forty years, and there is nothing in the way of signage or other materials within a Canadian franchise like this that tells you who the "Tim Horton" of Tim Hortons was.

The reasons Tim Horton is absent as a personality from the Canadian QSR colossus that bears his name are complicated. When I wrote his biography in 1994, it was clear that few customers of his namesake restaurants, which then numbered about 900, knew who he was. With more than four times as many outlets today, even fewer customers appear to know anything about him, if the occasional media street interview on this subject can be trusted. Tim Horton's commercial value as a public persona has also been seriously diminished, and in the minds of at least one brand and marketing expert I spoke with, had become too toxic to ever exploit—especially after Horton's autopsy report, secured through a freedom-of-information request by a journalist in 2005, revealed that his blood alcohol level had been more than twice the legal limit when he was killed in a single-vehicle crash in 1974.

But it's important that we don't forget who Horton was. For one thing, the legacy of Tim Horton as a name, as an absent persona, tells us much about the nature of brands, and of this particular brand, and about the company's relationship with its namesake. For another, Tim Horton was indeed a living, breathing person, with business ambitions that predated his coffee-and-doughnut chain. The story of how the chain was founded is not as simple as the standard-package tale of how a star hockey player teamed up with a cop. More than a narrative preamble to the story of the company today, the tortuous process Tim Horton went through to arrive in the coffee-and-doughnut business, and the way that business managed to emerge from the primordial ooze of franchising in the 1960s, illustrates how Tim's—and today's QSR industry overall—acquired its modern character.

The scattered, sometimes madcap effort to create a business—at times it seemed like *any* business would do—was the antithesis of Tim Hortons today: a corporate system that attracts franchisees like Cam MacDonald with the certainty of its model. Today's QSR sector actually is anything but predictable, and even now, at the height of its success, Tim Hortons has many challenges before it. But the business has become extremely refined in its analysis of costs and operating margins, sales and marketing, product development, franchisee relations and accountability to shareholders. The start of the chain, by comparison, was a raw, ad hoc, make-it-up-as-we-go sort of undertaking, involving people who have been forgotten by the neat recap of a corporation's history. The full story captures the messy nature of entrepreneurial ambition, and shows how Canadian franchising and Canadian eating habits were formed as suburbia came to define the lives of millions in a new, postwar middle class that included Tim Horton himself.

3

Tim's Tale: From Hockey Sticks to Stir Sticks

In September 2011, I walked into a co-branded outlet of Cold Stone Creamery and Tim Hortons on West Forty-second Street, just west of Times Square in midtown Manhattan, and ordered a medium coffee. The server surprised me by handing me a cup held in a sleeve, which you don't encounter at a Tim's back in Canada. The sleeve further surprised me by actually saying something about Tim Horton, which I never come across in Canada, either.

"FROM HOCKEY STICKS TO STIR STICKS" read the blurb title, which went on to explain: "Tim Horton, who was an NHL all-star defenseman for hockey clubs including the New York Rangers and the Buffalo Sabres, established his coffee and donut shop in 1964. Tim Hortons has since become the fourth largest publicly-traded quick-service restaurant chain in North America"—a boast that remained true in terms of market capitalization based on share price, but not on overall chain size or revenues, as the much larger Dunkin' Brands Group, Inc., owner of Dunkin' Donuts and Baskin-Robbins, had gone public on the Nasdaq exchange in late July.

Horton's likeness and information about him—mainly captured in a fundraising poster for the Tim Horton Children's Foundation camps—had begun to disappear from Tim's outlets soon after the poster itself was created in 1992. The poster's presence had been doomed by ongoing legal actions launched by Horton's widow, Lori, over the terms of her sale of her half interest in the restaurant company to Ron Joyce in 1975 and what she claimed was an unauthorized use of her late husband's image for the poster. The posters came down, even though both of Lori Horton's suits failed in court. By the time Tim Hortons had merged with Wendy's in 1995, what little material about Tim Horton had previously existed in the restaurants had all but disappeared from his namesake QSR chain.

Today, Tim Horton is recognized on the corporate website as a co-founder of the chain, with Ron Joyce. The website also offers a clip from a 1968 *Hockey Night in Canada* appearance. Interviewed between periods by Ward Cornell, Horton, dressed in his Toronto Maple Leaf uniform, is personable, bright and amusing as he thanks the customers of what Cornell calls his "doughnut emporium." The accompanying description on the website says: "Tim Horton was known for his generosity, modesty and quiet confidence. You can see for yourself, that he brought great passion and determination to his budding business. And, true to form, Tim Horton always had time to thank his loyal fans on and off the ice." But Horton is otherwise absent from the Canadian consumer experience.

This is what made a few brief words about Tim Horton on a cup sleeve in midtown Manhattan such a surprise. Tim Horton the living, breathing individual, however tersely, had resurfaced in company consumer packaging. Back home, I knew Tim Horton would still be missing from the stores in the chain he helped found, beyond the highly stylized script of his autograph that served as its logo.

THE BASIC RECAP of Tim Horton's life is that he played twenty-six seasons of professional hockey as a right defenceman: the first three in the American Hockey League, from 1949–50 to 1951–52, the last twenty-three in the National Hockey League, from 1952–53 to 1973–74. His three AHL seasons were with one of the Toronto Maple Leafs' minor-league affiliates, the Pittsburgh Hornets. Late in his nineteenth season in Toronto, he was dealt to the New York Rangers. This move was followed by a three-season shuffle that took him from New York to Pittsburgh and, lastly, to Buffalo. He won an AHL championship, the Calder Cup, with the Hornets, and four Stanley Cups with the Leafs. He was a Junior A first-team all-star with the St. Michael's Majors, a first-team all-star with the Hornets, and with the Leafs he made three second-team and three first-team appearances. In the 1962 playoffs, he set a record for points by an NHL defenceman, with three goals and thirteen assists in twelve games. He never won the NHL's Norris Trophy as its top defenceman, although many people thought he should have. He was forty-four years old, and had just played in his fifty-fifth game of the 1973–74 season for the Buffalo Sabres, when he was killed in a single-vehicle accident on the Queen Elizabeth Way at about four-thirty in the morning on February 21, 1974. He was inducted posthumously into the Hockey Hall of Fame in 1977. His number 7 is "honoured" in Toronto (the Leafs do not officially retire numbers anymore); his number 2 is officially retired in Buffalo.

None of that tells you a thing about why his stylized signature is on the signage and products of Canada's most successful QSR chain.

PROFESSIONAL HOCKEY PLAYERS of the 1950s and '60s did not live in multimillion-dollar condos or estates in gated communities. The ones who married and started raising kids often lived in the new suburbs comprising modest bungalows, side-splits and ranch houses, and they rubbed shoulders with the rest of the middle-to-upper-middle class. Dad might have an oddball job and be starring on television's

Hockey Night in Canada two nights a week, but the kids went to public schools like their friends, and the families attended the neighbourhood church. Having an unlisted number (as Horton did) was one concession to privacy in a job that could encourage half the country to phone your house when you accidentally put the puck in your own net.

The 1960s were a last gasp for the idea of professional hockey players as national celebrities who also lived pretty well as ordinary Canadian folk. Their values may have remained very much of the communities and families they came from, but their lifestyles would change tremendously. Horton lived through those changes, and embodied them. When he died, he had just begun to make what, at the time, seemed like astronomical amounts of money for a professional hockey player: $150,000 a season. And since the 1971–72 season, which he spent with the Pittsburgh Penguins, he had split his hockey salary with his restaurant partner, Ron Joyce, to keep Joyce working on the growth of the chain while he continued to star in the NHL.

When Horton's speeding Pantera sports car went off the QEW in St. Catharines, rolled on the median and flung Horton out the passenger door, his own life had accelerated to a precarious velocity. His wife, Lori, was battling alcohol and prescription pills, and according to Ron Joyce's memoir, Horton had an apartment in Oakville, Ontario, near the restaurant company's head office, where he was carrying on an affair. Horton himself had begun drinking again—his blood alcohol level at the time of his death, as noted, was more than twice the legal limit—and traces of barbiturate in his bloodstream and pills in his pocket indicated he had been taking the same highly addictive diet pills, Dexamyl, as Lori. He also had amphetamines in his pocket, which suggested that he had been using uppers to get through the grind of the NHL season at age forty-four.

He had been on his way back to Buffalo, after a losing effort against the Maple Leafs, to his suite in the Statler Hotel. It was suspected he had been playing with a broken jaw, and Horton wanted to keep a ten o'clock appointment that morning with the team's doctor, John Butsch. The doctor instead ended up identifying his body at the hospital in St. Catharines, and the autopsy indicated the jaw was not in fact broken.

Horton had been on the road at such a late—or early—hour because he had been holding an impromptu meeting with Joyce at the Oakville office. Horton had knocked back vodka and soda while they hashed out issues; a vodka bottle, its neck broken off, was found on the median at the crash site. The conversation, according to Joyce, was testy at times, but they had parted amicably, with Horton declaring, "I love ya, Blub"—a nickname that poked fun at Joyce's waistline—and planting a kiss on his cheek before getting behind the wheel of his Pantera and speeding into oblivion—and a peculiar mix of posthumous fame and infamy.

THE PARENTS OF TIM HORTON'S ERA did not dote on their hockey-playing kids. There were no Timbits minor sports programs, and moms and dads didn't necessarily even bother seeing their sons play, defying today's clichéd image of parents clutching a Tim Hortons coffee and cheering them on from the stands of a community rink. Horton's only sibling, his younger brother, Gerry (who died suddenly of a heart attack a few months after I interviewed him), doubted that their parents saw Tim play much as a kid, as they weren't interested in standing around in an unheated arena in sub-freezing weather.

Horton was born in 1930 in Cochrane, Ontario, to Aaron Oakley ("Oak") and Ethel Horton. He was christened Miles Gilbert; tradition has it this was his father's doing, but his mother made sure he was known as Tim. Cochrane had sprung up in 1910 at the junction of two railways, the Temiskaming and Northern Ontario and the National Transcontinental. The town failed to deliver on the promise of becoming the Winnipeg of northern Ontario. In the Depression, Oak Horton moved from job to job, distributing pop with a beverage company, working in the lumber business and moving the family to the Quebec mining town of Duparquet, about twenty miles north of Rouyn-Noranda (which gave the Leafs Horton's teammate and friend Dave Keon) so he could work in the Beattie gold mine. The family was in Duparquet from the time Horton was five until he was about eight, and it was where he began playing hockey, according to Gerry.

The Hortons returned to Cochrane in the late 1930s, when Oak landed a patronage job with the provincial highway department. After that job vanished, Oak got on as a railway mechanic with Algoma Central, which meant he had to be away from his family for extended periods in Sault Ste. Marie. In 1945, he quit the Algoma Central and got a mechanic's job with the CPR's Sudbury District, and moved his family to the city.

It was next door to Sudbury, in the Inco mining town of Copper Cliff, that Horton began his rise to NHL stardom. In the fall of 1946, he made the Redmen of the Northern Ontario Junior Hockey League, where he impressed observers with his rushing and scoring ability, his devastating hitting and his willingness to fight.

The overwhelming sources of new talent—even after NHL expansion in 1967—were the junior amateur leagues of Canada, and the NHL was in firm control of the pipeline. As with the Tim Hortons chain and its pool of wannabe franchisees in Canada today, there were far more prospective players in the amateur system than there were NHL jobs. Until a universal amateur draft was introduced in 1969, NHL teams had formal affiliations with particular junior clubs, and before kids appeared on these teams, their professional services were already spoken for. Scouts bird-dogged the hinterlands, securing rights when prospects were as young as fourteen.

Horton's rookie performance with the Redmen was impressive enough to get him transferred to St. Michael's College School in Toronto, despite the fact he was a churchgoing Protestant and St. Mike's was run by the Basilian order of Catholic priests. St. Mike's was home to the Majors, who had just won the Memorial Cup, the national junior championship, and had produced a number of Leaf starters since the 1930s. Horton began to round out his game, playing more in his own end of the rink.

Horton was not a big man. He stood five foot nine and in his prime was about 180 pounds. Like many players of his era, he would be hard pressed to make the NHL today, as any defenceman less than six feet tall now has a lot of proving to do. But he was incredibly strong, built like a Y. He could deliver clean, devastating hits and was impossible to move from out front of his own net. As a minor pro in Pittsburgh, he mastered a new tool of the game, the slap shot, which made him so effective on the point, especially on the power play. He was also bright, and coachable, and he made friends readily, both inside and outside the game, never limiting his social circle to hockey players.

Players could stay in Canadian junior hockey until they were twenty-one, the promising talents being routinely fed into the professional system at eighteen or nineteen. Few graduated directly to the NHL: they first needed to continue maturing, physically and mentally, in the minor pros while also furthering their craft, although being sent far from home as a teen to do so could wind up being their undoing. Education was not an overwhelming concern, either for players or the hockey system. Prospects might have been able to finish high school, but it was a tall order to play top-tier junior hockey and excel scholastically. Rare were the players who managed to attend a Canadian university or a U.S. college, play hockey there, and then have a professional career. A precious few savvy and ambitious NHL players, like Billy Harris and Carl Brewer on the Leafs, managed to pursue university degrees part time, although the culture of the game meant management (which seldom had any post-secondary education itself) frowned on this sort of egghead behaviour.

In the fall of 1949, the Leafs assigned Horton full time to their AHL farm team in Pittsburgh, the Hornets. As a result, he never did get his high school diploma, although his marks before he started playing junior hockey with the Redmen and then the Majors had been those of a solid "B" student with a few moments of brilliance that had included a 93 in geography in Grade 9.

Horton wrapped up his third season with the Hornets by winning the league championship, the Calder Cup, on the road in Providence, Rhode Island, against the Reds in April 1952. He returned to Pittsburgh to marry an American Ice Capades skater he'd met in Pittsburgh, Delores ("Lori") Rose Michaelek, who was his first true girlfriend. He never danced and had no fashion sense, and she was nineteen and didn't know a thing about hockey.

That fall, Horton made the Leafs lineup. The newlyweds rented a basement apartment where the only entertainment, as Horton would recall, was the radio. After about a year in the apartment, they ordered a bungalow, without even inspecting the lot on which it was to be built, in the Scarborough neighbourhood of Wexford. Only when they moved in did they discover that the house, on the west side of Warden Avenue, south of Ellesmere Road, was just a few doors down from a railway that cut across Scarborough en route from Toronto to Peterborough. Regardless, they would stay there from 1953 to 1959 as they began to raise a family of four daughters. Had Tim and Lori Horton not bought that bungalow and moved to Wexford, and stuck with it long enough to meet a crucial circle of small businesspeople, Tim Hortons the modern QSR restaurant phenomenon would not exist.

SCARBOROUGH'S GRID of major thoroughfares today is thoroughly staked out by the company Horton founded, with outlets commanding vantage points on virtually all the main intersections where retail space is available. In this classic example of suburban sprawl, the standard QSR restaurant format with drive-through is king.

Driving the rectilinear perimeter of Horton's old neighbourhood in 2011, I visited six Tim's in prime locations on the thoroughfare box (a little more than one mile long on each side) marked by Victoria Park Avenue to the west, Birchmount Road to the east, Ellesmere Road to the north, and Lawrence Avenue to the south, with Warden Avenue running north-south through the middle. There are another twenty Tim Hortons locations within a major block or so of this perimeter. To the south of Lawrence, for example, there are seven (counting the outlet at Victoria Park and O'Connor) along less than two miles of Eglinton Avenue east of the Don Valley Parkway. My native Hamilton proudly claims bragging rights as the most Tim's-intensive (and loyal) place in the world, yet one would be hard pressed to find a place more infused with Tim Hortons outlets that cater to car-ensconced consumers than this area of west Scarborough. Were Tim Horton today for some reason wishing to escape his old neighbourhood from his Warden bungalow without encountering a namesake restaurant, he would have only one way out: north on Warden, because the corner at Ellesmere, with its high-banked ground and a trestle carrying the trains that run past what was once his home, is hostile to any sort of commercial development.

Down the street from Horton's Wexford home, at the northwest corner of Lawrence and Warden, is a compact drive-through of the chain that outlived him. It is a mere doughnut toss from the place where Tim Horton's QSR adventures began.

PLAYING FOR THE LEAFS had brought Horton to Wexford and Scarborough's incessant sprawl. Houses had become more than shelter, meals more than sustenance, cars more than transportation. Entertainment had emerged as a common denominator.

Horton may never had understood it, or tried to articulate it, but the concepts outside of hockey that he found attractive were all about mobility. Cars were about speed and freedom, and Horton's father had made the switch from trains to automobiles as he opened a Shell station in North Bay, Ontario, in 1953, to provide the fuel for the growing ranks of tourists and vacationers. From the fuel to power them, Tim Horton migrated to selling cars before hitting upon further commercial possibilities of such a mobile culture. He was also focused on the urban/suburban landscape of opportunity of his adopted home, Scarborough, which included an emergent middle class.

In twenty years, from 1946 to 1966, the average weekly pay packets of hourly-rated wage earners in Canadian manufacturing tripled, from $30.15 to $91.65. Weekly salaried employees (both sexes) in manufacturing similarly leapt from $43.85 to $128.79; the men among them had seen their average weekly pay packet grow from $53.21 to $147.95. Postwar manufacturing—much of it in Ontario, tied to the auto industry—was creating this new middle class and a new streetscape for their historic affluence. Scarborough's housing development had taken off after the Second World War when what had initially been a site of munitions production was transformed into a manufacturing colossus known as the Golden Mile along Eglinton Avenue, to the south of where Horton came to live. Housing was affordable in the new suburbs, with bungalows like Tim and Lori's costing two to three times an annual salary, and mortgage interest rates were low. Multilane highways were connecting distant centres as well as encouraging urban sprawl.

The nuclear family was the paramount institution of society, and it had not yet relinquished its central role in daily life. Divorce, for good or ill, was rare before Canada introduced the first comprehensive national divorce law in 1968. The urban society in which Horton launched his business ventures very much was a mirror of his own life. Dad earned the money, and Mom stayed at home in suburbia, raising the kids. Meals—above all, dinner—were a family affair, prepared from scratch and served at home. If you were away during the day, at work or school, lunch was something your wife or mom made at home and packed in a lunch box for you.

Truckers, salesmen and other mobile types had their diners. Travellers had restaurants in hotels. The mobility of the family changed restaurant offerings in two ways, both of which were tied to urgency. People on the move wanted (or appreciated) food that was made and served quickly—in other words, that was fast. They began to distinguish between restaurants as a destination that could be a focal point of an evening's entertainment and socializing, and one that was a rapid calorie-consumption stop that could double as its own sort of entertainment. The grill and the deep fryer turned the meat and potatoes of a dinner of roast beef and mashed potatoes into a burger and fries—food that didn't necessarily require a table, a plate and cutlery and could be carried away or eaten in a vehicle, even while driving.

Drive in restaurants had begun appearing in the 1920s in lockstep with the proliferation of the automobile, the number of which increased 300 percent in the United States between 1915 and 1920. These restaurants evolved from simple roadside stands in more rural areas, migrating into (or being absorbed by) the sprawl of suburbia. The most elemental aspect of the drive-in was that it was a roadside attraction with enough real estate for a stand-alone building and space that allowed patrons to park on the property.

The first roadside McDonald's drive-in opened in San Bernardino, California, in 1946. In the 1950s, the drive-in restaurant proliferated, with or without carhops or interior seating, wedding the grill menu produced by a compact kitchen with the mobility of the consumer who was either passing through or was so enamoured of car culture that their eating and their driving fused in a new form of recreation. Land in the suburbs was initially cheaper than in city centres, or at least was more available, and a restaurant with a generous parking lot could be conceived. Although the drive-*through* restaurant was pioneered by the In-N-Out Burger chain in 1948—on the outskirts of Los Angeles in what is now Baldwin Park, California—the concept would not begin to flourish until the mid-1970s.

One of the appeals of this new restaurant business was the favourable relationship between income and receivables. Customers paid cash: you didn't have to invoice them and then try to collect thirty days later. Bad debt with customers thus was virtually unheard of. Suppliers, on the other hand, generally invoiced you and gave you time to pay, and if you bought more of what they were selling, you got volume discounts, whereas the customers collectively didn't pay you less for buying more. Seasonality could be a problem, and so could competition, especially with a customer that was by definition mobile and could easily take their business elsewhere. In the sprawl of suburbia, a drive-to/drive-in enterprise was generally one of many ranged along a major road or secondary highway. It didn't adhere to the normal criteria of restaurants that thrived by being in the heart of a business district, or near a theatre, train station, courthouse or library. These new enterprises weren't particularly anywhere, other than on the road to somewhere, and so were broadly accessible. You could pass by them as easily as you could go to them.

The quick-service restaurant was a gathering place, a social event. It was especially associated with youth culture: kids who grew up knowing only suburbia and cars, not Depression and war, in a period of burgeoning postwar affluence, with discretionary income of their own in the form of allowances and wages from part-time jobs. The baby boom was creating a new consumer group, and quick-service restaurants were largely catering to their tastes, or at least giving them tastes of their own that they would pass on to their children.

In postwar culture, the consumer's ability to move quickly between once-distant (as measured by travel time) locations created an appetite that paradoxically desired both the exotic and the familiar. People travelled because they wanted to experience different things, but when they got there, they often proved happy to experience exactly what they had at home. This was particularly true of businesspeople who began to travel because they had to, not because they wanted to. The human need for predictability, for familiarity, helped give rise to franchise motel and hotel chains, and to restaurants that served essentially the same menu, with essentially the same prices, with essentially the same level of service. People didn't just want something to eat. They wanted to scarf down a Big Mac or (eventually) savour a Tim Hortons coffee and a snack pack of Timbits.

Concepts and mini-chains of QSRs came and went in these primordial days of a restaurant business model that tried to find the sweet spot between convenience, entertainment and service. Their fare was ultimately a discretionary purchase: people stopped at service stations to fuel up their cars because they had to, whereas QSRs in urban or suburban settings were rarely a necessary visit. People could always eat at home if they really tried, or if they had to when money was tighter, but those conditions also applied to more formal, sit-down restaurants. QSRs, while discretionary, offered a competitive advantage over casual and fine dining concepts. They could endure through harder times if they had the right sort of product: a food, beverage or treat that was inexpensive, that was capable of staying on the personal or household budget as a minor form of entertainment and that could be scaled back if necessary, but not completely eliminated. A half-century before Tim Hortons chased consumers with television advertising campaigns in uncertain economic times to get them to part with a dollar or two for a discretionary summer treat like a smoothie or a box of Timbits, the essential strategic advantage of its QSR niche was waiting to be exploited on a chainwide scale.

One of the first such chains to do so was Dairy Queen, a departure from the standard drive-in grill menu that was founded on a soft ice cream product introduced in 1938. The first franchise opened in Joliet,

Illinois, in June 1940, and the chain began expanding massively after the war. From 100 stores in 1947, the number ballooned to 1,446 in 1950; five years later, there were 2,600.

Dairy Queen in particular, and ice cream in general, proved to be elemental to the Tim Hortons story. They were front and centre in the founding of the coffee-and-doughnut chain, and ice cream has returned to the forefront of the corporate narrative as the company has sought new growth by co-branding Tim Hortons and Cold Stone Creamery outlets.

It is common knowledge among those familiar with the essential Tim Hortons story that Ron Joyce, the partner of Horton who built the chain into a national phenomenon, was a Dairy Queen franchisee when he decided to try his luck with the hockey player's new concept. It is far less well known that Dairy Queen and ice cream, along with drive-ins, were on hand at the very start of Tim Horton's efforts to find a long-term alternative to life in professional hockey. To see how, we have to meet the Hannigan boys.

4

Hustling: How NHL Players Looked to Life Beyond the Rink

Gord and Ray Hannigan were brothers in Schumacher, a northern Ontario mining town in the greater Timmins area, who came up through the Toronto Maple Leaf system at the same time as Tim Horton. Ray was already playing for the St. Mike's Majors when Horton arrived along with Gord for the 1947–48 season, and they all played together when they turned pro with the Pittsburgh Hornets of the AHL. Horton was extremely close to the brothers, practically living with them in the summer in Schumacher in those years and sometimes visiting on weekends as well. In the fall of 1951, Gord was promoted to a line in Pittsburgh with centre George Armstrong, the future Leaf captain. While Armstrong moved up to the Leafs late that '51–52 season, Gord stayed in Pittsburgh with his brother Ray and Horton and won the league championship, the Calder Cup, that spring.

The Hannigans and Horton were all hoping that their Calder Cup performance could secure them starting jobs on the Leafs. Gord and Ray were driving to Leaf training camp together in September 1952 when they heard on the car radio that the Leafs had just secured goaltender Harry Lumley from the Chicago Blackhawks, giving up in return four players that included some minor leaguer named Ray Hannigan.

Gord, along with Tim, made the Leafs, while Ray was sent to Chicago's farm team in the Western Hockey League, the Edmonton Flyers.

Spend enough time around men who aspired to professional hockey careers in the postwar years, and you will gather the impression that for many, not having their playing careers unfold quite as planned was the best thing that happened to them. While still in their twenties, they got the message that they should busy themselves finding alternate employment that served them and their families well for their entire working lives. In contrast, many players who did make the NHL and stuck with it found themselves not especially well paid—certainly not well enough to retire in comfort—and not especially well prepared for life after hockey.

Enjoying anything like a full career in the National Hockey League of the "Original Six" era was a privilege reserved for a fortunate few. The NHL had emerged from the Second World War with only six teams and was a railway league run by arena owners. Because of league limitations on the number of players that could be suited up for a game (teams weren't even required to dress a backup goaltender until 1965), there were only about a hundred starting jobs in professional hockey's top tier until the 1967–68 season when the NHL doubled in size through expansion. The rival World Hockey Association, which appeared in 1972, forced the NHL to continue expanding to prevent the upstart league from dominating the available urban markets. The new league also ignited a bidding war for top talent, and even journeyman players reaped the benefits of a sudden seller's market. Between 1960 and 1970, salaries easily increased tenfold. Veterans like Tim Horton who were able to hang in long enough enjoyed an income windfall in their final seasons that allowed them to make as much in one season as players only recently had in an entire career. That sudden surge in income played a significant role in the initial growth of the restaurant chain Horton co-founded.

NHL expansion, the birth of a players' union in 1967 and the concomitant rise of the WHA dramatically changed the dynamics of the profession. Until then, it wasn't enough to be talented and to avoid injury to have a long (never mind prosperous) career. A player had to stay out of trouble, as the ones that got on the wrong side of management could effectively be buried in the minor leagues, sent down to a farm team and left there to stew or rot, all offers of trades from NHL clubs being declined. Short of quitting the game altogether, players had very little control over where they played and their terms of employment.

NHL players were not necessarily well prepared for life beyond the rink. They were certainly not well prepared for it by the professional system, which tied up their rights when they were young, brought them into professional service at the earliest opportunity, had nothing formal to offer in the way of career counselling, and in fact used the ever-present threat of demotion or termination as a management tool and a contract bargaining strategy. The better, more established players were able to secure one-way contracts, which meant they played only for an NHL team or were still paid their NHL salary if sent down to the minors for any reason, but otherwise players—especially young ones signing their first professional deals—were routinely signed to two-way deals, which specified terms (including pay) for their services in the NHL as well as one or more minor pro tiers. Demotion could come as a result of the marginality of their talent, misbehaviour or injury, as players were sent down to recover and regain top-tier ability. Players feared injury because of the likelihood of demotion. Some had gotten their big-league break because of an injury to a starter—Horton's full-time Leaf job in 1952 was partly due to the death of defenceman Bill Barilko, who had scored the Stanley Cup–winning goal in overtime against Montreal in 1951, only to be killed in a plane crash a few months later.

"People will never understand how badly these guys wanted to play hockey, or what they would play for in order to get there," Tim

Horton's Leaf teammate Dick Duff (a Hall of Famer who won a total of eight Stanley Cups with Toronto and Montreal) told me. "And having arrived there, somebody's going to give you $7,000 for being a national hero."

RAY HANNIGAN was one of those postwar prospects who shed his youthful ambitions for hockey early, sensing during his first Edmonton Flyers season that the professional game was not a long-term prospect where he was concerned. He was on a road trip to Seattle when he got talking with a director from the Edmonton exhibition board, which ran the Flyers, about what sort of business a fellow like himself could get into without a lot of cash. When the director spotted a Dairy Queen somewhere in the northwestern U.S., he told the bus driver to pull over.

"That's the kind of business that would go well in Edmonton," the director told Hannigan.

Ray got in touch with his brother Gord, who was having a terrific season with the Leafs and would finish second to New York Rangers goalie Lorne "Gump" Worsley in rookie-of-the-year voting. Like Ray, Gord harboured no illusions about the job security that hockey offered, and he agreed that a Dairy Queen was worth looking into. The brothers wrote the parent company, asking for a franchise for Edmonton. Dairy Queen hadn't yet opened a franchise anywhere in Canada, and though it was persuaded to add the first one, in Estevan, Saskatchewan, in 1953, the company wasn't taken with Edmonton. "They wrote back and said they felt we lived too close to the Eskimos," Ray Hannigan told me.

Still certain that ice cream was the way to go, Gord and Ray pooled $2,000 each and opened Hannigan's Dairy Freeze on 109 Street in Edmonton in 1954. It only lasted a year as an ice cream venture, suggesting that the Dairy Queen people had been right about Edmonton and frozen treats. The store was switched to a burger format, and in honour of the fact that they had been spurned by Dairy Queen, they called it Hannigan's Burger King. People with fast-food concepts in those days loved names with connotations of royalty. The Hannigan business was no relation to today's QSR chain of the same name, which had opened its first outlet in Florida in 1953.

The switch to burgers was a hit. Through a combination of owned-and-operated outlets and franchises, the Hannigans soon opened two locations in Edmonton and expanded into Wetaskiwin, Red Deer and Whitecourt, Alberta. They had found success selling burgers in cattle country, grinding their own meat for their signature Hannigan Steer Burger. They also added a Heavenly Chicken franchise—the running joke was that they called the restaurant that because they burned the hell out of the food.

The success of the Hannigan restaurants was a vivid demonstration to Horton of the career possibilities beyond hockey, and of the need to plan for that day, sooner rather than later. Gord's career reiterated that need: after his sparkling rookie season, he couldn't stick with the Leafs. He moved up and down between the Leafs and the AHL; when the Pittsburgh Hornets folded in 1956, he moved to the Leafs' new AHL farm team, the Rochester Americans. As their captain, he had a 61-point season, then decided it was time to follow Ray's example and commit himself to a productive life away from the rink. Both he and Ray were devout Catholics with big families. Ray had seven kids, and when Gord left Rochester he had five, with four more to come. Gord moved to Edmonton and played one season for Ray's old Flyers in 1957–58, then joined his brother full time in the restaurant business.

Tim Horton remained close to both Hannigans, and would visit with them in Edmonton whenever the Leafs passed through on a preseason exhibition tour. They in turn kept him apprised of their business, showing him plans as they expanded. The Hannigans were innovators, using modular restaurant designs that were set on cinder blocks and especially suited to small towns. The outlets were also all drive-ins, except for one Edmonton store that had interior seating.

By the time I tracked down Ray and interviewed him in 1993, life had taken a radical change of course. After Gord died suddenly of a heart attack in 1966, the restaurants were wound down; there would never be a Canadian QSR restaurant chain called Hannigan's that is as ubiquitous as Tim Hortons. Ray moved back to Toronto, and after his wife died in 1971, he entered the priesthood; he was a diocesan priest in Montana when I located him. "Tim was like a brother to Gord," Lori Horton told me. It is not hard to imagine that, but for Gord's untimely death, they might have ended up in the restaurant business together.

"Gord encouraged him to think about getting into business because of the uncertainty in hockey," Ray told me. "Tim was really, really interested in what we were doing."

IF TIM HORTON HADN'T been sufficiently inspired by the vicissitudes of the playing careers of the Hannigan boys to consider alternatives to hockey, his own career delivered a jarring reminder to make alternative plans. On March 12, 1955, Horton was crossing the New York Rangers' blue line in a game at Maple Leaf Gardens when he dished off the puck and made the classic error of admiring his pass and not watching where he was going. Rangers defenceman Bill Gadsby lined him up: the collision fractured Horton's jaw and cheekbone, and as he spun awkwardly and collapsed, he fractured the tibia and fibula of his right leg.

Horton spent a month in Toronto East General Hospital, with pins holding his leg together, sustained on a liquid diet. An off-ice friend of

Horton's from Sudbury, Dick Trainor, a lawyer who became a provincial court judge and had been at the game, recalled for me his shock at seeing Horton drinking chocolate milk through a straw and hearing this seemingly indestructible figure mumble through his wired jaw, "I'll never play again."

Horton did play again, but it was a near-run thing. The cast didn't come off his leg until July. Leafs impresario Conn Smythe gave him a desk job that summer at a sand and gravel quarry he owned, and arranged for a publicity photo of Horton behind the wheel of a dump truck. Smythe professed to be willing to sit him out for an entire season if it meant having him healthy enough to play again, and took his rehabilitation seriously, but after returning to play in the fall of 1955, Horton was damaged goods.

He was twice almost traded, but then managed to recover his form and stick with the Leafs to be part of the four-Cup run of the 1960s. By the time he was winning Stanley Cups, he was fully determined to establish himself in a business outside of hockey, and his efforts had undergone several permutations.

HORTON'S RECOVERY from the Gadsby hit coincided with the Hannigan brothers' shift into restaurants out west. Horton was also introduced to a new circle of Leaf players and their off-ice associates, partly because of his recovery regimen, partly because of the ongoing rebuilding of the Leafs lineup. The point man in this change was defenceman Bob Baun.

Horton was a transitional talent on a 1950s Leafs roster that wasn't winning a lot of games. He bridged the generation of players that had secured a string of Stanley Cup wins (1947, 1948, 1949 and 1951) and the fresh prospects, many of them from the Toronto Marlies (who won the Memorial Cup in 1955 and 1956) and the St. Mike's Majors.

These new players would help the Leafs return to the Stanley Cup finals in 1959 and 1960 (losing on both occasions to Montreal) and hoist the cup in 1962, 1963, 1964 and 1967. Among this fresh blood was Baun, a Memorial Cup–winning Marlie who played his first Leaf games in 1956–57, spending part of that season with the Rochester Americans, where Gord Hannigan was his captain.

Baun was still a Marlie when Conn Smythe chose him at age nineteen, in the summer of 1955, to help get Horton back in playing shape after the Gadsby hit. Six years apart in age, Horton and Baun had followed different tracks upward through the Leaf system, but those tracks had been running parallel for several years. Baun was a Scarborough native and had risen through the local Marlies system, with Maple Leaf Gardens as his home ice. At sixteen, in September 1952, he had attended his first Leaf training camp, which was the start of Horton's first full season in Toronto. The two were not destined to be defence partners—at the start of the 1959–60 season, the Leafs hit on a winning rearguard formula by pairing Baun with Carl Brewer, newly arrived from the Marlies, and Horton with Allan Stanley, a veteran acquired from the Rangers. But Horton became a close friend of Baun's, as their common interests didn't end with keeping opposing players away from the Leafs net. Baun would become a Tim Hortons franchisee, operating two stores in Pickering, Ontario, to the east of Toronto. But long before the restaurant chain existed, Baun was making connections for Horton within the business community.

In the mid-1950s, a close nucleus of Leafs players began to form, men who were as much interested in life away from the game as within it. They congregated at George's Spaghetti House, a jazz venue that opened in 1956, where Baun found a role as a sort of host, maître d' and bouncer. "It was our main meeting place after practice," Baun told me as we spoke in the cramped office of one of his Tim Hortons outlets in 1993. "A lot of things were decided there. Most of us worked at the time, so we didn't have that much time to be together. The team was very much a 'together' team. So we'd meet there at lunch and have a couple sandwiches. Some of the guys were hangers-on and stayed much longer, but Tim and I were always hustling."

"Hustling" was a good word for what they were up to. Hockey players with hustle were self-starters in constant motion who led by example. In the business world, hustle suggested entrepreneurial verve, a knack and yen for deal-making that could be a little rough around the edges at times. Risks were necessary and worth taking. The hustle off the ice was a natural continuum of their hustle on it. They had avoided the workaday world of salaried desk jobs and the hourly wages of mining and manufacturing. Some came from farming families, but many young players were from small northern mining communities. They had no desire to go into the mines like their fathers, uncles or brothers. George Sukornyk, president of Harvey's Foods, spoke in 1969 of prospective franchisees looking for a business opportunity that would save them from the uncertainties of old age. Professional hockey players were looking for something that would save them from the uncertainties of middle age.

Having made it in the NHL, these players were anything but financially secure. Beyond the lack of job security, professionals like Horton were paid surprisingly poorly, despite their celebrity and the wealth they generated for team owners and the media that broadcast and covered them. In 1960, male salaried employees in Canadian manufacturing had an average weekly take of $116.47, or about $6,000 a year. The stars of the Leafs weren't doing all that much better. Leaf earnings averaged about $12,700 in 1960–61, although the spread was considerable. Leonard "Red" Kelly, acquired mid-season from the Red Wings, earned $20,000 in salary and a $1,000 bonus for the team's second-place finish to Montreal in the overall standings. Horton made slightly more than the team average: a base salary of $12,000, with a bonus of $500 for the team's finish, another $500 for his plus-minus record, and a discretionary $100 bonus on the recommendation of coach and general manager

Punch Imlach. The rookie John MacMillan barely stayed ahead of a manufacturing job with a draw of $7,000. Players who were amply aware that their time in the limelight could end with the next debilitating check hustled as hard as ever to find other opportunities.

ORIGINAL SIX PLAYERS had much more time on their hands than modern NHLers. Training camp occupied September, the seventy-game season began in October, and playoffs were held in April. With only four teams involved, the league ran two semifinal best-of-seven series and a best-of-seven final. If your team didn't make the playoffs, you could be on vacation before Easter, and even if you played in the finals, you could count on having May through August to yourself. Off-season fitness routines weren't what they are today (a lot of players smoked), which meant players weren't tied up in conditioning regimens.

With little to occupy their time, players found ways to make extra cash in the off-season. One of the more prevalent jobs was that of a "beer traveller." Players were basically roving ambassadors for breweries, driving from one tavern to another and hoisting glasses with patrons thrilled to be in the presence of an NHLer. It was easy work, but some who tried it found it demeaning. It was also a good way to develop a drinking problem and pack on debilitating pounds.

For some of the Leafs, cars were a common off-ice pursuit. Horton's dad, Oak, had already opened Horton Shell in North Bay in 1953. The gas station was ideally located, on Lakeshore Road near Lake Nipissing, and well known to anyone coming to or going from Toronto along Highway 11. Bob Baun's family ran a Texaco on Kingston Road (Highway 2) in Toronto's east end, which until the Macdonald-Cartier Freeway (Highway 401) was completed in 1956 was the main thoroughfare from Toronto to all points east. In 1941, Baun's dad was the largest Texaco dealer in Canada, a feat attributed in part to the way Baun's mom would attract customers by putting on a short skirt and standing by the side of the road. The Bauns lived on the second floor of their station, and also operated a service garage at Cornell Avenue and Kingston Road.

Baun hooked up with Herb Kearney, a friend of fellow Leaf Bob Pulford, whose Hearn Pontiac Buick dealership on Lake Shore Boulevard West sponsored Milt Dunnell's "Hearn Sportscast" on radio station CHFI. Baun started selling cars at Hearn, then spent several years at Addison on Bay, a Cadillac and Buick dealer in downtown Toronto, before joining Alex Irvine's GM dealership in Scarborough when it opened in 1961. Along the way, Baun attended GM's management school. Among the Leafs who congregated off-ice with Horton and Baun were the brothers Brian and Barry Cullen. The Cullens also joined the Hearn operation, after Baun moved on. Barry Cullen became general manager of Hearn's leasing operation, and the leasing business there provided Brian's living after his wife's poor health compelled him to leave hockey in 1962. In 1966, Brian would open Brian Cullen Motors, a Pontiac-Buick dealership in Grimsby, Ontario.

As young men with disposable income, Baun and Horton had a taste for fast cars. Baun was a Corvette man, and he introduced Horton to his first sports car, a Sunbeam Alpine. Horton followed Baun into the car business, but on the second-hand side.

After the Gadsby hit, Horton started picking up extra cash selling classified advertising for the Toronto *Telegram,* driving around and calling on the city's used car dealers. He picked Baun's brains about the car business in general. "Tim was a very astute guy," Baun stressed to me. Horton started an ad-hoc used-car business of his own, selling some of them out of his driveway. According to Baun, Horton got his start by "buying old junkers and selling them to rookies who came into camp." He developed a reputation for dumping lemons on hapless rookies.

Sometime in the late 1950s—the date is not clear, but it was probably 1958—Horton teamed up with one of his contacts from selling *Telegram* classifieds, a car dealer who had been working at Anderson Pontiac GMC named Fred Care. They bought a BP station together on the east side of Yonge Street in Willowdale, just south of Steeles Avenue. While the station continued to pump gas, Care and Horton opened Tim Horton Motors. It had a repair garage and used cars, and repped the Triumph sports car line.

It was a short-lived venture, and probably didn't last past 1961. Horton's brother, Gerry, meanwhile, opened another Tim Horton Motors in 1960, on the family's Shell property in North Bay. Gerry managed it, while Tim found used cars and sometimes ran them up to North Bay himself, otherwise paying drivers $20 to do it for him. The North Bay operation also offered sales and service on Hillman, Sunbeam and Triumph models, although Triumph was replaced by Studebaker in 1963.

Horton hustled constantly. Teammate Billy Harris (who died in 2001) told me how Horton would play precisely one golf game every summer, a tournament supporting NHL old-timers for which he would be part of a foursome with Harris, the Leafs' team doctor, Jim Murray, and the trainer, Bobby Haggert. "Tee-off time was eleven-thirty. The three of us would be on the tee. Thirty seconds before eleven-thirty, Tim would show up in a pair of running shoes with a golf bag he'd take out once a year. He was a respectable golfer, considering he only played once a year. Tim always had other projects. He was going to car auctions. To give up five or six hours to play a round of golf was ridiculous to him."

IN WEXFORD, TIM HORTON forged friendships with a network of small businesspeople who cross-connected with his hockey life. They were fundamental to his transformation into a restaurateur in the

1960s. Some would play an active role in the business; others helped create and sustain the entrepreneurial climate of hustling.

One of them was Russ Gioffrey, an appliance dealer Horton probably met through Bob Baun. Horton would drop by the Bestway TV and Appliances store on the south side of Lawrence, near Warden, after Saturday practices to have a coffee with the friend he called Rooskie, and they also rendezvoused for lunches at Fran's on Eglinton. Gioffrey, who shared Sudbury roots with Horton, admired him tremendously. "I used to try to model myself after him. I never thought I could. I thought you had to be a saint. He never said a bad word against anyone." When he marvelled at how Horton allowed his food to sit uneaten at Fran's as he signed autograph after autograph, Horton would explain, "These are the ones that like me."

Horton connected with Gioffrey's brother-in-law, John Dywan, a licensed real-estate appraiser with a keen sense for the value of small industrial buildings. Gioffrey also introduced Horton to Ed Siekierko, who developed and managed the sorts of properties Dywan appraised. After the 1963 Stanley Cup win, the second in a row for the Leafs, Horton had enough cash to form a real estate investment company, Tim Horton Holdings Ltd., with Siekierko and Dywan. It never had more than a few properties in its portfolio, but it introduced Horton to a critical aspect of the restaurant business, to which he paid great attention: real estate. His eventual partner, Ron Joyce, is generally credited with having the sense to build a vertically integrated restaurant chain with properties at its core, yet it was Horton who brought the experience of property development and investment to the business and had already surrounded himself with expertise. And through Gioffrey and Bestway—which at its height had four stores, two associate outlets and a trade-in depot—Horton had begun to learn more about how a retail chain operation could work, complementing the reports he gathered from the Hannigan brothers on their restaurant mini-empire in Alberta.

Another key figure in Horton's entrepreneurial life was the lawyer Ken Gariepy, who would carry forward prominently into the coffee-and-doughnut years. Gariepy was part of the Dywan-Siekierko-Gioffrey circle, and his office was near Horton's new home: in October 1959, two months before Tim and Lori Horton's fourth and final child was born, they had left Scarborough for a larger home on Wedgewood Drive, north of the 401, in the new suburban community of Willowdale. The house was also around the corner from the BP station Horton had bought with Fred Care in 1958. Business mixed readily with pleasure as well as friendship in Horton's world. Whenever papers had to be signed for the real estate holding company, there was a good excuse for a dinner party at Gariepy's home with all of their wives.

Horton might have moved to the newer, more upscale Willowdale in 1959, but he had not left Scarborough behind. For one thing, he still got his haircut (a flat-top brush cut) at a barbershop called Benny's in the Colony Plaza strip mall on Warden near Lawrence, close to Gioffrey's appliance store. Two units down from Benny's was a business called Your Do-Nut. In the spring of 1963, Horton walked into the doughnut shop, and the world of QSR changed.

5

Jimmy: A Jazz Drummer Gets the Doughnut Rolling

On the surface, Tim Horton and Jim Charade could not have been more different. Horton was an anglophone professional hockey player from northern Ontario, a conservative dresser with no interest in fashion; Charade was French-Canadian, a part-time jazz drummer from Montreal who favoured bright ties and silk suits and had no burning interest in hockey. But they weren't as far apart as outer appearances suggested. For one thing, Horton had done passably well in French at St. Mike's (he got a grade of 65 for term work in composition in Grade 12, but didn't write the final exam), and occasionally stunned people by speaking and understanding it. Most important, Horton and Charade shared a dedication to hustle, to finding avenues of opportunity beyond those that currently occupied them. For Horton, that was professional hockey. For Charade, that was serving as an account rep for the Vachon family in Toronto.

Charade and Horton had both found their feet in Toronto in 1952, with Horton securing his starting job with the Leafs and Charade arriving at eighteen to try to make it as a drummer. When drumming didn't work out as a full-time profession, Charade went through a series of jobs before finding a place with the Vachon Cake Company in 1955. The parent company, J.A. Vachon & Fils, in Sainte-Marie-de-Beauce, a suburb of Quebec City, had been founded by Joseph-Arcade and Rose-Anna Vachon in 1923. The company's control had shifted to their four sons after Joseph-Arcade's death in 1938. Vachon made cakes and pastries for stores, caterers and restaurants, and was probably best known for its Jos. Louis snack cake, a 1932 invention. Vachon had 350 employees and 125 delivery trucks by 1952, and its steady expansion across Canada led to the Vachon Cake Company plant in Toronto on what was then Crockford Crescent, in the industrial corridor that ran between Warden and Birchmount, south of Lawrence.

As an account rep, Charade's bilingualism allowed him to bridge the operational worlds of Toronto and Sainte-Marie-de-Beauce for the Vachon brothers. His years in Toronto also made him understand that tastes in anglophone Ontario were different from those in francophone Quebec. It's a lesson that the restaurant industry continually has had to learn, often the hard way, especially when English-Canadian or American restaurant chain concepts have tried to establish themselves in the Quebec market. But the differences cut both ways, and Charade felt the Vachon product line was too sweet for English-Canadian tastes. That was partly because Quebec consumers overall had a sweeter tooth, and because sugar was a basic preservative in baked goods that had to have shelf lives of up to four weeks. (Today, Tim Hortons is striving to make inroads into Quebec with specialties like a meat spread called cretons and beans on toast on the breakfast menu.)

Charade (who died in 2009) told me that he persuaded Vachon to expand its product line to doughnuts and butter tarts, which could be wholesaled to Dominion supermarkets and corner stores. By 1958, Charade was running a new plant on the other side of Crockford dedicated to doughnuts. Having married his wife, Claudette, in 1956, with whom he had one child, André, Charade in 1959 bought a bungalow around the corner from the doughnut plant on the west side of Warden, above the Lawrence intersection.

Vachon's Toronto business expanded to the point that a single delivery truck in 1955 had become a fleet of twenty. The doughnut offerings were basic: some were made with lemon and jelly fillings, and there were also honey dips and honey buns. Charade told me they didn't make Vachon much money, but did open doors for the company. In hindsight, what was most important about these new products was that they weren't typical fried cake–type ring doughnuts that were best known to English Canada. These were generally baked yeast-based doughnuts, made by the same process as the *beignets* of Quebecois and Acadian/Cajun heritage that English-Canadians would come to know as fritters, and the filled doughnuts popular in eastern Europe and widely known as Berliners.

The positive reception of the new Vachon doughnut products made Charade think that there was an opportunity to sell them directly to the consumer through retail shops rather than to grocery stores. He decided to look into getting a business of his own, and in 1960 flew to Boston to see one of the first franchise operations in North America, Mister Donut.

Mister Donut was the result of a falling-out between the brothers-in-law who founded Dunkin' Donuts in 1950. The two rival operations were duking it out from headquarters in the Boston suburbs, with Dunkin' Donuts in Randolph and Mister Donut in Westwood. Charade toured some of the Mister Donut shops and the training centre. "I was impressed with them and wanted a franchise, but on my way back to Toronto, I thought, 'Why do I want a franchise? I can do it myself.'"

Initially, at least, Charade thought he could do it himself with a big assist from Vachon. Charade approached one of the Vachon brothers, Paul, who ran a side business of his own called Diamond Products, which made condiments like ketchup and mustard. Charade wanted Vachon Inc. (as the company became known in 1960) to help him launch a new retail chain. They'd call it King Donut. Jo-Lo Corp., a

Vachon offshoot that made the baking equipment and provided the mix to the parent company, would do the same for King Donut.

Charade said Paul Vachon couldn't get the retail concept past the Vachon Inc. board because of concerns it would compete directly with wholesale customers. "I was sort of pissed off. I started looking for a place myself."

Without quitting his day job at the Vachon doughnut factory, Charade secured a retail space around the corner from his house, in the Colony Plaza strip mall. He called his new business Your Do-Nut, and he opened the doors to the public for the first time on February 21, 1962. It was an auspicious date in Canadian doughnut history. February 21, 1965, would be the day Charade and his partner Tim Horton signed a franchise deal for the first franchise in Hamilton with Ron Joyce. February 21, 1974, would be the day Tim Horton was killed in a car accident. Charade would spend that February 21 shut in the bathroom, not wanting anyone to see his face swollen with tears.

THE COLONY PLAZA is a reminder of the character of Canadian business a half-century ago, when such strip malls provided retailing space in suburbia where no stock of street-front brick establishments in a typical town core existed. Developers starting with a clean sheet of drawing paper and cheap land recognized that the automobile now defined the consumer experience. Just as drive-in restaurants were proliferating, so were what amounted to drive-in stores, chained together in a strip of units that shared a generous parking lot. And just like drive-in restaurants, these early malls had begun to spring up as cars became popular after the First World War. The celebrated Golden Mile Plaza, built in the mid-1950s to the south, along Eglinton Avenue (and visited as a marvel of the Commonwealth by

Queen Elizabeth II in 1959), was essentially the Colony Plaza writ on a grander scale.

I had not visited Colony Plaza in eighteen years when I dropped in on the Saturday of the 2011 Labour Day long weekend. It is at the very heart of what the City of Toronto identifies as neighbourhood 119, Wexford-Maryvale. Stretching from Highway 401 in the north to Eglinton Avenue in the south, and from Victoria Park Avenue in the west to Birchmount Road in the east, this core area of Scarborough's postwar suburban sprawl and industrialization was home to 26,430 people, according to the 2006 Canadian census. Its ample stock of bungalows has helped attract a slightly higher than average proportion of immigrants: 27 percent of residents in the census spoke neither French nor English. There was a significant number of Arab and West Asian immigrants, 1,525 in all, and for Iranians especially the Colony Plaza had come to serve as part of their commercial centre along Lawrence Avenue.

The entire western half of Colony Plaza was now Rami's Market, a supermarket specializing in eastern Mediterranean groceries with a restaurant at the east end. Next came units 2010, 2012 and 2014. These had been the Bennett & Lane dry cleaners, Ted Swimmer Smoke Shop and Douglas Plumbing *circa* 1963. A restaurant, Filarkia ("A True Taste of Greece") now occupied units 210 and 212, and a pharmacy, called Quints Remedy's RX, had moved into 214.

That left the three units at the eastern end of the mall. The end unit at 220, which had been Benny's barbershop in the early 1960s, was the quick-serve restaurant Farhat ("Felafel, Shawarma, Kebab"), with a patio area that spilled onto the parking lot, where it wrapped around the side of the mall. At 218 was The Hair Affair's; the location's usage had been remarkably enduring, having been Howard's Beauty Salon some fifty years earlier and a Cyndy and Lynsey Unisex Hairstyling Salon when I visited in 1993. And at 2016, where I had found a real estate office in 1993, was Ladan Pastry and Bakery.

This marvellous Iranian bakery featured a display of specialty breads in the front window to the right of the central door. It was also stocked with Middle Eastern foodstuffs as well as open bowls of nuts sold by weight. I later learned that, among Toronto foodies, Ladan is considered a hidden gem of nuts.

A handsome, gracious woman of late middle age appeared from the rear of the bakery and took up station behind the counter. She told me her name was Touran and that she ran the store with her husband, Mhedy.

I told Touran that her bakery was the site of the original Tim Horton doughnut shop. Her intrigued but quizzical expression suggested she thought I was a little daft. "No, I think you must be mistaken." When they came from Spain and opened the bakery in 1993, she explained, the property was a real estate office. I agreed; she and Mhedy must have taken over soon after I had seen the office that year. It was a fluke of commerce that a doughnut shop in the early 1960s had become a bakery again in the early 1990s, albeit a very different one.

Touran fetched from the glass display case a free sample of one of her pastries. It was small, though not as small as a Timbit, and its honey-sweet flakes were topped in finely grated coconut. It was delicious, and when I asked her what it was, she had to take the pen from me and think of an English equivalent for its name in Farsi script. *Kareiy,* she wrote in my notebook.

I ordered a snack pack of Iranian pastries and left it to Touran to choose an assortment. "When was the Tim Hortons here?" she asked, seeming to warm to the idea I was actually correct. I told her the dates in the early 1960s as she filled a clear plastic clamshell container with a variety of small goodies, mainly featuring flaky pastry saturated with honey and sprinkled with nuts. Ladan doesn't sell baked goods in a way that a Tim Hortons regular would recognize. Touran put the container on a weigh scale and then rang up the result: $5.64. When I handed her two five-dollar bills, she handed one right back. "That will be fine," she said.

As I drove away, I noticed a man walking up to Farhat, where Benny's barbershop used to be. Even from a moving vehicle, I could tell he was carrying a Tim Hortons coffee. He had just walked about 100 yards from the outlet at the northwest corner of Warden and Lawrence. It was one of the restaurant chain's new concepts, a drive-through with walk-in counter service. The company had managed to squeeze the building, a tightly coiled drive-through lane and a handful of parking spots into a lot that, in Charade and Horton's day, had been home to a service station operated by Greg Williams. No one in this neighbourhood apparently had a clue that the corporate QSR giant that had placed this clever, hyper-compact outlet at the northwest corner of Warden and Lawrence had gotten its start virtually next door, behind a glass-front bakery where Touran and Mhedy were making a delectable bite-sized pastry called a *kareiy*.

THE BLUSTERY WINTER WEATHER on opening day was so bad that in the short walk from his house to Your Do-Nut, Jim Charade managed to lose his watch. But the store performed well enough that Charade added a satellite store in Toronto on Avenue Road, near a Loblaws supermarket and Harvey's burger outlet. It was an approach used by Mister Donut and Dunkin' Donuts; the Tim Hortons chain would adopt it years later, with individual franchisees operating a standard store with baking facilities that supplied smaller satellite franchises with delivery runs a couple times a day. But the Avenue Road outlet proved a mistake, and Charade retreated to Scarborough, relocating the satellite to a location south of his main store, on Danforth Avenue near Warden.

It was a little more than a year after Charade opened the first Your Do-Nut that he met Tim Horton. How they met is a matter of some debate, but to hear Horton tell it, they never met at all. In a profile of Horton by Lawrence Martin published by *Canadian* magazine in January 1973, the hockey player turned restaurateur streamlined the foundation story of the restaurant chain so aggressively that he pretty much mythologized it. His inspiration dated back to his days as a Pittsburgh Hornet in the early 1950s: "There was this big, beautiful donut shop on the outskirts of town. I had never really thought of being anything else but being a hockey player before, but the first day I walked into that shop, I thought that I would really like to own my own donut shop some day." (In her book, *In Loving Memory,* Lori Horton moved this inspirational doughnut shop on the outskirts of Pittsburgh all the way to Erie, Pennsylvania, which is now a hub of American Tim Hortons outlets.)

In an interview in 1969, Horton had also quipped: "I love eating donuts and that was one of the big reasons that I opened my first donut shop. Buying donuts was costing me too much money." In the *Canadian* magazine profile, he told Martin that Ron Joyce, his partner in the chain, had been an old friend who was on the Hamilton police force when they went into business together. In fact, Horton didn't know Joyce at all when he emerged as a franchisee in Hamilton—and as we'll see, Joyce wasn't even the first (or even the second) franchisee for the Hamilton store. And in Horton's version of events for Martin, there was no room for the fundamental founding role played by Jim Charade. But without Charade, there never would have been a Tim Hortons chain.

The different stories of how Charade and Horton connected all have the common denominator of a young man named Dennis Griggs, whom Horton had met when living in Wexford. Horton always had time for kids, whether they were clamouring for autographs in a restaurant, invading his backyard with his own daughters or playing road hockey out front of a friend's house.

He initially made a friend of Dennis Griggs in the summer of 1956 by agreeing to help the sixteen-year-old Griggs coach a neighbourhood baseball team in Manhattan Park, even though baseball wasn't something Horton had ever really played seriously as a kid. Griggs helped paint the picket fence at the short-lived Tim Horton Motors in Willowdale and joined Horton on *Telegram* ad sales calls, as well as on some of his high-speed car delivery runs to the North Bay dealership. They jogged together, and when they met kids who wanted Horton's autograph, Horton would whisper to him, "Sign 'Kent Douglas,'" and Griggs would obligingly impersonate the defenceman who joined the Leafs in 1962–63 and won the Calder as the league's top rookie. Horton was probably even closer to Dennis's older brother, Gordon, who after a delinquent streak as a teen decided to become a Presbyterian minister, a feat he achieved in 1967 after a significant amount of financial help from Horton to attend Waterloo Lutheran University (now Wilfrid Laurier University) and the University of Toronto. Gordon Griggs was very much the model of a muscular Christian, shy of neither swearing nor drinking. He would preside over Horton's funeral.

Dennis Griggs had a one-year stint as a Toronto police officer in 1960, before chucking life as a cop to establish a business called VIP that made signage, coupons and flyers out of his home on Tweed Crescent, close to Manhattan Park. When Charade started Your Do-Nut, Griggs produced the promotional materials and also came to manage the satellite operation. The two became so close that Charade served as Griggs's best man.

Charade recalled for me that he met Horton in May 1963, when he wanted to buy a car and Griggs obligingly made the connection with the Leaf defenceman, who sold him a used Pontiac. Both Griggs and Horton's widow, Lori, however, assured me that Tim met Jim because, despite the fact he hadn't lived in the Wexford area for more than three years, Horton was still getting his signature brush cut at the barbershop called Benny's in the Colony Plaza. In the spring of 1963, when the Leafs were en route to a second straight Cup win, Horton dropped in on the doughnut shop two units down after a practice, and Griggs introduced him to Charade.

"I told him what we were doing and I set him up with Jim," Griggs told me. "Jimmy was the brains behind it, the one who started the first doughnut shop, but it was me that got Tim involved. I'm one of the founding fathers."

BY THE SPRING OF 1963, the Your Do-Nut venture was emerging from one of several star-crossed episodes that would mark Charade's entrepreneurial career. Unable to both run the doughnut plant and attend to his retailing ambitions, Charade had left Vachon in September 1962. There was chain competition on the rise. Dunkin' Donuts opened its first Canadian outlet, in Montreal, in 1961, the start of its long-standing prominence in the Quebec market. Mister Donut had carried on with plans for Canada without Charade. There was at least one store in the Toronto area by 1963, in Scarborough on Eglinton Avenue East, near the intersection with Midland Avenue.

Charade hooked up with a group of Ottawa investors that had turned a single Royal Burger Drive-In Restaurant in Ottawa into a chain of seven outlets around the capital and had also entered the Kingston market. The Toronto market was next: an outlet opened on Dundas West, near Kipling, and in 1963 they added a walk-in outlet downtown, on Yonge near Shuter, across from what is now the Toronto Eaton Centre.

Charade told me he signed an employment contract with the Ottawa investors, and was to begin establishing a chain of Royal Donuts in Ottawa. They, in turn, would buy his Your Do-Nut operation for $20,000 and change his outlets to Royal stores. Over the winter of 1962–63, Charade went to Ottawa and opened the first Royal Donut Shop, on Richmond Road. Back in Toronto, the signage on Your Do-Nut was changed to Royal Do-Nut as planned, but Charade then decided to bail out on the Royal people. "They were wacko and they worked with other people's money."

Charade now had signage on his Toronto doughnut stores for a chain he wanted nothing to do with. He obviously couldn't go on being Royal Do-Nut, and continued to resist the idea of joining the Boston-area concepts of Mister Donut and Dunkin' Donuts as a franchisee. Charade wanted his own business, and the business needed a new name.

Charade also needed a competitive edge in a market that was increasingly becoming known by chain brands. By 1964, Mister Donut had three Toronto outlets. Joining the original franchise at Eglinton East near Midland was one in North York on Wilson Avenue, just west of Bathurst, and—most alarmingly—one on Lawrence East, less than a quarter-mile to the west of Charade's doughnut store and on the same side of the street. A Canadian doughnut chain, Country Style, was founded by Alan Lowe in 1963. By 1964 there were two in Toronto's west end.

Jim Charade knew all about baking doughnuts, and was learning quickly about consumer retailing. What he didn't know a whole lot about was branding, but he thought he could do better than reverting to Your Do-Nut as a business name. The solution he hit upon was to make his product not *your* doughnut, but *Tim Horton's* doughnut.

6

What's in a Name? The Persona of a Restaurant Brand

A restaurant's name is the foundation, the organizing principle, of its brand. I discussed the importance of brand with John Rothschild, president and CEO of Prime Restaurants of Canada, at his Mississauga office in the summer of 2011.

Prime's portfolio of franchised casual-dining and pub concepts has more than 160 outlets. On the casual-dining side are the original concept, Casey's (launched in 1980), and East Side Mario's (1987). The basket of pub concepts includes Pat & Mario's, Fionn MacCool's, D'Arcy McGee's, Paddy Flaherty's, Tir nan Óg, and the Bier Markt. Trading on the TSX under the ticker symbol EAT, Prime had enjoyed solid 2.5 percent growth in same-store sales* in the first half of 2011, opened two new East Side Mario's and another pub in the second quarter, and come away with pre-tax profits of $1.9 million on revenues of $15.3 million, which had been generated by $86.8 million in reported sales by the restaurants. In the midst of a shaky economic recovery, Prime was doing fine with a discretionary consumer product.

* In retail accounting, "same-store sales" compares year-to-year revenue changes at outlets that have been open at least one year. (Tim Hortons uses stores open thirteen months or more.) It filters out the revenue bump caused by new outlet openings and provides a clearer indication of how a chain is performing.

A chartered accountant with an MBA from Western University, Rothschild had been with the company that is now Prime since 1988. He also enjoyed the rare distinction among senior executives of Canadian public companies of having his family's name on the Stanley Cup.

"Sam Rothschild was my great-uncle," he told me, waiting until the end of our conversation to share this family lore. "He played for the Maroons. His name is on the first band of the Stanley Cup. He didn't play that many games, but he was in the right place at the right time."

Rothschild may have been one of the first Jewish players in the NHL, coming out of the Sudbury amateur game and joining the Montreal Maroons in 1925–26. As a member of the 1926 Cup-winning Maroons, he appeared in four playoff games without recording a goal, an assist or a penalty minute. Rothschild logged three seasons with them; the Hockey Hall of Fame's "Legends of Hockey" database indicates that he signed with the Pittsburgh Pirates as a free agent in November 1927, only to be suspended after a dozen games on December 26 for "breaking training rules." He joined the New York Americans that January and finished out his playing career with them after appearing in five games.

Sam Rothschild returned to Sudbury and joined Sam Bronfman's distillery company, Seagram, as a salesman. "I used to go to Sudbury as a kid and go fishing with my Uncle Sam," John Rothschild recalled. "We called him 'Hunk of Ham,' because he was a short little guy, a round, roly-poly kind of guy." The fact that Uncle Sam had gone from playing for the Americans, a team owned by a notorious New York bootlegger, Bill Dwyer, to selling liquor for Seagram, a distillery owned by the bootlegging Sam Bronfman, was an intriguing career trajectory that I had no time to explore.

Casey's, the original restaurant in what has become the Prime portfolio, coincidentally started in Sudbury in 1980; Rothschild joined the company that became Prime in 1988. He has seen many concepts come and go, and his own company's founding restaurant, Casey's, recently went through its fourth reconception. What began as a roadhouse was turned into a bar and grill, then into a "diner house" and finally back into a bar and grill with a new prototype in 2006. Change and adaptation is the nature of the restaurant business. Tim Hortons might be very different from how it was originally conceived, as a walk-in doughnut shop in Scarborough's Colony Plaza, but it exists because its successive owners and management have striven to retool it while—hopefully—maintaining and even enhancing the underlying value of its brand.

"The thing that we all have in common," Rothschild said as he considered the full gamut of the restaurant industry, "is we have brands. That's the only asset we have. A brand has to be meaningful. If you're not meaningful or relevant to your customers, you're a dying brand. Every brand has a life cycle, and it has to keep changing."

Precious few restaurant brands have endured as long or as successfully as Tim Hortons. A plethora of franchise concepts from its first years in business—remember Red Barn? Mother's?—have not survived. Others have risen along the way and failed to challenge Tim Hortons' market dominance.

Franchise concepts crash and burn because of a failure to adapt to changing consumer tastes, to meet the challenge of rival concepts, to manage the delicate power relationship between the franchisor and the franchisee, to expand with the right locations in the right markets with the right product and the right franchisees—or even to forgo franchisees and use corporate-owned locations. Tim Hortons' franchise classmates from the 1960s, Harvey's and Swiss Chalet, are still with us, having been part of the portfolio of Cara Operations since 1978. And Boston Pizza, which dates back to a single restaurant in Edmonton in 1964, continues to expand its casual-dining concept in North America. All of them have experienced hiccups in their growth, and concerted competition from American chains.

Alone among other concepts that endure, Tim Hortons was named for an actual living person, a co-founder that the concept has long outlived. The franchised stores were initially named "Tim Horton" or "Tim Horton's." They changed to a plural "Tim Hortons" to satisfy Quebec language laws in commercial signage. Semantically, it meant that the chain no longer *belonged to* Tim Horton, but was rather *of* Tim Horton. However it was spelled, I have long wondered how much that name ever mattered, and how much it matters anymore.

I remarked to John Rothschild that, like Tim Hortons, many of his restaurant and pub properties are named for somebody, even if they're just imaginary people. That made his stable of properties different from, say, Swiss Chalet and Boston Pizza, which conveyed places. Did he think a restaurant had to have a person's name in its signage? A human entity with which the customer could identify?

"A restaurant has to stand for *something,*" Rothschild said, "and by giving it some personality, that starts to help it stand for something." He turned his thoughts to Tim Hortons. Rothschild had actually known Tim Horton as a kid. His great-uncle Sam was in Sudbury when Tim Horton was living there and playing his junior hockey in Copper Cliff, but the connection to Horton was made by Rothschild's father, a professional photographer who worked with Horton's wife, Lori, in Toronto while she was still doing the odd modelling job. "I got to know them on a personal basis."

Rothschild was introduced to the inner circle of players of the celebrated Leafs, the ones who were hustling, like Horton, Baun and the Cullen brothers. "After the game, the players would go to a restaurant called the Honey Dew. As a kid I would go. We would have drinks, coffee and stuff, and so I got to know Tim Horton. I was in awe, being surrounded by these heroes. He was a great guy, a terrific guy. To me, Tim Horton was always a person first, and an entity second. He was a quiet man, a more or less introverted man, and on the ice he was a tiger, a tough guy."

Rothschild, now a sixty-two-year-old restaurateur and not an awestruck young hockey fan, could offer me no recollections of

Horton's namesake restaurants from those days. It was the memory of the human being behind the signage that endured. "I remember his death vividly," he said, correctly recalling that Horton had been driving a Pantera, "an Italian racing car with a Ford engine."

"When does a name change from being a personality to being a word in a dictionary?" Rothschild wondered aloud. "'Tim Horton' is no longer the name of a human being, it's a word in a dictionary. It's understood to be what it is." He left aside what he thought that might be, and instead turned to the example of his flagship chain. "East Side Mario's, to us, that says a couple of things. It says Italian, it says there's a guy named Mario, it says that it's from New York, the east side, and it's differentiated from the other Italian dinner houses. It says there's a personality. It's going to have good food, it's from New York, so it's kind of in your face, and it's going to be a kind of fun-type place. And it's going to be casual. It's a name that helps to identify our brand and to tell you what to expect."

A brand, as East Side Mario's amply demonstrates, can be named for no one—or at least for someone who might as well be no one. Such was the case with McDonald's, which was a drive-in business founded by Richard and Maurice McDonald. After franchisee Ray Kroc won a struggle for its ownership, the name stayed. "McDonald" has long ceased being a person in any meaningful way. People don't visit McDonald's because they have fond memories or associations with the brothers Richard and Maurice. It is a nameplate in which the franchise giant has infused particular brand values and from which it derived the *M* of its signature golden arches, and has also used to generate a fictional spokesperson, the clown Ronald.

As Jim Charade searched in 1963 for an identity for his doughnut store, as well as for a drive-in restaurant chain of his own that he hoped to launch after splitting with the Royal people, an instructive naming precedent was growing around him in Greater Toronto. It was the burger drive-in Harvey's, a chain that would prove to be a more significant factor in the ongoing Tim Hortons story than has been recognized.

Harvey's was the brainchild of partners Richard Mauran and George B. Sukornyk. Mauran had arrived in Toronto to open a version of a rotisserie chicken restaurant he'd developed in Montreal that featured interior seating as well as takeout and home delivery. In 1954 he opened one downtown on Bloor Street West, across from Varsity Stadium, and called it Swiss Chalet. A few years later, he added one in Buffalo, New York, and about this time he acquired as his partner Sukornyk, a lawyer who had been taking care of his paperwork. Together, around 1957, they began looking for another concept.

The story has been told that while in Buffalo one of them happened upon a one-man burger joint called Pat's that was making flame-broiled burgers with an interesting assembly-line counter system that allowed the customer to choose their garnishes. Mauran and Sukornyk decided to try the concept in Canada. The partners bought land in Richmond Hill, along the east side of Yonge Street, which did double duty as Highway 11. Highway 400 did not yet exist, which meant Highway 11 was the main route north out of Toronto into vacation country.

In 1959, they built an A-frame roadside grill, but didn't know what to call it. The lead candidate was Humphrey's. The actual person didn't matter: the name just had to sound friendly and unpretentious. They were fretting about the expense of the sign, with all the letters in the name, when they read in the Toronto *Telegram* (Harvey's corporate website today says it was specifically the July 11, 1959, edition) about a car dealer at 2300 Danforth Avenue, at the intersection of Gledhill, a site now occupied by Toronto Honda. The car dealership was called Harvey's.

The foundation stories get a little tangled here. One version has it that Mauran bought the Harvey's sign and modified it slightly. By one account, he stuck it up at the outlet he opened way out on Eglinton

Avenue East, between McCowan and Markham roads. But that outlet doesn't materialize in a city directory until 1963. It seems more likely the salvaged Harvey's sign was used for the original A-frame in 1959, on the location that came to serve as corporate headquarters for both Harvey's and Swiss Chalet. In any event, thus was branded one of today's most recognizable QSR chains in Canada, which also repeatedly crossed paths with Tim Hortons in their corporate histories.

If Charade simply wanted a personable sounding name for his doughnut shop, he could have followed the Harvey's example, or even used his own name. He could have done worse than to call the place "Jimmy's." But in the spring of 1963 he had just chanced to meet Tim Horton through Dennis Griggs. The Leaf defenceman brought to mind Gino Marchetti, a defensive end and team captain of the National Football League's Baltimore Colts.

A burger outlet had been started in 1957 by one of Marchetti's teammates, running back Alan Ameche, and a mutual friend, Louis Fischer. After the Colts won NFL titles in 1958 and 1959, Ameche and Fischer enlisted Marchetti as a partner and front man, and turned the single original store into a franchise chain of drive-in restaurants known as Gino's Hamburgers. Gino's had grown to 359 corporate-owned outlets in the eastern United States, including a Rustler Steak House division that was launched in the 1960s, when it was acquired by Marriott Corp. in 1982.

Charade sized up Horton and believed he had a Marchetti of his own. Like Marchetti, Horton had just won two back-to-back league titles. Horton wasn't a team captain like Marchetti, but he was an assistant captain. He was named to the second all-star team in 1963—his first all-star appearance since 1954—and was elevated to the first team in 1964. Horton was thirty-three, which was getting old for a professional hockey player, and he had never been more marketable as a name.

Horton also had a long-standing interest in getting a business going, and at that moment had little to show for his constant hustling. Tim

Horton Motors in Willowdale had flopped. Tim Horton Motors still existed in North Bay, though Lori Horton told me that it belonged to Tim's brother, Gerry, who ran it as part of the family Shell station with help from Tim in sourcing vehicles around Toronto. Horton, meanwhile, had the Hannigan boys whispering in his ear about their plans for Hannigan burgers and Heavenly Chicken in Alberta.

Charade saw Horton at the very least as a celebrity brand waiting to be exploited, the way Marchetti was. "People always feel you can't just go from sport, if you have another name, into another business," Charade told me. "But I thought Tim could do it, if you took care of things and did it well and didn't mess people up and had the right attitude. I took him as a partner for his name, for his autographs. Even if you don't have the product, if you have the name, at least you'll get them in the door."

In July 1963, only months after the two men met, Tim Horton and Jim Charade were in business together. At the same time that the lawyer Ken Gariepy handled the documentation creating the commercial real estate investment portfolio, Tim Horton Holdings Ltd., he marshalled a restaurant business partnership between Horton and Charade, called Timanjim Ltd. Charade also arranged a separate licensing agreement for Horton's name for his doughnut store and its satellite outlet.

"Tim didn't know a doughnut from a hockey puck, but he liked them," Charade told me. Horton was intrigued by the possibility of doughnuts, but was really more interested in beef and chicken, and so was Charade.

The Timanjim restaurant business was a hybrid of inspirations: the burger outlets of Gino Marchetti, the Hannigan burger and chicken restaurants, and the two Richmond Hill–based chains, Harvey's and Swiss Chalet. In fact, Greater Toronto was full of drive-in barbecue concepts offering chicken, beef and pork, all struggling to stake out a territory, with little variance in the essential model to distinguish one from the other.

Having bailed on the Royal Burgers initiative that had just arrived in Toronto, Charade wanted to get a rival operation quickly up and running. A local insurance executive with commercial real estate investments had opened a pair of drive-in restaurants in Scarborough call Johnny Johnson's. He was shutting both down, and Timanjim leased the site on Kingston Road east of McCowan Road. The executive had another property, formerly a Biff Burger, on Lawrence, across the street from Charade's Your Do-Nut in the Colony Plaza, which was now called Tim Horton Do-Nut. Timanjim took this site too, and with those two locations the Tim Horton Drive-In Restaurant chain was launched.

Timanjim added a third outlet, on the opposite side of the city, on Lakeshore Road in the heart of what is now Port Credit. Finally, it took over a storefront space downtown, near Ryerson Polytechnical Institute on the Yonge Street strip above Dundas, that was occupied by a restaurant called Stop and Go. The owner was Benny Winbaum, whose Winco Ltd. owned the Steak N' Burger franchise rights. The open grill shared a front window with a display case for doughnuts driven down from the Colony Plaza store, and in the back was a space that served as the head office of both the Horton restaurants of Timanjim and the real estate portfolio, Tim Horton Holdings.

Horton's drive-ins didn't have carhops. They were drive-ins in the concept's earliest sense of having on-site parking space for customers. The general floor plan featured stand-up eating at counters, but the Kingston Road outlet (which, at last inspection, was the site of a Hardee's) had indoor table seating that, it was hoped, would increase the appeal in winter, as the Hannigans found with their Edmonton outlet's indoor seating. The Port Credit store offered home delivery of chicken on the Swiss Chalet model. Horton found an old VW van and crowned it with a Tim Horton Chicken sign, but it did double duty as a family car for the Charades because Tim had sold Claudette Charade a Karmann Ghia that hardly ever ran.

The chain was fully in place by late 1963, when the flyer shown to me in 2010 by the vintage paper collector was created, most certainly by Dennis Griggs. But the Timanjim drive-in restaurant adventure was over virtually as soon as it started. By the time the city directory of 1964 was issued, there was only one Tim Horton Drive-In Restaurant, the outlet on Lawrence East across from the doughnut store in Colony Plaza. The rest had disappeared; the Kingston Road outlet, for one, had become a Chick-N-Burger Drive In.

When Lawrence Martin interviewed Horton for the 1973 *Canadian* magazine profile, he refused to discuss the drive-ins: "Let's just leave it at that. They flopped."

7

Industrial Sales: Staking a Chain's Future on Hamilton's Shift Workers

At the end of the 1963–64 season and after a third consecutive Stanley Cup win for the Toronto Maple Leafs, Tim and Lori Horton celebrated with a Caribbean cruise. They returned to financial disaster at Timanjim. "When we got back," Lori told me, "the money was all gone."

Some of Tim Horton's business friends suspected that Jim Charade was scamming him. Russ Gioffrey confronted Horton directly with that possibility, and told me that Horton was stunned and managed only "I guess he needs it more than I do" in reply.

Lori told me her husband never believed Charade was taking advantage of him. "I always found Jim easy to get along with. And I didn't believe it, either. I still don't believe it. I don't really think Jim was that kind of person. There was somebody working for them who was lifting money, but it wasn't Jim."

Charade was so drained by the restaurants that he had to sell his house to cover personal debts. That didn't mean Charade had been wholly above board. He had withdrawn money from Timanjim, but it was to address a cash-flow crisis in his doughnut stores. The problem was that Horton didn't have any equity in those stores, only in the burger and chicken operations owned by Timanjim. But the incident fuelled speculation that Charade was bleeding the profits from the Timanjim partnership to cover his losses in his doughnut enterprise.

According to Charade, there were never any profits to bleed. "There was a lot of money coming in," he told me, "but no profits. We did a lot of specials—buy one, get one free. We used to have chicken at special prices, and the places would be just loaded with people, but we weren't making any money. We tried to get some business, let people know where we are, and if they liked it, maybe we'll get some repeat business.

"We never had an argument," Charade stressed. "Tim was enthusiastic. He would call me in the middle of the night and say, 'I saw this in Chicago . . . I picked up this coffee cup . . . ' It was always something like that. And people would bring him things because they knew he was enthusiastic."

That Horton considered himself more than a celebrity brand name on a sign is indisputable. The Hannigans knew of (and fuelled) his interest in restaurants. The small circle of businesspeople he turned into good friends was well aware of his acumen and curiosity. Among his fellow Leafs, Bob Baun witnessed it regularly, and so did his defence partner, Allan Stanley, who recalled Horton taking business ledgers to review on road trips. "On the road," Stanley told me, "there was always a restaurant he wanted to see. He had his interest in fast food for a long time. I used to go with him. We'd go in, and he'd talk to the owner and ask them about their business."

What Horton wanted above all was not a doughnut store, or a chain of drive-ins, but a casual-dining restaurant. "He really had his mind set on a steak house," Charade told me. Horton was impressed with the Tad's chain in New York City, where for $1.59 you were served a steak and then moved through a self-serve buffet to load on salad and a baked potato. The steak house plans got as far as picking a potential site in downtown Toronto: the Rutherford's Drugs lunch counter on Yonge Street, south of Queen, across from the Simpsons department store. Lori Horton told me that the steak house would have been developed in association with Benny Winbaum, who had the Steak N' Burger chain and had leased Timanjim the site of the former Stop and Go outlet on Yonge. But the steak house never came to pass, and by 1964 the drive-ins were failing.

Horton had one more restaurant venture that moved to the front burner in the summer of 1964. A burger outlet was opened on the Horton Shell property in North Bay; its history is murky, but it was informally called "Number 7," or "The Big 7," in honour of Horton's Leafs number, which was the focal point of the sign. The design was based shamelessly on the A-frame of the original Harvey's on Yonge Street, which Tim patronized on trips to North Bay. Tim's brother, Gerry, built and staffed it; Tim provided the signage and the design knock-off of Harvey's.

Some people thought that the ownership of Tim Horton Motors in North Bay created a rift between Tim and his brother, Gerry, but Lori Horton told me this was never the case, that the car dealership was Gerry's. It was the little A-frame restaurant that ignited the fireworks. A family conference appears to have settled the matter of who owned Number 7 in Gerry's favour. But it was right after the ownership dispute that Gerry had his first heart attack. "Tim was really broken up about his little brother," Lori told me.

Gerry would continue to run the restaurant as a Number 7 until his brother's sudden death. After that, he would turn it into a German restaurant, declining the opportunity to operate a sort of fast-food shrine to his late brother's memory. The burger and chicken outlets around Toronto that had started Tim Horton's restaurant career were dismal failures almost from the beginning. And Jim Charade's doughnuts were the last things left on which Tim Horton could pin his restaurant hopes.

Tim Horton wasn't interested in putting any money into doughnut shops, but was agreeable to his friend Charade continuing to license his name for them. To raise the capital necessary for new restaurants, Charade decided to go the franchising route. To play this last card, Charade knew he had to get out of town.

CHARADE TOLD ME he picked Hamilton for the first Tim Horton doughnut franchise because it wasn't Toronto, where doughnut chain competition was mounting. By 1964, Country Style had two outlets in Toronto's west end, and Mister Donut was expanding, with two Scarborough outlets and another in North York. Hamilton was virgin territory as far as the nascent doughnut chains were concerned. Charade was willing to go there, even though it meant abandoning the city in which Horton's name had the greatest cachet. The Leafs, however, were well established as a national sports phenomenon, having won three consecutive Stanley Cups between 1962 and 1964. They were the showcase team of *Hockey Night in Canada* in English Canada, and Horton was one of the team's—and thus the program's—star players. There would be no name-recognition problems with Horton in the steel city forty miles west of Maple Leaf Gardens.

Apart from the fact that Charade must have been rattled by the impact that the Mister Donut outlet right down the street on Lawrence Avenue was having on his doughnut store in the Colony Plaza, he chose Hamilton because Greater Toronto was becoming far too expensive as a place of business for drive-ins, whatever they were serving. But what Charade didn't tell me is that he had an obvious inspiration for where he started looking for a franchise doughnut store location. Harvey's had just opened its first outlet outside Greater Toronto in a very different sort of spot: the industrial north end of Hamilton. The Harvey's Drive-In at the corner of Barton Street and Rosslyn Avenue was open in time to be listed in the Hamilton business directory of 1964—before

Charade showed up to open his first Tim Horton franchise, just a few blocks away.

WITH THE SUBURBAN LANDSCAPE having been pretty much filled in by 1960, land costs in Scarborough were soaring as drive-in developers vied for property with each other and with rival businesses like gas stations. By 1967, there were an estimated thirty different drive-ins along Lawrence Avenue East and Eglinton Avenue East alone in Scarborough. Residents were getting fed up with the increased car traffic, trash, cooking odours and teenage tomfoolery, including street racing. Frustrations would reach a peak in the summer of 1966, when police reported making twenty arrests and laying 270 charges, which ranged from "ability impaired" to "excessive noise," over the course of twenty days in the vicinity of two Harvey's Drive-Ins. On August 25, Scarborough's executive committee put Harvey's on four week's notice to see if it could clean up its act. Security guards were hired, and hours of operation were cut back from a 4 a.m. closing to 2 a.m. Harvey's held on to its existing locations, but decided not to build on land it had acquired at Ellesmere and Bellamy roads for a third outlet, in the face of opposition from the Woburn Gate Community Association.

The Harvey's and Swiss Chalet chains expanded through the shrewd guidance of partners Mauran and Sukornyk, who understood the two most critical aspects of drive-in restaurant siting. One was the importance of locations in high-traffic areas that were preferably right at, or very close to, major intersections: easy to find and to access for drivers going in four different directions. Not surprisingly, drive-in developers found that old gas-station service centres made for profitable conversions, both because of their siting (oil companies followed the same logic of traffic patterns) and their generous parking lots. It would take another few decades, but the people in the gas station business and the people in the QSR franchise business would finally realize that they should be developing these high-traffic locations together, as in the case of Tim Hortons kiosks being added to Esso's On the Run retail outlets.

The other key aspect of the Mauran-Sukornyk business plan was the importance of owning the property wherever possible, or at least holding the head lease on the land and owning the building, even when franchising. A real estate portfolio gave the restaurant company some gravitas of reliable, long-term assets that, in the right location, could appreciate regardless of the actual business. And when the parent company, or franchisor, controlled the property, it also remained firmly in control of the outlet's destiny. Franchisees with fixed-term agreements could be replaced without the location losing stride. It was a fundamental operating principle that Tim Hortons too embraced, turning the chain as much into a real estate portfolio as a restaurant franchise company.

In coming to Hamilton, the site Mauran and Sukornyk chose for Harvey's was profoundly at odds with where restaurant drive-ins were supposed to be located, and who they were supposed to serve. Hamilton and environs certainly had suburbia. The land south of the main city, on the escarpment, which became known colloquially as "the Mountain," had experienced a massive buildup of bungalows typical of those in Scarborough in the 1950s and into the early 1960s, with more development coming steadily on stream and pushing the city's settled boundaries ever farther south. Yet by 1964 there was only a handful of drive-in restaurants—the Millionaire and Rendezvous chains, and an A&W in the East End on Queenston Road, on the doorstep of Stoney Creek, to name a few. On the Mountain, Upper James Street, which became Highway 6 leading south out of town, was gathering momentum south of Mohawk Road as a strip of drive-ins and other conveniences. But Mauran and Sukornyk put their Harvey's deep in the industrial heart of the city—on the very frontier of it, in fact, as the land north of Barton Street was mostly one vast sprawl of foundries, rolling mills and associated industries.

This was nothing like the emerging suburbia to the south, above the escarpment. But there was life along Barton Street. The Forum, the hockey arena that was home to the Junior A Red Wings, a farm team of the NHL's Detroit Red Wings that won the Memorial Cup in 1962, was about a mile and a quarter down the road on Barton Street. Ivor Wynne Stadium, home to the Canadian Football League's Tiger-Cats, was only about a half-mile drive away. The Harvey's was also just west of Centre Mall, one of the largest shopping centres in North America, which had opened in 1955 and was the first such enclosed indoor mall in Canada. Furthermore, the drive-in was sited right on the doorstep of all those industrial jobs. Men—and they were virtually all men in the industrial pursuits—could be catered to as they came on and off shift.

Jim Charade followed hard on the heels of Mauran and Sukornyk in coming to Hamilton to try to make a go of the concept of a drive-in doughnut shop that also sold coffee. Hamilton was bereft of doughnut competition; the closest concept was the Coffee House Pastry Shop, which was downtown, at the corner of King and Walnut. He looked for a property that would distract the round-the-clock flow of shift workers and accommodate a typical drive-in restaurant plan: a small building with plenty of on-site parking.

It's hard to overemphasize how absolutely critical the selection of this franchise location was to the Tim Hortons saga. Charade was running out of chances to make a Tim Horton restaurant concept work. He didn't have the luxury of another failure. He was trying to create a doughnut drive-in concept of his own that was playing catch-up with rivals like Mister Donut and Country Style. Charade didn't have any money, and Tim Horton's own ability to raise capital was limited. They already had been through the debacle of the chicken and burger joints in Toronto. Now Charade had followed Harvey's to Hamilton's industrial East End, a place utterly foreign to him and Horton, to try a restaurant concept that was utterly foreign to the people who lived and worked there. A location one block in the wrong direction could have been fatal. There may well have been no repeat opportunity.

Charade found a former Esso service station on the northwest corner of Ottawa Street North and Dunsmure Road. It was a half-mile south of the intersection of Ottawa and Barton; the Harvey's Drive-In was three short blocks west of the Ottawa-Barton intersection. Ottawa Street led into Hamilton's industrial heart, straight to the front gates of the Dofasco steelmaking complex. Today, the Harvey's site is a convenience store with more than enough parking in a dilapidated neighbourhood. The site Charade chose is Tim Hortons store #1, a veritable national shrine to a cultural phenomenon. The jazz drummer from Montreal who had turned to doughnut retailing could not have stuck a pin in a map in a better place in choosing where to make what was likely the last stand for Tim Horton as a restaurant entrepreneur.

More than a site that finally got a restaurant chain launched, Charade's choice came to define the fundamentals of the company that arose from it. Store #1 was the model for Tim Hortons going forward. The interior may have been completely remodelled since then, and counter seating has been eliminated in favour of tables, but to many people, this store (which has no drive-through) remains what a Tim Hortons should be: friendly and local; a place where you park and get out of your car, or arrive on foot; where you order your coffee, treat or meal, and then sit down at a table, with friends or total strangers. A gathering place. Tim Hortons has greatly diversified its store concepts, especially with dedicated drive-throughs and self-serve kiosks, but the core idea of a Tim Hortons, which the company itself seems to realize it cannot drift away from, is store #1.

8

Steeltown: How Store #1 Became a National Shrine to Our Caffeine Habit

I came into Hamilton, the city in which I was born and raised, to visit Tim Hortons store #1 by driving along the Queen Elizabeth Way over the Burlington Bay James N. Allan Skyway, with its aerial view of the industrial sprawl of the city's north end along the harbour shore. The view used to be much more impressive (or daunting): Hamilton's industrial glory days are behind it. Mills and factories have closed, and the downtown is struggling to shake off a shabbiness that is disconcerting for a city so large.

There are brownfields in the north end where there used to be plenty of jobs. The two major employers, Stelco and Dofasco, no longer dominate the life of the city. The health-care industry is now the single largest local employer. Stelco was already shrinking when it was acquired by U.S. Steel in 2007. The Hamilton operations were mothballed in 2010 in a contract dispute that saw the workers locked out. Non-unionized Dofasco was bought by what is now Luxembourg steel giant ArcelorMittal in 2006 and had outlived its unionized rival Stelco to become the sole presence of steelmaking in what had been a major North American production centre.

Exiting Burlington Street, the main thoroughfare through the industrial north end, the drive south along Ottawa Street takes you past the Dofasco cold rolling mill and, in two places, beneath the overreaching structure of its waste-water treatment plant. On your left, after crossing the railroad tracks, is Centre Mall, recently completely made over as a big-box retail site.

Crossing Barton, now a half-mile from the original Tim's franchise, brings you into the enduring shopping strip of Ottawa North, then as now jammed full of fabric retailers. I knew this area well as a kid. The cross street of Cannon Street is a quarter-mile north of the doughnut shop, and my dad had been raised three side streets west of Ottawa, in a house near the corner of Cannon on Rosslyn Avenue. A quarter-mile north on Rosslyn, at the corner of Barton, was the Harvey's Drive-In. My grandmother, who had been widowed in 1963, still lived in that house when I was young, and we visited regularly. My mom would drag me along on shopping trips to the fabric stores for materials to make our clothes. My dad then was a tool-and-die maker employed by American Can, which was to the west, on Victoria Avenue. As a result, his shift-work commute (and the drives I made with my siblings as Mom picked him up at the end of a shift there until 1966, when he moved to the Westinghouse plant near the old Forum) didn't take him up and down Ottawa Street, past the new Tim Horton Donut Drive-In.

I can't recall a specific visit to the original Tim's as a kid—one Tim's blurs into another—although I would have been there after a hockey practice at nearby Scott Park Arena, a roofed outdoor rink that was brutally cold on an early winter morning. My dad recalls that when he was coaching teams my goaltending brother Andrew played on, he would take carloads of kids into the place after a Sunday practice at Scott Park. Where Tim's was concerned, we otherwise waited for the chain to follow the workers' diaspora to the suburbs of Hamilton Mountain, once the restaurant concept had proven itself in a promising if fitful start on Ottawa Street.

My family was part of that great middle-class diaspora, settling on the west side of the Mountain, not the east side from which steelworkers especially made the run down the Kenilworth Access and onto Ottawa Street, past that Tim Hortons and down to the gates of Dofasco. My parents moved into a three-bedroom bungalow in 1959, when I was born—a home much the same as the one Tim and Lori Horton had bought on Warden Avenue in Wexford in 1953. The second Tim Hortons location was placed on Concession Street, a business district of the Mountain suburbs that ran along the escarpment brow. When Tim's opened its sixth location, at Upper James Street and Mohawk Road, the coffee and doughnuts arrived in my neighbourhood. By the time I was in my teens, it seemed that if you wanted a coffee and a doughnut in Hamilton, you pretty much only had to point your vehicle down a major street and wait for the telltale double ovals of the franchise's signage to guide you into the parking lot.

As my dad is not a coffee drinker (and when I was young, he would valiantly try to buy tea to go at Tim's that met his standards), I did not question the idea, proposed to me many years after I first began to frequent the restaurants, that coffee had not been a popular drink of Canadians when Jim Charade opened the first franchise on Ottawa Street. I didn't even taste coffee until I reached university in the late 1970s. According to Charade, coffee only contributed about 20 percent of revenues in that franchise, whereas today, depending on the outlet, it accounts for perhaps 50 to 75 percent, and an even greater share of profits.

Nevertheless, in perusing the city directory of 1964 after visiting store #1, I was impressed by two things about Hamilton where restaurants were concerned. One was how crazy we Hamiltonians evidently were for fish and chips, judging by the enormous number of restaurants dedicated to them. The other was how many coffee shops the city already had when Charade brought his drive-in concept to town: forty restaurants in the city directory had "coffee" in their name, and that tally didn't include diners and lunch counters that also served the beverage. Ron Joyce would say that he considered Tim Horton outlets to be gathering places like bars, only without the alcohol. In 1964, there were in fact nine businesses in Hamilton calling themselves "coffee bars" before Charade showed up with his Tim Horton coffee-and-doughnut concept.

In the nascent doughnut franchise business, coffee and doughnuts were considered inseparable. Dunkin' Donuts was so named because customers were expected to dunk their small rings of cake into the coffee as they consumed both. And while coffee was supposed to be a hard sell to tea-sipping Canadians, Hamiltonians already appeared to be slugging back java at a rate out of all proportion to their neighbours down the road in Toronto.

About half of Hamilton's coffee shops and bars were clustered around the downtown, but half a dozen were so deep in the industrial north end that they suggest shift workers were already mainlining caffeine from coffee rather than tea. Two coffee shops were on Ottawa Street, and were closer to Dofasco's gates than the location Charade chose for the doughnut drive-in. But they lacked what Charade was about to provide: on-site parking that made it easy to pull in and have a cup, either at the counter or as takeout, either to or from work. In the early days of steelmaking, workers' pay was such that they expected to live close enough to the mill to walk to their jobs. With increasing postwar labour affluence, industrial workers had moved to the new suburbs as they could afford cars that delivered them to the factory gates. Those same cars could propel them into a drive-in restaurant. And Charade had another draw that these other establishments did not: sweet, fresh-baked doughnuts, especially yeast-based ones that you didn't dunk and were a real novelty. They could be eaten one at a time or driven away by the boxload.

Ottawa Street was a main arterial road leading from the factories and mills of the East End, south through the city's older, working-class residential area, before it gained the emerging suburbia of the East Mountain via the Kenilworth Access. The traffic along Ottawa was significant enough to warrant the first Tim Hortons franchise, but its position in relation to the east-west routes was also critical. In the name of efficient movement of shift workers, Hamilton is a warren of one-way streets. The two principal arteries that cross the city from east to west are one-way: Main Street runs east; King Street runs west. Main meets Ottawa just a block south of the restaurant, which took care of easy access to the store for people coming out of the centre of town. Westbound King Street, the old settler road, curves in the East End and crosses Main at a neighbourhood junction called the Delta, to the west of the store. Dunsmure Road is a two-way secondary street that runs parallel to Main, one block north, and feeds into King less than half a mile to the west of the store, near the Delta. So anyone coming south on Ottawa from the plants that wanted to access King Street to go west into the city centre hung a right at Dunsmure. They couldn't help but see the restaurant and would have to resist the temptation to pull into its parking lot and partake of its doughnuts and coffee.

Charade still fretted about his choice of location, recalling for me how, shortly before the drive-in opened, he spent an entire night counting the cars on Parkdale Avenue, another major north-south street servicing the industrial sector a few blocks to the east. This was the basic tool of franchise siting: the drudge work of observing traffic volumes at different times of day, to see if a location met minimums a franchise operation considered necessary. "I watched the traffic at 3 a.m., 4 a.m., because it was going to be open twenty-four hours. I thought, 'I've got to be crazy.' But there was nothing to compare it to." Charade was praying there was enough commuter volume of shift workers in the entire East End that he could deflect it to the store if word got around that the doughnuts were worth the detour.

There was one other traffic draw for the location: it was right across the street from a Canadian Tire that occupied a modest ground-floor storefront space in a two-story building. This was the first franchise (or "associate") outlet opened by the Toronto-based company, and it had been there since 1934. (At last inspection, the spot was a Chinese restaurant.) The demographics of Canadian Tire customers and shift workers had considerable overlap. Someone visiting Canadian Tire could be tempted to use the doughnut drive-in's parking lot, patronize the restaurant and walk across the street to buy auto parts, hardware and whatnot. Another neighbouring business was Quondamatteo Real Estate, run by Jim Quondamatteo, a former CFL star who had started his career in Hamilton in the 1940s but won Grey Cups with Montreal and Edmonton. Quondamatteo was also involved in the restaurant business, and he arranged the lease on the Concession Street property that became the second Tim Horton's franchise.

All of these elements in Charade's first franchise outlet in Hamilton—the store location that leveraged commuter traffic of shift workers and local shopping, the on-site parking that made it convenient to frequent, a combination of counter-seating service and takeout, the essential product offerings of coffee and doughnuts—created the foundation of the chain's success. All of these elements also continue to inform the debate over what Tim Hortons has become, and where it is headed. In the beginning, the product draw was supposed to be doughnuts, augmented by coffee. Tim Hortons quickly became a doughnut store renowned for its coffee. Even today, as much as Tim Hortons has diversified its menu offerings, coffee remains its overwhelming revenue generator and profit centre. Jim Charade took a doughnut drive-in concept to Hamilton; from it, a coffee juggernaut emerged.

TIM HORTONS STORE #1 is at the corner of what the street signage proclaims to be Tim Hortons Way ("Site of the First Store"). There is no trademark double-oval signpost at this franchise. It didn't exist when Charade opened the outlet, and the company has respected that fact. But authenticity only goes so far: the building has not been returned to its original bleach-white exterior and purple interior, or to the lava rock of the interior that was left over from the Esso station days. The standard red Tim Hortons script logo is installed on the facade of the building, accompanied by a replica of the original pole sign, mounted flush. It featured an early version of Tim Horton's signature-as-logo, above the word DONUTS, along with an illustration of Horton on the ice in his blue at-home Maple Leafs uniform—trademark protection was less earnestly pursued in those days. Horton is depicted shooting three brown doughnuts. Later signs (which did not feature a drawing of Horton) would add another doughnut. Tradition has it that those four doughnuts represented Horton's four daughters. But as he already had four daughters when the sign with three doughnuts went up, the story might be apocryphal. "WE NEVER CLOSE," the sign promises. "OPEN 24 HRS. A DAY."

The counter seating is gone from store #1, and so is the original counter: when the store was renovated and a local resident discovered the company was throwing the counter away, he salvaged it and installed it in his house as something of a sacred relic. Joyce has written how the original store had a few stools at a counter and a walled-off baking area with a window through which customers could watch the doughnuts being made. There are now a handful of tables and chairs, and a thoroughly modern interior, with digital menu boards.

Two older ladies were working the counter as the late weekday morning brought on the lunch trade. The grandmotherly woman who served me was sharp, personable and just a little combative as she tried to build a coherent order out what I wanted: the chili combo for a sit-down meal, coffee in a takeout cup and a French-toast bagel for the road. Most people lining up—a couple on a motorcycle, a guy driving a service van, a young woman dressed for white-collar work—

were placing orders for takeout. A young mother with a toddler in a stroller took a table at one end, and I settled into one at the other end, beneath a portrait of Ron Joyce. Three young women next to me, fresh out of high school, carried on a spectacularly profane conversation about former teachers, the CBC's *Battle of the Blades,* paleontology and their past pregnancies.

The weirdness of life can and does surface at Tim's. A guy in Bracebridge was convicted for appearing stark naked in his car at the drive-through, startling the window attendant, who was on her first day on the job. But Tim's are overwhelmingly safe and congenial places. Crimes occasionally crop up in and around franchises, but rarely do you hear about them being consistently associated with any sort of dubious behaviour. (Mind you, a storefront Tim's in downtown Hamilton has been known to hire security guards.)

Store #1's front door is flanked by two display cases stuffed with memorabilia; curio cabinets without a curator's intervention of explanatory labels. There are pictures of Horton playing in the NHL, pictures of Horton and his partner Ron Joyce, newspaper clippings, cups and mugs, an old promo sign offering pie and a coffee for $1.49, a Ti-Cat helmet and jersey, and a letter from local MP Sheila Copps saluting the company on the thirty-fifth anniversary of the outlet as it reopened on October 22, 1999, after its memorabilia-laden renovation.

"There have been great beginnings in Hamilton East," Copps observed. "Tim Horton's just happened to be the best of the lot." That was saying something, considering that Canadian Tire, which, like Tim Hortons, has long been one of Canada's most recognized and respected consumer brands, opened its first franchise right across the street. "Just think, you're standing in the birthplace of one of the greatest Canadian cultural institutions," Copps wrote. "A place with a new face, but with the same values."

Copps called Tim Horton more than "just a great Canadian hockey icon. He was a visionary." She passed on mentioning Ron Joyce at all.

There would be no praise for the man who became a franchisee of this original outlet and built the chain; whose portrait hangs on the end wall, in a business suit with an Order of Canada pin in the lapel; and who is mentioned front and centre in the bronze plaque on the front wall commemorating the store's opening, which it says was on May 17, 1964 (Charade told me it actually opened in April).

In Hamilton's East End, politics is played for keeps. Sheila Copps was (and is) a hardcore Liberal, and Joyce, whose home in Burlington, on the north shore of the harbour, takes in a gritty view of the East End's steel mills, was (and is) a Conservative. Not only did Sheila Copps pass on mentioning Ron Joyce, but neither her letter nor the plaque had anything to say about Jim Charade. The guy who brought doughnuts and coffee and Tim Horton to Ottawa Street had disappeared from the narrative of a national consumer icon.

Copps attributed the growth of the chain to Horton's qualities as a "visionary entrepreneur." She cited the wisdom of Wayne Gretzky, who had once said, "You miss 100 percent of the shots you never take." Horton's conviction "that you had to seize opportunities" led to "a nationwide trend . . . that has never lost its momentum. There's proof in that. No matter where you travel in Canada, it seems as though one of the first things you do is locate the nearest Tim Horton's. And you do it for more than a coffee and a doughnut. You do it because it makes you feel a little at home. It's a gathering place for Canadians. It's because we're friends—everywhere we go."

That Horton was a business visionary was probably a little overly salutary. He certainly took much more than a figurehead's interest in his namesake outlet, and may have been involved in choosing the location with Charade, but the first franchisee for this store didn't even meet Horton until the restaurant had been open for a week, instead dealing entirely with Charade and Dennis Griggs. As well, the idea that Tim Hortons had become a national gathering place is something Canadians like to assert, without any proof that Tim's is more fundamental a meeting spot than any other restaurant chain or independent operation. There are certainly a lot of Tim's, but that doesn't mean Canadians instinctively huddle in them. And the more drive-throughs and kiosks the company installed, the less priority there was for accommodating huddling. Even Joyce has recalled in his memoir that three-quarters of the doughnut sales in the original store were takeout. Customers paid their money and left.

The company has either been neglecting the essential huddling nature of its own restaurants in expanding with drive-throughs and self-serve kiosks without seating, or it understands better than do Canadians just how much huddling they're actually willing to do. The company seems confident that it continues to be a communal hive. "We are the meeting place," CEO Paul House said in the conference call with analysts following the release of third-quarter results in November 2011. "'I'll meet you at Tim's' is pretty much a popular line that's right across this country. So, I think the ambiance is the friendship of the staff and the friendship of people you meet there. And the great quality products that we serve there are more important than the design ever would be. I think that's the reason why people come visit us with such great regularity."

Still, the Tim Hortons restaurant as a focal point of Canadian life is to some degree a nostalgic ideal. We want to think there is a single physical space, one hut in the nation of small huts called *kanata,* where we gather to chew over the weighty and the trivial with our fellow citizens. If Tim's is more likely to be that place than a McDonald's, or the outlet of another Canadian coffee chain like Second Cup, or a mom-and-pop diner, or a shopping mall food court, then perhaps it is because of the sheer number of outlets.

The idea of Tim's as an unpretentious national communal gathering place also draws on the ideal of what sort of people Canadians think they are: unpretentious people who like to gather communally. As we'll see, in Canadian electioneering, politicians on the hustings reached an extraordinarily consensual status—at least in English Canada—that the true Canadian of mushy-middle values can be found in a Tim Hortons. That these Canadians often insist instead on grabbing their Tim's coffee and Dutchie or breakfast sandwich from a drive-through window and speeding away into their hectic, cocooned lives suggests that, like many other aspects of modern life, the idea of Tim's as a local social hive is one that some of us like to keep alive rather than actually practise regularly. But when we need a place to meet, be it to sign papers for a real estate deal or a divorce, meet a stranger in a safe, quasi-public space or arrange the drop-off or pickup of a kid, we do tend to turn to Tim's. With Tim's serving 1.5 billion customers a year, a lot of us end up at one. Unlike Cheers, it may not be a place where everyone knows your name, but it is a place whose name everyone seems to know and trust.

9

The 100 Percent: Tim Hortons Becomes the Inclusive Canadian Experience

IN HAMILTON, as in other Canadian centres like Moncton and St. Catharines, Tim Hortons became the overwhelmingly dominant purveyor of coffee. Nationwide, the company has said it sells eight out of ten cups of coffee served in Canadian restaurants (77 percent of servings, to be precise, in fiscal 2010, compared to 7 percent for McDonald's and 3 percent for Starbucks), which helps it account for four out of ten visits by Canadians to a QSR outlet. Tim's is routinely said to have inspired the Canadian "double double" of two creams and two sugars, although when the editors of the *Canadian Oxford Dictionary* recently tried to verify this, they couldn't nail down an indisputable source. And where people tend to congregate for coffee, they tend to congregate, period.

As noted, before Tim Hortons arrived at 65 Ottawa Street North and began expanding across the city, and then across the country, Hamilton already had forty coffee shops, coffee bars and cafés that were allowing locals to gather. Those coffee purveyors are all gone now. A few independent cafés have come along in their stead (as well as chains like Starbucks, which has a half-dozen outlets within the city limits and in neighbouring Ancaster and Stoney Creek, and Second

Cup, which has five in the same area), but Tim's dominates Hamilton's QSR landscape and the coffee habits of its citizens and visitors, with some sixty outlets in the city at last count.

If Tim's drove the original coffee shops of Hamilton out of business, it did so fundamentally through good product and a ready embrace of car culture. Today, the arrival of a Tim's in smaller communities has been a cause for civic celebration, and not merely because of a desire to have coffee and doughnuts.

Two small Saskatchewan communities were head-over-heels thrilled with the appearance of a Tim's in 2011. "It's just one of those symbols [to have] a Tim Hortons in your community," Greg Schoonbaert, general manager of the Pineland Co-op Marketplace, said when it was announced that a Tim's with a drive-through had received the green light for the co-op property in the town of Nipawin (population 5,052). Mayor Sheryl Spence called the opening that September of a Tim's in her town (population 4,655) "a very exciting day for Warman. When I look out and see the Tim Hortons sign lit up, it shows me how much the community has grown, and how it continues to grow and prosper."

Tim Hortons is targeting rural communities for the growth that can take its Canadian store total to 4,000. Its 2010 analysis showed that it was present in only 40 of 324 Ontario towns of less than 5,000, and a mere 10 of 1,100 such towns in Quebec. It seems confident it can find growth in these small populations because it has already achieved high market densities overall in Atlantic Canada (about one store per 6,500 people) and Ontario (one per 8,100). As a result, western Canada (one per 15,500) and Quebec (one per 18,600) beckon. More small towns thus stand to be delighted by the arrival of a Tim's as a symbol of their own commercial arrival.

Other locales have been less enthusiastic about the appearance of a Tim Hortons. Robin's Donuts had its share of defenders when Tim's began to move more aggressively into the Thunder Bay and Winnipeg markets. Detractors otherwise have included neighbourhoods in large urban centres that champion localism and resist what they see as creeping suburbanization and corporatization by QSR chains in general.

That sentiment was already clearly alive in Toronto's Greektown, where franchisee Cam MacDonald—as noted, the son of Jack MacDonald, who as a Ward 8 councillor in Hamilton had finessed the permit that allowed the original Tim Hortons to be converted from a gas station to a restaurant—spoke frankly with me of the resistance to his presence that he has had to work to overcome.

When he took over a corporate-owned outlet as his first store in February 2003, MacDonald quickly realized that the ubiquity of Tim Hortons in Canada was not necessarily going to work in his favour. Greektown, like the Beaches neighbourhood, is one of those Toronto enclaves that prides itself on local character, on having a village feel within the greater metropolis. The Danforth strip has lost some of its distinctive Greek flavour as other chain outlets have moved in, raising local hackles. Both the Beaches and Greektown are also east-end strongholds of Toronto's urban left, which harbours a general hostility to corporations. Toronto-Danforth would soon become the federal riding of NDP leader (and leader of the Official Opposition) Jack Layton. The provincial riding (called Toronto-Danforth as well) has been an NDP stronghold since 1999.

"I've had two neighbours," MacDonald said, gesturing from his seat south along Logan Avenue as we spoke, "tell me their aim is to put me out of business." He shrugged it off. Urban politics are nothing new to his family. And he had managed to make a go of it in Greektown.

But to thrive in the neighbourhood, MacDonald knew he had to make his presence known and felt as a local proprietor. "I'm just another small businessman," he said. The Tim's at Danforth and Logan, in the very heart of Greektown, had to be a local gathering place, and he had to be seen in it, meeting customers and getting to know and work with neighbouring business owners through the local business improvement association.

Considering his Cold Stone Creamery counter, I had noticed a Baskin-Robbins just down the street, which was of course a major international franchise system owned by Dunkin' Brands. But I also wondered about the competition right across from his Tim's: a café called Leonidas advertising gelato. In name and décor, it looked like a classic independent Greektown restaurant.

Cam MacDonald grinned when I pointed it out. "That's a European chain." It was a franchise of the Belgian chocolate and café company Leonidas, which was founded by a Greek-American confectioner, Leonidas Kestekides, who settled in Belgium early in the twentieth century and began opening tea rooms there in which his chocolates and patisserie were served. Leonidas is hardly a corporate giant, but in pointing out that it is a franchise of a European company (there are several outlets in Toronto), MacDonald made his point: looks can be deceiving in the restaurant trade, and his was not the only business on the Danforth creating a corporate presence.

The issue of Tim Hortons as a corporate intruder surfaced again as we drove down Danforth Avenue and he pointed out a storefront on a corner location.

"That could have been a Tim Hortons," he told me.

The problem, he explained, was that the doorway wasn't wheelchair accessible and needed to be modified to meet the company's standards. Tim Hortons wanted the property owner to undertake the remodelling before the site could be considered as a Tim's outlet. As MacDonald explained, if it had been left to Tim's to do it, the moment the permits were applied for, individuals hostile to a corporate outlet in the neighbourhood might start agitating. The landlord refused to undertake the work, and Tim's looked elsewhere for a new location.

One of the remarkable things about the growth of Tim Hortons from that single franchise outlet on Ottawa Street North is how it has managed to avoid—so far—the broader condemnations of an anti-corporate zeitgeist. Like other QSR chains, the company is vulnerable to the buy-local movement on two fronts. One is on the issue of vertical integration of supplies, the other on its corporate character.

Tim Hortons franchises have some flexibility in sourcing goods locally, but a Tim Hortons manager does not head to the nearest farmer's market in the morning to buy lettuce and tomatoes when they're in season for the BELTs. The "buy-local movement" is increasing in strength, especially among urban foodies, in a convergence of anti-corporatism, localism and green-living sensibilities.

Buy-local activists favour independently owned enterprises, and the movement has spawned the crowdsourcing initiative known as the 3/50 Project ("saving the brick and mortars our nation is built on"). It began in the United States in 2009, has been spreading to Canada and has a free smartphone app that allows users to share information about favourite independent businesses, many of them in the bakery and café sector.

The project's name draws on two propositions. It asks people what three independently owned businesses they would miss if they disappeared, and to patronize them. It says that if half the employed population spent $50 a month in locally owned independent businesses, more than $4.6 billion in revenue would be generated in the U.S. The project further argues that for every $100 spent on such businesses, $68 is returned to the community through taxes, payroll and other expenditures, compared with $43 for a national chain.

The 3/50 Project was starting to breach Canada in 2011 in its crowdsourcing of local businesses showcased in its smartphone app. A writer for B.C.'s *Salmon Arm Observer* in October 2011 liked what she read about the project. "The group has an extensive definition of what makes it a local business, but comes down to the owner being directly connected to the community where the business operates—not a national chain, like Safeway, or a franchise, like a Tim Hortons." And Salmon Arm has two Tim's outlets.

For Tim's and its QSR rivals, the buy-local movement may prove to be a minimal threat. Beyond the issue of local sourcing, it is largely an urbanist movement, concerned with preventing the brick and mortar of downtown areas of smaller centres and hip neighbourhoods from being corporatized. The suburbs and highway rest stops are a place apart, as are the steel-and-glass commercial centres of large metropolises: Toronto's business district is so infused with outlets of Tim Hortons, Starbucks and other chains in modern commercial buildings that it is difficult to imagine them being displaced. And so far, small Canadian communities have been fairly thrilled with the idea of a Tim Hortons arriving in their midst, exhibiting the sort of local pride a large city would show in landing an NHL franchise. Still, independent cafés have been trying to fight back against the ubiquitous chains with innovative promotions. In 2010, Indie Coffee Passport was launched in Toronto. For $25, a passport buyer was entitled to $120 worth of coffee at thirty participating independents. The concept spread to Ottawa in early 2012, where $14 could get the bearer a drink (tea, coffee or espresso) at each of twelve participating shops.

Tim's has also come under criticism for its hiring practices. In March 2009, Chief Glen Ross of Opaskwayak Cree Nation complained to CBC News that the Tim Hortons outlet at Otineka Mall, a development owned by the band and located in The Pas, on the First Nation reserve, was hiring Filipino migrant workers when unemployment on the reserve was "skyrocket high." Said Ross, "They should help the regions where they're raking in the money from, you know?" He wanted Tim Hortons to try harder to train local people. "I just can't understand why Tim Hortons would be doing that. They should figure more on training people and spending some money on getting those people lined up on the weekends, instead of spending tons to ship people here from wherever."

Tim Hortons defended the hirings, saying that because it had been unable to find and keep reliable local help for night and weekend shifts at the busy twenty-four-hour drive-through outlet, it was bringing in six Filipino workers that summer to help alleviate the rest of the staff. Coincidentally or not, the company ramped up its efforts in Aboriginal sensitivity training for franchisees and employees.

Tim Hortons turned to Millbrook Technologies, owned by the Mi'kmaq Millbrook First Nation near Truro, Nova Scotia, to develop an online Aboriginal awareness program for staff. Millbrook had just developed such a training tool for provincial employees in Nova Scotia in June 2009. More than 120,000 Tim Hortons staff had gone through the program by the end of 2010, and another 37,000 completed it in 2011.

Tim Hortons also looked to the Aboriginal Human Resource Council, based in Saskatoon, for help in creating a two-day pilot cultural-sensitivity training program held in November 2011 for about fifteen franchisees in Alberta, which included strategies for local recruitment and employee retention in Aboriginal communities. "Companies like McDonald's, Loblaws, Tim Hortons . . . have stepped forward in their industry to say, 'We see and want the Aboriginal market as a workforce, as customers and as partners. Let's work together to make it happen,'" Kelly Lendsay, president and CEO of the Aboriginal Human Resource Council, told *Canadian HR Reporter* in March 2012.

Tim Hortons now runs a diverse initiative in Aboriginal relations it calls Horizons, which it says focuses on education, empowering youth, economic development and employment. Among other undertakings, it was a founding sponsor of the Assembly of First Nations' IndigenACTION sports-and-rec initiative. The company also says it is looking to create more opportunities for Aboriginal ownership of stores. By year-end 2011, Tim Hortons said it had stores on eleven reserves, with four Aboriginal franchisees. (In September 2011, Tarbell Management Group, which runs several family-related enterprises on the St. Regis Mohawk reserve in upstate New York, announced it would be opening a Tim Hortons on the reserve as well as kiosks at two of its retail operations.)

The controversy at Opaskwayak Cree Nation was one of the periodic exposures of the fact that, like most of the QSR industry in Canada, Tim Hortons depends to some degree on the temporary migrant worker program of the federal Department of Human Resources and Skills Development. In October 2011, the issue surfaced in the south Okanagan region of British Columbia, where rumours held that the local Tim Hortons franchises were laying off local hires to bring in cheaper offshore labour. A company spokesperson told the *Osoyoos Times*: "The temporary foreign workers program is used by our owners in order to keep our restaurants operating, when local applicants are not available to work these hard to fill shifts. In certain areas, temporary foreign workers are crucial to our operations because they work shifts that are difficult to staff locally, such as nights, overnights, early mornings and weekends."

Paul Stawarz, the owner of seven Tim Hortons outlets in the Okanagan, reiterated this position. "Of our 240 to 250 employees, about eighteen have come from the foreign workers program. All of them fill jobs that we posted but simply couldn't fill." Stawarz said the foreign worker program was the opposite of bringing in cheap labour. "This is not a cheap program. You have to go through a lot of hoops to hire these workers." Stawarz said the foreign workers were essential to keeping a business with long hours open.

Temporary foreign workers, who are not eligible for landed immigrant status, have proved critical to the Canadian restaurant industry, including its QSR sector, although their employment has been highly regional, rather than a systemwide corporate response to filling low-paying jobs—and keeping those jobs low paying. Tim Hortons is one of many franchise companies that have looked to the federal program to secure low-cost labour in semi-skilled positions that federal bureaucrats determine cannot be filled by existing labour supplies. With labour one of the most significant costs a franchisee needs to control to achieve reasonable profitability, and with unions having failed to organize its workers, the temporary foreign worker program arguably has served as a safety valve for the QSR industry to avoid labour shortages that would otherwise drive up wages and benefits.

In 2010, "Food Counter Attendants, Kitchen Helpers and Related Occupations" was the second-largest category of temporary workers in Canada (after "Babysitters, Nannies and Parents' Helpers," but not counting farm labour), with 9,175 positions. That was up from 6,685 in 2009, but well down from 15,450 in 2008. Relatively rare in the restaurant industry in eastern Canada, these temporary workers were being used far more prevalently in British Columbia, Saskatchewan, and above all in Alberta, which is chronically short of service workers and accounted for 7,720 of the 9,175 positions nationwide in 2010. Still, in October 2011, Tim Hortons was one of a rash of QSR and casual-dining franchise businesses (not to mention independent operations and other hospitality enterprises, tourist attractions and universities) registered as a potential employer in the temporary foreign worker program in the Toronto region.

In May 2012, in the midst of the controversy surrounding the Harper government's plan to tighten employment insurance qualifications and make it easier for employers to use foreign workers, Stephen Breed, who runs eight Tim Hortons franchises in Nova Scotia through Down East Hospitality Inc., told CBC News that he had hired twenty-four temporary foreign workers from the Philippines to staff the outlet at Halifax Stanfield International Airport because he couldn't fill the full-time minimum-wage jobs with Nova Scotians. Breed said he had been using temporary foreign workers for four years. He said the staffing problem was unique to the airport Tim Hortons—public transportation was inadequate, and Nova Scotians with cars couldn't accept a minimum-wage job. According to Breed, he had no shortage of applicants for jobs at other locations.

The reality of counter-service QSR jobs is that they pay minimum wage. At the time of the debate over the Harper government's changes to employment insurance and foreign worker rules, the online job bank managed by Service Canada featured an opening at a popular Halifax Tim Hortons on Dutch Village Road. The advertisement offered $10.15 an hour, regardless of day or night shift, for a permanent full-time position. In addition to a wide range of benefits—medical, dental and vision coverage, as well as life and group insurance—the posting by Tyeco Investments promised "great tips every shift." Yet more than ever, Tim Hortons became synonymous, for some critics, with low-paying service-sector work. Responding to the proposal to require unemployed Canadians seek out (and accept) new work more rigorously, federal NDP finance critic Peggy Nash asked, "If you are a computer software developer, will you be working at Tim Hortons?"

On a more positive note, Tim Hortons franchisees have quietly gone about running their own affirmative-action programs in hirings. Dan Hardiman, who has three franchises in Columbus, Ohio, stepped into the limelight in May 2012 to announce he was publicly backing a state bill that would make it easier for businesses to hire ex-convicts. He revealed that more than half of his fifty employees were convicted felons. "They have worked out," he told television station WBNS. "In many cases, better than people coming off the street."

One Toronto franchisee has aimed to level the playing field for people with disabilities. Mark Wafer, who was born with a hearing capacity of 20 percent, has been a strong advocate of proactive hiring. About one-quarter of his 120 employees at six outlets in the summer of 2012 lived with disabilities; in all, he hired 82 people with disabilities between 2005 and 2012, he explained to journalist Alison Griffiths in June 2012. Wafer also helped design a Rotary International program called Rotary at Work to urge other employers to follow his lead.

I have heard rumblings of discontent among the young (enough of whom nevertheless form lineups to get a Tim's coffee at campus outlets) with Tim Hortons' corporatist ubiquity. But it is going to take a major groundswell of consumer hostility in Canada to break the widespread Tim's habit. Tim Hortons maintains a Facebook page that has about 1.8 million "likes," a phenomenal total for a Canadian company. The Facebook page of its Canadian-owned rival, Second Cup, in comparison has about 23,000 likes, and many of its wall postings are by Second Cup or its own employees. (Mind you, Starbucks' likes exceed 29 million, although that is on a global scale; its Canadian page has more than 300,000 followers.)

How much consumer loyalty a company's Facebook following represents is debatable. A study produced in January 2012 by an Australian marketing think tank, the Ehrenberg-Bass Institute, determined that only 1.3 percent of the people who "like" a corporate Facebook page are actually "engaging" with the brand, as it compared the ratio of "People Talking About This" incidents to overall likes. At that time, Tim Hortons was par for the course, with a frequency of 1.2 percent. As with other companies, contests make a big contribution to the number of likes on the Tim Hortons page.

But to judge by the amount and the nature of postings on its wall, many Tim Hortons customers are highly and vociferously engaged, with a large number of bracingly unhappy customers. A random sampling includes a complaint in October 2011 by a Hindu customer in an undisclosed location that her family repeatedly was served beef in soup and noodle products and that they were never going to eat there again. (Tim Hortons does list on its website the menu items, including soups, without animal products.) An Ohio customer demanded in 2010: "Why doesn't Tim Hortons offer its customers satisfying coffeehouse 'perks' like free coffee refills and free wireless Internet? How can they compete with the make-yourself-at-home atmosphere of Panera Bread Company, or some of the smaller independent coffee houses across the country?" A Calgary customer complained in August 2011 that her drive-through order is served wrong half of the time. Such consumer griping is not unheard of on corporate Facebook pages. On the Starbucks page, a customer in Portland, Oregon, groused in October 2011 about the "really horrible, chemical aftertaste" of the pumpkin spice latte.

The nature of Facebook means that consumers can start unofficial pages of their own dedicated to Tim's, but enthusiasm is minimal. Curious about the issues that might concern it, I was one of only 249 people to have joined the group Boycott Tim Hortons by the fall of 2011. One page member had already quit on March 17, 2011, with a dispirited: "This will be my last post here because, quite frankly, I don't support this 'lost cause.' Just FYI—the Tim Hortons page now has 1,386,186 people who like them. That's an increase of 4,157 since Monday [she posted on Thursday]. This group, on the other hand, has gained how many? Good luck with the boycott." Tim's added another 300,000-odd likes over the next seven months. When I checked back in late January 2012, membership was down to 246, and there hadn't been a posting in three months.

As Tim Hortons grows in the U.S., it will increasingly learn how advocacy groups target large chains for action or public shaming. In February 2012, the Humane Society of the United States filed a shareholder proposal for the company's annual general meeting in May, calling on Tim's "to disclose to shareholders the feasibility of ensuring that the bacon and other pork products used for its U.S. locations does not come from pigs bred using gestation crates—cages that virtually immobilize breeding pigs for much of their lives." The society wanted Tim Hortons to follow the lead of McDonald's in calling for a phasing out of such rearing methods in its supply chain.

The U.S. campaign was expanded upon by the Vancouver Humane Society. Its director of farm animal programs, Leanne McConnachie, posted an online petition at Change.org that soon had more than 20,000 signatories calling for Tim Hortons CEO Paul House to "stop supporting farm animal cruelty." Stated McConnachie's petition: "Tim Hortons, Canada's largest restaurant chain, currently serves eggs and pork from farms that use battery cages and gestation crates, extreme practices that treat chickens and pigs like machines—and *that other major fast food chains have already committed to abandoning!*"

As the petition gained momentum and threatened to create an ad hoc boycott of Tim Hortons, the company responded one week before its annual general meeting with the announcement of a comprehensive plan for sourcing eggs and pork. The company announced it was asking the pork industry and suppliers "to eliminate gestation stalls for sows and to develop clear plans and timelines by the end of the year to phase out these housing systems. We have also set a goal of purchasing at least 10 per cent of our eggs, representing significantly more than 10 million eggs, from enriched hen housing systems by the end of 2013. We plan to actively evaluate the industry's capacity to provide eggs from enriched housing systems, and to progressively increase our commitment beyond 2013 as additional supply becomes available."

Tim Hortons went further, saying in 2012, "We will commission scientific, fact-based animal welfare research with leading academic institutions on sustainable, humane animal housing systems. Further, we plan to call for a North American–wide summit of restaurant companies interested in the humane treatment of animals in the restaurant industry supply chain." As a result of the company's announcement, the Humane Society of the United States withdrew its petition prior to the annual general meeting.

Tim Hortons' response to the animal welfare campaigns was typical of its response to other controversies. Rather than simply accede to demands of critics, the company has made an art of exceeding basic expectations and creating comprehensive initiatives that are much more than feel-good corporate window-dressing. Such has been the case with its First Nations programming, and as we'll see, its drive to reduce waste through recycling and its own answer to ethical coffee sourcing.

So far, Tim's has avoided the status of pariah that still haunts Starbucks within the anti-globalization movement. Two days after I visited Tim Hortons store #1 in Hamilton, a judge in a Toronto courthouse handed down a sentence of twelve months' house arrest and twenty-four months' probation to one of the so-called black bloc rioters at the G20 summit in Toronto in June 2010. The young man from London, Ontario, had been part of the masked mobs that went on a vandalizing spree, targeting retail stores on Yonge Street and Queen Street West. He had helped smash the plate-glass windows of a Bell Mobility outlet and a Starbucks on Yonge Street above Dundas. Others took out the window of the Adidas store in the same location. (Coincidentally, this new building occupied the site of the Tim Horton walk-in store that Charade and Horton had leased from Benny Winbaum.)

For many violent urban anarchists, Starbucks long has been name-checked as *the* symbol of global corporate hegemony, the logo of choice on which to vent tantrums. A Tim Hortons outlet was in the very same building as the trashed Yonge Street Starbucks, around the corner on Victoria, but no one apparently thought of hurling bricks through its windows. The contrite young man, who avoided jail time, had come to Toronto from a Canadian city with nine Starbucks but more than two dozen Tim Hortons in the greater area.

Apart from the sheer size and international notoriety of Starbucks, the Seattle-based chain differs from Tim's in that its outlets are owned by the company or operated by corporate licensees within other stores, whereas Tim's relies almost entirely on franchisees. The ability of Tim's to avoid being tarred with the same corporate hegemonic brush as Starbucks, even among hardcore activists, nevertheless is impressive. At Occupy Toronto in November 2011, a *Toronto Star* reporter, Stephanie Findlay, noted the masses of discarded coffee cups from corporate QSR outlets in the trash cans. One activist was sufficiently frustrated to go out and buy two French presses to make coffee for fellow protesters, but others were trying to patronize the right corporation: Tim's.

Findlay wrote that drinking Starbucks was "the real Occupy faux pas." A thirty-four-year-old Occupy Toronto police liaison who identified himself as Antonin told her, "We don't police that matter, but it's frowned upon." Antonin volunteered, "I drink at Tim Hortons, double-double," and he reasoned, "One percenters don't go to Tim Hortons."

That may be wishful thinking. The Tim Hortons brand is about inclusion, I was told at the time of Occupy Toronto by Alan Middleton, an assistant professor of marketing and executive director of the Schulich Executive Education Centre at the Schulich School of Business at Toronto's York University. Middleton paraphrased an insight into Tim's of the anthropologist Grant McCracken: a rich businessperson and the unemployed worker can both walk down the street carrying a Tim Hortons coffee and feel comfortable. That's a unique brand proposition that Tim Hortons does not want to harm. Tim Hortons has always been after the 100 percent.

Starbucks and its many competitors in the coffee and overlapping QSR concepts all bend over backwards now to project their corporate virtues, and Tim Hortons has worked assiduously on initiatives that elevate its brand image as caring and socially responsible. In July 2005, Tim Hortons launched an anti-littering campaign with the environmental group Clean Nova Scotia; the CBC reported at the time that its takeout cups accounted for 22 percent of all the litter in the province. Its cups, however, were not recyclable, and Tim's also was being criticized elsewhere in the country for the amount of garbage, buried in landfills and strewn across the landscape, it was generating, especially during the annual Roll Up the Rim contest.

Targeted by the City of Toronto over the amount of trash produced by its cups, which did not meet local recycling requirements, Tim Hortons responded by developing its own program in 2008 with

Turtle Island Recycling and offering customers ten cents off a cup of coffee if they used a refillable container. The company now has a trash–recycling bin system at drive-throughs that puts most QSRs to shame, and has developed cups and packaging that are more recycling friendly (including a process that recycles cups into takeout trays).

The cups are still not recyclable with all municipal waste programs in Canada, and the company continues to attract flak for the amount of trash and litter its sales generate. It does, however, reduce waste volumes by using washable cutlery, dishes and china cups within restaurants, and gives a discount to customers who use refillable travel mugs for orders. McDonald's, for one, has refused to fill travel mugs in the escalating coffee war with Tim's, asserting that it is a hygiene issue.

Tim Hortons produces a sustainability report on energy usage and carbon emissions in its corporate and franchise operations. It joined the Carbon Disclosure Project and dispatched its director of sustainability and responsibility, Tim Faveri, to a panel discussion at the Toronto Stock Exchange when CDP released its 2011 Canada report, in which Tim Hortons was reporting for the first time. Faveri called brand reputation the "big elephant" that is always in the room. "Anything that has to do with brand reputation, we have to look into it."

The company doesn't participate in various virtuous coffee schemes, including Fair Trade, Rainforest Alliance, and Organic Crop Improvement Association, which is an annoyance to activists and some consumers. In 2005, the company instead created the Tim Hortons Coffee Partnership, working with the Hanns R. Neumann Stiftung Foundation, a charitable group set up by Germany's Neumann Kaffee Gruppe, a green (arabica) coffee service group controlling 10 percent of the world's production. It's not clear, however, how much of the coffee Tim Hortons sells comes from this program.

"All of the mainstream coffee certification models including Fairtrade [*sic*], Rainforest Alliance, UTZ Certified, 4C Association, etc., should be commended for the good work they are doing to improve social and environmental issues in the coffee growing regions of the world," Tim Hortons states. "We developed the Tim Hortons Coffee Partnership to address important philosophies relating to sustainable coffee production that we believe are not as prevalent in other programs." The company's website provides links to these other programs and encourages consumers to compare Tim Horton's initiative with them.

The company says its coffee partnership program is built on three pillars—economic, social and environmental—and that since 2005 it has worked with more than 2,500 farmers in Brazil, Colombia, Guatemala and Honduras on projects with three- to five-year commitments. One of its program's advantages, the company says, is that the farmers, who are mainly small-scale producers that it helps work in cooperatives, do not have to pay a certification fee, which it says can be up to $3,000 under some models. And Fair Trade coffee, which involves such certification fees, certainly has its critics. Colleen Haight, writing in the Summer 2011 issue of *Stanford Social Innovation Review,* acknowledged the positive achievements of Fair Trade but also stated "the system by which Fair Trade USA hopes to achieve its ends is seriously flawed, limiting both its market potential and the benefits it provides growers and workers. Among the concerns are that the premiums paid by consumers are not going directly to farmers, the quality of Fair Trade coffee is uneven, and the model is technologically outdated." Haight argued that "Fair Trade coffee has evolved from an economic and social justice movement to largely a marketing model for ethical consumerism."

Tim Hortons is not the only coffee purveyor to try to design a socially responsible sourcing program of its own. Starbucks, for example, has created C.A.F.E. Practices as a guideline for its bean buyers, to favour sustainable best practices according to social, economic and environmental criteria. Unlike Tim Hortons, which offers one standard brew, Starbucks, for one, gives customers the option of buying Fair Trade coffee.

Other Tim Hortons initiatives include the network of children's foundation camps that serve about 15,000 underprivileged kids and youth leadership trainees a year. (See Chapter 25.) The Timbits minor sports program involves about 300,000 kids, and not just in hockey, in community-based recreation.

Still, if lashing out at corporate retailing in Canada is your game, Tim's should be your whipping boy of choice. But the idea of Canadians forming angry mobs to wreak havoc on Tim's would strike most people as absurd. If Tim's is a corporate monolith dominating the Canadian retail landscape, it's *our* corporate monolith. And at the heart of its image—despite its own proud boasts of having more than 3,000 outlets in this country, and of being one of North America's largest publicly traded QSR companies by the measure of market capitalization—is the enduring idea of the friendly neighbourhood gathering place, run by a local entrepreneur/franchisee, that Jim Charade planted at Ottawa and Dunsmure.

Muffie's Coffee Shop, which stood at the north end of Ottawa Street, near the Dofasco gates, when Charade opened his drive-in, is long gone—there isn't even a building anymore on that side of the street. Charade's brilliant hunch endures as an unofficial tourist attraction and a national shrine not only to the resulting chain and the national QSR habit it spawned among consumers, but also to that beloved notion that Canadians are by nature people who gather in such a place, to sip coffee, chew on a cruller and hash out the issues of the day, large and small, public and private. Some of those issues might even be the buy-local movement and the recycling challenges of takeout coffee cups.

Tim's *is* Canada, many people have decided, and Canadians are Tim's. Jim Charade just wanted to sell some doughnuts.

10

Partings: Casualties in the Making of a Dream

Narratives can be messy; foundation stories can demand streamlining. This may make them easier to tell, but we lose what historians call the granular level of detail, the stuff that might actually tell us what happened, rather than what can be reduced to a neat paragraph.

The bronze plaque on the side of store #1 is not an official historical marker but rather a creation of Tim Hortons that dedicates the site to "The Making of a Dream." It reads in whole: "This site is dedicated to the dream that lived in the hearts of Tim Horton and Ron Joyce; to the commitment and dedication of the operators who have built the Tim Hortons chain; and to the people of Hamilton, whose undying loyalty has been the backbone of our chain's success. This location signifies the history and heritage of Tim Hortons and will serve as a monument to even bigger dreams yet to come."

What it says is fine for the purpose of inspiration and giving civic thanks. But there is no room for Jim Charade in this dream, or for any of the other characters in the sputtering start to the restaurant chain's story. The plaque does not tell you that the store-opening date it celebrates fell almost a year before Ron Joyce became involved; that it was Charade, largely independently of Horton, who conceived of and set up this store; and that there were two franchisees before Joyce. The name of the second franchisee has been forgotten, but the first has not.

From a strictly corporate point of view, the Tim Hortons story has a vague beginning. Sometimes it is said to have been in 1964, when store #1 opened. Sometimes it is in January 1965, when the company Tim Donut Ltd., still the basis of the enterprise, was incorporated by Charade and Horton, with Ron Joyce arriving on the scene as the third franchisee for the troubled outlet about one month later. The compressed story of the chain's beginning tends to make Horton and Joyce partners from the get-go, even though they did not become partners in Tim Donut until December 1966. The misfires of the Toronto burger outlets, or the Tim Horton Do-Nut at the Colony Plaza dating back to 1963, never figure in the narrative.

Joyce himself well understands that the story of Tim Horton's restaurant aspirations, and of the drive-in at Ottawa and Dunsmure, runs deeper and wider than his own arrival. When I interviewed him in 1993 for Horton's biography, Joyce made a point of putting me in touch with both Jim Charade—who was working for Tim Donut at the time—and the original franchisee, Spencer Brown, who had gone on to preside over a portfolio of Best Western hotels, so that I understood the backstory he himself could never tell. And there was a parting of ways between Charade and Brown to be negotiated in the retelling.

As it happened, there were more partings to come after Brown split with Charade: Charade parted with Horton and Joyce, Horton and Joyce parted through a violent death and Joyce parted with Horton's widow in the ownership of the company in what at first seemed an amicably negotiated buyout that, more than a decade later, turned into an acrimonious lawsuit. Two years after I first met and interviewed Joyce, he merged Tim Donut with Wendy's, and while he became Wendy's single largest shareholder and a very rich man, he was on his way to his own parting with the company he had built up from that modest location at Ottawa and Dunsmure. Soon after he resigned his board position in 2001, Tim Hortons parted with what Joyce considered to be a fundamental character of the restaurant chain: on-site scratch baking, which Joyce had learned at store #1, in favour of the parbaking system that largely inspired a 2008 lawsuit filed by his cousin—and former Tim Donut senior executive—Archibald Jollymore, against the company. Finally, Tim Hortons parted with Wendy's, spun off in a distribution of shares as dividends and an IPO in 2006. After all that parting, there was at least one significant joining, as Tim Hortons was repatriated as a Canadian corporation in 2009, thus reuniting the restaurant chain as a legal entity with the customer base that had long supported it.

But first, the joining, and the parting, of Jim Charade and Spencer Brown.

SPENCER BROWN (who died in 2010) couldn't even recall for me precisely how he got involved with Jim Charade and wound up as the original franchisee of that first doughnut drive-in in Hamilton. It was early 1964, though. He was only twenty years old, still living at home near Lawrence Avenue and Markham Road, working as a clerk at a Bank of Nova Scotia branch in Scarborough for $40 a week. "To this day, I don't know how it all happened. One thing came to another, and before I know it I'm in the car with Dennis going to Peterborough."

Dennis Griggs's exact role in the founding of Tim Hortons is a little elusive. In her book, *In Loving Memory* (written with Dennis's son Tim), Lori Horton said Dennis became a full business partner of Charade and her late husband in Timanjim Ltd. But neither Charade nor Dennis Griggs himself ever told me that Griggs had equity in the company. Griggs asserted he was a "founding father" of the chain in the sense that he introduced Horton to Charade. In taking over the operation of Charade's Colony Plaza doughnut store, Griggs was issued a business licence by the city and had been producing promotional materials and looking out for the interests of Tim Horton, although Charade was also a close friend of both Horton and Griggs.

Peterborough, like Hamilton, seemed to provide an expansion opportunity outside the competitive froth of Toronto; it was also where Horton's Maple Leafs held their training camp each autumn. Horton's defence partner, Allan Stanley, told me how for years Horton eyed a particular site in Peterborough, but dithered so long that a competitive concept finally opened on it. In any event, nothing in Peterborough met the fancy of Griggs. At which point he told Brown about a restaurant they were launching in Hamilton. It was mere weeks away from opening, and Charade didn't even have a franchisee in place.

So they drove to Hamilton to have a look. Spencer Brown tore his arm up on the lava rock in the interior, and saw a coffee-and-doughnut shop with used kitchen equipment ready to go. The property owner, a Ukrainian fellow from Kitchener, had been riding a bicycle back and forth—in the winter—on a round trip of about eighty miles to keep tabs on the build-to-suit renovation.

Brown was convinced Charade was on to something. He agreed to a franchise fee of $1,500 and a royalty rate that he could no longer recall but was probably the standard 2 percent that the early franchisees would pay. He borrowed the entire down payment from an uncle, quit his bank job, moved into the YMCA in Hamilton for a week while he found a room closer to the store, and opened for business in April 1964, one month after his twenty-first birthday.

He didn't meet Tim Horton until the store had been open for a week, and as he told me, Brown himself knew as much about doughnuts as he did about tires—both were round and had a hole in the middle. Charade sent him his Scottish baker to get him started.

The restaurant, Brown recalled, was an immediate success. A dozen doughnuts were sixty-nine cents; a quarter got you a cup of coffee and a doughnut. "It went super well. It was busy, busy, busy. For a kid that had been making about forty dollars a week in the bank, all of a sudden I'm making four hundred a week." Running a twenty-four-hour restaurant, he would fall asleep for a few hours on a bag of flour in the kitchen and then go right back to work.

The fresh-baked doughnuts were a hit. "The big things were jelly and condiment-filled doughnuts, the yeast-based ones that were pumped full of filling and sprinkled with sugar. It was a really big deal: Venetian cream–filled, jelly-filled—apple and spice was a big seller—and honey-dipped. Cake doughnuts were the only type people knew, and we didn't sell much of those. We had peanut crunch, macaroon, coconut crumble, you name it. We tried really hard to have at least forty different varieties there at any one time. You ordered what you needed from a supplier for that week, and sometimes we had to order a second shipment because we were really selling a lot of product. It was terrific. It just went gangbusters."

Business was so good that they didn't need to bother selling off the day-olds at a discount or dumping them, creating the wastage known as "throws." Around 5:30 or 6:00 a.m., before the shift changed at Dofasco, they'd put doughnuts back in the proofer—the oven in which yeast doughnuts rise—to keep them warm, then parade them past the counter as if they were fresh. The workers snapped them up.

But as successful as the business was, after only a few months, Brown began to grow fed up with Charade. "Quite frankly, I got the impression that maybe [Charade] was a little underhanded or having a bit of a problem with Tim. Tim was off playing hockey and making a good name for himself that way, and Jim was screwing him in business. At least that was the impression I had." Brown had tapped into the suspicions circulating among some of Horton's friends that Charade was taking advantage of his celebrity business partner.

Brown felt he was being taken advantage of by Charade as well. He was dismayed to be paying blatant markups by Charade on supplies for his store, for which he could see no justification, as Charade's business had no warehousing or delivery costs. Goods were shipped directly from the supplier to the restaurant on Ottawa Street, the invoices going to Charade, who would add a profit margin for himself as the franchisor and then forward the final bill to Brown.

Brown's dispute with Charade was an enduringly fundamental one of franchising. Franchisors are entitled to profit from captive sales to franchisees, as Tim Hortons does today through "distribution sales," which account for more than half of its revenues. This aspect of the business was legally murky in the mid-1960s. Brown's unhappiness was just a few years ahead of its time: in 1969, a group of Mister Donut franchisees in Toronto, Jirna Ltd., filed a landmark suit against their franchisor. The franchisees were annoyed by the fact that Mister Donut was receiving volume rebates from suppliers of the goods that its franchisees were required to purchase from Mister Donut, and that Mister Donut wasn't sharing those rebates with them, instead booking the rebates as pure profit. The franchisees won their case in 1970, and although the lower court ruling would be overturned, the initial victory sent shockwaves throughout the North American franchise industry.

Back in June 1964, the Ottawa Street restaurant was doing so well, and Brown was so incensed with the markups on invoices, that Charade tried to buy him out. "I said, no, no," Brown recalled. "I wanted to buy *them* out . . . 'Take down your sign and I'll try this on my own.' Well, that didn't fly. A lot of people were nosing around because the place was busy. George Sukornyk, who was president of Harvey's, was very interested in the whole deal. He'd just opened a place on Barton Street."

Indeed, in April 1964, just as the first Tim Horton Donut Drive-In franchise was opening on Ottawa Street, Sukornyk and his partner Mauran had taken Harvey's public (as Harvey's Foods Ltd.). It remained an over-the-counter stock until 1967, when it was listed on the Toronto exchange and the partners' other venture, Swiss Chalet, was folded into the company. The share issue gave Harvey's a capital injection to fund an expansion spree based on property acquisitions.

Whether Harvey's was interested in taking on a doughnut operation or simply acquiring a prime site in Hamilton, no deal was done. Instead, Brown sold his interest in the franchise back to Charade, who recalled the parting completely differently. "I sold him the franchise, but he was really nervous. He didn't think that he would make it. I had to take it back from him."

Brown told me he got back his $1,500 franchise fee from Charade and another $5,000 from the new franchisee, an Englishman with an older, wealthy wife. With $6,500 now to his name, Brown did not go out and open a doughnut store of his own. Instead, he met with Sukornyk to see about a Harvey's.

After turning down a chance to open a Harvey's in Ottawa and Montreal, Brown went to work for the Steak N' Burger chain being run by Benny Winbaum's Winco Ltd. Winco fired him when it learned he was looking into the possibility of bringing the Arby's roast-beef QSR concept to Canada on his own. He found his way into the hospitality trade and acquired a portfolio of hotels in Kingston, Cornwall, North Bay and Kirkland Lake, operating under the Best Western marquee. A Tim Hortons franchisee in Kingston was a friend of his when the twenty-fifth anniversary of store #1 was approaching in 1989. Brown attended the celebration as a guest of honour.

"It was a novel concept," he told me, looking back on the Tim's doughnut debut in Hamilton, "ideal for a cooler climate. It could be a big winner in northern Europe and Russia. A friend of mine from Oslo would come over with his kids, and they'd go nuts over filled doughnuts. There's nothing like that over there." But apart from some kiosks in England and Ireland, Tim's has not made it to northern Europe—or to Russia, where a number of American QSRs have been turning for fresh expansion opportunities. George Cohon of McDonald's Canada led the way in 1990, and McDonald's has since been joined by such brands as Starbucks, Burger King, Carl's Jr., Wendy's, KFC, Papa John's and Subway (which has 200 outlets there).

Dunkin' Donuts tried Russia initially in 1996, but withdrew in 1999. Dunkin' went back in April 2010, announcing a new master franchise agreement. Dunkin' Brands already had 143 of its Baskin-Robbins outlets in Russia, and hoped to open twenty Dunkin' Donuts stores in its first year. The pace of openings hasn't met this projection—thirteen were open in September 2011. But even for Dunkin', whose international sprawl eclipses that of Tim Hortons, Scandinavia remains *terra incognita*. As for Tim Hortons, almost fifty years after the franchise chain was born in Hamilton, the United States—home turf of Dunkin'—remains both a challenge and a riddle as a new territory. Tim's is more likely to conquer Russia before it does New England.

THE ENGLISHMAN WHO TOOK OVER the Ottawa Street franchise from Spencer Brown was a disaster. Charade was getting calls in the middle of the night from staff, complaining about his behaviour. They said that the man was scooping money out of the till and wandering down to Barton Street to drink away the revenues in the Jockey Club tavern and that the franchise was getting shabby. Charade's coffee-and-doughnut concept nevertheless managed to survive the new franchisee's incompetence and continued to do business through the rest of 1964, whereas the Timanjim partnership's chicken and burger drive-ins back in Toronto flamed out.

"The burger places were a mess," Brown recalled. "Winding them down was the best thing that could happen." He watched the new Red Barn concept, with its fifteen-cent hamburgers, make life miserable for Timanjim. One opened at Pharmacy and Warden, just down the street from the only Tim Horton drive-in still in business in 1964. Charade agreed that Red Barn was a principal nemesis, but really, Scarborough was lousy with drive-ins.

"We needed more promotion, more capital, more advertising." Charade especially needed more money, but didn't have any. With the burger and chicken drive-ins a lost cause, its last outlet limping toward closure, Tim Horton agreed to inject some capital into Charade's doughnut venture. On January 27, 1965, they formed a new partnership, Tim Donut Ltd., the company that remains the legal heart of the modern chain. Where he had previously licensed his name to Charade for the doughnut stores, Tim Horton now had half the business.

For all the misadventures that accompanied the opening of the first Tim Hortons franchise outlet in Hamilton, Charade had done brilliantly in siting the concept. He had chosen a city that was already keen on coffee, which would give the franchise chain critical momentum as it built its initial customer base and network of stores. And although the immediate future of the business would not be kind to Charade, Tim Horton was incredibly fortunate that Charade had placed this first outlet in the one-store chain of which he was now part owner just a quarter-mile from a house on Kensington Avenue, near the Delta, where a cop named Ron Joyce lived.

11

Ron:
An Ex-Cop Takes Charge

If ever there were a boilerplate example of the sort of fellow who made an ideal franchisee as defined by George Sukornyk in 1969, it would seem to have been Ron Joyce. A guy who had never made more than $8,000 a year, who was staring at the prospect of poverty in old age . . . Joyce had those bases covered. As a beat cop in Hamilton, Joyce was making about $5,600 a year in 1964. He was also on his second marriage, and would have a total of seven kids to support.

But the big difference between Joyce and Sukornyk's model franchisee is that Joyce was not a guy who could be pushed around or who would ever put up with the abuse Sukornyk said his own Harvey's franchisees had to endure from head office. Joyce's ambition, and the ragged opportunity the Tim Horton Donut Drive-In represented, saw him rapidly change from being the third franchisee to try to make a go of Charade's concept on Ottawa at Dunsmure to becoming Tim Horton's business partner and the driving force behind the chain's expansion into a national phenomenon.

Joyce's great-great-grandfather, Thomas Joyce, was an Irishman from Waterford who arrived in northern New Brunswick early in the nineteenth century and settled at Botsford Portage, near the shore of the Northumberland Strait. Joyce's ancestors spent three generations in northern New Brunswick, around Botsford Portage, Moncton and Shemogue, before working their way a few miles east to the Northumberland shore of Nova Scotia. His father, Willard (Bill), arrived in Tatamagouche from Westville to help build a bank, and there he met Grace Jollymore, who was only seventeen or eighteen when they married in 1929. Ron Joyce, born in 1930, had two siblings: a brother, Willard Jr., and a sister, Gwenythe.

When Joyce was four, his father was killed when a barrel of oil rolled off a truck and crushed him. His mother, pregnant with Gwenythe, moved back to her hometown of Tatamagouche, where she raised her kids in a house without plumbing or electricity. Ron Joyce would spend years knocking around from job to job. As he related in his autobiography, he pitched in at the farm of his uncle Stan Jollymore during the war, then worked in a canning factory in the Annapolis Valley, and after that plant abruptly shut down he returned to Tatamagouche, to a job in a creamery. He saved up thirty-five dollars, which was enough for a thirty-dollar train ticket to Hamilton, where he thought there might be work in industry. He arrived in 1946, at the age of sixteen, with nothing to his name, having spent his last five dollars en route on beer and sandwiches.

Joyce held an assortment of low-skill industrial jobs—including at American Can, where my own father would work as a tool-and-die maker—before returning to Tatamagouche in 1949, marrying his first wife, Lynda, at nineteen, and deciding to join the Canadian navy. His tour of duty took him to the Korea conflict, but the fighting was over by the time he arrived in 1953. Leaving the navy, he headed back to Hamilton in 1956 with Lynda and two boys. He promptly was taken on by the police force, and twin boys arrived soon after that.

Joyce wrote that his marriage collapsed in 1958, and that he met his second wife, Theresa, who was separated from her husband, in 1960; they would marry in 1963. Both worked in order to make ends meet, and Joyce, who was paying support to his ex-wife, moonlighted in a variety of jobs, among other things driving a banana truck for Sam Netkin's wholesale fruit and vegetable business.

In the fall of 1962, Joyce and Theresa took a walk from their house on Kensington, east along Main Street. One block east of Ottawa Street, at the corner of London, was a little Dairy Queen that still exists. Joyce discovered it was being run by an old navy shipmate, George Otterman, and his wife. Otterman persuaded Joyce that Dairy Queen was his future. He went out and bought a Dairy Queen of his own, an existing franchise on Queenston Road near Stoney Creek, out where A&W had opened a drive-in, and started running it when the snow began melting in March 1963.

"I was a policeman, and frankly I wasn't very happy with it," Joyce told me. "I really fell in love with the Dairy Queen, because you are selling fun. It's pretty hard to sell a traffic ticket, or sell locking up a drunk. Your product isn't fun at all, and I really didn't enjoy it. Then I got into selling food. People come to you, and it's a minor form of entertainment. People want a nice experience, and it was fun to sell Dairy Queen. I started looking for another one."

Joyce was offered a new location in Bronte, a suburb of Oakville, about ten miles east of Hamilton. Money was hard to find, and despite having secured an approved loan from the federal government's Industrial Development Bank, Dairy Queen turned down his application, saying he was undercapitalized. He still had the Queenston Road outlet, but it was a seasonal operation, and he was also still working the beat, which he wanted to quit. Joyce was convinced that fast-food restaurants were his future, in part because he had gotten to know the brothers who owned the local Millionaire Drive Inns. "Not only were the brothers successful, but they were having fun managing their restaurant," he would write. "While I was working to survive, these guys were having the time of their lives *and* making money doing it."

Then Joyce walked by the Tim Horton Donut Drive-In near his

house. He had never been inside it, but he spotted a sign in the window that said the franchise was for sale. He dialled the Toronto number and got Jim Charade.

PROSPECTIVE FRANCHISEES today are exhaustively counselled to seek legal advice before signing an agreement. Tim Hortons' own franchise agreements include an affidavit signed by the franchisee acknowledging that the company has advised them to take the stack of paper to a lawyer. Ron Joyce sought such advice from his lawyer, Buck Bennett, who went on to become a judge in Hamilton. Joyce also ignored his advice.

"He tried to talk me out of buying the store," Joyce told me. "'There's nothing there,' he said. But I wouldn't listen to him. I was determined to buy the damned store." Joyce also ignored standard advice many aspiring franchisees receive today: don't buy into an unproven concept just because you think you're getting in on the ground floor of something big. But Joyce did, and he was.

He went to a local credit union and borrowed $10,000 to buy the whole place, and agreed to a 2 percent royalty. Charade had assured him that the store would gross $1,000 a week, and in that he proved to be correct. He took over as the new franchisee in February 1965—Charade would recall the date for me as precisely February 21—and immediately began to run into problems.

There was no manual (Joyce would later see a manual that Spencer Brown had been given, which was four pages long), and Joyce was not a baker. Already on the premises were Charade's little Scottish baker, and another baker named Jeff. They were, as Joyce would write, an openly gay couple. The Scotsman was supposed to be there to train Joyce, but according to Charade, the baker's extremely effeminate manner drove Joyce nuts. Joyce called him up and said: "If you don't get this bastard out of here, I'm going to kill him. I'm telling you right now, I'm going to choke him."

But Joyce had an altogether different version of why he was so angry. He was convinced that the Scottish baker was sabotaging him so that he could take over the franchise himself. Joyce would write about the baker's oddball behaviour—among other things, consulting a Ouija board to decide how many pounds of flour to prepare for a night's baking and telling Joyce that eating an orange in the presence of the doughnuts would spoil them. Finally, Penny Spicer, who had been working at the store under both previous franchisees, called Joyce at home and told him that the Scot was mocking him behind his back and setting him up to fail.

"I threw him out the damned door," Joyce told me. "He was deliberately teaching me to fail."

Other things going on made Joyce wish he had taken Buck Bennett's advice. "When I got in the store," he told me, "the sheriffs were coming in, trying to seize the cash register, the hot chocolate machine . . . They tried to seize the equipment a couple times, but I had a quit-claim deed* on the equipment. One sheriff came in, and me being an ex-policeman and young and healthy, we had a pretty good confrontation."

In his memoir, Joyce accused Charade of outright fraud in issuing a quit-claim deed to him on restaurant property to which he did not have clear title. By this time, Joyce, not surprisingly, didn't entirely trust Charade, and decided he had to speak with Charade's partner, Tim Horton. Joyce had not dealt with Horton at all in securing the franchise, and only met him when a grand opening was held for him.

Joyce was not much of a hockey fan. He had never been to an NHL game, but he knew that Horton was a star. Horton was in the latter part of the 1964–65 season when Joyce reached him and unloaded.

---

* A basic legal instrument by which one party transfers an unencumbered right to property to another party.

"Tim said, 'I'll clean it up,'" Joyce told me. "Once Horton got involved, that was the beginning of the end for him and Jim, because Jim didn't have any more money. Tim went out and borrowed the money to clear up all the debts against the equipment I paid for. The money I'd paid for the franchise went out to pay other bills. It was just coming down in all directions."

THE END FOR JIM CHARADE did not come right away, but it was coming fast. He had no money, and neither did Horton. The Leafs failed to make it four Stanley Cups in a row in the spring of 1965, losing a bloody semifinal series to the eventual winners, the Canadiens. Tim and Lori were also building a custom home in Willowdale, on Bannatyne Drive, which they weren't entirely sure they could afford.

Charade recalled for me constantly driving around with Horton, trying to find new sources of capital. "I remember going to Canada Permanent Trust, sitting in the car in the parking lot with Tim, waiting to meet a guy. Things were rough, saleswise and with the money. I was saying, 'Regardless of what happens, you'll be fine. Your name is there. We didn't do anything bad. We tried.' He said, 'Well, I always say, I can always dig ditches.' I said, 'Tim, Jesus Christ, you've got it made. It's me that's got trouble. I'm not a hockey player. Nobody's going to want my autograph anywhere.'"

They stuck it out, opening the second franchise, on Concession Street in Hamilton, with the help of Jim Quondamatteo. Ron Joyce bought the franchise, borrowing the money from his mother, his sister and others. "The store was built," Joyce told me, "but there were some financial problems, and the suppliers wouldn't release the furniture to them [Tim Donut Ltd.], so for some reason they released it to me. I think they'd become disillusioned with Jim a little."

Things soon felt apart for Tim Horton on both fronts of the doughnut business. Charade had to back out as a business partner, and Joyce was fed up with the lack of support he was receiving for his two franchises.

Over Christmas 1965, while visiting the Hortons in their new home, Charade capitulated. "I said, 'Jesus, I'm not going to make it this way. I'm working night and day and nobody realizes it and they think I'm screwing around anyway . . .' But when you have to run away from bill collectors and meet payrolls, and cheques are bouncing, what do you do? You have to rob Peter to pay Paul. It was not the easiest time."

In order to extricate himself from the disaster of the burger business, Timanjim Ltd., Charade had to walk away from his equity in both Timanjim and Tim Donut Ltd. "I signed over. I resigned as president [of Timanjim Ltd.] and surrendered my end of it. Tim would own it, as long as I wouldn't have the debt. Even at that the restaurants were closing, step by step. I had to go to these examinations with an arbitrator. They wanted to see the books. I was not going bankrupt. I was surrendering the charter and just saying that we couldn't make it, unless the creditors could make some other arrangement. People from the coffee company, Mother Parkers, Jo-Lo Corp. [which supplied the doughnut ingredients], would be there. And that was rough, to do that and to try to operate also."

"It became very clear after the second store opened," Joyce told me, "that there was no input from Jim, and he became a source of frustration for me, because I'd look for help, he'd come in, and with his limited knowledge of the business he would do what he could, but when he got in a corner he would just have to leave. I was always struggling, trying to find my way through this business that I knew nothing about. Tim knew nothing whatsoever, and Jim a little bit."*

---

* The sequence of events of Jim Charade's departure is far from clear. Charade told me he let Horton know he would have to bow out of their ventures during Christmas 1965. In *Always Fresh,* Ron Joyce wrote that Charade had surrendered his half of Tim Donut Ltd. in "early 1965" (p. 48). Joyce also stated in *Always Fresh* that Charade was gone before he took ownership of the second outlet, on Concession Street, which created problems because both

With Charade gone, Tim Donut Ltd. became an equal partnership of Tim and Lori Horton. Ron Joyce, meanwhile, was unhappy paying royalties to Horton for what he saw as no discernible return. Like Spencer Brown before him, Joyce wanted to buy out the franchisor, take down the Tim Horton sign and go it alone. Instead, Horton offered to sell him 10 percent of Tim Donut. Joyce wasn't interested in buying a minority interest, and Horton in turn—now trying to run Tim Donut on his own while playing for the Leafs—wasn't interested in buying back Joyce's two franchises. So Joyce decided to sell them, and was gone from the chain.*

With both Joyce and Charade gone, Horton tried to proceed on his own with a third outlet, in Kitchener, at a commercial property being developed by Dore Carnahan, who already had several Dairy Queens, one of which was on the site. He was leasing out space for a variety store and now a Tim Hortons. Horton was too busy to manage the project himself, and got in touch with Joyce, asking if he was willing to take it on. Carnahan happened to be a friend of Joyce's, and Joyce "reluctantly agreed" (as he put it in *Always Fresh*) to step back in to get it up and running. They then found a franchisee in a former Hamilton cop named Pat McGrinder.

How Joyce and Horton then ended up as partners is as murky as many other aspects of the chain's early history. Joyce told me that he wanted to be a partner and nothing less, but that Horton demurred and Lori wasn't keen on the idea of giving up her half of the company.

Horton and Charade's names were on the lease. But Joyce told me (as I have quoted) that his problems with Charade continued after the Concession Street store was open.

* Like other aspects of the early story of Tim Hortons, this chain of events is unclear. In his memoir, *Always Fresh*, Joyce wrote that he sold his two Hamilton outlets, only to come back to help set up the Kitchener outlet at Horton's request. When I interviewed him in 1993, Joyce recalled still having the two Hamilton outlets when he pitched in with the Kitchener store: "I was living in Stoney Creek, trying to run my two stores in Hamilton, plus my Dairy Queen, plus that store [in Kitchener]. It was one of the worst years of my life." However, I have accepted the timeline in this instance from *Always Fresh*.

"He needed somebody who knew a little about the business, and I was working there all the time," Joyce told me. "Once Tim accepted the fact that I wasn't going to stay there just as an operator, that it had to be more than that, because he wasn't contributing anything—he wasn't, because he didn't know anything about the business—once he accepted that, we became partners. That was done very amiably, and we became good friends." He said they shook hands on the partnership at the Leafs' training camp in Peterborough in the fall of 1966.

Joyce's version of events was a little different in *Always Fresh*. He had planned to break with Horton once the Kitchener store was running, but when it opened in September 1966, "Tim had come to realize he had reached an impasse and couldn't continue to operate. He called me from training camp and indicated that he needed to have a partner; if I reconsidered [leaving], he said, he would sell me half the company. I drove to Peterborough and met with him."

However it came about, Joyce agreed to buy Lori's half of Tim Donut Ltd. for $12,000, with a right of first refusal on Horton's half for $12,500. The deal was signed on December 1, 1966. Joyce wrote in *Always Fresh* that he didn't have the money, and in lieu of cash agreed to take on company debt and pay the remainder over a period of years.

Charade found new work out of his Toronto home, selling franchises for Mister Donut in the United States on trips that took him as far afield as Colorado. Despite the unhappy events of 1965, Charade remained on good terms with both Horton and Joyce, dropping in at the head office they established in Oakville. In 1970, Charade returned to Toronto and for about nine months went to work with Horton and Joyce, selling franchises for them.

Charade recalled for me standing in the parking lot of the headquarters while Horton and Joyce could not decide how to go forward with the company. "It was just on the edge. I wanted to stay with it and expand, but money was tight. There was a recession. Maybe we shouldn't go so fast, maybe we should slow down. We were opening shops, but only one to four a year. I wanted to go faster. I thought there was no job for me. Tim was agreeing with me and Ron was disagreeing with me about the way things were going to turn out."

Charade left, heading to Philadelphia in 1971 to sell franchises for AAMCO. Best known for its transmission stores, it also had the franchising rights for a gift shop called Plum Tree, a women's clothing chain called Red Rooster and a wicker-import retailer called Cargo 7. He spent twenty-three years in the franchise business in the United States; after his wife, Claudette, died in 1988, he returned to Mississauga to open an office for AAMCO. He was playing drums in a jazz group in his spare time at Hy's in Toronto when Ron Joyce walked in one night.

"Maybe you should come back with us," Joyce said, although by then the only "us" left from the old days was Joyce himself.

While Jim Charade was away with AAMCO, Tim Horton's widow, Lori, had launched a spectacularly corrosive lawsuit in 1987 over her sale of her inherited half of the company to Joyce in 1975. To believe Lori Horton's world view, Joyce was a Svengali-like character who forced her late husband to take him as a partner, made him share half his NHL salary in his final playing seasons, and hoodwinked her out of her share of the company a year after her husband's death by taking advantage of her mental incompetence at the time due to her drug and alcohol dependencies.

Lori Horton's legal action failed resoundingly. To try to make her case that she had been taken advantage of in the sale of her interest in the company, she had to sue the lawyer who had represented her, as well as Joyce. Two independent valuations had been secured for the company, which led to an offer of $850,000 for Lori's half. At the eleventh hour, Lori's lawyer upped the demand to an even $1 million. Joyce would recall how he had to scramble to borrow the money to close the deal, and threw in Lori's company car, a Cadillac. In her suit, she asked for $10 million, or half the company back. The defendants built a counter-case of reckless spending by Lori in the years following the sale, arguing that she only filed the suit after she had burned through the money and sold such assets as the family home in Toronto and the cottage at Peninsula Lake.

Lori Horton died in 2000, felled after Christmas dinner by a heart attack. There would always be people who felt, notwithstanding the outcome of her suit, that she got a raw deal in the buyout of her half interest. But there were also people who felt that her suit had been a huge miscalculation, that in arguing on the basis of temporary mental incompetence she had exposed her life, and that of her family, to intense public scrutiny. In the process, her husband's legacy had been seriously tarnished, as Lori resisted the role others assigned to her of having been the difficult partner in the marriage—hooked on diet pills and other medications prescribed for depression and anxiety, overly demanding of her husband's attention (pouring a drink over his head at a party when she decided he'd had enough fun and it was time to leave). In her pushback, Lori recounted Tim Horton's own struggles with alcohol, his predilection for crashing through the front door when she locked him out, and his frightening behaviour in the summer of 1973, which led to him agreeing to seek psychiatric counselling.

Many old friends and teammates stood by Lori, but the airing of so much dirty laundry angered others. One former friend and teammate of Horton's told me after her appeal was launched: "I personally think the suit is baseless. I don't know where it started, but I have an idea of where it started, and it was badly thought out. It did nothing but harm her and harm their family, and it dragged Tim's name through all kinds of crap that needn't be." Joyce, for his part, suspected that Tim Horton's former teammate Eddie Shack and his wife, Norma, who remained close to Lori, helped persuade her that she'd gotten a raw deal.

Lori Horton's suit over the sale of her half of Tim Donut to Joyce in 1975 had been dismissed on February 1, 1993. The judge's decision in its quick recap of the company's history erroneously referred to Charade as "Charet." Invited back by Ron Joyce, he started work in the company's real estate department on March 1, which is where I met him a few months later.

Charade lasted until 1996, a year after the merger with Wendy's, when the new ownership group terminated him. He suffered a heart attack, accepted a $75,000 severance, invested it in part in a tanning salon scheme, and ended up having to declare bankruptcy because of his debts to Canada Revenue Agency. He died in Jonquière, Quebec, in 2009, after suffering from Parkinson's and Alzheimer's.

His son André told *The Globe and Mail* that his father had long lamented the fact that Joyce had gotten rich from the doughnut idea whereas he did not: "I think Ron [Joyce] has always wanted to be noted as the co-founder of Tim Hortons and that frustrated my father a bit. I told him, 'Ron was a vital piece and so were you.' My dad wanted to be known as the key person at the start and it was very difficult for my father to accept that he left the company before it became successful. He was like the fifth Beatle, not getting enough credit. He's the forgotten one in the founding of the chain."

"Jim was the idea guy," Joyce told me in 1993. "You've got to give him a lot of credit. The Tim Horton chain wouldn't be here today without him. Even though he couldn't execute, he was the guy who got it started. The one who made it run was me."

When he learned of Charade's death, Joyce was magnanimous. "It wasn't Tim Horton. It wasn't Ron Joyce. It was Jim," he told *The Globe and Mail.* "Jim was the gambit behind the concept. He doesn't get enough credit, but I have always acknowledged him. Without him, it would never have happened."

*

ONLY TWO YEARS after Jim Charade opened his doughnut drive-in on Ottawa Street, the Tim Horton restaurant venture was completely transformed. Gone were all of the Toronto drive-ins as well as the doughnut stores Charade had opened there with Dennis Griggs. Gone, too, was Charade, and in his stead was a new partner for Horton, with very different ideas from those of Charade about how to move forward, and how much value Tim Horton's celebrity actually contributed to the venture.

12

The Human Factor: Tim Horton Becomes the Ghost in the Corporate Machine

On January 20, 1997, Justice Joan L. Lax of the Ontario Court (General Division) heard a motion from lawyer Paul Bates on behalf of his clients, Tim Donut Ltd. (TDL) and Ron Joyce, requesting that a suit filed on June 20, 1995, by Lori Horton be dismissed. Tim Horton's widow had launched the action three months after a final unfavourable result for her more notorious earlier action over the sale of her half interest in the chain to Joyce in 1975.

Lori had appealed the 1993 decision, alleging Joyce had financing lined up at the time of her sale in order to begin expanding the chain, and thus knew the company was about to be worth much more than its appraised value. The appeal court judge dismissed the appeal on March 9, 1995, saying this was a new allegation that had not been part of the original suit, and so could only be the basis of a new suit. Lori didn't follow through on the claim, instead launching the fresh suit on another matter entirely.

Like the relationship between a franchisor and a franchisee, the dispute between Ron Joyce and Lori Horton in the initial suit over her sale of half the company was ultimately a matter of power and obligation, of fair dealing, of contractual good faith that cannot cross the threshold into what the law calls "utmost good faith," which would demand that Joyce have dealt with Lori with the selflessness of a trustee or guardian. He was not the keeper of the widow of his late partner, although he would voluntarily pay a regular stipend to Horton's daughters. But in the process of fighting her lost legal causes, Lori Horton would inadvertently establish that her late husband's public persona—the persona that had been battered by revelations arising largely from Lori Horton's legal actions—belonged to the company whose owner she had come to despise.

The follow-up suit was scarcely noticed or commented upon by the media, lacking the initial suit's bait of a (now) wealthy corporate owner, a widow allegedly wronged, and tales of alcohol abuse and drug addiction. This second suit concerned the use of Tim Horton's likeness for a portrait created by the artist Ken Danby for a 1992 fundraising poster for the Tim Horton Children's Foundation, which Lori Horton and Ron Joyce had co-founded in 1975 following Horton's death. Yet this suit, lacking the personal pyrotechnics of the first, was far more instructive about Tim Hortons as a commercial and cultural phenomenon.

What was the legal relationship between a human being and a brand? Could the personality of an individual named Tim Horton be permanently, irretrievably fused with an enterprise he founded, to the point of being transformed into an intellectual property, an intangible asset to which an accountant could assign a value? And was this preserved-in-amber immortality of his commercial personality what Tim Horton had in mind when he got into the restaurant business?

I MET LORI HORTON in late 1993, almost a year after she suffered the expensive loss at trial of the first suit over the sale of her interest in the company. Joyce has written that in mid-trial the judge had urged Joyce to consider settling, and he had made an offer of an annuity of

$100,000 for the rest of Lori's life. She turned it down, gambling on winning all at trial. In September 1993, the court had ordered her to pay costs of $307,823.15 arising from the failed suit; the failed appeal would cost her another $28,604.93. Lori had no means to comply, and was essentially destitute, supported only by a $2,100 monthly annuity. She was living in a north Toronto home that I understood was provided by a former teammate of her late husband. An alumni group of these teammates had loaned her $21,000 for the appeal and was unlikely to ever see it again.

Lori was already making clear her displeasure over the fundraising poster when I met her. She was generally unhappy with the children's foundation she had co-founded with Ron Joyce. The first camp for underprivileged children, which had opened at Lorimer Lake near Parry Sound, Ontario, in 1975, in her mind was the true memorial; the rest, she thought, were just promoting the restaurant business. Joyce would concede in his memoirs that without consulting Lori, who was supposed to be the foundation's co-chair, he had agreed to persistent requests by Moncton super-franchisee Gary O'Neill that a second camp be opened in Atlantic Canada. Lori withdrew from the foundation in 1986 and the following year launched the suit over Joyce's purchase of her half interest.

In her mind, Ron Joyce, the company carrying on business as Tim Hortons and its franchisees had appropriated the memorial foundation and turned the original camp into a chain that really served to promote their collective business interests. She told me she wanted the franchisees to take the poster down from the restaurants. As it turned out, her lawyer had already written a letter to the company in October 1991, objecting to the fact that certain photographs had been provided to Danby for the fundraising portrait by her daughter, Jeri-Lyn—who, to complicate matters, was married to Ron Joyce's son, Ron Jr., ran a Tim Hortons with her husband and had testified on her mother's behalf in the 1987 suit.

Lori Horton's portrait suit came early in the bench career of Justice Lax; she had been appointed a judge of the Ontario court in January 1996, after ten years as the assistant dean and director of admissions at the University of Toronto's Faculty of Law. It took seventeen days from the hearing of the defence motion for dismissal for Justice Lax to render judgment. In agreeing to the dismissal, Justice Lax delivered a withering critique of Lori Horton's case, rather strongly suggesting that the latest suit had arisen because of her failure to succeed with the first one.

Although Lori's conviction that the foundation was no longer truly a charitable memorial to her husband seemed genuine, it was tempting to view this second suit as a last-gasp attempt by Lori to exact some retribution for the fact that the company her late husband had co-founded was in the hands of a man she had plainly come to loathe. She had filed the suit not only a few months after losing her bid to overturn the terms of the 1975 sale of her half of the company, but also (coincidentally or not) about six weeks before Wendy's and Tim Hortons announced that they were merging in a deal that made Joyce the single largest shareholder of the new QSR company, garnered Joyce an $850,000 annual salary and ultimately netted him hundreds of millions of dollars when he cashed in shares.

The portrait suit appeared to hinge on whether or not the artist Ken Danby, caught haplessly in this legal firefight (although he was never a party to the action), had infringed on copyright in photographs used as the basis for his Horton portrait, which Lori Horton claimed belonged to her. In the whipsawing of alliances in Lori Horton's life, her daughter Jeri-Lyn's behaviour was now somewhat at issue, as Jeri-Lyn had provided the photos for the portrait that Lori now claimed were her intellectual property.

The intellectual-property claim failed to withstand scrutiny. A fundamental issue instead addressed by Justice Lax was whether or not Horton, while alive, had willingly exploited his own name and likeness in launching and developing the Tim Hortons restaurant chain, and in the process had granted the business he co-owned, Tim Donut Ltd., the right to continue exploiting this "commercial personality." Lori Horton could not claim ownership of her husband's commercial personality if it had already been assigned to the company, her half of which she in turn had sold to Ron Joyce.

The issues of the use, meaning, and relevance of Tim Horton's name, likeness and reputation are at the heart of the failures of his initial businesses, the doughnut chain's founding and growth, and the ongoing opportunities (and implicit limitations) of the brand that so dominates the Canadian QSR landscape and is pursuing growth in the United States.

AS I TRIED TO NEGOTIATE MY CAR out of the bewildering sprawl of the AMC Plaza in Vaughan, north of Toronto, in the summer of 2011, another contender in the crowded field of bar-and-grill concepts appeared: Wendel Clark's Classic Grill and Sports Lounge. It turned out to be one of two that had opened (the second one was in Oakville), and was part of a greater 12,000-square-foot complex at AMC Plaza called Entertainment Central, owned by Dynamic Hospitality & Entertainment Group.

Wendel Clark was not the only Leaf to follow Tim Horton's example and become a name on a restaurant sign. John Anderson, who played with the Leafs from 1977 to 1985, opened a chain of burger diners. One of them used to be on Warden Avenue, coincidentally only a few doors from the location of one of Tim Horton's ill-fated burger drive-ins and across the road from where Jim Charade's Tim Horton Do-Nut stood in the Colony Plaza. It's gone now, but other locations endure in Scarborough, North York and Mississauga.

More germane to the Tim Horton saga is Eddie Shack Donuts.

Horton's friend and old Leaf teammate was suspected (especially by Ron Joyce in *Always Fresh*) of encouraging Lori Horton to pursue her suit against Joyce over her sale of her half interest in Tim Donut Ltd. After Lori lost the suit, Shack lent his name to a new, erstwhile chain of doughnut shops in 1994. Lori agreed to come out for the opening of the first one, but on the condition that Eddie pledge not to open an outlet that competed directly with any Tim Hortons being run by her daughter, Jeri-Lyn. Eddie Shack Donuts has never caused any loss of sleep at Tim Hortons corporate headquarters. There's still one in Caledon, Ontario.

When Wendel Clark turned out for the opening of his first namesake bar and grill in January 2008, the *Toronto Star* reported that he was under contract to put in an appearance "a few times a year" in exchange for a share of the revenues. Clark avowed that since he only lived ten minutes away in King City, he planned to actually show up "every week or two," and quipped to the reporter, "More than Wayne. I've got a shorter commute." It was a jab at Wayne Gretzky, who had recently sold his Los Angeles mansion to live in Phoenix, where he was part of the troubled ownership of the NHL's Coyotes. The Great One was unlikely to be spotted on anything like a routine basis at his namesake restaurant in downtown Toronto.

The Wendel Clark opening came about two months after the Painter family of Parry Sound acquired rights to Don Cherry's Sports Grill concept. What had begun as a franchise chain called Don Cherry's Grapevine in the 1980s had been converted to a new system in 1995, whereby existing restaurateurs licensed the right to brand themselves as a Don Cherry restaurant in exchange for a percentage of receipts. There were seventeen Don Cherry's Sports Grills listed on the licensing company's website when I last checked in April 2012, predominantly in small Canadian towns like North Battleford, Saskatchewan; Parry Sound, Ontario (hometown of Don Cherry's all-time favourite hockey player, Bobby Orr, where William Painter is the licensee); and Goose

Bay, Labrador. With that many sports grills in that many far-flung locations, and with Don Cherry being the national media celebrity he is, customers in North Battleford are assuredly not expecting to find Grapes himself behind the bar whenever they walk into their local version of his sports grill.

There has long been an irresistible attraction between retired professional athletes and the bar business. Call it the Sam Malone Effect, in honour of the fictional Red Sox reliever Sam "Mayday" Malone, who was found faithfully tending glass in the Boston bar called Cheers in the long-running sitcom of the same name. The idea of the celebrity sports bar is predicated on the notion of mutual need: fans need (and will pay for) contact with sports heroes, and sports heroes either need ego-stroking or ongoing contact with fans, or are just savvy enough to know they can charge for it.

The deals that have put Wendel Clark's and Don Cherry's names on sports bar-and-grill concepts are in the same vein as Jim Charade's original licensing agreement with Tim Horton for his doughnut stores. Unlike Wendel Clark, though, Horton had no contractual obligation to show up in the doughnut outlets. With the drive-in restaurants owned by Timanjim, Horton had equity, management oversight and a greater incentive to make his physical presence felt among the customers. Horton certainly understood (or was under the illusion) that his name had a marketplace cachet, otherwise he would not have founded a succession of businesses with his name and likeness in the signage.

At the least, he was persuaded of the marketability of his name by business partners. Jim Charade was convinced that Horton's mere ability to sign autographs would generate beneficial publicity. But Horton's previous partner in the car business, Fred Care, could have told Charade otherwise. Hughie Phillips, a resident of Bloorview Hospital's Home and School whom Horton had befriended in the 1950s, recalled for me hearing Care grouse. "I remember he said, 'Tim Horton Motors. That name has done nothing for us.' I'm only a kid, and that really hurt me. I felt like punching him. Tim used to work like hell."

Horton did work like hell, but only sporadically, given that for the better part of the year, from September through April, his main job was playing professional hockey. Charade imagined Horton being in the restaurants they would open together, maybe not flipping burgers full time but at least dropping in to meet and greet the public. It was an emcee role not unlike the one fulfilled by Bob Baun at George's Spaghetti House in his spare time, but Horton was not a glad-handing public figure.

"Tim *never* saw himself as a public persona," Lori Horton insisted to me in 1993. A more nuanced interpretation would be that her late husband understood the exploitability of his public persona, but had little stomach for the sausage-making machinery of fame and exerted the least possible effort to cultivate the persona on which others wanted to help him capitalize. Bob Baun saw this early, when as a young player he would go out on speaking engagements with Horton. Baun would end up doing all the talking while Horton hung back and, when required, signed autographs.

Horton's old Leaf teammate Dave Keon considered what Charade had told me about being inspired by the example of Gino Marchetti and the Gino's burger chain. Keon had been quite familiar with Horton's business ambitions, having introduced him to Mel Rothwell of the firm Dunwoody, who became the accountant of Horton personally as well as of the business partnership, Tim Donut Ltd., that Horton formed with Ron Joyce. (Keon also had a Tim Hortons franchise in Nova Scotia from 1977 to 1982.) "Gino Marchetti didn't only lend his name, he ran them," Keon told me. "If you're going to be in that type of business, you're going to be a guy meeting the people, and it takes a certain type of person. A guy like Bobby Baun could do that, but Timmy felt uncomfortable.

"He was happy to have somebody else take credit for things," Keon went on. "Playing hockey, he enjoyed being an all-star, but he didn't particularly care for all the trappings that went with that. He would much prefer that when he stepped off the ice, it was over. He was a really humble guy. He enjoyed excelling at hockey, but I don't think he ever took it to be any more than it was."

"I look at the picture of him sometimes in the doughnut shop that says 'The Legend,'" Charade told me of the Danby fundraising poster that was still visible in some restaurants in the early 1990s, "and I think: 'I don't know. He was just real people.'"

The Leafs of the 1960s were a tight-knit bunch when it came to helping out friends and each other in off-ice promotions. Brian Cullen recalled for me how, when he opened up his car dealership in Grimsby in September 1966, "I brought in Tim, Bobby Pulford, Bobby Baun, Frank Mahovlich, Eddie Shack, seven or eight more of the Leafs . . . You couldn't get within four miles of the dealership. They couldn't do enough for you when you went into business and needed a boost to get off the ground and be well known." Long into retirement, they continued to do the same.

Charade learned quickly that Horton, who had become a good friend, was just about as immovable when it came to getting him to appear at a restaurant as he was when parked in front of the Leaf goal. And when he did appear, Horton typically shied from the limelight. When Charade and Horton started opening the namesake drive-ins, his Leaf teammates dutifully turned up. But when players like George Armstrong and Dave Keon would be mixing with the crowd and signing autographs, Horton would find some excuse to go back in the kitchen and watch over the chicken.

The Canadiens great Jean Béliveau, a regular opponent of Horton over their long careers, touched upon the difficulty of fulfilling the expectations of namesake celebrity for me. John Bitove, a Torontonian of Macedonian descent who built a catering empire from a fourteen-stool lunch counter (and who would make overtures to acquire Tim Hortons in the late 1980s), had secured the Canadian rights to the Big

Boy burger chain. He tagged his initials onto the chain, and for his JB's Big Boy in Scarborough, Bitove made the inspired decision to bring in another JB—Jean Béliveau—for the grand opening.

"I became very close with the Bitoves," Béliveau told me. (John Bitove Jr. partnered with Allan Slaight of Standard Broadcasting to secure the National Basketball Association franchise, the Raptors, for Toronto in the mid-1990s.) "We've always been good friends. I almost had the Big Boy franchise for Quebec and the Maritimes. At the last minute, I stepped out. It's nice if, after several years, you end up with a few stores, but people would think that I should be there all the time, and that would be impossible if you have five or ten stores. You'd have to be everywhere."

IN CONSIDERING THE MOTION to dismiss Lori Horton's suit over the use of her husband's likeness in the foundation fundraising poster, Justice Lax had to rule on whether the defendants had "unlawfully appropriated the commercial personality of the late Tim Horton." At issue was the degree to which Horton willingly made himself, including his likeness, a commercial property.

The judge was satisfied that Horton well knew what he was up to. The concept of Tim Donut Ltd., she ruled, "was developed by Tim Horton and Ronald Joyce with a view to exploiting the commercial personality of Tim Horton in the restaurants which bear his name and image. Representations of Tim Horton, including his name, signature and photographic likeness in hockey uniform, were part of the early marketing initiatives of the company. By 1974, there were thirty-nine restaurants which were well known in southwestern Ontario and elsewhere under the trade names 'Tim Horton Donuts' and 'Tim Hortons.' The trade names continue to this day. Prior to his death, this was done with Tim Horton's consent."

To the extent that the Danby portrait actually represented a commercial exploitation—which she decided it was not—Justice Lax ruled: "The commercial personality of Tim Horton was one which was licensed to the business of TDL since its inception. This was done directly through trademark registrations and through Mr. Horton's conduct in permitting the use of his personality in the development of the business in which he was a 50 percent partner. By these actions, TDL acquired the personality rights of Tim Horton which, if they continue to exist, have been carried on, in one form or another since his death."

Justice Lax concluded "it was the intention of Tim Horton to exploit his commercial personality in this way. There is no evidence to suggest otherwise. During his life, he benefited from this. That benefit passed to his estate, and ultimately to Mrs. Horton on the sale of her shares in the business for $1,000,000 in 1975."

Justice Lax went on to reject Lori Horton's contention that her October 1991 letter, objecting to the use of photographs to which she argued she owned the copyright, put the defendants in her impending 1995 suit on notice that (as Justice Lax summarized) "she was revoking whatever licence had been obtained, either expressly or impliedly to use the commercial personality of Tim Horton." The judge found this argument "has no merit." The right of commercial personality had belonged to Tim Horton himself, and she was satisfied that while Horton was alive "he had given over that right to TDL, as he was entitled to do." Nor was there evidence that TDL or Joyce appropriated his commercial personality for the portrait, as they did not commission it. If any appropriation occurred, it was by the Tim Horton Children's Foundation and the artist, Ken Danby, who weren't even defendants in the action.

What was particularly interesting about Justice Lax's granting of the motion for dismissal was her conclusion that the stores in the Tim Hortons chain "represent the commercial personality of Tim Horton."

Dead for more than twenty years, he still somehow haunted the drive-throughs, a ghost in the corporate machine. Although she also questioned whether Tim Horton's "personality rights" continued to exist, it seemed that in her judgment, the company that by the time of Lori Horton's suit had merged with Wendy's essentially owned his marketable persona.

The judge concluded that Horton had, while alive, willingly and deliberately exploited his own likeness, name and signature. Yet as soon as Joyce was his partner, Joyce started persuading Horton that if they were to be successful, Charade's fundamental strategy of exploiting his hockey celebrity would have to go.

Insofar as the name on the restaurant sign (and doughnut boxes) represented Horton's signature, it was a stylized script that became increasingly bereft of personality. Horton's own likeness was only briefly a part of the promotion of his businesses. One longer-standing exception was the restaurant that had nothing to do with Tim Donut Ltd., the "Number 7" or "Big 7" in North Bay. But the signage for the franchised stores that were organized as Tim Donut Ltd. rapidly abandoned the Horton likeness. The image of him in Leaf uniform, reproduced in the replica sign at store #1, was only used for the first three outlets. Once Joyce was Horton's partner in December 1966, the imagery of hockey and of Horton's persona, beyond the stylized signature, was phased out. When the fourth outlet opened in Hamilton's Westdale neighbourhood in 1967, the signage with Horton in a Leaf uniform was gone. The new design, which endures, was two ovals joined by vertical stripes of brown and yellow, a palette that was more reminiscent of the Boston Bruins than the Toronto Maple Leafs. The signature "Tim Horton" (or "Tim Horton's") appeared in the upper oval, with four doughnuts beneath it, and the word "donuts" appeared in the lower oval until it was replaced by the slogan "Always Fresh."

When Joyce began opening stores with Horton, they benefited from the usual flying squad of teammates who could draw a crowd. But that only filled a restaurant for a day, and Horton himself continued to be uncomfortable in the celebrity role. The fact that Horton had such a difficult time adopting a public persona "didn't bother me, but I think it bothered him a little bit," Joyce told me. "When we were doing a grand opening in Belleville, we announced he was going to be there. He had an awful time. He was very uncomfortable, and he showed it."

Joyce itemized the many reasons he had for advocating the abandonment of the Horton hockey persona in *Always Fresh,* all of them sensible. Foremost among the image's problems was that using Horton's likeness in a Leaf uniform was going to raise trademark issues—and, as it turned out, Horton was not going to remain a Leaf until retirement, as he played for the New York Rangers, Pittsburgh Penguins and Buffalo Sabres for the last five seasons of his career, beginning in the fall of 1969. The blue-and-white livery of the Leafs was felt to be too "cold" for a restaurant. The new signage had the warmth of yellow and brown, colours associated with coffee and baking, and the interiors employed gold and red.

But above all, Joyce firmly believed that they could not build a viable business together based on athletic celebrity. "The name was not important," he told me. "It was operations. How do you make it work? How do you make it happen? We developed the manual, the systems, because there was nobody there to teach us." Apart from deciding to call an ill-fated sandwich-spinoff concept "Breakaway" in 1977, the company steered clear of the hockey imagery where it didn't involve sentimental images of kids in winter. Joyce led a failed bid to secure an NHL franchise for Hamilton in the early 1990s, but only when the restaurant allied with Sidney Crosby in a multiyear partnership in December 2006 did a strong NHL connection emerge in its marketing. In Crosby's case, though, the aim has been to leverage his roots in the Timbits minor sports program—he played for Nova Scotia's Cole Harbour Timbits at age five. Crosby was enlisted to sell Tim Hortons' association with minor hockey and the program's philosophy of putting fun first, not to link

Tim Hortons with the professional game. During the 2010 Olympics, Tim Hortons built television marketing around Crosby, leveraging his stardom on Canada's national team, but again used it to promote the Timbits minor sports connection and philosophy. And nowhere in a promotional spot has Crosby ever uttered words about the restaurant's namesake star NHL player.

In successfully securing a dismissal of the second Lori Horton suit, the lawyer for TDL and Joyce had to argue that the company possessed the rights to the image of Horton that it has never really exploited. Which isn't to say that it never will. The cup sleeve on the medium coffee I ordered from the outlet on West Forty-second Street in Manhattan, with its description of Horton the hockey star, showed that the persona beneath the otherwise depersonalized name is capable of being deployed where necessary by the company—especially now that Lori Horton has died and Ron Joyce is no longer involved. Hockey in general is critical to the brand's marketing and retailing. Through Tim Hortons' relationship with Crosby, the company cemented its association with both moms and dads and kids in local hockey rinks. A dad and his own dad at a small-town hockey arena have been featured in Tim Hortons television advertising.

The company has struck partnerships with American NHL teams like the New York Islanders, Crosby's Pittsburgh Penguins and the Columbus Blue Jackets, which also involve retail presences in their arenas.* It has sponsored the NHL's Winter Classic outdoor games, and in 2012 was the lead sponsor of the NHL All-Star Game and related activities. These links with the NHL are critical as McDonald's forges a promotional partnership with *Hockey Night in Canada*, yet

* A branding confusion kerfuffle emerged when St. John's, Newfoundland, announced in July 2011 that its AHL affiliate with the NHL's Winnipeg Jets would be called the IceCaps, in honour of a former senior amateur team, the Caps. More than a few people thought the team had been named for a Tim Hortons beverage, even though Tim's has nothing to do with the club's ownership or operations.

they need to be considered as one aspect of a larger effort to associate the Tim Hortons brand with major sporting events and leagues.

In August 2011, the company struck a sponsorship deal for the remainder of the professional baseball season that allowed it to sell coffee and Cold Stone Creamery ice cream at two kiosks at the Rogers Centre, home field of the Toronto Blue Jays, in what was expected to be the start of a multiyear relationship. Tim's is also involved in promotions with Canadian Football League teams, producing themed gift cards (and special doughnuts) for the Hamilton Tiger-Cats, Winnipeg Blue Bombers and Toronto Argonauts. (CFL quarterback Kevin Glenn even became a partner in two Detroit-area franchises when he was on the Ti-Cats roster.) The company is the marquee sponsor of the national curling tourney, the Brier, and in Michigan it has been building bridges to college football. In 2007, it sponsored Michigan State's homecoming game against the Indiana Hoosiers, and in 2011 announced that would be the official coffee served throughout Michigan State's Spartan Stadium in East Lansing, Michigan. Tim's coffee and other menu items would also become available at the college's student centre and Munn Ice Arena, home to hockey's Spartans.

So far, despite the company's efforts to associate its brand with hockey, both amateur and professional, in Canada and the United States, the commercial persona of its namesake has remained almost entirely untapped. Its value may be seriously underestimated. If the marketing wars for consumer loyalty, especially in Canada, ever become dire for Tim Hortons, that persona could be called upon. With McDonald's turning to minor hockey sponsorship and co-promotions with *Hockey Night in Canada* as a means to win back QSR market share (and sell coffee) in Canada, Tim's could be nudged closer to showing that Timmy, not Ronald, has the *real* hockey restaurant chain.

Comedian Mike Myers already has created the Tim Hortons that never was, that many people surely wish there could be, for his film *Wayne's World*. Riffing on memories of his Scarborough upbringing,

Myers constructed an alternate-universe Tim's in the form of Stan Mikita's Donuts in Aurora, Illinois, placing a statue of the former Chicago Blackhawks great, laced up in team livery, a bent stick in hand, on the roof. Myers also named a police officer who appears in the doughnut shop Koharski, a reference to NHL referee Don Koharski, at whom New Jersey Devils coach Jim Schoenfeld—who was Tim Horton's defence partner on the Buffalo Sabres—once famously yelled, "Have another doughnut, you fat pig!"

Fans of all things related to Mike Myers, *Wayne's World,* hockey and doughnuts are tenaciously fond of Stan Mikita's Donuts. You can find deliberately cheesy T-shirts on sale on the Internet purporting to be from this restaurant, and discussion boards produce the occasional wistful query as to whether it actually exists. (Reads one such posting: "Me and my husband are taking a trip to Chicago and we were hoping to hit up this little known *Wayne's World* doughnut shop but could not find it! I know it is suppose [*sic*] to be in Aurora but that is as far as we got.")

A *Wayne's World*–style Tim's is not entirely out of reach. According to the logic of Justice Lax's 1997 ruling, Tim Donut Ltd. could conceivably aggressively reinvent the chain (or a few outlets) as a wink-and-nod retro tribute to its namesake, riffing on the Mike Myers riff of the past that Tim Hortons never had (the aesthetic near-miss of Number 7 in North Bay excepted).

In five, ten or fifty years, Tim Horton might emerge as a retro icon, in what would amount to the nuclear option for the company: a measure of last resort that could be as devastating to itself as to its brand competitors. For if the company owns the commercial personality of Horton, it also bears the burden of his tarnished personal legacy.

But just to be safe, Tim Hortons has a fallback position. When Ron Joyce retired from Wendy's International in 2001, the company acquired the rights to the continued use of his name as well as his likeness. Spun off from Wendy's in 2006, Tim Hortons assigned an intangible value of $6.455 million to what it called Joyce's "persona" when it was acquired in 2001. Its value would be amortized over a period of twelve years, ending in 2013. Tim Hortons has nothing on the books for the persona value of Tim Horton himself. As it stands, Horton's legacy is literally worthless to the present company. But that doesn't mean Tim Horton's commercial personality is bereft of value. You never know: someday, the faces of Tim and Ron may be united on the sign, the menu board or the coffee cups—ghosts in the machine together, forever.

13

The Stealth Chain: Tim Hortons Quietly Conquers Canada

ANYONE MULLING OVER THE FUTURE of the fast-food industry *circa* 1970 would have been astonished to know how the business was going to turn out in Canada—that coffee in general and Tim Hortons in particular would become so predominant in the coming decades, and that they would do so by building momentum before the 1970s were over. It is safe to say that no one, not even Tim Horton himself, saw Tim Hortons coming. His eponymous brand managed to survive the turbulence of its own beginnings and the many uncertainties of the QSR industry to become a Canadian giant with international aspirations. It did so through shrewd strategic decisions, the quality of its product and people, and more than a little serendipity.

At the close of the 1960s, the fast-food industry was undergoing a rapid transition into its modern form, accompanied by a lack of clarity over where the industry was headed, or what it even was. And the business Tim Hortons was in—at that time, doughnuts, with some coffee on the side—was seen as a dead-end concept that showed little if any opportunity for growth.

Tim Hortons and its winning formula of coffee and doughnuts was deep in the weeds when the trade magazine *Canadian Hotel and Restaurant* surveyed 1,948 fast-food chain outlets operating at the end of 1969. Of the fourteen companies that controlled two-thirds of the outlets, all but two came from the United States. The only two Canadian chains in this elite were Harvey's of Toronto and Dixie Lee, a fried-chicken concept based in Belleville.

Tim Hortons was not only absent from that list of key players; it implicitly had no future. In February 1970, Harvey's Foods president George Sukornyk dismissed the future of doughnuts in a seminar on fast food he delivered to the Ontario chapter of the Canadian Restaurant Association. "Obviously, the public is willing to accept only some things in fast food," he assured the audience. "You don't see people opening pancake houses and doughnut houses," he offered as examples, observing there had been a flurry of such openings a few years earlier.

As president of Canada's largest domestically owned fast-food chain, and with a stock that traded on the Toronto exchange, Sukornyk's opinion verged on the prevailing media wisdom. In a two-part article on the state of fast food in Canada published that August, *The Globe and Mail* parroted Sukornyk's line on the industry's future, stating that some concepts "had apparently passed the peak of their popularity, including doughnuts (4.5 per cent) and pancakes (1.5 per cent), with little indication that they will increase their market share."*

The general lesson of popular food groups proved enduring. In 1969, three products dominated Canadian fast-food chain outlets: chicken (32 percent), hamburgers (29 percent) and ice cream (about 23 percent). The distinctions weren't totally cut and dried—there were hamburger joints that also sold chicken or hot dogs, and ice cream parlours that were fighting the seasonality of their business by adding hamburgers (as Dairy Queen recently had done, with its brazier

* Sukornyk—and those who abided by his opinions—wasn't entirely wrong about pancake houses. Although the Golden Griddle concept of family restaurants, established in 1964, is still very much alive in Ontario (with eighteen outlets, about half of them around Toronto), it never reached the scale of, for example, Harvey's sister restaurant Swiss Chalet as a sit-down eatery.

menu). But it was still true that about 85 percent of fast-food outlets were geared to those three basic food groups. The other 15 percent was a free-for-all food fight—hot dogs, roast beef, fish and chips, pizza and, yes, doughnuts, among others—struggling for market share.

The fast-food industry was anxiously seeking a breakthrough food fad because competition within the dominant concepts was ferocious, as Horton and Charade had already learned with drive-ins devoted to hamburgers and barbecue chicken. The industry also feared consumer fatigue. Customers were thought capable of tiring of the same old combo of burger and fries and craving new taste experiences. While the public has proved to be overwhelmingly faithful to burgers and fries, it has also proved to be true that there is far more room in their diet for novel choices than the standard fast-food fare of the 1960s offered them. As the 1970s dawned, the fast-food business was determined to figure out what those choices might be.

For the dominant players that were offering one or more of the standards (chicken, burgers, ice cream), it meant experimenting with new offerings. That compulsion has not changed, and if anything has accelerated. For people looking to get into the fast-food business, novelty meant finding a concept that was underexploited and relatively low in competition within its own sector. It might be one of the many concepts fighting for a small share of the marketplace left untapped by the chicken–burger–ice cream colossus, but the upside potential of picking the right one was huge.

Exploiting new food possibilities meant addressing the temporal and demographic aspects of the business. The standard drive-in of the 1960s, as exemplified by Harvey's, was an evening (and late-night) business. It was welded to car culture, and most firmly to a youth culture built around cars. For the drive-in business to grow, it had to find customers other than teenagers with tight budgets whose antics (as Harvey's had discovered in Scarborough) annoyed the neighbours to the point of blocking the development of new restaurants. The industry had to do more with grown-ups and with families. It also had to do more to exploit what are known as "day parts," the different time periods of an average day, and the retailing possibilities each one represented in terms of discrete meal, snacking and entertainment windows.

Sukornyk advocated the Harvey's model of simplicity, to which Tim Hortons adhered. A fast-food operation had to have a very limited menu, which permitted efficiencies in purchasing, staffing, kitchen design and preparation. Tim Hortons mainly did coffee and doughnuts, which were snack-category offerings. Harvey's was focused on hamburgers, hot dogs, french fries and milkshakes. Harvey's *had* experimented with fish and chips and ice cream, but those forays had required no significant changes in the essential restaurant set-up. An outlet needed no more than half a dozen people to fill its staffing needs. Harvey's also didn't believe in seating areas. It increased the necessary real estate footprint (or robbed available space from parking) and inflated construction and fixture costs. Since fast food was predicated on the notion of not having the expense of table service, tables themselves seemed extraneous. Providing parking space for cars was more important than seating space that encouraged people to loiter.

Fast food was poised to diverge in two predominant (but not exclusive) directions. One was toward self-service seating areas that went beyond a simple counter with stools, which Harvey's would begin to adopt in the mid-1970s. The other was to allow customers to forgo the inconvenience of getting out of their vehicles by serving them through a drive-through window. But already the idea that fast food was exclusively linked to car culture was being challenged by urban locations that relied on pedestrian traffic.

The common denominator of fast food, then, was not necessarily the automobile, but convenience. The food, as the label indicated, had to be fast. It had to be easy to order, quick to be made and served, and quick to be consumed, generally without a need for cutlery and dishes.

It was usually hand food, which the customer could carry away, and the lack of cutlery and dishes (beyond disposable utensils, cups, plates and containers) meant the restaurant didn't need a dishwasher on staff, or dishwashing equipment, beyond what was required to maintain the kitchen itself.

As time proved, the automobile remained an important factor in the convenience denominator of fast food, but it would not be the sole factor. That said, the automobile was overwhelmingly responsible for creating a culture of convenience in consumption where food is concerned, which then migrated into other aspects of life where no cars were present, such as food outlets in concourses of office towers and institutional settings like airports, hospitals, museums and colleges and universities, most of which Tim Hortons would exploit as it sought new territorial opportunities.

The relationship between suburbia and the automobile was symbiotic. The automobile made the sprawl of suburbia possible, and the sprawl of suburbia made the automobile necessary or at least highly desirable. Life itself sprawled along with the suburbs. Commuting ever-greater distances to work as well as play became part of the postwar routine. People spent more time in cars, which meant less time for other aspects of life, one of which was meal preparation. People had begun to sacrifice sit-down meals at home out of harried necessity rather than choice. Where restaurants had once been a form of entertainment for most people, they began to fulfill a primary role in the daily routine of a modern household.

The restaurant industry is still said to be supported by "discretionary" consumer spending. While it is true that much of what the QSR business especially is constantly trying to sell us is essentially unnecessary—and no QSR business is more reliant on indulgence than Tim Hortons—it is also true that the business occupies a place in the typical consumer's life that is close to indispensable. No one really "needs" a Happy Meal, or a bucket of fried chicken or a coffee and an apple fritter. But between force of habit (and in the case of caffeine, an actual addiction) and the pressures of household scheduling, fast food has become ingrained in modern urban and suburban life to the point that it can no longer be considered a mere indulgence or frivolity.

This was not universally understood or foreseen in 1970, not even by the leading members of the fast-food business. George Sukornyk's complaints at the Canadian Restaurant Association seminar in February 1970 about unsupportable levels of competition are particularly revealing. Sukornyk recounted how, eight months earlier, he had opened a Harvey's in Chatham, Ontario, in competition with a "root beer drive-in" (A&W, obviously), two fried chicken operations and a number of sit-down restaurants. Business was fine until two independent operations, a takeout hamburger chain restaurant, and three soft ice cream vendors, one of them also selling hamburgers (which must have been a Dairy Queen) opened. Sukornyk declared that every resident of Chatham would have to eat out once a week just to give all these establishments a volume of $1,000 a week, which he considered marginal.

Sukornyk plainly thought that no one could expect the typical resident of an urban centre to patronize any fast-food outlet more than once a week. In an astonishingly short period of time, his perspective would prove to be obsolete. (And before 1970 was out, Sukornyk would be gone from the helm of Harvey's Foods, as a stock that had soared above $20 crashed below $1.) Today, plenty of Canadian consumers visit a QSR business once a *day*, if only to get a Tim's coffee. Fifty-seven percent of Tim Hortons' customers visit one to three times a week, 17 percent four to six times, and 26 percent seven or more times. The frequency of visits, and the profit margins on coffee especially, allows a Tim's outlet to make a healthy return despite the fact that an average "cheque," or order, *circa* 2010, totalling $3.23, lagged the $3.95 at Starbucks and the $5.46 at McDonald's.

But forty years ago, the restaurant industry lacked hard numbers on consumer spending. In 1969, the Dominion Institute estimated that

Canadians were spending about $1.2 billion annually on food outside the home, which was about $57 per person. Colin McLaren, editor of *Canadian Hotel and Restaurant Magazine,* ventured that the number was closer to $80. He thought 16 to 20 percent of that was going to fast food. Canadians were about to rapidly change the way they ate. In 2001, 26 percent of household restaurant spending was devoted to fast food or takeout (with another 10 percent spent in cafeterias and snack bars and at vending carts). An average Canadian household was spending 30 percent of food purchases in restaurants, a pattern that was already fairly well established by 1981. The amount of spending was disproportionate to the actual number of meals. A 2008 NPD Group report indicated 11 percent of Canadian household meals were taken in restaurants, another 6 percent from cafeterias, vending machines and the like, and 3 percent brought home as takeout.

A spokesperson for the Dominion supermarket chain—about three-quarters of which had snack counters—told *The Globe and Mail* in August 1970 that his company considered fast food "oriented at present to the young, unmarried set, whereas supermarkets are oriented to the family trade." Dominion had seriously misread the rapid changes already occurring in the fast-food business. George Cohon, a thirty-three-year-old lawyer in charge of the new Canadian division of the Chicago-based McDonald's Corp., explained to the newspaper his company's strategy in choosing restaurant sites: "We count the church steeples and station wagons."

The menu at McDonald's was narrow by today's standards. Cohon's Canadian restaurants offered hamburgers and fries, a new fish-on-a-bun concept called a Filet-O-Fish (doubtless inspired by Burger Chef's own fish-on-a-bun concept, but nevertheless created by a Cleveland franchisee who wanted a meal for Roman Catholics on Fridays), milkshakes, drinks and pie. The Big Mac had arrived in 1968; the Quarter Pounder would not appear until 1973. McDonald's was already a highly systematized operation. Cohon was running a staff training centre called, with whimsy, the McDonald's Canadian Institute of Hamburgerology. Its idea of a fast-food hamburger outlet was significantly different from the one Sukornyk espoused through Harvey's. McDonald's had seating, and much higher staffing levels. Cohon stated that an outlet needed a pool of fifty to sixty staff to keep running—in other words, ten times the number of people Sukornyk said a Harvey's required—and this was when a McDonald's didn't open until 11 a.m., not yet having introduced a game-changing breakfast menu when the original breakfast sandwich, the Egg McMuffin, debuted in 1975.

The QSR industry in which Tim Hortons would come to compete, and dominate in outlets and sales volumes in Canada, began to coalesce in the 1970s while Tim's itself was very much a fringe player. Tim Hortons was able to build a commanding QSR presence precisely because it was in a niche market of coffee and doughnuts, which meant that competition from the major chicken, burger and ice cream categories went no further than the broader vying for discretionary consumer dollars. Its menu was highly distinctive, with little to no significant overlap with major players like McDonald's. Tim's could grow by installing new franchises right next door to a McDonald's if it had to, in a way that Harvey's never could. Its direct competitors instead were doughnut chains like Country Style, which it managed to surpass in total outlets (fifty) in 1975, growing until it dominated its sector.

By focusing on the niche of coffee and baked goods, Tim Hortons was able to create a major chain of outlets in well-chosen locations, building up an enviable level of goodwill among consumers along the way with product and service. When the urge struck to increase revenues by diversifying the menu with meals in 1986, Tim Hortons had pulled off what amount to a stealth expansion. It had acquired prime sites, strong customer loyalty and a discipline of operating twenty-four hours a day, which gave it access to (and experience in) every possible day part. Where its QSR competitors tried to figure out a breakfast menu that would warrant them opening in the early morning rather than for the lunch hour, Tim's restaurants were already open all night, building a following from the snacking trade. Today, no three-hour interval represents more than 20 percent of Tim Hortons' business, yet the company manages to utterly dominate certain parts of the Canadian QSR day cycle. It claims to command 67 percent of the Canadian morning day-part traffic as generated by the top ten QSRs (a day part that represents 45 percent of its own business), and about 55 percent of evening snacking traffic.

UNTIL THE TRAGIC EARLY MORNING of February 21, 1974, the most important ingredient in the company's growth and success was the partnership of Tim Horton and Ron Joyce. They were an interesting pair. Joyce was highly driven and a little excitable, Horton more laid back, with four Stanley Cups having instilled in him an enviable grace (and good humour) under pressure.

Joyce likes to tell the story of store #7, on Queenston Road in Hamilton near Stoney Creek. The property was a great buy, but it pushed their cash flow to the limit. "The money crunch was coming down on us," Joyce told me. "Everything had to work. We had to get the building permit in a hurry. We had to get the building up. It was bleeding us." Joyce decided to flip the floor plan so the restaurant would have a view across the expansive lawn of the Gulliver's Travels motor hotel next door. It was typical of Joyce's attention to detail, and he explained to Horton, whose customary role was to deal with contracting for fixtures, to adjust the orders accordingly.

"Somewhere along the way he forgot to do it," Joyce recounted. "He screwed up." The fixtures arrived and wouldn't fit the new, mirrored plan. "The problem was no money. The moving truck is there with all the equipment, and we have to find a place to store the stuff. I'm livid." Joyce phoned Horton and lit into him.

"Tim said, 'Ron, hold it. As I see it, we've got two choices. Either I'll drive down to the Skyway Bridge and jump off if that solves the problem, or I'll order new equipment. Now it's your choice. You tell me what to do.' He got it back in perspective. He didn't really lose his cool, and he got a little humour in there."

Horton worked hard at developing the business, but not as hard as Joyce. "They were different people," Charade told me. "Tim was soft, and wanted to enjoy life." Horton's friend, the Scarborough appliance dealer Russ Gioffrey, told me, "I don't think Tim thought the doughnut business would ever get to the size it is today"—and the business is now almost four times as large, in total outlets, as it was when Gioffrey said that. "He wasn't looking for prestige, to be recognized like Conrad Black. With Tim, it was something to do to keep himself occupied. He always let Ron Joyce run the business, even though he had control—he told me he had control. Ron, I think, had a lot of respect for Tim, not just as a hockey player but as a human being."

They did not always agree on the direction to take. The initial decision in the Jirna Ltd. case of 1970 rocked their plans and tested their relationship, with each other and with franchisees. The Jirna plaintiffs argued that the franchisor, Mister Donut of Canada, had a fiduciary duty of care to the franchisees. By "fiduciary duty," they meant that because of the unequal power relationship in a franchise agreement, the franchisor was in a position of trust that required it to act selflessly in the best interests of the franchisee, who relied entirely on the franchisor to secure the best prices possible for goods the franchisee was contractually obligated to buy from the franchisor. To secretly make profits, by keeping for itself volume rebates from suppliers, thus would be a breach of that trust.

Jirna won the case in 1970, which was a shock to the franchise industry, but that decision was overturned on appeal in 1972.

However secretive Mister Donut might have been about securing volume rebates from suppliers (and not revealing the fact to franchisees), the appeal court rejected the idea that there was any fiduciary duty. Instead, the relationship between franchisor and franchisee was a contractual matter. The appeal court ruling was upheld by the Supreme Court of Canada in 1975. The Jirna case remains the only franchise suit ever to have reached the highest court in Canada.

Mister Donut's volume-rebate practices were common in franchises, and were followed by Tim Donut as well. When the lower court ruling threatened an end to this practice, Joyce proposed to franchisees that the parent company would end its rebate profiteering if the franchisees agreed to a higher royalty rate. In response, the franchisees formed an association and began threatening a legal action of their own. Joyce's solution—which, he would write, Horton balked at—was to adopt a more vertically integrated model by establishing a central warehouse and distribution system to take direct control of the supply chain. Horton was reluctant to abandon the rebate model of profit-making, which was allowed to continue in the franchise business after the Jirna ruling was overturned. Today, Tim Hortons franchisees acknowledge in their franchise agreements that the company has the right to such volume rebates on goods that franchisees are required to purchase from it. But by the time the overturn of the Jirna ruling was upheld by the Supreme Court, Tim Donut was committed to the distribution model that continues to give it firm control of the purchase and delivery of goods and equipment that franchisees require, and also the majority of its sales revenue.

The partners also stuck to the practice of acquiring real estate, either as property or head leases, in expanding the chain. This strategy proved to be of enduring importance to Tim Hortons' success and stability. But initially it was an expensive way to grow, and the company's cash burn rate on real estate acquisitions outpaced its income flow from franchisees. Joyce and Horton were constantly under pressure to find new sources of capital and having to borrow at near-usurious rates of up to 20 percent. At one point, Horton turned to Maple Leafs owner Harold Ballard, and borrowed $25,000, no strings attached.

Joyce, for his part, began to feel some of the desperation, and opt for some of the corner cutting, of Charade. He recalled for me how, in the early expansion of the chain, "we had no money. We were borrowing it, signing notes. I was the one doing it, and Horton would get mad at me. It was a snowball effect. A whole lot of things we were doing were, not dishonest, but probably unorthodox. There were things we did to get money. We'd sell something and then mortgage it. It was never to defraud anybody, but we probably shouldn't have done that. We were just trying to get money to get the chain going." It was a time, he said, when they were "always financing backwards, to pay for what we'd already spent."

Joyce's pledging of property they no longer owned did not sit well with his partner. Horton's daughter—and Joyce's daughter-in-law—Jeri-Lyn told me that Joyce "was doing that without Dad knowing. And when he found out, Dad hit the roof." They cleaned up the problem, and moved on.

In the last few years of Horton's life and his partnership with Joyce, the two men did their best to accommodate each other, while moving the company forward. "They were very close," Horton's friend Dick Trainor, who was practising law in Sudbury at the time, told me. "Tim spoke to me often about it. He made a point of saying he wanted me to meet Ron." Trainor and Joyce became good friends, sharing a love of flying (Joyce became a pilot in 1968). "Tim really admired him. They got along very, very well." Even Lori Horton allowed to me, "For years and years, they were very close friends."

"He brought a lightheartedness to the office," Joyce recalled of Horton for me. "He was a very, very kind man. I used to get all the dirty looks, and he used to get all the smiles, and I had to live with that. But I loved Tim, and we had a lot of laughs. We'd have moments with mistakes being made, and we'd always cover each other's ass."

Joyce summed up Horton as "honest, fair, intelligent, astute. He very rarely spoke ill of anybody. He was really at his best when someone was doing a number on him, if he thought he was being taken advantage of. When I first got involved with him as a partner, he insisted we share the same office. Our desks faced each other." That way, the two men had to look each other in the eye when working together.

Horton had fallen into an annual ritual of agonizing over whether to continue playing professional hockey, a summer drama that would end with Horton being offered more money than he had ever earned to come back for another season and serve as a mentor to younger players and a stalwart presence on the blue line. Early in their partnership, the limited revenues of the start-up company led Joyce to be compensated by running one of the outlets. Once they had established an actual office in Oakville, and introduced warehousing and distribution as a solution to the Jirna case, that was no longer possible. Joyce had to be running the parent operation full time. Joyce demanded he be paid a salary, and Horton accommodated him by splitting his own hockey salary with him. Although Joyce personally benefited from Horton's extended NHL career, he was also waiting for Horton to leave hockey behind and focus full time with him on making the chain grow.

But Horton wouldn't leave the game behind. One reason was his sheer love of it: the fans, the camaraderie, the routine he had known since he was in his teens. But a key reason was the money: it was too much to turn down, and he needed it to keep the restaurant business going. To get him to come back for the 1973–74 season with the Buffalo Sabres, general manager Punch Imlach (who had been his coach and GM in the Leafs' glory years) offered him $150,000 and a new car, the Pantera in which he would be killed.

"I think Tim had wanted to retire the last three years or so, but Punch kept stuffing his pockets with money," his Leaf blueline partner, Allan Stanley, told me. "The money, I think, was the thing that kept him there. They were a new business [Tim Donut], and they needed the money. I know Tim told me his cheque went straight into the business, and he'd draw from the business."

Had Horton lived beyond 1974, he most certainly would have remained involved in the restaurant business, but never as a day-to-day presence. His daughter Jeri-Lyn thought he wanted to coach hockey; Lori agreed that Tim wanted to stay in the game, but as a general manager.

Horton had fought the bottle in recent years, though friends and teammates told me he'd been on his best behaviour on his return for the 1973–74 season. "Tim was a pretty good drinker at times," the Sabres goaltender Dave Dryden told me. But in the season leading to his death, "he had been on the wagon for a fair length of time." The Reverend Gordon Griggs had visited with Horton over Christmas 1973, and had been told by Tim that he hadn't had a drink since September.

Lori told me he had made a firm decision to stop drinking at training camp, after an incident that summer when he went into a hotel in Huntsville, near the cottage he had just acquired on Peninsula Lake, and started to trash the place, an outburst that was followed by more riotous behaviour at a neighbour's cottage. "The next day, he was ready to see a psychiatrist," Lori recalled. She contacted Dr. Jim Murray, whom Horton had known as the Leafs' team doctor, and they arranged counselling for him. "I never saw Tim drink again. I know he did with the guys, but he never *drank*."

When the end came, Horton was running on empty. The sudden death of his father, Oak, on January 23, 1974, soon after his own forty-fourth birthday on January 12, was a tremendous blow and may well have helped to send him back to alcohol. Horton's marriage was on the rocks, if not effectively over; he had declined to renew an insurance policy that named Lori as his beneficiary. Physically, he was living on borrowed time. The stay-at-home blueline duties Imlach required of him were manageable at his age, but he wasn't in top shape. The coroner would list his weight at 210 pounds, which was fifteen pounds heavier than the Sabres media guide claimed and about twenty-five pounds heavier than his peak fitness level as an all-star with the Leafs. Lori had told the media while her husband was still alive that she and Punch always had him on a diet. The presence of amylbarbital in his blood, and the Dexamyl pills (which contain amylbarbital) found in his possession, indicate that at the time of his death he was taking the same diet pills to which his wife had become addicted. The coroner noted an enlarged liver and an enlarged heart: the congenital heart disease that had just killed his father, and had already caused heart attacks that would eventually claim his brother, Gerry, was stalking him as well.

Horton and Joyce had prepared for an untimely death of either partner. In 1970, they had created a share trust agreement. Each partner purchased ninety-six common shares, for a dollar each, from the company treasury; each then sold one of their shares to the other. Those two shares were then placed in trust. When one of the partners died, the share he had purchased and placed in trust would be released and transferred to the surviving partner, giving him ninety-six common shares. The heirs of the deceased would inherit ninety-five. (The remaining share, meanwhile, was still in trust while the other man remained alive.) The surviving partner thus would have control of the company, with 50.5 percent of the common stock.

In the event of the death of Horton or Joyce, the survivor would not have to run the company as an equal partner to the other man's wife or children. Lori Horton knew nothing about the trust, and would suspect that Joyce insisted on it so he wouldn't have to share power with her. But Horton had his own reasons for wanting the arrangement:

his name was on the sign, and he didn't need a power struggle with Joyce's heirs over the business's direction. In 1973, Joyce's marriage failed; he would write that he returned from a business trip to discover that Theresa had left with the children and provided no forwarding address. He blamed the failure on his obsession with growing the restaurant business. Had Joyce been the one to die first, Horton would have found himself trying to agree on the company's direction with Joyce's seven children, if not Joyce's estranged wife.

At around four-thirty in the morning on February 21, 1974, the share trust agreement was triggered, handing control of the company to Joyce.

14

Base Hits: Fast-Following to Consumer Success

Following Tim Horton's death, his restaurant chain grew in popularity because of its system, which was ultimately about delivering quality product, consistently and affordably. That system was marshalled not only by Ron Joyce but also by the professionals he began to recruit to the company, including Paul House, who joined Tim Hortons in 1985 as vice-president of marketing. Before that, House, who had grown up on a farm in Stoney Creek, had been a senior executive at Dairy Queen Canada, where he had started as a district manager in 1972 after earning a BA in economics from McMaster University in Hamilton in 1969 and managing a franchise for Shell Oil. When Wendy's absorbed Tim Hortons in the 1995 merger, House was named president and chief operating officer of TDL Group, the division devoted to Tim's. In 2006, when Wendy's began to spin off Tim Hortons, House became president and CEO of TDL Group, and chairman of the board as well in 2007. He moved to executive chairman in 2008, when Donald Schroeder got the top job. After Schroeder's abrupt departure in May 2011, House returned to the roles of president and CEO while the board conducted what proved to be a protracted search for Schroeder's successor.

Regardless of the growing ranks of professionals at head office,

Joyce deserves abundant credit for turning himself first into a bona fide baker (Horton never did learn how to bake), and then into a coffee connoisseur, to develop signature products that customers loved. Joyce's efforts would be formally recognized in 1999, when he was named Canadian Entrepreneur of the Year, an award overseen by Ernst & Young.

Coffee became the chain's key differentiator and profit centre. Joyce tried having beans ground on the store premises, the scent of which he thought would add to the outlet's atmosphere, but inconsistency in results led him instead to develop a signature blend with its supplier, Mother Parkers. Eventually, the company fully integrated its coffee production, with its own roasting facilities. The famous twenty-minute rule—no pot of brewed coffee is kept simmering for more than twenty minutes, after which it is tossed out—assured customers that the quality of brewed coffee would always be high. (The twenty-minute rule invokes the skepticism of some Tim's customers, who have asked me if the carafes really are chucked that regularly. I cannot speak to the practices of every outlet large and small in the chain, but while touring Cam MacDonald's store at Danforth and Logan, I did see the time marked in white grease pencil on a carafe, indicating when it had to be dumped.)

Coffee has long been an important factor in the Tim's brand image in that it serves a no-nonsense, drip-brewed product made from quality arabica beans. Unlike competitors such as Timothy's, Treats, Second Cup, La Prep and above all Starbucks, Tim Hortons does not offer an array of brewed coffees of different flavours, roasts or geographic origins. Its menu of hot and cold drinks has been expanding steadily, yet Tim's for the foreseeable future likely will remain a place where a customer can order a cup of coffee without first deciding whether it should be a particular mountain, regional or breakfast blend, or of a particular roast, or be flavoured with mint, and especially without having to say, "I'd like a Guatemala Casi Cielo," as they can at Starbucks.

Despite that the sheer variety of blends and roasts (along with the barista service and the vocabulary that accompanies the orders) is a key appeal of a competitor like Starbucks, and has been adopted by McDonald's for its McCafé, so far the lack of choice in the core drip-brewed product has allowed Tim's to diversify the drink menu into relative exotica without harming its reputation as a place for regular folks who just want a decent cup of joe. Coffee is still coffee at Tim Hortons. The 2011 espresso additions—the espresso shot and espresso-based latte, Americano and cappuccino—are grouped with the French Vanilla Cappuccino and Mocha Latte (and hot chocolate) in "Tims Café Favourites Specialty Hot Beverages."

Consumers nevertheless are finding they can become more sophisticated in their brewed coffee tastes without becoming more pretentious. Even Dunkin' Donuts has a medium roast and a dark roast. Tim's is becoming increasingly isolated in QSR coffee retailing with its one-size-fits-all brew, while offering a line of specialty "gourmet" teas. It may not be able to go on forever selling something dark brown in a carafe it just calls "coffee."

Tim's followed a fairly conservative approach to growth, doing very little to the essential product lineup or store concept. It stuck to what it knew—sweet baked goods and roast coffee—and in avoiding head-on clashes with McDonald's and other QSRs in the dominant food and meal categories, spread through suburbia, second-tier cities and mid-sized towns. Both Charade and Joyce told me that Tim Horton feared Toronto and avoided it as a place of doing business. With Joyce as his partner, Horton finally returned to the city where he'd had his hat handed to him in burger and chicken drive-ins with stores in the early 1970s. Both outlets, as it happened, were in Scarborough, and one of them failed, a rare experience for the company. After the stores enjoyed acceptance in southern Ontario, Horton wanted to try B.C.'s Lower Mainland next, but Joyce won out in insisting that they should go to Atlantic Canada instead. It was a small bone of contention between the partners at the time of Horton's death. Given the incredible per-capita density the chain enjoys in Atlantic Canada, Joyce called it right.

Despite its menu diversification into meals, Tim Hortons continues to be driven by snacking. Eighty-five percent of its traffic comes from morning and evening snacking, compared to 28 percent for the rest of QSRs; main-meal traffic amounts to only 14 percent of Tim Hortons' traffic, compared to 65 percent for other QSRs. Meals appear to be the chain's relative weakness, but they are also its greatest opportunity: the one sure way it can turn already healthy levels of traffic into higher revenues by bumping up average cheques. At the same time, McDonald's has become a much more serious rival as it recognizes the opportunity to boost sales by targeting the lower-ticket sales items of snacking dominated by Tim's, in coffee and other specialty beverages and baked goods.

Tim Hortons developed a strong group of franchisees, rewarding them with additional outlets, and avoided the legal and media pyrotechnics that plagued some of the Canadian franchise industry in the 1990s. True, Lori Horton's lawsuits were heard in the 1990s, but they had nothing to do with relations between franchisor and franchisee. And the collateral damage the personal revelations of the suits inflicted on Tim Horton's commercial persona mattered little when the company had long ago decided, while he was still alive, not to build its business plan around his hockey notoriety.

Tim Hortons is probably best described as a "fast follower," a company that has watched trends carefully and added products to its mix when new concepts come along that either threaten its market share or suggest a new revenue stream. (McDonald's at times has been no different. Some of its signature products were inspired by the offerings of Burger Chef, which had once been a serious contender for the American QSR crown. Burger's Chef's fish sandwich and the Big Shef were inspirations for McDonald's Filet-O-Fish and the Big Mac, while the Happy Meal, introduced in 1977, owed a debt to the Fun Meal of Burger Chef, developed earlier in the decade.) Its recent introduction of hot meals like beef lasagna casserole and (in the U.S.) macaroni and cheese, which complement existing offerings of soups and chili, indicates the company sees a future in sit-down meals served in a bowl, a strategy that, as we'll see, dovetails with a renewed emphasis on the consumer's experience of the restaurant interior while also increasing the average cheque price.

Tim Hortons has been most innovative in its systems: the vertical integration of product and supply chain, and its recent QSR leadership in recycling and energy audits, for example. One of its most important innovations had nothing directly to do with food, but everything to do with positioning the chain so that it was able to dominate the snacking sector without become trapped by the more down-market aspects of coffee-and-doughnut houses.

In 1984, Joyce decided that the chain should start converting to non-smoking outlets, after the format was tested in Hamilton, at the Main and Wellington outlet, the previous year. Restaurants would be cleaner and more welcoming, and the baked goods on display would not be contaminated by the taste of second-hand smoke.

Getting rid of smoking may well have made outlets more welcoming to women. A 1985 survey of Canadians age fifteen and over found that 38 percent of males and 32 percent of females smoked. Many young women were not going to become the next generation of Tim's customers if they had to contend with treats that tasted like burned tobacco and also had to confront counters lined with chain-smoking men and women in order to place an order. Coincident with the chain's effort to get rid of smoking was the introduction of a lunch menu and a new wave of store designs that eliminated counter seating (where a wall of smokers could sit, tapping into ashtrays right where people were trying to order, their second-hand smoke wafting into the doughnut displays) and provided more table seating. Beyond the health and aesthetic issues, eliminating smoking also served to reduce loitering, as customers could no longer hang around, nursing a cigarette, long after they drained their cup of coffee.

Ontario, where the chain remains strongest, had one of the lowest smoking rates in the country in 1985, at 32 percent. The Atlantic provinces collectively had the second highest, at 38 percent, exceeded only by Quebec, at 40 percent. Tim's was weak in Quebec, but strong down east, which was where the switch to no-smoking was the most challenging to pull off. Joyce would recall in *Always Fresh* that the conversion of outlets in P.E.I. (which led the country in adult smoking rates in 1985, at more than 43 percent) went so badly that it quickly cost the Charlottetown franchisee 30 percent of his business, forcing a reversal of the policy and a public apology by the company for what it said was a corporate initiative. Glassed-off smoking areas also were tried in some outlets; it would take until 1999 for the company to banish smoking from all of its Canadian outlets, with the notable exception of those in Quebec. Although tobacco use had fallen ten percentage points in Quebec since 1985, that province still led the country with 30 percent of adults smoking in 1999, whereas Ontario was down to 23 percent and B.C. a nation-leading 20 percent.

By the time Tim Hortons had eliminated smoking everywhere in Canada but Quebec, in 1999, the rest of the country was only beginning to catch up with its corporate initiative. A slew of municipal and provincial laws would begin to ban or restrict smoking in restaurants, starting with Vancouver in July 2000. Quebec and Ontario both banned smoking from indoor workplaces and public places, including restaurants, on May 31, 2006.

Tim's was pulling away from its coffee-and-doughnut competitors in ambiance, menu diversity and franchising reputation. At the legislative standing committee hearings in March 2000 into what would become Ontario's Wishart Act, Tim Hortons' Nick Javor took the opportunity to praise his company's high operating standards. "We have marketing managers in the field, as well as operations managers. They call on our franchisees for the purpose of helping them be more successful, following our national franchise standards." Franchisees sat on a national advisory board and a joint operations committee that met three times a year. There were regional meetings every spring and fall with franchisees. The advertising funds gathered by the franchise levy were audited annually by an independent third party. Ron Joyce's philosophy, Javor stressed, "has always been that 'the franchisee's success will help make the franchisor successful.' He has always said we will turn down a deal if it can't make the franchisee a buck in the long term."

Javor also freely volunteered how Tim Hortons had "copied other successful franchisors over the years." Indeed, it adopted the franchisee training centre concept and QSCV ("quality, service, cleanliness and value") mantra of McDonald's in the 1970s. From Dunkin' Donuts' Quebec restaurants it took the cue of diversifying its offerings into soups, and followed its lead on "doughnut holes," which Dunkin' called Munchkins, by introducing Timbits. Its cinnamon buns, introduced in the 1980s, were inspired by the offerings of the American chain T.J. Cinnamons. Bagels and muffins similarly were added as a response to their success with rival baked-goods QSRs.

In recent years, Tim's has appeared more reactive than innovative, but that is often the position of a market leader defending its turf against incursions and exploring opportunities suggested by the products and services of rivals. Tim's has been not unlike McDonald's in diversifying (or what is called "extending the brand") from a core-strength position, but if QSR were baseball, McDonald's is a long-ball hitter, willing to swing and miss a lot in hopes of knocking something out of the park, whereas Tim's has been more inclined to try for incremental gains through base hits and minimal strikeouts.

Alan Middleton of the Schulich School of Business at York University agreed with my baseball analogy for McDonald's and Tim's where product development is concerned when we discussed the two companies in the fall of 2011. But he also said: "Tim Hortons' product development is way above McDonald's. It constantly adds newness without having to rethink the brand." He also said Tim Hortons excels in constantly pressing its staff to generate those base hits.

The number of things McDonald's has tried and failed at is impressive—not as a measure of incompetence, but as a signature of relentless corporate determination to keep striving for a product segment breakthrough, which has usually meant a breakthrough into a rival QSR's market. When it comes to consumer demand for a niche product, if you prove it, sooner or later McDonald's will come and try to take it. From McPizza (introduced in the late 1980s) to hot deli sandwiches to the McRib sandwich (which makes occasional guest appearances on the menu) to the expensive flop of the more adult Arch Deluxe burger of 1996, Mickey D's has struck out on an array of offerings, sometimes at considerable expense to franchisees who had to invest in new equipment, such as pizza ovens. On the other hand, it has had great success with ice cream, isn't giving up on specialty sandwiches, and is inordinately determined to crack the premium coffee market that Tim's must defend in Canada.

Tim's has had precious few misfires. The stand-alone sandwich store concept called Breakaway, which originated with a pilot outlet at the training centre in Hamilton in 1977, was such a miscue. It is virtually unknown that Tim Hortons toyed with a similar spinoff strategy in the late 1990s. Ron Joyce's cousin and Tim's franchisee Archibald Jollymore—a plaintiff in the 2008 suit over the Always Fresh par-baking system and lunch menu—was the head lessee, through his company Brule Foods, for a commercial property on Walkers Line at Mainway Drive in Burlington, Ontario. Jollymore operated franchises there for Tim Hortons, Wendy's, Mrs. Vanellis and New York Fries. In June 1996, he opened for Tim Donut Ltd. a 400-square-foot concept store called The Bagel Café. Tim's used it to test new products (bagels had just been introduced to the chain) and to explore the possibility of launching an up-market QSR chain based on bagels and specialty coffees. Head office decided that the café's offerings, which included flavoured cappuccino, were better incorporated into the existing stores, and it pulled the plug on The Bagel Café in January 1999.

Following the misfire of Breakaway, the company tried again with sandwiches in the early 1980s, after croissants joined the baked goods lineup in 1983. (Burger King, meanwhile, was experimenting with a breakfast sandwich to combat the Egg McMuffin, and came up with a hit in the Croissan'Wich in 1983.) Some of Tim's franchisees began selling sandwiches made from croissants, and they had enough local success to persuade Tim's to introduce sandwiches chainwide. It was a rare example of franchisees going their own way and developing products that were not part of the franchisor-approved fare.

This second attempt to introduce sandwiches also failed, according to Joyce, because the decision to make them the night before and wrap them in cellophane failed to live up to the company's pledge of freshness. So the company tried again, this time with assembly stations that made sandwiches to order. Since then, the British-based chain Pret A Manger has shown that it is possible to live up to a freshness promise and also command upscale pricing by making all of its sandwiches en masse at the start of the day and displaying them in refrigerated self-serve shelving units. But this sort of preassembly requires a keen anticipation of daily demand and a willingness to discard potentially large amounts of unsold product. (Pret A Manger donates its unsold food at the end of every day to charity, to feed the homeless.) For Tim's, the enduring made-to-order method reinforces the freshness slogan and provides some interaction between server and customer that promises to be increasingly important as the company strives to stress hospitality as a differentiator.

When news emerged in 2003 that Tim Hortons had abandoned on-site scratch baking in favour of the Always Fresh parbaking system, the chain was ripe for a backlash that could have driven customers into the arms of a nimble competitor, had two conditions been fulfilled. The first was that customers had to notice enough of a difference in the baked goods to dump their Tim's habit in favour of a scratch-baking competitor with a decent cup of coffee. The second was that such a nimble competitor had to exist. By the time the negative PR began to build around parbaking, fed by the public disapproval voiced by Ron Joyce (who had departed in 2001), the coffee-and-doughnut sector in the Canadian QSR landscape was largely cleansed of serious competitors, as they had begun to succumb to self-inflicted wounds.

15

Pleasing the Market: Competitors Stumble and Tim Hortons Goes Public

Franchising is so varied as an industry that it is impossible to say anything unequivocal about the relative merits of franchising as a business option versus independent ownership. Franchising advocates are wont to claim that franchise businesses are more likely to succeed than non-franchise ones, and that bank loans to franchisees have lower default rates than those to independent businesses. In the 1990s, however, a Canadian academic, Francine Lafontaine, who is now the William Davidson Professor and chair of the Business Economics and Public Policy Group at the University of Michigan, conducted a study of U.S. franchise companies that found that 77 percent of franchisors failed over a five-year period. In other words, about three out of four companies selling franchises were going out of business, presumably taking the franchisees with them. That didn't begin to account for the attrition rate among franchisees who signed up with franchisors that managed to stay in business.

Clearly, there are different tiers of franchising. Some franchising concepts are promoted by franchisors with limited track records that offer the allure of lower introductory costs and that "ground floor" opportunity to be part of what is touted as the next big thing in whatever business sector they're targeting. There are many good franchise systems in Canada, but Tim Hortons and McDonald's represent the elite. They have been around a long time, have enjoyed strong, fairly steady growth and boast highly refined systems. Individuals fortunate enough to secure a franchise are getting a turnkey package of product and support that is second to none.

Franchisors don't make public their data on dud franchises, beyond saying (if it's a public company) how many outlets it has shuttered for largely undisclosed reasons. One expert to appear before Ontario's hearings in 2000 that prompted the passing of the Wishart Act ventured that the failure rate for McDonald's and Tim Hortons franchisees was down at the level of 1 percent. And even at that minuscule level, one has to distinguish between franchisees that fail because of something wrong on the franchisor end (for example, a poor site choice), and something wrong with the effort by the franchisee that had nothing to do with the franchise. Tim Hortons closed twenty-six stores in Canada in 2011, as well as two self-serve kiosks. The company says it typically closes between twenty and forty restaurants a year, mostly in Canada, and this generally happens not because of business failure but because a better location becomes available—one that will accommodate a drive-through lane, for example. Any new restaurant within one kilometre of an old one is considered a "relocation," but generates a new franchise fee.

No franchise concept, just like no business concept, is safe from reversals. All companies can miscalculate new product offerings, bobble their expansions into new territories, spend millions on ineffective advertising or fail to adapt to changing consumer tastes and threats from rival concepts. Franchisors like Tim Hortons are protected by strong corporate cultures, but all franchise systems are vulnerable to changes in corporate ownership, which can have different business priorities. In the worst cases, those can include a predatory realization that they can milk franchisees for profits over the short term, regardless of the long-term impact on the franchisee or the entire franchise system. Unscrupulous franchise systems have been accused of preying on vulnerable franchisees, which often have been new immigrants who rely on family-pooled funds and labour to try to make a go of a franchise in a system that is actually fleecing them and is only too happy to take back a franchise and sell it to another unsuspecting mark.

Changes in methods of capitalization can significantly affect the way a franchisor does business. When a franchisor goes public with a stock offering, or is purchased by a private equity group (that may have borrowed heavily to pull off the deal), the investment inevitably has strings attached. Investors pour funds into a franchisor because they expect a return on equity commensurate with the stock price or their cost of borrowing to invest. With franchise systems, such investment invariably can mean an aggressive growth strategy that focuses on adding franchises, as a fresh influx of franchise fees increases a business's top line of revenue at the same time that it adds revenues it collects on a percentage of a franchise's sales to customers. It can be far easier for a franchisor to grow the top line by adding franchises than by focusing on how to increase "same-store sales," which are year-to-year revenues of existing outlets that have been open for at least a year.

No sane franchisor will attempt to add franchises while allowing same-store sales to atrophy, but making a chain larger overall nevertheless is a revenue-growth priority. Thus, whether a franchising company is a publicly traded stock or a private equity holding, the arrival of investment capital can place heavy demands not only on revenue growth but also on the particular kind of growth. Such growth demands can hurt franchisees if expansion encourages a franchisor to cannibalize existing territories with new outlets, or if the franchise brand is compromised, to the detriment of the entire system.

Franchise systems are a delicate balancing act between a diverse bunch of interests. There is the franchisor as an operating business, the capital behind the franchisor, the individual franchisee and the collective interests of franchisees. Discussions of the rights of franchisees often focus on the relationship between the individual franchisee and the franchisor, including the right of franchisees to associate. Less appreciated is that franchisees as a group have a collective interest that may be at odds with the interests of individual franchisees.

In a system like that of Tim Hortons or McDonald's, not all franchise outlets are the same format or address the same target markets. Large chains like these have expanded by finding new niches into which to press their outlets. Formats differ, as can menu offerings. A franchisee with an outlet skewed to the care and feeding of commuters rushing through a drive-through line has a different notion of the marketplace (and how ad dollars should be spent and creative advertising shaped) than one in an urban setting relying on pedestrian traffic, another in a suburban outlet that is a combination of drive-through and interior seating with a broad swath of customer types and still another that is a counter-based service in a university or hospital food court. A large chain has to try to satisfy all of these franchise interests, and remain adaptable while being willing to experiment with different outlet formats and menu offerings that are not necessarily of interest to all existing franchisees.

It is a tribute to ownership, management and franchisees alike that Tim Hortons has managed to endure and grow while remaining in the elite ranks of Canada's most admired consumer brands and most sought-after franchise opportunities. At the same time, its growth has meant an accompanying complexity in its operations and opportunities—and in potential pitfalls. With a strong commitment to further growth, in both revenues of existing outlets and the addition of new stores in new territories, Tim's is a fascinating case of a company whose success breeds increasingly precarious possibilities. The chain has never lacked for challenges, or the resourcefulness to overcome them. And even though it may sound platitudinous, Tim Hortons has long insisted that its franchisees are the backbone of its success. Franchisees in turn should realize that, were it not for the company's rigorous system, they might long ago have gone the unhappy way of store operators in rival franchise concepts.

COUNTRY STYLE OF RICHMOND HILL, Ontario, was the first direct competitor to Tim Hortons in Canada to stumble. It had begun to do so right after Tim's, already on an expansion spree, merged with Wendy's International in 1995. Ron Joyce had previously considered overtures from Cara Operations, Scott's Hospitality and John Bitove Sr. With the Wendy's deal, Tim Hortons became an American company, registered in Delaware as Tim Hortons Inc., but operating as a distinct subsidiary of Wendy's International, with a head office still in Oakville, Ontario, and a U.S. office established near that of Wendy's, in Dublin, Ohio.

Outwardly, nothing about Tim Hortons really changed, but it had gained additional financial heft, which included the ability to enter into more expensive real-estate deals through co-branded outlets with Wendy's. It also now had a partner with experience in the U.S. market, where Tim Hortons' efforts had been lagging. The chain had surpassed 1,200 outlets in 1995, and with the aid of U.S. expansion would reach 2,000 by the millennium.

Country Style franchisee horror stories were related at the Ontario legislature's March 2000 standing committee hearings for the Wishart Act. The chain had trailed Tim's in introducing drive-throughs and a lunch menu, and suffered through a revolving door of corporate owners as parent Maple Leaf Foods was bounced from the U.K.'s Hillsdown Holdings to McCain Capital Corp. to the Ontario Teachers' Pension Plan Board. A plan by Maple Leaf to take Country Style public in 1998 was scuttled, and a majority interest in the chain was instead sold to a Montreal-based equity investment fund, CAI Capital Partners, which hoped to be able to sell it at a profit in a few years. But the stores already had become tired and outdated. A belated decision to follow Tim Hortons' lead and switch cold turkey to a no-smoking format in 2001, as a severe recession hit, didn't help. Indeed, as Tim's had driven off the dedicated smokers, outlets like Country Style had become something of a haven, making it even harder to impose a no-smoking regimen. As one franchisee, who had acquired a Country Style in 1991, told *Canadian Business* in 2002, "The first four and half years were really good. Then Hortons came in and kicked the shit out of us."

In December 2001, Country Style filed for protection under the Companies' Creditor Arrangement Act (CCAA). The company began terminating 102 of 277 franchise outlets, saying 52 had already been abandoned by the franchisees. CAI stuck with the investment, and by the time the parent, Country Style Food Services, was sold to Montreal's so-called "King of the Food Court," Stanley Ma, for his MTY Investments portfolio of two dozen franchise concepts, Country Style and its associated Buns Master bakery chain stood at 490 outlets. But in the meantime, Country Style had lost enormous ground to Tim's, which in 2002 wrested Canada's top-grossing QSR crown from McDonald's. Even had Tim's customers wanted to abandon it in droves over parbaking, there weren't enough Country Styles around to welcome them.

Another casualty of this doughnut-rationalization period was Robin's Donuts, which had caused Tim Hortons conniptions in northwestern Ontario and Winnipeg after it was founded by two former Tim's employees in 1975. Robin's hit the skids soon after Country Style got in trouble. The chain had joined 241 Pizza in the portfolio of Afton Food Group, headquartered in Burlington, Ontario, which traded on the Toronto venture exchange. Afton sought bankruptcy protection under the CCAA in July 2004, and limped along, shedding franchises and leaving gaps for Tim's to fill where it hadn't already prevailed over Robin's in head-to-head competition.

Robin's appeared to be suffering a slow and painful demise right into 2006. Tim's made considerable inroads in Winnipeg, where Robin's had been such a daunting competitor in the 1990s. At the University of Manitoba, franchise and food services management company Aramark had installed three Tim's franchises around campus by late 2005. There was still one Robin's outlet on campus, in the Fletcher Argue building, but as Brent Gilchrist, the university's director of food services, explained at the time, "Corporately speaking, Robin's Donuts is on the brink of bankruptcy . . . out in the marketplace, Robin's Donuts are closing left, right, and centre." He wouldn't rule out adding a fourth Tim's were Robin's to finally succumb. "You can certainly see what's happening out in the marketplace; every corner has a Tim Horton's almost."

Robin's Donuts did not disappear. Chairman's Brands, which owned Coffee Time, acquired it along with 241 Pizza in June 2006. Robin's remains a fixture in Winnipeg, where there are twenty-four—including the outlet in the Fletcher Argue building that had been living on borrowed time in 2005. And while it has loyal customers, it is no longer a significant impediment to Tim Hortons aspirations to affix yet more outlets to the Canadian streetscape and inside institutional settings like hospitals and universities.

To compete in a world dominated by Tim Hortons, Country Style repositioned itself as a deli-bistro café to get as far from a doughnut-shop image as possible. In contrast, Coffee Time, which started with a single store in Bolton, Ontario, in 1982, made itself into a mirror of Tim's (much like Joyce had accused Robin's Donuts of doing), following Tim Hortons' lead on menu diversity and promotions.

Like Country Style and Robin's, Coffee Time didn't have the market presence (or promotional budget) to move Tim Hortons customers en masse in its direction when the parbaking issue got sticky. And it soon had far more serious PR problems of its own. In February 2007, Coffee Time was rocked by a CBC *Marketplace* investigation that used Freedom of Information Act filings to gather health inspection reports for Tim Hortons, Second Cup, Starbucks, Country Style and Coffee Time. The investigative program said Coffee Time recorded 78 infractions for every 100 health inspections, and that 35 percent of outlets were put on probation over a two-year period. Coffee Time told *Marketplace* that problems at every location were fixed and that all restaurants were subsequently given a passing grade.

Publicity for Coffee Time hardly improved in January 2008, when Toronto police announced they had charged the owner of an outlet at Queen and Sherbourne with four drug-related offences and possession of stolen property—stolen food that he allegedly purchased from one of his customers. Police said they had seized 3.22 grams of crack cocaine and 192 dime bags, totalling 219 grams, of marijuana. The store was in a rough part of downtown; the city had been on the verge of ordering it closed three years earlier because of its notoriety as a haven for drug dealers and prostitutes when the owner at the time sold the business. With the latest franchise owner's arrest, Coffee Time head office ordered him out of the building, where he lived in the basement. In January 2009 the former franchisee was sentenced to a ten-year weapons prohibition and twelve months of house arrest on the charges of trafficking marijuana and possession of stolen property. Charges of possession (including crack cocaine) for the purpose of trafficking were withdrawn.

The Queen-Sherbourne outlet is no more, but Coffee Time and Robin's Donuts are still a going concern, with a level of devotion to Tim Hortons' methodology that is almost endearing. Tim Hortons has Timbits, Coffee Time has Coffee Bits and Robin's Donuts has Robin's Eggs. At least the two Chairman's Brands franchise concepts have salads, which haven't come to Tim's yet. (In recent years, Chairman's Brands also has been rolling out a new franchise concept aimed at the breakfast-brunch-lunch crowd, Eggsmart.) In the summer of 2010, Tim Hortons released TimmyMe, a store-finder app for the iPhone. In November 2010, Chairman's Brands announced for its restaurants "a new iphone web site so now customers can find them from wherever they are and get the latest news from there [*sic*] smart phone." This is not an actual mobile app that you get from Apple's App Store, but I will grant that the website is iPhone friendly.

All of Tim Hortons' Canadian competitors have had to come to terms with the promotional juggernaut that is the annual Roll Up the Rim contest. Coffee Time, Robin's and Country Style have resolved to counterprogram with cup contests of their own. Country Style launched Turn Up a Winner, and in 2008 also redeemed losing Tim Hortons cups for free coffee. In 2012, Turn Up a Winner ran head to head with Roll Up the Rim, from mid-February to late April, with a bevy of giveaways that included a $1 million grand prize. Chairman's Brands has also vied for attention with its cup contest (called Flip to Win at Coffee Time and Sip to Win at Robin's), which in 2012 ran from early February to mid-April. In the fall of 2011, both Coffee Time and Robin's ran a Fall for Cash promotion that required customers to "flip the rim" of cups.

Another domestic competitor to yield to the unstoppable force of Tim Hortons was the Canadian operation of Dunkin' Donuts. From a high of 210 franchises in Quebec in 1998, Dunkin' had been reduced to 11 in the province by 2012. In 2003, a group of Quebec franchisees (Bertico Inc. et al) sued Dunkin's Canadian operation (called Dunkin' Brands Canada Ltd. in the judgment), claiming the franchisor failed to protect the brand under increasing competitive pressure from Tim Hortons, whose expansion effort was described in the judge's ruling as a "phenomenon," a "wave" and an "onslaught." Judge Daniel H. Tingley of the Quebec Superior Court agreed with the plaintiffs in the June 2012 judgment, saying Dunkin' had "abandoned" the Quebec market in 2003. The judge awarded 32 franchisees $16.4 million and released them from their franchise agreements. "Allowing Tim Hortons to capture the lion's share of the Quebec fast-food donuts and coffee market between 1995 and 2003 was a huge and costly mistake," Judge Tingley ruled after a seventy-one-day trial. Coincidentally, Douglas Fisher, an expert witness for the franchisee plaintiffs in the Fairview suit against Tim Hortons, was also an expert witness for the defendant Dunkin' Brands Canada in the Quebec case. Judge Tingley ruled that Fisher "erroneously laid the blame for the franchisees' misfortunes on them." On June 25, 2012, Dunkin' Brands stated in a press release that it "strongly disagrees with the decision reached by the Court and believes the damages awarded were unwarranted. Dunkin' Brands is proud of its efforts to support all of its franchisees in Quebec and around the world, and the Company intends to vigorously appeal the decision."

If any coffee-doughnut chain were to capitalize on Tim Hortons' brand vulnerability at the time of the parbaking controversy, it was Krispy Kreme, headquartered in Winston-Salem, North Carolina. After going public in 2000, it was massively hyped through product placements in U.S. network television programs and a savvy PR campaign. The idea of an indescribably heavenly doughnut based on a recipe from the Old South, produced in an honest, old-fashioned way, arrived in Canada with absurd levels of media fanfare as it opened its first outlet in Mississauga. The company "carpet bombed" the *Toronto Star* newsroom with some of the 250,000 free doughnuts its distributed locally over the winter of 2001, and the media, in Toronto as elsewhere, stoked the consumer frenzy.

Krispy Kreme's simple product formula consisted of coffee and the Hot Original Glazed Doughnut that customers could watch rise in the proofer and roll off what the *Star*'s David Olive later described as a "quaint, faux-1930s assembly line." The company proclaimed a single-store first-day sales record of more than $70,000 when the Mississauga outlet opened, and the crowds made the figure believable.

Krispy Kreme appeared poised to challenge a Tim Hortons that critics thought had become too diffuse, too unfocused in its product line—and as the parbaking controversy surfaced, forgetful of its "always fresh" promise. Instead, Krispy Kreme was soon beating a retreat—not only in Canada but around the world as well—as a $45 stock crashed below $5 in 2004. Krispy Kreme has since been rebuilding, removing the bad taste left in investors' mouths by its overreaching ambition and an SEC probe into its accounting practices launched in 2004, which resulted in a cease-and-desist order in 2009.* With Krispy Kreme now having just four stores in all of Canada, journalists henceforth will think twice about proposing that the company's glazed doughnuts and its new line of coffee can ever make life unbearable for Tim Hortons north of the border.

By the time Krispy Kreme arrived and Robin's Donuts, Country Style and Coffee Time had their misadventures, Tim Hortons was sufficiently entrenched in Canada that it seemed unlikely any coffee-and-doughnut concept could ever displace it or impede its growth. And besides: Tim's no longer saw its main competition being the rest of the coffee-and-doughnut sector. Tim's still had coffee and doughnuts, but it also had meals, and bagels and muffins. The word "donuts"—and the image of doughnuts—had long since been removed from the signage, replaced by the "Always Fresh" slogan. Having passed McDonald's in Canada in revenues in 2002, in 2005 Tim's had 24 percent of Canada's QSR business by dollar revenue, which was 25 percent higher than any other competitor.

---

* In a release on March 4, 2009 ("SEC Approves Agreement with Krispy Kreme to Resolve Investigation"), Krispy Kreme stated it "consented to a cease and desist order against future violations of provisions of the Exchange Act and related rules concerning filing of accurate annual, quarterly and current reports with the Commission, the maintenance of accurate books, records, and accounts in reasonable detail, and the maintenance of a sufficient system of internal accounting controls. The Company did not admit or deny any findings in the Order and the Order does not include any monetary payments or other sanctions."

The chain was doing so well that Wendy's International shareholders began agitating for a spinoff of Tim's to release the value being suppressed within the larger company. At the end of the first quarter in 2005, Wendy's had 6,699 outlets worldwide, compared to 2,738 for Tim's, but Tim's (aided by an appreciating Canadian dollar) generated 70 percent of the franchisor's operating income that quarter. Where Tim's sales were growing, the Wendy's operation was on its way to a 3.7 percent decline in same-store sales in 2005.

In July 2005, Wendy's announced it would sell 15 to 18 percent of Tim Hortons at the end of the first quarter of 2006. Investor Nelson Peltz pushed harder. Triarc Companies, of which Peltz was chairman and CEO, was the franchisor of Arby's and was in the process of acquiring more than 1,000 Arby's franchises that it would operate corporately; Triarc was also the franchisor of T.J. Cinnamons and Pasta Connection.

There was a bit of history between Peltz, Ron Joyce and Wendy's. Joyce had never been comfortable at or with Wendy's. He would write that he was quickly disillusioned by its senior management and felt shut out by the board, which he thought kowtowed to Dave Thomas, even though Thomas held a fraction of the shares in Wendy's that Joyce, its single largest shareholder, did. Joyce hadn't liked the board's choice of Jack Schuessler (according to Joyce a Thomas "yes man") as CEO, and he had gone so far as to contact lawyers about mounting a hostile takeover. Around 2000, Joyce was put in touch with Peltz by NHL commissioner Gary Bettman. Joyce's bid to secure an NHL franchise for Hamilton in the early 1990s (when John Ziegler was the league's commissioner) had failed, but he had since become a minority owner of the Calgary Flames. Joyce agreed to meet with Peltz, who explained he was interested in mounting a takeover of Wendy's.

Joyce wrote in his autobiography that Wendy's directors were unhappy when they learned that Joyce, who had a seat on the board, had been speaking with Peltz on the matter. For whatever reason, no takeover arose, but Joyce was finished at Wendy's. Joyce withdrew from Wendy's board and entered into negotiations to sell most of his shares back to the company for $250 million, a deal concluded in late 2001. Joyce would dump the remainder of his shares in 2002.

In 2005, Peltz was back for another run at Wendy's. The announcement that 15 to 18 percent of Tim Hortons would be spun off the following spring wasn't good enough. That November, Peltz and other officers of Triarc formed the Trian group of investment funds. In mid-December 2005, one of those funds, Trian Partners, surpassed a 5 percent holding in Wendy's stock that, under SEC regulations, made it a beneficial owner; Peltz contacted Wendy's, requesting a meeting with Schuessler to discuss Trian's "value creation plan," which included "the immediate commencement of a 100% tax-free spinoff of Tim Hortons." Wendy's capitulated, agreeing to divest itself of all of Tim's by the end of 2006. In 2008, Peltz's Triarc would acquire Wendy's outright in a merger that created Wendy's/Arby's Group, Inc.

The first phase of the spinoff, the spring 2006 IPO, distributed 33.4 million common shares, representing 17.25 percent of Tim Hortons stock, which began trading on March 24, 2006, on both the Toronto and New York exchanges. Wendy's had decided to distribute most of the initial share offering in New York, although RBC Capital Markets got some of the issue for Toronto, and individual franchisees could buy up to $30,000 worth. In late September, the remaining shares were distributed as a dividend on a pro-rata basis to existing Wendy's shareholders. Tim Hortons was now a stand-alone company, though certain aspects of the business were still intertwined with Wendy's, and it remained incorporated in Delaware. A complete break would not come until 2009, when the company was repatriated as a Canadian corporation.

Some analysts fretted that Canadians especially would snap up Tim's shares out of emotional attachment rather than investor acumen, as shares reached an early trading high of $38 before heading below

$30 by year-end. Some fears of losing one's shirt in Timbits equity assuredly were assuaged by the company's announcement in August 2006 that it would launch a share repurchase program, which would support the share price by reducing the float; Tim's has continued to repurchase shares. But with systemwide sales growth of 9.5 percent in 2005 (and a boisterous 12.8 percent on the way in 2006), investors had good reasons for long-term optimism in this dividend-paying investment. Same-store sales grew 7.5 percent in Canada in 2006, and the 8.9 percent surge in the U.S. was the sixteenth consecutive annual increase in that market.

Ron Joyce was cautious at the time of the IPO, telling *Financial Post Business* he wouldn't be buying shares himself because he thought they would be fully valued when they hit the market. Joyce worried that since he had left the company in 2001, Tim Hortons had begun squeezing franchisee margins, which he said had been 20 percent when he ran the company. "It was my philosophy to treat the franchise owners as partners," he said. He warned that under public ownership, Tim's "could be forced to open more restaurants near existing ones or perhaps charge more for the services it provides to franchisees," according to *FP Business*.

Tim Hortons declined to get into a public argument with its retired co-founder over how an IPO could affect franchise operations and profitability. Which brings us to the fundamental issue of the Tim Hortons system today: What, exactly, is a Tim Hortons franchise, anyway?

16

Dollars from Doughnuts: The Tim Hortons Franchise System

Tim Hortons overwhelmingly uses franchising for its restaurant system: the company at year-end 2011 said 99.7 percent of outlets in Canada and 98.9 percent in the U.S. are franchised. There were on average about eighteen "corporate" stores operating in all of North America in 2011. Some are used for training; others are stores repurchased or taken back from franchisees, which the company converts back to franchise operation as soon as possible. Tim Hortons' franchising system is complicated, though, and the distinction between a franchise and a corporate operation is not cut and dried.

No single boilerplate franchise licensing agreement exists for Tim Hortons. Nevertheless, there are still general similarities between them all. Tim Hortons organizes its franchisees into two categories: "owners" and "operators." "Owners" are said to "own" their outlets, although they don't usually own the actual physical restaurant. With about 80 percent of its restaurants, the company either owns the actual land and the restaurant on which it stands, holds the head lease to the land on which it has built an outlet or (as in the case of Cam MacDonald's Danforth and Logan store) holds the head lease to a commercial space in which a restaurant has been installed.

"Operators" probably don't belong in the same breath as franchise "owners," as the former are really independent contractors running what amounts to a corporate-owned store. Tim Hortons, in its 2011 annual report, says, "These are not typical franchise relationships" and that "we do not consider our operators to be typical restaurant owners," but for the purpose of its filings includes them in the same discussion as owner franchisees.

The main difference between an "owner" and an "operator" franchise licensing agreement is that the "operator" doesn't pay the up-front franchise or licence fee, or an ongoing rental fee. These operator stores are known as "80/20s" in the Tim Horton vernacular because of the 20 percent royalty on gross receipts the operators instead generally pay, along with the usual advertising fee and an additional initial damage deposit. In the Murray case, in which Tim Hortons successfully defended itself against a suit by a husband-and-wife team that began running a new 80/20 store in Smithville, Ontario, in 1994, the operators agreed to a deposit of $20,000. The plaintiff Archibald Jollymore, in the 2008 suit over the lunch menu profitability and parbaking switch, stated that the damage deposit on his 80/20 store in Burlington, Ontario, was $37,500.

Tim Hortons generally (but not exclusively) uses 80/20s to introduce new franchisees to the system. As we'll see, they're the main way the company is expanding in the U.S. Tim's doesn't say how many of its franchises are actually run under 80/20 operator agreements, although president and CEO Paul House allowed in an analyst conference call following the release of first-quarter 2012 results that there were "a couple of hundred" in Canada. House credited Ron Joyce for having conceived of the concept "way back when," and said 80/20s are "a good way to bring new blood into the business that have got great energy, but are just a little undercapitalized." Added chief financial officer Cynthia Devine, "The goal is that we ultimately resell it back to the restaurant owner and make them a full franchisee at that point, and you'll see our Canadian history is like that."

Where Tim Hortons as franchisor would have to resort to legal action to extinguish an owner licence agreement prior to its end date, operator agreements typically can be terminated on thirty days' notice by either party. This means the company can swiftly replace underperforming or problematic operators with a new candidate, or turn the store over to someone willing to invest as an owner franchisee. But it's not always easy to draw a line between the ranks of operators and owners. Some franchisees with multiple outlets appear to have both "operator" and "owner" stores, and so wear both hats within the system.

The single largest cost faced by a new "owner" franchisee is the initial franchise fee payable under the licensing agreement. This "franchise" or "licence agreement" fee is not simply the up-front franchise licence cost (which is $50,000, according to the Canadian Franchise Association's member directory), but rather the all-inclusive turnkey cost for a franchisee getting a restaurant going. This includes all the equipment, signage, machinery and interior furnishings, which must be of an approved type and purchased through Tim Hortons. A new franchise also needs a decent pool of working capital in order to pay for initial inventory and meet payroll, among other start-up expenses. In the Murray case, the operators (led by a husband who had been a corporate employee) were allowed to borrow an initial $25,000 for working capital to get an 80/20 store going, but generally Tim Hortons wants a new franchisee to have a minimum pool of unsecured capital.

The total cost of a franchise varies according to the size, type and location of the outlet, and the duration of the agreement. The Tim Hortons listing in the CFA directory indicates an "all up cost" of $194,000 for a franchise, but it can certainly be much higher. Cyril Garland, a deponent in the 2008 "Fairview" suit (in which the judge dismissed the claims of the representative plaintiffs; the ruling was under appeal as this book went to press), paid $450,000 in 1988 for his licence agreement for store #385 in Brampton, Ontario, which covered a ten-year licence with a right of renewal for a further ten years, a typical arrangement. Not surprisingly, new franchisees generally have to borrow at least some of the turnkey franchise fee.

Canadian franchisees may still need to scrape every available barrel to find the necessary cash, but they also have Industry Canada's small business financing program, which backs loans by participating financial institutions to enterprises with less than $5 million in annual revenues. The loans of up to $500,000 can be used to finance up to 90 percent of approved costs. Although the loans cannot be used for franchise fees and working capital, they can be used for a number of expenses incurred by a start-up franchise, or by an existing franchise required to receive a refurbishing or upgrading. Those permitted loan costs include purchasing or improving land, real property or immovables; purchasing leasehold improvements or improving a leased property; and purchasing or improving new or used equipment.

Once an outlet is operating, Tim Hortons collects from the owner franchisee a basket of income known as RRA—rent, royalty and advertising. For an owner franchisee, this generally amounts to a total of 17 percent of gross receipts for a standard outlet. Rent and royalty, which Tim Hortons counts as corporate revenues, total 13 percent, with rent usually 8.5 percent of gross sales and the royalty, collected on weekly sales, 4.5 percent. In its 2006 annual report, the company said the typical U.S. franchise split was 10 percent for rent and 3 percent for the royalty. The annual report for Wendy's International in 2005, when Tim's was a subsidiary, said some Canadian franchises were paying a 3 percent royalty. It also said that where a franchisee owned the store property, the company tacked 1.5 percent onto the royalty.

The remaining four percent of the RRA is an advertising charge that is not accounted for as income by Tim Hortons. It enters a pool for promotions purposes, and is paid by corporate-owned as well as franchise stores. The ad charge in Canada was reduced to 3.5 percent in 2008, but remained at 4 percent in the U.S. The company reserves the right to increase it at its discretion, but has said it has no foreseeable plans for doing so. Even at that reduced rate, Tim Hortons raised a promotional war chest of $191.5 million in fiscal 2011 from its franchised and corporate stores in Canada (and another $18.1 million in the U.S.), which helps explain the constant television advertising, NHL rink-board ads and title sponsorships of events like curling's Brier and the NHL's All-Star Game. The fund is also used to pay for digital menu boards and rotating drive-through menu boards. In fact, the company planned to devote $100 million of the Canadian fund in 2012 to menu boards. With kiosks—which are considered to be more profitable for the franchisee (in terms of percentage of revenue, as opposed to absolute dollars), rent might be set at 13 to 14 percent, and the royalty at 4.5 percent or higher.

An owner outlet has about a 7 percent advantage in remittances to the company over an operator (80/20) outlet, which provides a little more wiggle room for profitability. In the Murray case, tried in 2002, a target profit margin of 5 to 10 percent on gross receipts of the 80/20 store was cited in the judge's ruling. Margins for owner stores are elusive, but higher. At a fiscal 2010 investors conference, the company indicated that U.S. stores achieving average unit volume sales of more than $1 million annually have a pretax gross margin of 17.4 percent before paying themselves for management-in-labour, which is usually 4.3 percent of sales, giving a net pretax margin of 13.1 percent. As Canadian standard outlets average about $2 million, a net pretax margin of 13 percent or more may be typical. Of course, an owner franchise must aim for this higher profit margin in order to secure an adequate return on a much higher initial capital investment, above and beyond what he or she earns as management-in-labour and must set aside for renovations and other upgrades.

As franchisor, Tim Hortons makes its money from the franchisees, and only indirectly from the customer at the counter or the drive-through. Of $2.85 billion in revenues in fiscal 2011, about $2 billion was generated by "sales." Of those sales, $1.7 billion (85 percent) came from "distribution sales" of goods to franchisees (products, supplies and restaurant equipment, except for initial equipment packages sold to restaurant owners as part of their start-up); most of the rest of 2011's "sales" was attributable to sales of parbaked menu items to franchisees produced by Maidstone Bakeries. The only sales not generated by franchisees were the $24 million contributed by the eighteen corporate-owned restaurants operating (on average) in 2011. Rent and royalties amounted to $733 million of revenues; franchise fees, which include goods sold for start-up, contributed $108 million. Against those revenues, Tim Hortons must cover its own costs. They include the expense of acquiring and developing property, the wages and benefits of a staff of more than 1,800, creating new food and beverage products, designing store concepts, the warehousing and distribution of food and other goods through five distributions centres, and production of food in its facilities.

Tim Hortons has become more vertically integrated in the past decade. The parbaking facility, Maidstone Bakeries, was set up as a joint venture in 2001, but Tim's no longer has an interest in it. The Maidstone Coffee roasting facility in Rochester, New York, was acquired in 2001, the fondant and fills manufacturing facility was established in Oakville in 2003 and a new coffee roasting facility opened in Ancaster, Ontario, in 2009. "We continue to believe that distribution is a critical element of our business model as it allows us to manage costs to our restaurants owners and service our restaurants efficiently and effectively while contributing to our overall profitability," the company stated in its 2011 annual report. In its franchise agreements, franchisees acknowledge that the company is entitled to volume discounts from suppliers, but the distribution model is supposed to secure for franchisees goods and ingredients that meet franchisor standards while providing some collective purchase advantage that franchisees wouldn't otherwise enjoy as independent restaurateurs. As well, Tim Hortons' agreements with approved suppliers places a ceiling on the amount they are allowed to charge franchisees.

Requiring franchisees to purchase essential supplies directly from the franchisor or a designated supplier is a much different model from the one used for Wendy's restaurants when Tim's was part of Wendy's International from 1995 to 2006. (As a separate operating unit, Tim Hortons maintained its own franchise agreements.) Wendy's generally did not sell supplies to franchisees. Instead, it arranged volume discount purchases from suppliers, as it ran a significant number of corporate outlets, and franchisees had the option of participating. Wendy's otherwise strove to ensure uniformity of its offerings in part by providing "detailed specifications for food products, preparation and service."

Tim Hortons will not allow outlets to become dated in design or furnishings or to lag behind in the most recent product offerings. In addition to selling the new franchisee the necessary start-up equipment, the company sells the new equipment a franchise must have in order to prepare new product-line items. The chain also stresses uniformity of consumer experience, as franchisees generally must sell the company's full product line. While there are regional variations in menu offerings, a franchisee cannot decide unilaterally to be just a coffee-and-baked-goods shop, and forgo the lunch menu or the smoothies, or whatever else head office adds to the offerings—although, as we'll see, in its expansion into New York City in 2009 with the powerful Riese Organization as its franchisee, Tim's was willing to allow individual outlets to offer selective parts of the full menu in order to make the franchise fit the Riese "food court" concept.

Franchisees are not supposed to skimp on offerings. They must keep a sufficient supply of approved products on hand, and traditionally have been required to display at least twelve varieties of doughnuts, for example. Franchisees, in short, produce and sell what they're told, essentially at a price determined by head office, as the company sets maximum pricing and also requires the outlets to participate in special offers. In its quest to provide "value pricing" to the consumer, Tim Hortons pretty much ensures that prices are uniform, that franchisees do not discount or undercut each other and that their prices are in line with national advertising promotions.

In addition to maintaining a store according to the company's high standards, a franchisee must be prepared at the company's request to undertake a refurbishment every five years at a cost of up to 2 percent of gross receipts for the previous five years. And as a condition of executing the franchisee's ten-year right of renewal, the company can require a substantial refurbishment to bring the outlet up to the chain's present image and configuration. The company generally shares the costs with franchisees: "We typically, but are not required to, contribute up to 50% of the funding required for certain front-of-restaurant construction costs incurred in connection with renovations on properties that we own or lease," the company explains in its 2011 annual report.

One of the key differences between Tim Hortons and some other franchise operations is that the franchisees do not build up any personal equity in their outlets. All "goodwill" is assigned by the franchisee to the company. Franchise agreements provide a sliding scale of depreciating equity value by which Tim's can repurchase a franchise during the life of the agreement, and the company has a first right of refusal in any effort by a franchisee to sell to someone else. Franchisees must make their money (and recoup their costs, especially the initial franchisee fee) from the cash flow of day-to-day business. It's not enough for a franchisee to be rewarded with the management-in-labour fee. The franchisee also has to consider the capital invested over the period of the agreement, and see some reasonable return on it as well.

The company's fiscal 2010 investors conference presentation indicated that for a U.S. franchise owner who generated more than $1 million in revenue, the costs typically broke down this way: 17 percent went to the company as RRA; paper goods, food and labour consumed about 60 percent; other operating expenses were about 11 percent. That left about 18 percent in gross margin, from which a franchisee usually collected a management-in-labour fee of a little more than 4 percent. So on sales of around $1 million, the management-in-labour would amount to $45,000. The pretax margin is around 13 percent, or $130,000. Taxes still have to be paid, and earnings need to be retained in order to pay for refurbishing (minor and major) and new equipment to prepare new products. As well, more than one person may be involved as a franchisee with a claim to both the management-in-labour fee and the gross margin. Consequently, really making money means getting sales up to the Canadian standard-store average of $2 million. From 2008 to 2010, a Burlington, Ontario, store belonging to Fairview suit plaintiff Fairview Donut averaged $325,000 in annual income on typical sales of almost $2 million, according to the judge's dismissal of the individual claims of the plaintiffs. The judge also noted a smaller Fairview Donut store was making about $100,000 on revenues of about $1 million between 2005 and 2007.

Tim Hortons' restaurants have struggled in what the company calls "growth markets," which are mainly in the United States, where standard unit sales have averaged half of what they do in Canada. I'll look at the specifics of the U.S. market in a later chapter. For now, because of the squeeze on gross margins in growth markets as well as in the case of new stores starting to find their feet, Tim Hortons must be flexible on the RRA assessment, offering a relief program that gives a break to franchisees. The company's executives were adamant in their testimony in the Zabco Holdings case (which dealt with Winnipeg franchises in the 1990s and was tried in 2008, with a result entirely in Tim Hortons' favour) that they would never give relief simply because a franchise was operating unprofitably. Tim's would do so only if relief would improve the profitability of an outlet that was already in the black or would aid a franchisee with a new outlet that showed the potential for achieving profitability.

The company doesn't ordinarily disclose publicly how much business a franchise has to generate to make a certain amount of money for the owner or operator, but it does provide them with guidelines that indicate targets for profit margins based on sales volumes. Although Tim Hortons profits from goods it sells to the franchise, and also collects a percentage of gross receipts, the franchisee cannot make money (and in fact can lose money) if a store's sales volumes are insufficient or if costs aren't carefully managed.

Franchisees face an assortment of costs that can or cannot be controlled. Paper goods, food and labour, the single largest group, is a mixed bag. The more a store sells, the more it needs to buy in paper goods and food, mainly from Tim Hortons. Because the franchisee cannot shop around for what might be a cheaper deal (or an inferior product) as a way to cut costs, limiting waste is vital. Labour costs are within the purview of the franchisee, and with low-wage, semi-skilled help, the key to keeping costs down is not so much finding cheaper help as it is ensuring that staff levels at different times of day are adequate to the customer flow, without being overstaffed. Cases where franchisees have run into profitability trouble have stressed the importance of carefully managing the costs of labour and food.

The company's RRA fees are all percentage based, and so are out of the franchisee's control. As a store's gross receipts go up, so does the RRA in absolute dollars. But if business slows down, RRA obligations decrease accordingly. In purely hypothetical terms, were revenues at a Tim's for a particular month to fall to zero, so would the franchisee's RRA obligations. On that front, the franchisee has an advantage over independent business owners and franchisees of some other systems: when business is suffering, either seasonally or during an economic downturn, the franchisee catches a break on some of its business costs.

Tim Hortons' control over what is sold, how it is prepared and how much the franchisee charges may be close to absolute, but this is part and parcel of a franchisee buying into a corporate system. Tim Hortons has been attractive as a franchise opportunity precisely because head office has a product and a means of marketing and delivering it to the public that is considered to be among the best in the QSR business. Franchisees don't have to conceive of their own systems or their own products. If they wanted to do those things, they wouldn't (or shouldn't) be a franchisee. At the same time, it means that Tim Hortons is the main supplier of most everything the franchisee needs, and has tremendous power in telling the franchisee what to sell, how to make it and what to sell it for.

It would be absurd for a franchisee to want to sell some brand of coffee other than what Tim Hortons itself makes in its own roasting facilities, given that coffee is such a signature product and drives the majority of revenues—and, for franchisees, it appears, the vast majority of profits. In addition to naturally only selling coffee supplied by Tim Hortons itself, Tim Hortons franchisees also cannot sell any coffee variations that head office has not conceived of, approved of or provided to them. A franchisee cannot decide to start offering a "dark roast" or flavoured alternative to the standard Tim Hortons fare. A franchisee similarly cannot go rogue on the menu and elect to get into burgers or tacos, even at their own expense. Nor can a franchisee operate any sort of business other than Tim Hortons on the premises. (Licence agreements can also forbid moonlighting on the part of the franchisee. They must be dedicated to their store.) Some stores—121 in Canada and 30 in the U.S.—are co-branded as a Wendy's and run by franchisees. There were also 232 co-branded Cold Stone Creamery outlets (133 in Canada, 99 in the U.S.) by the end of 2011. There are a few other cases in the U.S. of franchisees operating some sort of co-brand operation, but as with the Wendy's and Cold Stone cases, the joint premises are sanctioned at the corporate level.

All good franchising companies consult with franchisees, to understand regional variations in tastes and menu priorities and to get a grip on emerging trends and competitive threats. Tim Hortons experiments with new product offerings, trialling them in selected outlets and regional markets before deciding whether to add them to the overall product line. For example, the beef lasagna casserole introduced in Canada in October 2011 was initially tested in some U.S. outlets, and in August 2011, all 115 outlets in western New York began offering a significantly expanded drink menu: espresso shots in coffee as well as in a number of hot and cold cappuccino and latte drinks. The concept had been previously test-marketed in western Canada, as well as in Syracuse, New York, and at stores in Michigan and Ohio. This expanded drink menu was then introduced in Canada in November 2011. While in New York City in September 2011, I saw Tim's outlets there serving approved oddities (to a Canadian customer) like frozen lemonade (which was introduced to Canada in the summer of 2012) and macaroni and cheese.

Such rigorous control of menu offerings is par for the course in the QSR business. Franchisees are expected to master, benefit from and execute the franchisor's system. Long gone are the days when McDonald's franchisees took it upon themselves to experiment with new offerings that produced chainwide signature products, like the Egg McMuffin, Big Mac, Quarter Pounder and Filet-O-Fish, which came on line in the late 1960s and early 1970s. Today, the franchisor knows best, and the franchisee is paying for the right to benefit from that accumulated wisdom. As competition in the food-service industry has increased, it is probably true that restaurant franchising overall has become much more rigorously controlled by the leading franchisors, in an effort to protect their brands from wayward and undisciplined franchisees and to continue to provide franchisees with what they were looking for in the first place: a finely tuned concept and operating system, with centralized expertise in marketing, product development, human resources and management of chain expansion.

In addition to carefully screening prospective franchisees, Tim Hortons puts approved franchisees through a mandatory seven-week training course and requires them to work two to three different shifts under the watch of an established restaurant owner. Franchisees are responsible for hiring and training (and firing) staff, with the company providing prescriptive oversight in human resources and guidance on how to deal with franchise employees through its operations manual and direct advice from head office. This was especially apparent during the cutover from the traditional scratch baking to the Always Fresh parbaking system, when head office was providing advice to franchisees on how to deal with their trained bakers, whose talents (and higher wages) were no longer going to be required.

Franchise systems sink or swim according to the performance of their weakest operations. Individual franchisees may function locally, but the franchisor operates over large territories—sometimes globally—and customers expect similar levels and quality of product and service wherever they happen to find an outlet. Given the mobility of consumers, Tim's is well aware that a badly run franchise in Hamilton, Ontario, can negatively affect the profitability of an outlet in Calgary, Alberta. And dissatisfied consumers can spread their wrath to wherever social media extends—even through the company's own Facebook page, as is the case with Tim Hortons. A consumer who is served lukewarm coffee in Richmond, B.C., can influence purchasing decisions in Antigonish, Nova Scotia.

A franchisor, accordingly, needs to be rigorous in its quality-control inspections. Regional managers of Tim Hortons have the right, which they exercise, to drop in unannounced on franchises and assess their operations—above and beyond requisite visits by local health inspectors. (The company says it makes at least two unscheduled health inspections of its own annually at every operation.) Cam MacDonald pointed out to me a small plaque on a wall of the Danforth and Logan outlet at the entrance to the kitchen area. He had to score at least 85 (on a scale of 100) on a corporate inspection to earn the plaque for outstanding operational quality. Were he to score less than 85 on three consecutive inspections, the plaque would come down. When he scored 95 or better, he said, he paid bonuses to staff.

The Tim Hortons licence agreement extends beyond the company's right to inspect the physical environment. The franchisee also cedes corporate access to financial information, including sales reports, audited financial statements and tax returns. Tim Hortons has the right to know pretty much everything about how a franchisee is running an outlet, whenever it chooses to look or ask. This has a Big Brother air about it, but the necessity and benefits are twofold and far from unusual in franchising. First, the company has a timely and ongoing picture of how the company's products are faring in the marketplace—locally, regionally and nationally. Second, it has hard data to indicate how the franchisees are performing.

The least-appreciated benefit of the window into franchisee performance that head office demands is the saving of franchisees from themselves, which happens occasionally. There have been surprisingly few cases of a dispute between Tim Hortons and a franchisee ending in a courtroom, but in the case of two that arose in the 1990s and went to trial, both of which ended resoundingly in Tim Hortons' favour, it seems pretty clear from the judges' decisions that things might have turned out far happier for the failed franchisees had Tim's been even more involved in their day-to-day operations than it already was under the letter of the franchise licences.* Indeed, these cases leave an indelible impression of a franchisor that was working very closely with franchisees to ensure their mutual success and to stave off the failures they were unable to avoid. While the franchisees were left indebted to Tim Hortons and without franchises, the outlets involved survived and prospered.

These cases also refute the idea that securing a Tim Hortons store in Canada is an automatic licence to print money. Although a Tim Hortons has been one of the surest franchise opportunities in Canada, rivalled only by McDonald's, running one successfully is hard work—"overly onerous," according to the judge's estimation in the Zabco

---

* See *TDL Group Ltd. v. Zabco Holdings Inc. et al* and *Murray v. TDL Group Ltd.*

Holdings case. A franchise operator doesn't have to wander far off the prescribed, proven path to get into trouble. But it was with the filing of the Fairview suit in 2008 that two married franchisees made the most emphatic allegation that Tim Hortons' own policies were making the path much harder to follow than it should be, all while the franchisor and its investors continued to profit.

17

PARBAKED: ALWAYS FRESH AND THE FAIRVIEW LAWSUIT

THE $1.95 BILLION FAIRVIEW SUIT (*Fairview Donut Inc. v. The TDL Group Corp.*), was an exceptional public eruption of operator dissatisfaction in the Tim Hortons system. Although the claims of the representative plaintiffs would be dismissed on February 24, 2012 (an appeal was filed on March 23, 2012), the suit was made particularly alluring to the media by the fact that the two plaintiffs, Fairview Donut Inc. and Brule Foods Ltd., were associated with a former senior executive of Tim Hortons, Archibald Jollymore, who was also Ron Joyce's cousin.

Tim Hortons wondered whether Ron Joyce was playing a behind-the-scenes role in his cousin's legal action. During cross-examination, Jollymore was asked if he had any funding arrangement with Joyce. The plaintiffs, in response, said they were prepared to answer questions about whether or not they had control of the litigation but not about funding arrangements, which, they said, were protected by solicitor–client privilege.

The judge, George R. Strathy, disagreed on this point. Though he wrote there was "no question that the plaintiffs are substantial, motivated and competent representatives of the class" seeking to have the suit certified as a class action, he felt the court was "entitled to know whether some other party is funding the litigation and, if so, who is doing so and on what terms. The answers go to the independence and motivations of the representative plaintiff as well as the ability of the representative plaintiff to see the action through to completion." If it were established that a third party who was not a member of the class was supporting the litigation financially for "collateral reasons," the judge ruled, "that alone might be reason to question the independence and suitability of the representative plaintiff." Assuming all other issues were resolved in the plaintiffs' favour, Judge Strathy decided that he would order that the questions about Joyce's possible role be answered before he would approve certification of the class action. As it happened, the action was not certified, and the question of whether Joyce might be behind the lawsuit was never further addressed or resolved.

Archibald Jollymore had been an executive with his cousin's company since 1977 and was executive vice-president when he left to become a franchisee in 1994. As we've seen, he ran the experimental Bagel Café for Tim Hortons in Burlington from 1996 to 1999. He also operated three Tim's outlets in Burlington, Ontario, through Brule Foods (Jollymore grew up at Brule Point in Nova Scotia). At the time of the suit, he was still running two of them, having sold the balance of the term of the franchise agreement for the third one back to Tim Hortons in 2007.

Jollymore's wife, Anne, a pastry chef who married him in 1994, had run two franchises of her own through the other plaintiff, Fairview Donut. The first store she had opened with a former husband in 1988. The franchise for that store had been terminated by Tim Hortons in 2008, at the end of its ten-year franchise agreement, but she continued to run the second one, which had been relocated in 2001, through Fairview Donut. A deponent for the plaintiffs, moreover, was Cyril Garland, who was Tim Hortons' vice-president of finance when he departed in 1998 to become a franchisee. Garland had launched a similar suit and then settled with Tim Hortons, selling back his three stores, but was able to serve as a deponent for the Jollymores' suit in the context of his eligibility to participate in a class action should the suit be certified.

The bulk of the suit objected to the Always Fresh parbaking system Tim Hortons had switched to as on-site scratch baking was abandoned. The company had actually begun using parbaking for bagels when they were introduced in 1996, using a convection oven in the stores to finish them off. It began investigating parbaking for doughnuts and other baked goods in 1999, and signed a joint-venture agreement in late 2001 with Ireland's IAWS Group. The joint venture, called CillRyan's Bakery Group ("CillRyan"), established a parbaking production facility in Brantford, Ontario, called Maidstone Bakeries. Maidstone would sell parbaked goods to CillRyan, which in turn would sell them to a distributor (after 2006, this was Tim Hortons itself for the Ontario market), which in turn would sell them to the individual franchisees. In 2010, IAWS's new owners, Aryzta AG, triggered a buyout clause, offering Tim Hortons $475 million for Tim's half of CillRyan and the Maidstone facility. Tim Hortons had the option of buying out Aryzta for the same amount, but chose to sell (realizing a one-time gain of $361 million), and secured a supply guarantee from Maidstone that runs through 2016, with a further supply option into 2017.

The new parbaking system, which required franchisees to invest in special ovens, was introduced to stores between 2002 and 2004. Ron Joyce, who had departed the company in 2001, publicly decried parbaking's introduction when asked about it in 2003, saying it never would have happened had he remained in charge.

It's a matter of semantics whether or not parbaked goods are "baked" after they reach an outlet and are popped in the oven for final preparation. The biochemistry of parbaking says that with yeast-based goods like breads, bagels and doughnut varieties that aren't cake-based, the product has to rise completely before freezing shuts down the baking. It's essentially done on the inside; what remains is the final browning process that the specialized ovens take care of in a restaurant.

Parbaking is not a proprietary Tim Hortons concept. Developed in Europe, it is now employed widely through the food industry, allowing supermarkets, for example, to offer "fresh-baked" so-called artisan bread. "The quality of parbaked bread these days is unbelievable," Ric Scicchitano, senior vice-president of food and beverage at Corner Bakery, an American bakery-café chain, told *QSR* magazine in September 2011. Scicchitano was the original baker for Corner Bakery when it was founded in Chicago in 1991, and plainly believed in the new technology. "You would have a difficult time distinguishing it from bread made from scratch on site."

Another Tim Hortons competitor in the bakery-café sector, Panera Bread, has built its business on a parbake foundation. Tom Gumpel, head baker and vice-president of bakery research and development at Panera, has offered an explanation for parbaking that I'm sure someone in corporate at Tim Hortons wished they'd thought of when its parbaking controversy erupted and people started talking about frozen doughnuts being thawed in a microwave. Panera's bread, Gumpel told *QSR* magazine, is "made from scratch. It just goes for a little ride along the way."

When I met with Cam MacDonald at his store at Danforth and Logan, the Fairview suit was a few weeks away from a crucial hearing in a downtown Toronto courtroom. The suit also raised issues over the profitability of the mandatory lunch menu. The hearing would determine whether the suit should be certified as a class action, the way the plaintiffs wanted, or should be dismissed, the way Tim Hortons was arguing. In the end, Judge Strathy would emphatically dismiss claims of the representative plaintiffs.

In my tour of the back of MacDonald's restaurant at Danforth and

Logan, we paused before an Always Fresh parbaking oven. A chart on the top provided instructions for preparing different-sized batches of various products, which arrived frozen from the Maidstone plant in Brantford.

Cam MacDonald had no complaints about the parbaking system, ticking through the advantages he felt it had provided him. There was no baker to worry about relying on to show up for work (although he had been trained as a baker as part of the seven-week franchisee course). They no longer had to organize an early-morning bake, or leave product on display from such a bake for ten hours, going stale, in order to meet the minimum variety requirements. "We don't sell off boxes of day-olds like they did when you and I were a kid in Hamilton." When he needed to resupply the display, a staffer with minimal training could prepare fresh batches of as few as six Timbits to maintain variety. As far as MacDonald was concerned, that's what "always fresh" meant.

The statement of claim and the affidavit of analysis from Douglas Fisher of the food service and franchise management consulting firm FHG International painted a scenario in which Tim Hortons imposed on franchisees a new baking system and menu items at costs and retail pricing levels that made it harder, not easier, for franchisees to make money, while the company itself continued to prosper from the captive sales of food, machinery and the like to franchisees. Tim Hortons sounded like it had become a corporate equivalent of Saturn devouring his own children, using the vertical integration of operations and the terms of its franchise licence agreements to force franchisees to use an Always Fresh baking system that allegedly turned out to be less profitable than the old scratch-baking system for the franchisees, but highly profitable for the franchisor.

The parbaking switch was supposed to make life easier for franchisees by eliminating the need for skilled bakers at standard outlets and by reducing costs by eliminating wastage, or "throws." The plaintiffs argued that employing bakers had never been a big deal or expense, and that the new system actually was more expensive for the franchisees. The mandatory replacement of the old baking equipment with the new proprietary ovens was one cost issue, but essentially the case came down to dollars and doughnuts. The franchisee cost of making a doughnut was supposed to increase from about six cents to twelve, with savings to accrue through reduced wastage because of the small batches the parbaking ovens could produce on demand. Instead, the plaintiffs argued, the doughnut cost had increased to about eighteen cents, and despite wastage being reduced, because they were now throwing away eighteen-cent doughnuts, the new system was more expensive.

The company was also accused of making franchisees sell a lunch menu whose value pricing, prescribed by head office, meant there was little to no profit (or an actual loss) for franchisees. All the while, Tim Hortons as franchisor continued to earn profits on the goods that the franchisee had to buy from it, and on the RRA percentages it charged on gross receipts, before a franchisee paid its own costs. The plaintiffs were seeking damages for breach of contract, negligent misrepresentation and breach of the duty of good faith and fair dealing at common law as well as where applicable under the Wishart Act, the franchise disclosure law that was enacted in Ontario in 2000 in order to provide greater transparency for franchisees entering into agreements with franchisors.

It so happened that the Wishart Act had arisen from Bill 33, which had been drafted with input from an industry working group that included a senior Tim Hortons executive, Nick Javor. Today, Javor is senior vice-president, corporate affairs, but when he appeared before a legislative standing committee in March 2000 to urge that Bill 33 become law forthwith as it was already conceived, he was vice-president of southwestern Ontario operations, overseeing 375 stores operated by 160 franchisees. Had Bill 33 foundered in committee, there likely would not have been a Wishart Act in effect for the plaintiffs to cite where parbaking was concerned.

That Tim Hortons might end up being sued by one of its former senior executives, for allegedly violating a statute that another senior executive had helped to create and had pressed to be made into law, was presumably as unforeseen as it now seems surreal. Javor had even argued that Bill 33 was sufficiently worded for its "fair dealing" prescription to govern actions of a franchisor after a franchise licence agreement was signed. That formed the grounds on which the Wishart Act could be said to apply to Tim Hortons' ongoing actions under any franchise agreement entered into after the act became law and before franchisees were required to adopt the parbaking system in the rollout from 2002 to 2004.

In another case of déjà vu where the Bill 33 standing committee hearings were concerned, the allegations in the lunch-menu aspect of the Fairview suit were highly reminiscent of battles in the pizza franchise sector in the 1990s that provided impetus for the Wishart Act. Franchisees then had claimed that sales specials mandated by a franchisor eroded their profit margins when they were required to buy ingredients without any price relief from the franchisor. The franchisees were stuck delivering pizzas at little to no profit, while the franchisor made money off the sales of the ingredients to the franchisees. The Fairview suit plaintiffs, using analysis by Fisher, contended that Tim Hortons was keeping sandwich prices unnecessarily low to maintain its value-pricing strategy, causing franchisees to make little or no profit (or record an actual loss) on these items while the company itself profited from the captive sale of ingredients to the franchisee.

Fisher's analysis of sales figures for outlets of the plaintiffs and the deponent Cyril Garland proposed that franchisees were making thin profits on baked goods and minimal profits to actual losses on the lunch menu, and were overly reliant on the beverages menu, brewed coffee especially, for their profits. The profit margin on brewed coffee, according to the plaintiffs' evidence, ranged somewhere between about 15 and 35 percent, depending on the outlet.

Tim Hortons called the Jollymores' suit frivolous and without merit. It said it had a contractual right to determine the price at which franchisees purchase ingredients, that it exercised its contractual rights reasonably and in good faith and that, overall, the plaintiffs and all franchisees enjoyed an exceptional rate of return on their investments. All arguments over the enforceability of the franchise agreement aside, Tim Hortons wasn't about to abide the plaintiffs' allegations that it was making tremendous profits while franchisees suffered. (Nor were many franchisees. At an early stage of the suit, 436 franchisees operating more than 1,300 stores that called themselves the "Concerned Franchisees Group" tried and failed to secure intervenor status in support of the company.)

Tim Hortons had its own franchise production figures that showed, for example, that the reduction in "throws" in fact offset the increased unit cost of doughnuts. While the company quite correctly stated that nowhere in any franchise agreement is a particular level of profit guaranteed, the company insisted that all franchisees, the plaintiffs included, profited nicely. One of Tim Hortons' senior finance executives, Jeff O'Rourke, swore that its system produced "a return on investment for our store owners that is unmatched in the quick service restaurant industry."

The company also denied the lunch menu was a money loser (although it's generally believed that its margins in the highly competitive QSR meal sector are thin). The menu, which had been introduced in 1986, was necessary to the chain's competitiveness in the QSR sector, especially during other parts of the day, and not just during the lunch period on which the suit focused its analysis. The meals also were said to drive purchases of other menu items, the drinks and baked goods.

Judge Strathy overwhelmingly sided with Tim Hortons in dismissing, on February 24, 2012, in a summary judgment, the claims of the representative plaintiffs (who then launched an appeal on March 23,

2012). He came very close to striking the affidavit of Fisher, whose analysis was key to the plaintiff's case. "Mr. Fisher's opinion is prolix in the extreme, largely because he does not confine himself to expressions of opinion based on assumed facts or facts clearly established by other evidence. Instead, he undertakes his own fact-finding mission, relying on facts that have not been proven. His affidavit also includes improper legal analysis and contract interpretation and improper advocacy."

Expert witnesses like Fisher are supposed to be neutral "friends of the court." The judge noted how "Mr. Fisher could not resist assuming the role of advocate, something that occurs throughout his affidavit. This is perhaps not surprising, as the evidence shows that soon after this action was commenced, Mr. Fisher contacted Tim Hortons, unsolicited, and attempted to obtain a retainer, suggesting that he could assist in 'stifling this matter early on.' I agree with the submission of Tim Hortons that this sort of conduct by a putative expert should lead the court to approach his opinion with some degree of skepticism." Although he did not strike Fisher's affidavit, Judge Strathy wrote, "I give his evidence little weight."

The suit was assuredly doomed from the beginning, because the court was in no position to rewrite a valid contract, namely a franchise agreement. "What matters, at the end of the day, is whether the franchisee makes sufficient profit overall to justify his or her investment and to remain in the business," the judge concluded. "The suggestion by the plaintiffs that the franchisor has an obligation to price every menu item so that they can make a profit on that particular item is not supported by the contract, by the law or by common sense. It is simply not the responsibility of the court to step in to recalibrate the financial terms of the agreement made by the parties."

The judge rejected the idea that Tim Hortons' switch to parbaking took advantage of franchisees. "It has been established beyond dispute that the Always Fresh Conversion was a rational business decision made by Tim Hortons for valid economic and strategic reasons, having regard to both its own interests and the interests of its franchisees. The evidentiary record provides ample support for the conclusion that scratch-baking was unsustainable in the long run and that the move to Always Fresh baking was beneficial for franchisees."

The switch to Always Fresh "addressed legitimate problems experienced by franchisees with scratch baking and legitimate concerns by Tim Hortons concerning the long-term viability of the scratch baking method. The result was an improved method of producing donuts. The fact that the donuts may have cost more, and that this adversely affected the franchisees' bottom line, even if proven, was not a breach of any express contractual term." Judge Strathy cited franchisees that welcomed the switch and said that although the changeover initially impacted profits, the advantages of the new system were borne out. Indeed, if Tim Hortons hadn't made the change, Judge Strathy wrote, the cost of producing a doughnut using the old scratch-bake system would have increased to about thirty cents.

Judge Strathy accepted that the meal offerings were critical to Tim Hortons' competitiveness. "If [customers] cannot find the meal, or if it is too expensive, or it doesn't taste good, they will go somewhere else, like McDonald's or Mr.Sub. If they find the coffee in those stores is just as good, they may be lost forever as customers of Tim Hortons."

And losing coffee customers, in Judge Strathy's estimation, was the real risk franchisees like the plaintiffs faced. Judge Strathy portrayed a Tim Hortons outlet as a coffee cash cow. "There is one aspect of the Tim Hortons franchise that the plaintiffs don't complain about—coffee," he chided. "Coffee is what Tim Hortons has been about since the very first day. It remains so today. Tim Hortons owns the coffee brand. It owns the trademark. The franchisee acquires the right to use the trademark. To sell the brand. Tim Hortons calls its coffee 'legendary' and describes it on its website at [*sic*] 'the chain's biggest calling card.'" Selling Tim Hortons coffee, he reminded them, is "extremely profitable."*

JUDGE STRATHY FELT he could write with confidence that selling Tim Hortons coffee, in Canada at least, is "extremely profitable." How profitable the American arm of the company has been for individual franchisees and the company itself is another matter.

At the end of 2006, following the IPO and spinoff of remaining shares to Wendy's investors, there were 2,711 stores in Canada and 336 in the U.S. While Canadian operations dominated revenues and profits, the U.S. market whet the appetite of investors and analysts, who priced an aggressive American expansion into the stock's value whenever it rallied. The stock wobbled up and down for several years, bottoming out around $26 in late 2008 as a deep recession hammered markets overall and investors worried about even the short-term profitability of a restaurant company that thrived on sales of discretionary treats. But by mid 2009 Tim's stock was regaining traction and beginning a mostly steady climb toward $50 in 2011, as analysts on both sides of the border championed the stock as one of the surest—if not *the* surest—QSR restaurant plays.

In 2009, the company generated headlines by cutting two significant U.S. deals: the purchase of a chain of former Bess Eaton doughnut

* In the plaintiffs' notice of appeal, filed March 23, 2012, it was argued that Justice Strathy "committed two fundamental and overriding errors: (a) His Honour mischaracterized the plaintiffs' claims as being in essence a demand that every item sold by franchisees be profitable, and to a greater share of profits on [Always Fresh] goods and Lunch Menu items; and, (b) His Honour held that because each franchisee is, on the whole, profitable and making a 'reasonable rate of return,' the franchisee cannot have any cause of action for breach of contract or breach of the statutory duty of good faith." The plaintiffs also objected to the fact that the judge "held that this is a simple case that can be decided on a summary judgment basis without the benefit of a trial and the full appreciation of the evidence that comes with the trial process."

stores from a Rhode Island bankruptcy court that gave it an instant presence in the southern New England market, and a franchise agreement with the Riese Organization of New York that displaced about a dozen Dunkin' Donuts outlets in midtown Manhattan so that Tim's could make its debut in the Big Apple. By mid-September 2011, when I flew to New York City to visit the Tim's franchises, the Bess Eaton deal had already proved to be an abject failure. I wanted to see for myself how Tim's was faring in the Manhattan market, and what it could tell me about the chain's overall prospects for conquering America, as analysts and investors had been hoping since 2006.

18

To Take Manhattan: Testing the Limits of the Tim Hortons Brand

SHORTLY AFTER NINE-THIRTY on a hot and humid mid-September morning in 2011, my Air Canada flight touched down at New York's LaGuardia Airport. "Forty-second and Broadway," I told the cabbie, and we leapt into and lurched through the usual traffic morass leading into Manhattan. I had a lunch date at one o'clock, at Junior's at Forty-fifth and Broadway, and I was determined to use the intervening time to track down every Tim Hortons outlet in New York City I possibly could, save the lone one in Brooklyn. Of ten Manhattan outlets, I managed to see seven. By the time I had taken my seat at Junior's, my feet were aching from almost three hours of pavement pounding, and my impression of Tim Hortons' celebrated 2009 entry into the QSR battle of the Big Apple, and its prospects for American expansion, had been considerably affected.

For anyone who knows Tim Hortons from its Canadian outlets—and, for that matter, most of its American ones—the New York outlets are startlingly different in size, concept, menu items, signage and promotion. Tim Hortons may have done the best it could in taking advantage of an opportunity to enter the New York City market, but that entry cannot be called a roaring success. Not only has further expansion not come, but by the time I arrived, the number of outlets being operated by its franchisee, the Riese Organization, had dropped from thirteen to ten. Four of the original locations had closed and one had opened. The only two stand-alone, full-menu locations had disappeared. Three co-branded outlets with Cold Stone Creamery that were announced at the same time as the Riese Organization deal remained open, but there had been no additions. The chain also had undergone a curious local rebranding, at odds with the rest of its thousands of outlets, in a highly visible location. Worse, some of the Tim Hortons outlets had experienced problems with the city's restaurant health inspectors—one was even ordered shut down for a day.

Tim Hortons' decidedly mixed arrival in New York would seem to be of little consequence to the greater company. After all, the city only represents (depending on how you want to count the Cold Stone co-brands) about a dozen of more than 700 outlets in the United States. But in announcing the arrival in New York City, Tim Hortons then-president and CEO Don Schroeder had said in a company press release: "Coming to New York City is a significant milestone in our U.S. expansion and we intend to deliver on our lasting commitments to speed of service, fresh quality products and great value." As a market foray that generated much fanfare, both in Canada and the United States, New York City instead could be demonstrating the natural limitations of a strong and respected brand, while at the same time illuminating the risks a great brand has taken in order to enter one of the world's great media centres and tourism destinations. Manhattan is the first place I have ever seen Tim Hortons in action and wondered if it really had a fighting chance, although it has experienced outright failure in other U.S. markets. Manhattan is also where the future of urban QSR is brewing. The new concepts thriving there promise to be the challenges Tim's will face in other markets where it is already established or hopes to expand.

SOONER RATHER THAN LATER, even with almost 1,000 new outlets forecast north of the border, Tim's will exhaust its expansion opportunities in Canada. Despite some efforts to find growth elsewhere in the world (including a master licensing agreement with the Apparel Group for a projected 120 outlets in the Arab Gulf States, announced in 2011), America remains the great, largely untapped opportunity.

America is also an opportunity that eats Canadian retailing concepts as a between-meal snack and spits out the bones. The market is enormous, and because Americans famously love eating, it is crowded with competing niche players, some of which are national in scope, but many of which are regional. Tim Hortons is trying to adjust its game from being a dominant QSR presence (and cultural phenomenon) in Canada to competing as another QSR concept without a national brand presence in the U.S. Ken Wong, a Queen's School of Business distinguished professor of marketing and member of the Canadian Marketing Hall of Legends who has provided consulting services to the restaurant industry, including Tim Hortons' competitor Starbucks, for one, is skeptical of Tim Hortons' strategy for the U.S. market. "I don't think they have a brand in the U.S., outside the border areas," he said to me after I returned from my New York visit. "I don't think they have a plan for how they're going to roll this out regionally."

Wong was far from alone in criticizing Tim Hortons' American expansion plans. Kenric Tyghe, a consumer products and retail analyst for Raymond James in Toronto, has said that a "too big and too audacious" U.S. expansion has distracted the company and caused the core business in Canada to suffer. When we spoke in October 2011, Tyghe volunteered, "I have become progressively more negative over the past nine months" because of what he called "management missteps." Whether Tim Hortons can successfully (meaning profitably) expand its brand into a large part of the United States is something the company, its franchisees and investors are in the process of learning.

The company's message to investors is that it has adopted a

"challenger brand mentality" for the U.S. market and resolved that, in the U.S., it would position itself as a "café/bake shop." But from the moment I stepped into my first Tim's in midtown Manhattan, I was confused about what the company's brand actually was.

TIM HORTONS DID NOT CROSS the border until 1984, when it opened its first location in the Buffalo, New York, suburb of Tonawanda—ten years after Tim Horton died while on the roster of the Buffalo Sabres—but expansion didn't begin in earnest in western New York until 1992. An effort to establish the chain in South Carolina was a flop that required a total retreat. There were only seventy U.S. outlets in 1997, two years after the merger with Wendy's International, when Tim's embarked on its first U.S. television ad campaign, with spots airing in the Columbus, Ohio, and Detroit, Michigan, markets in support of a fresh expansion push. A U.S. headquarters was established in the Columbus suburb of Dublin, where Wendy's also had its head office. Store #100 in the U.S. appeared in 1998 in Columbus; Wendy's gave Tim's a shove forward by acquiring an existing QSR sandwich chain whose conversion immediately gave Tim Horton's more than forty outlets in Ohio.

Franchise counts are a moving target, but not including self-serve kiosks, Tim Hortons at year-end 2011 had 124 Ohio outlets (standard and non-standard) around Columbus and Toledo. The Ohio outlets form one of several border-region clusters in the U.S. market. Southeast of Columbus, West Virginia has half a dozen, around Charleston and Parkersburg, all standard format. Up the Lake Erie shore from Toledo, there are eight outlets in Erie, Pennsylvania. Outlets (161 standard and non-standard) have also spread into southeastern Michigan, a strong growth area, from the Windsor-Detroit border. Western New York (mainly Buffalo, Rochester and Syracuse) had 207, and Maine had 29.

Tim Hortons' numbers for year-end 2011 are a bit deceptive when it comes to the proportion of standard-format outlets. The U.S. overall lags Canada, with 61 percent of outlets in standard format, versus 72 percent in Canada. But that picture is skewed by New York State, which has 59 non-standard outlets as well as a huge number (148) of self-serve kiosks because of a franchise deal with Tops Friendly Markets.

Kiosks are used in the U.S. to introduce the company's products in markets where it is not well known. They represent 23 percent of all U.S. outlets, compared to less than 4 percent in Canada, where they're mainly found in Esso On the Run locations. "Our self-serve kiosks typically have single-serve hot and cold beverage offerings and a limited selection of doughnuts, muffins, Danishes, and other pastries, although the product offering varies with the size of the kiosk and is generally more limited in the U.S.," the company explained in its fiscal 2010 annual report. The main format is a self-pour coffee service.

The self-pour kiosk concept has also been exported to the United Kingdom and Ireland, where they formed the bulk of about 275 licensed outlets. Their performance is so inconsequential that Tim Hortons doesn't even count them in its outlet totals or break out their revenues. In March 2011, a *Toronto Star* journalist dropped in on one on Haymarket in the heart of London. Kiosks had been introduced to Spar outlets, a chain of small supermarkets and convenience stores, and as *The Star* discovered, the Tim Hortons presence in the small Spar on Haymarket (which since has closed) consisted of a self-pour kiosk offering coffee, cappuccino and hot chocolate near the cash register. A rack of baked goods offered seven doughnut varieties and three muffin types. The store manager explained that the doughnuts "were made in Portugal or Denmark and shipped frozen to the U.K." If nothing else, the outlet was a magnet for Canadian tourists.

In Ohio, Maine and Michigan, Tim's overwhelmingly is represented by standard-format restaurants with drive-throughs—more so than anywhere in Canada, where non-standard units have been increasingly deployed to infill established markets. This means the new food-court and co-brand franchises in New York City are even more of a surprise to many American customers than they are to Canadians.

I started my Tim Hortons walking tour of midtown Manhattan at a co-branded Cold Stone Creamery outlet at 253 West Forty-second, in the heart of the Times Square theatre district. The street was a notorious, gritty strip of adult entertainment and shuttered theatres when I first visited the city in the late 1970s. Thanks to an aggressive urban recovery plan, Forty-second Street (or "New Forty-second Street," as it is labelled) is now a family-friendly tourist mecca: a few doors to the east of the co-branded outlet is Foxwoods Theatre, where the *Spider-Man* musical was playing; across the street is Madame Tussauds wax museum and the New Amsterdam Theatre, where Disney's *Mary Poppins* was running. Cold Stone had already been doing its best to compete with the garish visuals of the Forty-second Street strip with a neon marquee. Now that it was a co-branded outlet, a neon Tim Hortons signature logo with a cup had been added to the marquee.

This was overwhelmingly a store selling Cold Stone ice cream, with a U-shaped counter dispensing cold treats on both sides. At the front, a display of muffins, bagels and doughnuts had been installed beside the cash. It also offered breakfast sandwiches, but not the lunch menu. An assortment of teas were displayed, and there were hot and cold coffee products.

It wasn't quite ten-thirty on a weekday morning, and while there was plenty of foot traffic on the street, I was the only person in the store: too early in the day for ice cream, too late apparently for breakfast sandwiches, and not much apparent demand for coffee. I ordered a medium brewed coffee from the young woman at the cash, which came in the fourteen-ounce cup that in Canada was a large; a week earlier, while in Kingston, Ontario, I had ordered a Canadian medium, normally ten ounces, and had been handed this size of cup as the company test-marketed an upsizing of its Canadian servings that it would finally adopt chainwide in January 2012.

The cup she handed me was a minor confusion of branding. The actual cup featured the standard Tim Hortons logo—red script in a pale yellow oval, with the "Always Fresh" slogan within it. Below the oval, a banner absent from Canadian cups read "Cafe & Bake Shop." The cup was held in a corrugated cardboard sleeve (also unfamiliar to Canadian customers), and it featured a different logo, created for the expansion into New York City.

In what I had heard described as a "retro" look, a trademark white Tim Hortons script was set in a red trapezoid, adorned with two additional mustard-coloured trapezoids. The signature "Always Fresh" slogan was in the smaller one on the upper left; the larger one on the lower right read "Coffee & Bake Shop." This retro logo adorned the signage of the New York outlets, an oddly divergent strategy that was made only further confusing by declaring this was a "coffee & bake shop," not (as the cup told me) a "Cafe & Bake Shop." The back of the sleeve surprised me by actually saying something about who Tim Horton the hockey player was, which you don't come across in Canada.

Even had Tim Hortons tried to go it alone in this location without the Cold Stone co-brand and the full lunch menu, it would have been tough. A massive McDonald's was right across the street in a former theatre, and it was more than big enough to swallow every Tim Hortons in the New York area. On that same side of the street were two other enormous chain operations, an Applebee's and a Dave & Buster's. On the Tim Hortons side of the street was a string of eateries: Pax Wholesome Foods, Dallas BBQ (whose space extended to the floor above Tim Hortons/Cold Stone), a Yoshinoya beef-bowl chain outlet, Chevys Fresh Mex, Crumbs Bake Shop, Stromboli Pasta and Villa Pizza. And among them, only a few doors to the west of the co-branded Cold Stone/Tim's, was the ubiquitous, inevitable, unavoidable Starbucks. And in case anyone, in their craving for a decent coffee, missed that modest storefront Starbucks, there was a major outlet nearby, on the northeast corner of Broadway and Forty-third, right on the pedestrian mall in the heart of Times Square.

"Do you get a lot of Canadians?" I asked the young woman who sold me the Tim Hortons coffee. She smiled and said yes, and didn't volunteer anything further. It occurred to me that I should have asked, "Do you get a lot of Canadians asking if you get a lot of Canadians?" I walked out the door onto Forty-second Street to continue my tour. I wouldn't see another person carrying a signature Tim Hortons cup of coffee for the rest of my day.

I headed south, into the Fashion District, where most of the other outlets were clustered. In so doing, I entered the decidedly complicated world of the Riese Organization, its ugly divorce from Dunkin' Donuts and the rebranding of outlets that not so much brought Riese into the fold of Tim Hortons franchisees as it brought Tim Hortons into the unique embrace of Riese's local franchise empire.

IN 1940, IRVING AND MURRAY RIESE, the sons of poor Russian immigrants, opened their first restaurant, a luncheonette in midtown Manhattan, using money earned in a Bronx ice cream parlour. By the late 1990s, the business, presided over by Murray's son Dennis as CEO, was the largest private holding of restaurants in America. The Riese Organization of companies, which themselves numbered in the hundreds, had more than 300 outlets centred on midtown Manhattan, most of them being franchises of national brands like KFC, Pizza Hut, Roy Rogers, Häagen-Dazs and Dunkin' Donuts. It also, coincidentally, owned the Tad's steak house chain, which had once fuelled Tim Horton's desire to open a steak house of his own in Toronto.

The Riese Organization developed an enviable portfolio of midtown retail properties that it either owned or controlled through leases. It also pioneered in 1983 the "food court" or "cluster" concept, in which a single collective retail space is shared by a group of Riese-held franchises. The Riese formula, which became widely imitated in North America, showed how franchises with limited menu offerings could be clustered together by a single franchisee, sometimes sharing the same kitchen, accessing prime locations that an individual franchise might not be able to afford.

The food-court innovation was the start of Riese's reputation for maverick behaviour, for writing its own rules on how the restaurant franchise business should operate, at least from the franchisee's point of view. By 1989, about half of Riese's restaurants were in food courts. It was willing to challenge franchising norms, in court if necessary, and its stable of properties and leases gave it considerable sway in the restaurant business around greater New York. In 1984 it became a Dunkin' Donuts franchisee, and had more than a dozen outlets around Manhattan by the late 1990s.

The legal feud that led to the convergence of Tim Hortons and Riese began in inimitable New York style. In late 1998, a photograph appeared on the front page of the tabloid *New York Post* with the heading "Under Mouse Arrest," showing a mouse munching on a doughnut in the window display of one of Riese's midtown Dunkin' Donuts outlets. More articles followed in the *Post;* Mayor Rudolph Giuliani called it a "disgusting, horrible story." The embarrassment for Dunkin' went national when David Letterman referenced it on a "Top Ten List" of things overheard in Times Square. Number nine: "It's so cold the rat on my doughnut just froze."

Dunkin' Donuts initially sued the Riese Organization on January 4, 2009, claiming a breach of contract because Riese had not met Dunkin's health and sanitation standards. Dunkin' sought a court order that would force Riese to close the now-notorious outlet at Forty-sixth and Fifth Avenue and remove the Dunkin' Donuts sign.

"Anytime someone laughs at your trademark and what's going on in your shops, you've been damaged," Jack Laudermilk, a lawyer for Dunkin', was quoted as saying by *The New York Times*. Riese also closed about half of its Dunkin' outlets in the midst of a financial reversal that saw the Riese Organization emerge with a much smaller portfolio of around 110 restaurants. Another suit from Dunkin', in 2002, sought to terminate the franchise agreement for Riese's remaining thirteen Dunkin' outlets, alleging violations of health, sanitation and safety.

In 2004, the suit was settled out of court, although what the two warring parties agreed to, beyond the fact that Riese's franchise agreements would end on July 31, 2009, was of enduring dispute. Dennis Riese claimed a victory. "They couldn't demonstrate [in court] that we weren't running clean and healthy restaurants," Riese told *Crain's New York Business* in 2009. A spokesperson for Dunkin' said, "We thought it was in our best interest to remove the Riese Organization from the system."

The Dunkin' "system" in New York was enormous, far eclipsing the thirteen outlets that Riese, a non-exclusive local franchisee, had to give up. Dunkin' was hands down the largest national chain retailer of any kind in the five boroughs of New York and had grown more than any other retailer in the previous year, despite the economic downturn. Even with the loss of the Riese locations, in one year Dunkin' had grown from 341 to 429 outlets (more outlets than Tim Hortons had in B.C. and Alberta combined) as of July 2009, when the Riese stores were cut over to Tim Hortons; 107 of those outlets were in Manhattan.

Five of the top six national retailers in New York were QSRs, with Tim Hortons' competitors from other markets well established and growing. Second-ranked Subway was up from 335 to 361 outlets, 151 of them in Manhattan. Third-ranked McDonald's had grown by 10, to 258, with 81 in Manhattan. And fourth-ranked Starbucks had closed some outlets but still netted ahead by 23, at 258, with

193 in Manhattan. The only top QSR retailer to decline was sixth-ranked Baskin-Robbins, which had dropped by 8 to 207, with 46 in Manhattan. But then, Tim Hortons' new co-branding partner, Cold Stone Creamery, had dropped from 15 to 14 outlets, 4 of them in Manhattan. And between Dunkin' Donuts and Baskin-Robbins, Dunkin' Brands had 636 outlets in New York (some of them being co-branded operations).

Watchers of New York's restaurant scene had to wonder if Tim Hortons really knew what it was getting into when it cast its lot with the Riese Organization. For one thing, Riese had that long-standing reputation for going its own way as a franchisee and fending off litigious franchisors who disagreed with it. That promised a very different sort of franchisor-franchisee relationship than Tim Hortons was accustomed to, as a vertically integrated operation with plenty of head-office control over its stores. The Riese Organization's own website celebrates the defiance of the brothers Murray and Irving Riese as they branched into operating franchises at the urging of Dennis Riese in the early 1980s: "They defended their tough reputations in the franchise market by explaining that the rules placed on them by franchisors did not apply to the Manhattan market, which was an entirely different market from the suburban family market pursued by most national chains. They talked about the franchise relationship in David and Goliath terms—with the national franchisors being Goliath." The national chains were "short-sighted" in not understanding the food-court concept. "Generally, [the Riese brothers] got away with their tenacious stance, since franchisors were eager to break into Manhattan, but had little experience in doing it. Rules were bent, fees were renegotiated, franchise agreements were pushed to the limit—and the Rieses acquired their reputation along with their restaurants."

And then, of course, there was the baggage of the doughnut-munching mouse. "The new Hortons joints will have the same problem as the Dunkin' ones—they're franchised to the Riese Organization, the restaurant-management outfit that consistently succeeds in making horrible national brands even worse," wrote *New York Post* columnist Steve Cuozzo on July 14, 2009, in a piece whose title ("Yecchh! Flunkin' Donuts") captured his disdain for both the newly arrived chain and its local franchisee. "I tasted a bunch of the Hortons products . . . I found them even lousier than Dunkin'—gummier in the mouth and with no discernible flavor improvement." No fan of Riese restaurants, Cuozzo wrote: "I wonder if the Hortons people ever took a stroll through any of them before signing on the dotted line . . . Hortons, schmortons—the upstart doughnut shops might have grease—whoops, 'Riese'—written all over them. Caveat emptor."

On August 18, 2011, the mouse that started the lengthy and messy departure of Riese from the Dunkin' universe again roared. The New York City Department of Health and Mental Hygiene ordered closed the Riese food court at Sixth Avenue and Thirty-eighth that included a Tim Hortons. Among the violations: "Evidence of mice or live mice present in facility's food and/or non-food areas."*

---

* The August 18, 2011, inspection recorded fifty-six violation points. The first four listed violations are considered "critical."

1) Hot food item not held at or above 140°F.

2) Evidence of mice or live mice present in facility's food and/or non-food areas.

3) Food not protected from potential source of contamination during storage, preparation, transportation, display or service.

4) Sanitized equipment or utensil, including in-use food dispensing utensil, improperly used or stored.

5) Facility not vermin-proof. Harborage or conditions conducive to attracting vermin to the premises and/or allowing vermin to exist.

6) Plumbing not properly installed or maintained; anti-siphonage or backflow prevention device not provided where required; equipment or floor not properly drained; sewage disposal system in disrepair or not functioning properly.

19

Making the Grade: Tim Hortons' Struggles in the Big Apple

Walking down Sixth Avenue, I arrived at my first Riese-operated Tim Hortons. On the northwest corner of Thirty-eighth Street was the Riese food court that the city's inspectors had ordered closed one month earlier. Tim's had arrived in the Big Apple a year before Mayor Michael Bloomberg unveiled, in July 2010, a new restaurant inspection and rating scheme that was designed to shame restaurants into improving their health and sanitation standards. Restaurants are now required to display prominently a letter-grade rating, based on inspection points for violations, and the results of inspections are available through a searchable online database. To encourage greater public awareness of the rating system, the city's Department of Health and Mental Hygiene offers a free search widget that can be embedded in blogs and websites.

I initially twigged to the significance of the restaurant grading system when I noticed that the co-branded Tim Hortons/Cold Stone Creamery I had just visited on Forty-second Street had a sign indicating it was "grade pending"—the status of a restaurant formally appealing an unfavourable rating. In six inspections since March 2010, this outlet had been awarded points worthy of a B or C rating. Evidence of mice or live mice sometimes had been cited, and twice the restaurant was cited for not having a supervisor of food operations with a Food Protection Certificate, which was considered a "serious" violation. (When I checked back in early March 2012, it was still "grade pending," as it appealed a C-worthy score of 33 from an inspection on December 6. By mid-March, it had secured an A.)

The Riese food court at Thirty-fourth and Eighth that had been ordered closed on August 18 was authorized to reopen after an inspection the next day; it had actually been doing fairly well on inspections until that black day.* The food court was still listed as "grade pending." Although the reinspection on August 19 had earned it an A-worthy 5 points, a follow-up inspection on September 19, only days after my visit, would earn it a B grade. (It would be back to an A grade on March 15, 2012.) Customer traffic was minimal. Across the road was a bustling, A-grade Pret A Manger ("Pret"), the British import specializing in fresh soups, salads, sandwiches and beverages, backed by private equity, that has thrived in Manhattan, with twenty-nine outlets in prime locations.

Many good restaurants are capable of having a bad day right when the inspector arrives. Later that day, I had lunch at the popular Junior's, an A-rated destination that had been rocked by a few shaky inspections, including a whopping 64-point debacle in March 2010. (A score of 14 to 27 yields a B; 28 and up warrants a C.) But the top chains were fastidious about earning A ratings. McDonald's often scores zero inspection points, and Pret and Au Bon Pain outlets were

---

* New restaurants are expected to earn an "A" (0–13 points). If, on a first inspection, the restaurant can't make the A grade, it is given an "ungraded" rating and is subject to an unannounced follow-up inspection. At that point, if it still doesn't make an A, it is assigned the appropriate letter grade of B or C—unless, of course, the place is so bad that the inspector shuts it down. (The department advises "closures are typically brief.") The restaurant has the option of displaying the B or C card, or a "grade pending" card, while it appeals its case. Restaurants are wont to appeal immediately an unfavourable letter grading and display a "grade pending" rating in the meantime.

all sporting A grades. At the time of my visit, 188 of 195 Starbucks in Manhattan were A-listed. The fact that Tim Hortons would even have health-inspection troubles in New York City is a shock to anyone accustomed to the high standard the chain maintains elsewhere. Because the Tim's outlets in New York are either co-branded with a Cold Stone Creamery or operated in conjunction with other franchises in one facility by Riese as a single franchisee, inspection issues are shared across all operations inside the front door. Other locations with a Tim Hortons had experienced inspection problems. Later that day, I would visit the Riese food court across the street from Macy's on West Thirty-fourth. Even though this outlet had an A rating and a mostly good track record, in November 2010 it was cited for a "critical" administrative violation: "Nuisance created or allowed to exist. Facility not free from unsafe, hazardous, offensive or annoying conditions." When I last inspected the restaurant ratings (March 15, 2012), every Tim Hortons outlet in New York City but one (a B-grade co-branded Cold Stone Creamery with mice issues on the Upper West Side) had an A grade. Mice have been a chronic problem for the city's restaurateurs. Before the new inspection regimen was introduced, 32 percent of new restaurants were cited for mice on their first inspection. That had dropped to 22 percent in the first eighteen months. By the spring of 2012, the facilities featuring Tim's appeared to have largely turned the corner where restaurant ratings were concerned. How much business had suffered in the meantime in trying to establish the brand in New York City is a good question. A survey conducted for the city indicated that almost 80 percent of restaurant-goers paid attention to the letter grades.

My visit to the outlet at Thirty-eighth and Sixth was my first look at a Tim Hortons reconceptualized for a Riese food court. Give Riese its due: every food court I visited placed Tim Hortons closest to the door. A small Tim's counter displayed a selection of doughnuts and muffins and offered breakfast sandwiches, but no lunch menu. Next to it, an Original Soupman set-up was selling soup and sandwiches, and on the end wall a Tasti D-Lite handled desserts. These three counter-service mini-outlets shared an interior with three tables totalling twelve chairs and two window counters with stool seating; there was also a sheltered patio area out front. Looking in two directions, there was solid competition: the Pret across Sixth Avenue, on the northeast corner; and across Thirty-eighth, to the south, Bryant Market, with salads and sandwiches on offer.

The Riese Organization was attracted to Tim Hortons because of its ability to plug a hole in the QSR breakfast and lunch day parts. But Dunkin', with which the Riese Organization had so rancorously split, had also shifted in the direction of breakfast with its own sandwiches, and was about to take its coffee offerings up a notch with the Seattle's Best brand from Starbucks.

In war, victory often depends on who gets to choose the field of battle. For Tim Hortons, moving into Manhattan has meant confronting its competitors on what, for them, is comparatively secure, high ground, a strategic disadvantage it faces in making inroads into some other U.S. markets. Tim Hortons' broad menu makes enemies of a multitude of independent and chain operations, and the most prominent brands, like Dunkin', Starbucks, Subway and McDonald's, were well established with extensive outlets, and still growing. It has also meant confronting the entrenched positions of popular local enterprises, when many New Yorkers have been rebelling against the proliferation of national-brand chains in their neighbourhoods. Midtown Manhattan is full of coffee shops, bake shops, sandwich shops and combinations thereof. In addition to the aforementioned Pret A Manger, the café–bake shop chain Au Bon Pain has almost fifty locations around New York City, many of them in airports and subway and ferry locations, and in institutions like hospitals and universities.

On the beverages side, Starbucks is the chain coffee king, but above and beyond the many independent cafés and coffee shops, Manhattan has been witnessing the arrival of strong new players with their own aspirations for conquering more of urban America. The Coffee Bean & Tea Leaf, a Los Angeles–based chain, opened its first New York outlet in the summer of 2011 on the east side of Broadway north of Thirty-ninth, on Golda Meir Square. And there is Argo Tea out of Chicago, which has opened six outlets in Manhattan. Like Pret, it is a private-equity chain, without franchises. They have similar urban-trendy target markets, play up their corporate virtues, and not surprisingly have deployed similar game plans in the United States: avoid the burbs, stay true to store formats and conquer one major urban centre at a time. Argo Tea has established outlets in New York, Boston and St. Louis. Pret has crossed the pond from England to open outlets in New York, Chicago and Washington.

To the Queen's distinguished professor of marketing Ken Wong, Tim Hortons' recent performance in the U.S. appeared symptomatic of a company that has gone public and is under pressure to constantly post higher numbers for revenue and earnings, which for a franchise-based operation means constant geographic growth. He thought the entry into New York City had been "less a planned assault, like that of other foreign competitors, than acting on an opportunity." He was thinking in particular of Pret, which has stayed true to its basic store format, whereas Tim Hortons agreed to scale down to Riese food-court size.

One wonders if Tim Hortons, having dared to tackle Manhattan in a format that so compromises its proven store formats and full-menu offering, has a chance of establishing itself as a café/coffee-and-bake-shop concept in this overheated competitive environment. Panera Bread, with a bakery-café concept offering soups, sandwiches and baked goods, avoided Manhattan entirely, instead establishing twenty outlets within seventeen miles of New York City's commercial core. In 2010 it was ranked first in customer satisfaction among QSR chains in the New York area by J.D. Power. (In June 2011, Panera's executive vice-president and chief concept officer, Scott Davis, received the MenuMasters Innovator Award from the National Restaurant Association, which saluted Panera for being "one of the first chains to pioneer fast casual with upscale sandwiches and salads in a higher-end setting.") Only when Panera was well established in the surrounding terrain did it open its first Manhattan outlet, in February 2012.

Whether it likes it or not, Tim Hortons is locked in a head-to-head struggle with Dunkin' in the U.S. A large part of this is media perception: however much Tim Hortons might be trying to rebrand itself as a café/coffee and bake shop, the press is wont to see it as a doughnut store invading from the Great White North. When Tim Hortons started operating in Nassau Coliseum, home of the New York Islanders, in fall 2010, the *Long Island Press* opened its story with "Watch out Dunkin' Donuts: The Canadians are coming." *The New York Times* announced on July 9, 2009, the imminent arrival of Tim Hortons in Manhattan with the headline "Let the Doughnut Wars Begin," explaining that Riese "is ending its affiliation with Dunkin' Donuts and hoping it can make more money with a chain named after a dead hockey player." The press didn't care about the breakfast sandwiches, and precious little about the coffee. This was a food fight in which Tim Hortons' Timbits were going up against Dunkin's Munchkins.

Given that Tim Hortons accepted its role in the Riese system, with reduced menus and compact outlets in food courts that often focus on a display case of baked goods, it's hard to shoot the messenger when media outlets don't portray the chain as an up-market café. Tim Hortons is not competing in New York on the same playing field as Au Bon Pain or Pret A Manger where lunch-menu cafés are concerned. Nor is Tim Hortons projecting an upscale urban ambiance like Pret, The Coffee Bean, Starbucks or Argo Tea, as it rubs shoulders with the Soupman, KFC, Tasti D-Lite, Pizza Hut and Nathan's Famous in the Riese food-court portfolio. For the savvy Riese Organization, Tim Hortons presented the right product mix to plug the gap in its Dunkin'

Donuts vacancies. For Tim Hortons, Riese was an experienced franchise operator that could provide instant access to Manhattan locations. Riese also appeared to work hard to promote the new brand. In addition to giving Tim's prime positions in the food courts, in September 2009 Riese sent employees (some dressed as coffee cups) onto the streets of Manhattan to give away 7,000 gift cards worth $5 each. But the question remains: At what price to the Tim Hortons brand position and overall up-market strategy has the company tried to take Manhattan?

FOR TIM HORTONS, Manhattan provides a perturbing parallel with the Bess Eaton misadventure in Rhode Island and Connecticut: instead of simply moving into new locations, it was displacing a brand in the same category. In the New England case, it was a local chain called Bess Eaton, and securing the outlets of a doomed chain involved a battle with Dunkin's franchisees and ultimately a struggle for market share with Dunkin' that Tim Hortons could not win. It's possible that Tim Hortons' devastating success against Dunkin' in Quebec made it overconfident of its prospects against Dunkin' in New York City and New England; it's also possible that Dunkin' learned dearly from its Quebec drubbing and was better prepared to withstand the Timmy Ho juggernaut on its home turf. Indeed, in his 2012 ruling that Dunkin' had failed to protect market share for Quebec franchisees, Judge Tingley cited Dunkin's subsequent ability to "contain" Tim Hortons in New England as evidence that it should have been capable of doing so in Quebec.

The Bess Eaton chain (whose name punned on "best eating") was a New England phenomenon run by the fractious and mutually litigious Gencarelli family for fifty years. When the chain fell into bankruptcy in early 2004, Tim Hortons—still part of Wendy's International—struck a tentative deal of $35.5 million for forty-two of the chain's forty-eight outlets. Of that price, nearly $15 million would go to satisfying Bess Eaton's creditors, and another $14 million would cover owner Louis Gencarelli's personal debts. But when a U.S. bankruptcy court decided to open the assets to competitive bidding, a group of fourteen Dunkin's franchisees came forward with an offer of $36 million on April 21, 2004. Tim Hortons carried the day with a final offer of $42 million in a bankruptcy court auction on April 23.

In moving into the former Bess Eaton outlets, Tim Hortons had to displace consumer memories of the venerable Bess Eaton (which included idiosyncratic biblical quotes placed on cups by its born-again owner) while also contending with Dunkin's overwhelming dominance of the New England market. In late 2008, Tim's resolved to close eleven of those outlets, ten of which had been company-operated, recording $21.3 million in closure costs and asset impairment charges. In October 2010, Tim's lowered the boom on the entire Bess Eaton–related New England gambit. Another thirty-six outlets, as well as eighteen kiosks it had opened at gas stations, were shuttered around Hartford, Connecticut, and Providence, Rhode Island, along with two stores in Portland, Maine. The company said it had lost $4.4 million running these outlets over the past year, and was taking total closure and asset impairment costs of $28.3 million. Apart from Maine, Tim's was pulling out of New England entirely. In September 2011, a group of Dunkin's franchisees bought sixteen of the abandoned restaurants from Tim Hortons, with plans to convert five to Dunkin' outlets and lease out the others to non-competing businesses.

When Tim's moved into the former Bess Eaton stores, the displaced brand of doughnut shops was at least doomed, but when Tim's agreed to have Riese swap over its Dunkin's outlets in Manhattan over the course of a July 2009 weekend, loyal Dunkin' customers suddenly discovered that their daily Dunkin' fix had been replaced by a Canadian import they had largely never heard of. Tim's was at once behind the eight ball on two measures of consumer brand loyalty: one to Dunkin', the other to America. Customers had not only been suddenly deprived of their Dunkin' baked goods, they were being deprived in favour of a *foreign* doughnut chain.

Tim's has been trying to have it both ways in its North American marketing: a proud Canadian company and cultural icon at home, but an American company south of the border. The American cups tell you right below the logo that the coffee is "Roasted in Rochester, NY." The fact that the U.S. headquarters are in the Columbus suburb of Dublin has encouraged Tim's to position its java locally as "Hometown Coffee." A May 11, 2011, press release for a store opening included a quote attributed to Mike Meilleur, senior vice-president: "We're thrilled to bring Columbus' Hometown Coffee to those who live, work, and visit downtown Columbus."

The sleeve on my cup in New York City mentioned that Tim Horton had played for the NHL's New York Rangers and Buffalo Sabres, saying nothing about his nineteen seasons with the Toronto Maple Leafs. But in New York City, neither customers nor media were buying the American angle. Tim's was a Canadian import, straight out of the land of lumberjacks and dangerous wildlife. In a *New York Times* article a few days before the chain breached New York, an Ottawa tourist was quoted explaining the appeal of Tim's back home, in what seemed like a mischievous freelance variation on Rick Mercer's *Talking to Americans:* "When you're crossing the prairie and going through bear-infested territory, Tim's is your friend."

Tim's did find a devoted following for its iced capps; the prospect of them showing up in New York was one of the enthusiasms more consistently expressed online. (The other aspect of Tim's that excited people was things maple flavoured, especially maple-dip doughnuts.) By and large, though, the response of New Yorkers to Tim Hortons as the media reported it (beyond the ranks of expat Canadians) was middling to poor. *The New York Times* called the coffee "serviceable though not particularly distinctive," and the bagels "pallid"—this, after all, is a major bagel town—and it implied the doughnuts were nothing special. In a nod to the parbaking controversy that had erupted in Canada, the paper said Tim's doughnuts were "not exactly what they once were there, either." To be sure, Manhattan wasn't looking to a foreign chain operation to rescue it from some deficit of quality baked goods. From-scratch bakeries abound in Manhattan, and the doughnut is something of an art form. You can pay three dollars for just one at a number of gourmet bakeries.

Blogger Krista Garcia at newyork.seriouseats.com panned the Canadian company's effort in July 2010, a year after its arrival: "Some international chains seamlessly adapt to New York City; others botch the spirit of the hometown original. Canadian doughnut shop Tim Hortons has always been a fun pit stop when travelling north of the border, but after underwhelming experiences in both Brooklyn *and* Manhattan, I'm sad to report that this franchise falls into the latter camp."

Garcia criticized the lack of menu items and seating as compared to Canadian outlets, and a poor selection of product. Of the Brooklyn outlet she reported: "On a Sunday afternoon, the glass display case was alarmingly barren with only a few ancient chocolate-glazed specimens holding ground on the bottom rack. Strike out." She found the outlet next door to the Hotel Pennsylvania, across from Penn Station, disappointing. This outlet occupies one of the tiniest spaces in which I've ever seen a Tim's. "They did have a better, albeit limited, selection compared to the Brooklyn branch," she reported, "but oddly, the famous Timbits, or doughnut holes, were nowhere to be seen. Company literature states that a minimum of eight varieties will be offered at all locations."

Garcia had hit upon something crucial about Tim Hortons' foray into the Big Apple. Some Americans knew Tim's from trips north, and they wanted the real thing, not a denatured version with a different logo and a limited choice of offerings. (A Californian in May 2012 sang the praises of a Victoria, B.C., outlet on the rating website Yelp, declaring, "Each time I visit the Great White North, this pilgrim walks the Camino de Hortonago to Tim's.") In coming to New York, Tim's might have brought Tim Horton the hockey player with it, but it had left Canada behind. What some people seemed to crave was the Tim's they already knew from elsewhere. Adapting the brand to Manhattan had created a Tim's I did not recognize. The coffee tasted the same, but the essential flavour of Tim's was gone.

20

Going Big, or Going Home: The Struggle for American Market Share

Whether or not Tim Hortons' Manhattan gambit goes the way of the New England misadventure, the company must resolve essential problems in the U.S. The company, as franchisor, has been unprofitable for the most part in the U.S. since the IPO in 2006.

Some hope began to shine through the historically discouraging American numbers at the end of fiscal 2011. There was solid annual same-store sales growth in the U.S. of 6.3 percent, including 7.2 percent in the fourth quarter, its strongest since the IPO (versus a healthy 5.5 percent for Canada for the year and 4 percent for the fourth quarter). The U.S. also turned a $15.1 million profit for 2011, as Tim's opened 114 more locations there. The improvement continued in the first quarter of 2012, when same-store sales increased 8.5 percent over the same quarter in 2011.

Still, the average standard restaurant in the U.S. only pulls in about half the revenue of a Canadian counterpart: $1.06 million versus $2.13 million (all Canadian dollars) in fiscal 2011. Non-standard restaurants (not including self-serve kiosks) similarly lag in the U.S., doing about $447,000, compared with $870,000 in Canada. Average sales at non-standard U.S. stores have been flat since 2008 (as measured in U.S. dollars), whereas they've increased 16 percent in Canada. According to figures in a 2010 investor conference presentation, American stores that break through the $1 million sales threshold are nicely profitable. But where the million-plus store has a pretax operating margin of 13.1 percent (after management-in-labour costs of 4.3 percent), an emerging-market store is negative by 2.3 percent (after management-in-labour costs of 4.6 percent).

In 2006, 19 percent of Tim Hortons' 336 U.S. outlets were corporate. As part of its expansion plans, in 2008 and 2009 the company converted virtually all of its existing corporate stores to franchise (owner or operator) outlets, and along the way the number of outlets has more than doubled. The resulting average U.S. standard-format franchise is said to be profitable, despite much lower revenues than an average Canadian store, but the "emerging market" U.S. store franchises have needed a lot of help to keep the heads of franchisees above water.

To attract franchisees, Tim's offered new owners (not 80/20 operators) a franchise incentive program (FIP) with interest-free loans for "equipment packages"—equipment, furniture, trade fixtures and signage—and gave them a 104-week holiday before payments had to start. Franchises granted FIPs also didn't have to remit the rent and royalty fees. This assistance, the 2011 annual report explained, was part of the "additional relief and assistance to restaurant owners in developing markets in the U.S. where the brand is not yet established and the restaurants have lower sales levels. This additional relief may include assistance with costs of supplies, certain operating expenses, including rents and royalties, and, in certain markets, labour and other costs."

At year-end 2011, 88 percent of the FIP notes were past due. The gross value of notes more than ninety days past due was almost $20 million. While the outstanding notes were collateralized by the restaurants and equipment, the company set aside $2 million as an allowance for FIP notes it considered impaired, up from $265,000 the previous year.

The company says almost 99 percent of U.S. outlets are franchised, but 165 are "variable interest entity" (VIE) outlets, in which the franchise owner has little to no equity interest, either because the store is an 80/20 or an FIP agreement is in effect. At the same time, Tim Hortons was getting out of the business of lending new U.S. franchisees interest-free money that most plan participants were having trouble paying back, and instead would rely on contracting operators to run new stores. The company has allowed that in fiscal 2011, "we began entering into operator [80/20] agreements more frequently than full franchise agreements when opening new restaurants" in the U.S. The particular reliance on 80/20s in the U.S. underscores the fact that the emerging-market American stores are a risky proposition for franchisee capital. The rise of VIEs in the Tim Hortons system is also proving costly for the franchisor. The company noted in its first-quarter 2012 results that an increased number of VIEs meant rent and royalty growth was 7.4 percent, when it otherwise would have been 9.1 percent. Cost of sales also grew 15.7 percent in the quarter, which the company said was "primarily due to higher distribution cost of sales and higher cost of sales from VIEs."

Tim Hortons is probably doing better in core U.S. markets than its own general figures have said; the 2010 fiscal numbers, for one, included the poor-performing New England outlets it shut down that fall. Those shutdowns helped increase subsequent revenues in rents and royalties because of lower overall relief costs for struggling outlets. Analyst Kenric Tyghe, who was otherwise quite critical of the company's recent performance, told me in the fall of 2011 that he thought the border-area franchises around Buffalo and Detroit were doing well. Still, franchisees of growth-market stores have been kept afloat through a variety of corporate assistance programs that ultimately require profits to be redirected mainly from Canadian operations, and also have required investors to be patient. Another concern is that if the company becomes too focused on resolving its

American challenges, it could take its eye off the considerable competitive challenges emerging in Canada, which in 2011 accounted for about 94 percent of reportable segment revenue and about 98 percent of operating income therefrom.

As New York City demonstrates in one capsule view, America is crowded with fierce competition among chains, and boasts a near-infinite variety of them, in addition to thriving independents. In *QSR* magazine's 2011 Top 50 rankings (admittedly based on 2009 sales), Tim Hortons squeaked in at number 49, behind its co-branding partner Cold Stone Creamery, at 47, and just ahead of Einstein Bros Bagels, a rising player. McDonald's utterly dominated the rankings with $31 billion in U.S. sales, three times the revenues of the nearest competitor, Subway, at $10 billion. Tim Hortons ($410 million) ranked fifth in "snack" brands, with the giants Starbucks ($8.4 billion) and Dunkin' ($5.7 billion) first and second respectively, Dunkin's co-brand Baskin-Robbins ($570 million) third, and Tim Hortons' co-brand Cold Stone Creamery ($430 million) fourth. One positive is that despite its corporate-support challenges for stores in new markets, Tim Hortons already led the other snack brands in average unit store sales—$957,000 versus $952,000 for Starbucks and $820,000 for Dunkin'.

Tim's nevertheless is hard pressed to find American markets not already crowded with major competitors, who have much bigger promotion budgets, better brand recognition and loyalty, are tinkering with their offerings and are conducting their own expansions, along with refurbishings of existing outlets. And for all its efforts to redefine itself as a café/bake shop, Tim Hortons in the U.S. appears locked in a consumer brand-recognition struggle not with Starbucks or Panera Bread, but with Dunkin' Donuts, the nation's favourite coffee-and-doughnut purveyor.

In February 2012, the consulting firm Brand Keys released its sixteenth annual "customer loyalty engagement index" based on a survey of 49,000 American consumers. Dunkin' topped the coffee purveyors ranking for the sixth year in a row, and also tied with Starbucks atop the home-brewed coffee ranking, while finishing second in the overall restaurant category. Tim Hortons failed to register in any category except coffee, where it ranked fourth, behind Dunkin', Starbucks and McDonald's. The fact that Tim's even made the coffee rankings may be a good sign: fourth is certainly better than nothing when you're a strictly regional player and your own 2011 annual report concedes of U.S. operations: "We still have limited brand awareness, even in many areas where we have a presence."

Like Dunkin' Donuts, which has been co-branding outlets with Baskin-Robbins (which is also owned by Dunkin' Brands), Tim's has chosen to co-brand with an ice cream parlour, Cold Stone Creamery. Cold Stone's average unit sales outperform Baskin-Robbins, and analysts have been hopeful that the typical strong performances of Cold Stone outlets could increase overall revenues in co-branded U.S. Tim Hortons stores, allowing franchisees to increase or even achieve profitability. But Cold Stone will not change the profit picture overnight: of seventy-two standard or non-standard restaurants opened in the U.S. in 2011, only nineteen were co-branded Cold Stone outlets, bringing the total co-branded outlets south of the border to ninety-nine. And although Tim Hortons' same-store sales showed promising growth in the U.S. in 2011, the company allowed that this growth was mainly due to the improving performance of its top outlets, as opposed to across the system. The good stores (some of them aided by Cold Stone) are getting better; the weak stores in "emerging markets," not so much. The company's U.S. growth focus has shifted to infilling areas where it is established and giving these core regions marketing support. Don't expect Tim Hortons to make a leap into Phoenix or even Minneapolis anytime soon.

Whether co-branding with an ice cream parlour is the best strategy for a coffee/bake shop remains to be seen. In Tim Hortons' case, CEO Paul House indicated in the February 23, 2012, conference call with analysts following the release of fourth-quarter and year-end 2011 results that co-branding was no longer a driver of U.S. expansion. Jim Durran of Barclays Capital asked if Cold Stone's role in new-store growth is "fairly done at this point in the U.S." House replied: "Done. It's a select type of thing that we will do strategically wherever it makes sense. Our main thrust is Tim Hortons and Tim Horton locations. If Cold Stone happens to play, then that's great."

In Dunkin's case, it inherited the ice cream through its history of corporate takeovers that began with British food and hospitality conglomerate J. Lyons & Co., which operated a chain of eponymous tea room/bakeries once as ubiquitous in England as Tim Hortons is in Canada. Pumped with American investment capital, it went shopping for assets stateside. In 1972 it bought DCA (Doughnut Corporation of America), which had a near lock on doughnut-making machinery and also produced mixes. Baskin-Robbins (which had arrived in Canada in 1971 through a master franchise agreement with Silverwood Dairies) was then acquired in 1973. After struggling financially, J. Lyons was swallowed in 1978 by Britain's Allied Breweries, which became Allied-Lyons.

Dunkin' and Baskin-Robbins might never have become a co-branded entity that in turn inspired Tim Hortons to co-brand with Cold Stone Creamery were it not for a hostile bid for Dunkin' launched in 1989 by Toronto businessman George Mann through Kingsbridge Capital, which had amassed 6.5 percent of its stock. When Dunkin's management and its powerful franchisees rejected Kingsbridge's $272 million offer of $42 a share (and Dunkin' adopted a poison-pill defence), Kingsbridge enlisted Cara Operations as a partner and took the offer to $43 a share, or $278 million. Under the revised Canadian proposal, Cara would operate the 1,455-unit Dunkin' chain.

Had the Kingsbridge-Cara bid been successful, the future might have turned out very different for Tim Hortons, as Dunkin' would have entered the portfolio of an experienced Canadian chain restaurateur that was already operating Harvey's and Swiss Chalet and would have pushed for franchise growth beyond Quebec, the one Canadian market where Dunkin' had a reasonable toehold. But the actual circumstances of the deal are cloudy. Dunkin's chair and co-founder, Bob Rosenberg, suspected Tim Hortons was involved somehow, according to Ron Joyce's memoir. Joyce also wrote that he personally held shares in Dunkin', but had no prior knowledge of the Kingsbridge-Cara offer. The offer in any case was fended off, as Dunkin' found a white-knight buyer in Allied-Lyons. As it already owned Baskin-Robbins, Allied-Lyons stuck the doughnuts and the ice cream in one operating unit, Dunkin' Brands. According to Joyce, Allied-Lyons also made overtures about buying Tim Hortons.

The corporate migrations of Dunkin' and Baskin-Robbins were not over. In 1994, Allied-Lyons merged with the sherry and brandy producer Pedro Domecq and became Allied Domecq, headquartered in Bristol, England. In 2005, the French beverage giant Pernod Ricard swallowed Allied Domecq. Pernod Ricard had already bought the beverage assets of the venerable Canadian distillery, Seagram, in 2000, after the Montreal-based company made a disastrous diversification into entertainment and chemicals. As well, Pernod Ricard now owned the former Hiram Walker of Canada, which Allied-Lyons had swallowed in 1986. In order to pay down the debts of the acquisition and focus on the drinks business, Pernod Ricard off-loaded overlapping alcohol brands and opened bidding on Dunkin' Brands, which by then included a California soup/sandwich/salad chain called Togo's.

In December 2005, a trio of American private-equity firms, Bain Capital Partners, the Carlyle Group and Thomas H. Lee Partners, agreed to buy Dunkin' Brands for $2.425 billion in cash, in a highly leveraged deal that was finalized in early 2006. Dunkin' Brands by then consisted of more than 6,500 Dunkin' Donuts outlets in twenty-nine countries, more than 5,600 Baskin-Robbins outlets in thirty-four countries, and more than 350 Togo's restaurants in the U.S.

The new private-equity owners launched an aggressive expansion of Dunkin', both domestically and globally, in restaurants and menu items. In July 2011, Dunkin' again went public with a share issue on the Nasdaq exchange that raised a $423 million war chest. In the ensuing turf war to establish American outlets, Tim's keeps making headlines as a Dunkin' rival—not only in the failed New England expansion and in the takeover of the Riese Organization's Dunkin' outlets in Manhattan, but in places like Columbus, Ohio, where Tim's wrested away a prime downtown location at Broad and High streets in 2011 after the landlord evicted a Dunkin' franchisee who in turn was being sued by Dunkin' to terminate the franchise agreement. Dunkin's for its part has declared its intention to consolidate its dominance of its core New England territory before making a serious westward push.

Being locked into a brand war with Dunkin' may not be in Tim Hortons' best interest if it wants to move up-market, in the direction of the likes of Panera Bread, while retaining its "value pricing" reputation. Dunkin' is under its own growth pressures from whip-cracking analysts and shareholders after the IPO, and Tim's has generally been looked on far more favourably by both Wall Street and Bay Street. Analysts have been impressed by Tim Hortons' low corporate debt–equity ratios, cash flow, return on capital investment and increasing dividend payouts, and its consistent ability to increase same store sales in defiance of economic downturns as well as a recent spike in global coffee prices. At times, Tim's has been proclaimed the best QSR stock buy in the U.S.

Both Tim's and Dunkin' have been trying to outgrow their coffee-and-doughnut images. Dunkin' has added espresso drinks, a Coolatta line of frozen drinks, the Seattle's Best brand of coffee from Starbucks, chicken salad sandwiches, flatbread sandwiches and breakfast sandwiches. Tim's in turn has been chasing Dunkin' in the U.S. with frozen lemonade, along with its established iced capps to counter the Coolatta line. There is constant pressure on these chains to introduce new product, and Tim's rolls out around twenty to twenty-four new offerings a year.

Dunkin' needs to push into the American Midwest if it is going to live up to its expansion hopes. If it beats Tim's there, the Canadian company may find itself hemmed in around the Ontario border regions. The Midwest already has a strong regional competitor with big aspirations: Minneapolis-based Caribou Coffee, which was founded in 1992 and trades on the Nasdaq. In 2008, it hired as its president and CEO Michael Tattersfield, the former COO and vice-president of the yogawear phenomenon Lululemon Athletica.

Caribou did not start franchising until 2004 and now has about 150 of its more than 500 outlets (including kiosks) franchised. More than 200 Caribou outlets are in Minnesota, and around 120 are in Illinois, Wisconsin, Michigan and Ohio. "It's very good," an American friend assures me. "Very Minnesota-nice. Like Starbucks, but with a homey, Midwest, Pottery Barn kind of feel." She gave me a bag of Caribou's Rainforest Alliance–certified Sidamo beans, whose tag promised "organic, natural processed Ethiopian coffee." It brewed up nicely. In 2011, Caribou was the only U.S. food-service company to earn one of forty J.D. Power awards for "achieving excellence in customer service."

Caribou's growth-strategy playbook for its "lodge-like" coffee houses—hot meals, inviting interiors, kiosk outlets and an increasing diversity of hot and cold specialty drinks—is much like the one Tim Hortons is following for the U.S. market. Caribou also signed a master franchise licensing agreement for up to 250 outlets in twelve Middle Eastern countries in 2004. Sixty-nine had been opened, as well as six in South Korea, by 2010. Tim Hortons only announced in 2011 a master franchise agreement of its own for up to 120 outlets in the Arab Gulf States, and had opened five by year-end. (Canada's Second Cup, for that matter, had opened its first international regional franchise, in Dubai, in 2003, and now has a presence in sixteen countries, most of them in the Middle East.)

Tim Hortons' American expansion has been unfolding much differently from its incremental, sequential growth in Canada. Tim's was long established in Canadian suburbia, with its standard format of a sit-down restaurant with parking and drive-throughs, when it started diversifying into other formats and locations. It was able to introduce self-service kiosks and drive-through-only outlets because the brand's reputation and product were well established among a customer base that was prepared to accept a different outlet experience, provided it satisfied convenience without compromising product quality. Tim's similarly was able to wait to enter the downtown Toronto market until relatively late in its history, introducing walk-in storefront outlets after establishing the brand in the suburbs. Tim's followed its suburban customers to their white-collar places of work, and in the process found more customers among urbanites.

In the U.S., Tim's has been willing to try everything, all at once, going into new markets with self-serve kiosks before it has standard stores in order to increase brand awareness, and developing institutional locations in parallel to traditional outlets, where in Canada the institutional market was a later development that built on existing brand awareness. Almost one in four U.S. outlets in 2011 was a kiosk, and the company allowed they "contribute minimally to systemwide sales and operating earnings."

One criticism of its U.S. strategy is that using down-market self-serve kiosks to increase brand awareness is no way to introduce a premium brand. The use of such kiosks in gas stations, with self-serve doughnuts in a display case, has been cited as a contributor to the company's failed New England gambit. Tim Hortons' number-four ranking among coffee purveyors in the 2012 Brand Keys survey may be telling us that more Americans are becoming aware of Tim Hortons coffee in part because of the kiosk initiative, but unfortunately are thinking less of it than Dunkin', Starbucks and McDonald's. Still, it was ahead of Caribou, which bodes well for it.

Tim's has made known its willingness to tinker with its format in breaching new markets. In New York, Tim's tried to take the brand into a new territory with food-court outlets, and without the benefit of a suburban beachhead of the full-menu, drive-in and drive-through restaurants that made the company's reputation in Canada.

Securing Riese locations near Grand Central Terminal and in and around Penn Station did place the company's product within ready reach of millions of commuters and travellers. I visited the Tim's on the Long Island Rail Road (LIRR) level of Penn Station, one of four close at hand. (Other Tim Hortons were on the Amtrak level at Penn Station, the taxi stand at Madison Square Garden and across the road at the tiny outlet next door to the Hotel Pennsylvania.) It was in a 12,500-square-foot Riese food court that Riese had renovated in 2009. Riese had placed Tim's in a prime position, the first counter in a grouping with Taco Bell Express and Colombo Frozen Yogurt.

Penn Station is an uninviting subterranean labyrinth beneath Madison Square Garden, but it is also an unavoidable experience for hundreds of thousands of commuters. LIRR is North America's busiest commuter railroad, with about 280,000 riders per weekday on the system. Tim's may be able to sell coffee and breakfast sandwiches to those Long Island commuters at Penn Station, but when they are back home, there is as yet no way for them to shift their brand allegiance from other coffee and baked goods purveyors. Dunkin' especially dominates the suburbs that feed commuters into the Big Apple. Long Island is saturated with Dunkin' outlets. Tim Hortons has no presence in Long Island (save inside Nassau Coliseum) or suburban New Jersey. Its nearest restaurant in New York State is seventy-five miles north, in Albany.

Tim Hortons' Manhattan incursion of 2009 was marooned by the decision to abandon the southern New England market in October 2010 as the Bess Eaton takeover failed. The Manhattan outlets of Riese—above all, the ones in and around Penn Station—became a hub without any complementary sales points at the end of the commuter spokes, and no prospects for those spokes to connect to suburban outlets any time soon.

A year after arriving in New York City, its U.S. operations declared a goal of going up-market in image and service with a new format it began testing in Ohio and elsewhere. Tim Hortons' presence in the Big Apple has shrunk since then. Established competitors (Dunkin' included), already larger, have continued to expand, while emerging competitors have secured excellent locations with enough floor area to offer a diverse menu and an up-market experience.

I came away from New York disappointed that Tim's had not arrived in the city with a strategy as bold as that of other newcomers. Despite the high price of Manhattan real estate, new concepts like Argo Tea and Pret (and the start of a chain presence for the Coffee Bean & Tea Leaf) have been able to establish themselves rapidly with strong locations. Tim's has shown in Toronto and other Canadian cities that it can do urban locations, as storefronts with seating and without parking or a drive-through. I thought of Cam MacDonald's outlet, in a former bank in the heart of Greektown, as I flew home, and wondered what Tim's could accomplish, and could yet accomplish, if it set its mind to transplanting that experience into the Fashion District, instead of muddying its brand image with food-court outlets and a confusing signage change that promised it was a coffee and bake shop but was actually little more than a service counter next to a counter-sized KFC or Soupman.

Tim's, I thought, can do better. On the other hand, maybe a Riese food court is the best it is ever going to do in pricey Manhattan if it stays with its value-pricing image. (The stand-alone outlets Riese tried opening are among those that closed.) Pret sells individual sandwiches for as much as six dollars; at Argo Tea, I bought a fruity iced-tea concoction that cost more than four dollars. Such menu pricing is anathema to Tim Hortons' price-point strategy (and its average cheque of

$3.00 to $3.75 in 2011, depending on region and store type), but without a decent revenue stream, a restaurant model won't work in Manhattan. Something has to give, and with Tim's, it was the full-menu, stand-alone restaurant package.

In the U.S., Ken Wong advised, "you either go appropriately big, or you go home." There's nothing wrong with being a strong regional competitor, he suggested, and knowing one's geographic limits.

At the time of my Manhattan visit, American analysts were fairly bullish on Tim Hortons stock. A research note to investors by equities research analysts at Bank of America Merrill Lynch on September 7 had reiterated a "buy" rating. On the Motley Fool website on September 13, Dan Caplinger wrote an article called "How the Wrong Stocks Can Get You in Trouble," comparing a basket of equities with a price–earnings ratio of around 12. His table indicated Tim Hortons (12.1) had shown the best growth trajectory among them in price change over fifty-two weeks and in earnings per share over three years.

Writing about the shocking collapse of Nortel in my book *The Bubble and the Bear,* however, has probably scarred me for life where enthusiasm for hot stocks is concerned. Tim Hortons is no Nortel, but I have developed a healthy respect for contrarian voices. At the least, they inject necessary caution into potentially runaway enthusiasm, and they need to be listened to, especially whenever the consensus of the Street threatens to move in herdlike optimism. Analyst Kenric Tyghe of Raymond James in Toronto, for one, was fairly unsparing in his criticism of Tim Hortons, and in its U.S. operations especially, on my return from New York. "I think that the Street is giving them way too much credit for that business," he said to me of other analysts' enthusiasm for the stock, based on U.S. prospects for growth and profitability. "To a fault, the management team all seems hopeful. They labour under the illusion they're running a North American business. They're not. They're a Canadian business, a Canadian icon, that is increasingly under threat from McDonald's." Six months later, though, the bullish Tim Hortons investors had been rewarded, at least in the short term. A stock that had been trading around $46 during my New York visit was approaching $60 the following spring. The P/E, however, had almost doubled. When the company missed the consensus earnings estimate of 59 cents a share by three cents with its first-quarter 2012 results, the price immediately backed off a few dollars. Still, the company had posted an 8.5 percent increase in U.S. same-store sales over the same quarter in 2011.

Tim Hortons is a long way from succumbing to the irrational exuberance that had swept up Nortel executives, investors and analysts en route to a stunning comeuppance. And the cash-based nature of the restaurant biz is far more reassuring to investors of the fact that customers really have been spending ever-increasing amounts of money every quarter, and the company continues to impress by meeting fundamental growth objectives. Maybe the foray into New York City can be categorized as an episode of irrational exuberance by a Canadian company whose U.S. growth opportunities lie elsewhere. In announcing its first-quarter 2012 results, Tim Hortons attributed its strengthening numbers in U.S. sales to its decision to allocate the majority of restaurant development capital to "core growth markets." Arriving in New York City may have been heralded by the company as a milestone achievement in 2009, but in 2012 it could no longer be imagined as key frontier of expansion.

When I returned home from New York City, it seemed that I had only partly grasped the struggle for growth and market share. Yes, franchise companies like Tim's are expected to conquer new territories in order to drive revenues and profits, and the pressure to do so is especially acute when they're public companies and are beholden to the incessant growth demands of the Street. But there was another struggle going on within the QSR industry, and it was taking place on a different topography. The quest for more customers had turned inward, to the restaurant experience.

21

Ambiance Chasing: How QSR Chains Are Rediscovering the Importance of Their Interiors

By the summer of 2010, the Tim Hortons outlets in the Riese food courts of New York City were looking particularly out of synch with Tim's up-market café/bake shop plans for the rest of the United States. A new store format had entered testing in Dayton, Ohio, which featured coffee stations where staff would prepare beverages in a barista-like manner reminiscent of Starbucks, which was also a lot like the new McCafé concept that would be introduced to Canada. Tim's was hoping to combine a more intimate and upscale experience with the company's signature value pricing: looking more like a Starbucks wouldn't mean charging for drinks like a Starbucks.

"What we're trying to do is really dial up the in-store experience to call out that something different is going on here," David Clanachan, chief operating officer for U.S. and international markets, told *Nation's Restaurant News* in the summer of 2010. If the test marketing proved positive, Tim's planned to role out the concept across the U.S. In November 2011, Tim Hortons announced that new formats (including free Wi-Fi) also would be introduced to Canada, along with an expanded drink menu that included espressos and espresso-based lattes and mochas. True to its value-pricing strategy, an espresso at Tim's would cost about 40 percent less than one at Starbucks.

Canadian cultural theorists were still earnestly digesting the significance of the introduction of the beef lasagna casserole in October 2011 when they were left reeling by the announcement of fancy new beverages and the promise of a more upscale interior with free Wi-Fi. In his conference call with analysts following the release of third-quarter results in November 2011, CEO Paul House stressed that Tim Hortons' restaurant designs were undergoing an "evolution" rather than a wholesale change. "The restaurants we are building today are very different from the restaurants we built five years ago, and I suspect they will be very different five years from now, as well." But the promises of a "coffee theatre" (as trialled in the U.S.) where new espresso-based drinks would be prepared in a barista-style manner, naturally brought to mind Starbucks. How could Canada's beloved Timmy Ho's be transforming itself into Starbucks North?

Starbucks, for its part, was said to be fighting back when in January 2012 it introduced its "blonde roast," a mellower bean more akin to the Tim Hortons brew. Starbucks' concern about Tim's is debatable: it was mainly responding to long-standing criticism that its standard brew is over-roasted to the point of burnt, and the product was not aimed specifically at Tim's drinkers. If anything, it gave Starbucks another product for different palates in the increasingly lucrative grocery retail market. Still, the move came just as Tim's was topping Starbucks' twenty-ounce Venti cup by introducing the bladder-busting twenty-four-ounce extra-large cup in Canada. But it wasn't Starbucks that the new interior Tim Hortons concepts resembled, or that Tim Hortons needed to be worried about. It was McDonald's.

McDonald's in 2007 had begun a multiyear "Forever Young" refurbishing of its 1,400 Canadian stores from coast to coast. The design by Toronto's deSignum Interior Planning features grey and earth-tone colours, gas fireplaces, free Wi-Fi and flat-screen televisions, and also incorporates the McCafé coffee stations trialled in Canada in Burlington, Ontario, in May 2011. McDonald's made its own announcement of espresso for McCafé a week after Tim's said it was introducing its espresso drinks in Canada in November 2011.

McDonald's was spending $1 billion at the corporate level on the Canadian remodellings, and in the space of about two and a half years gave away an estimated 50 million cups of its improved arabica coffee in a quest to grab some of the commanding share that Tim's has, not only of coffee sales but of the breakfast day part in Canada. Tim's claimed to have 78 percent of restaurant coffee servings in the year leading up to November 2011, as well as 41 percent of all QSR orders. Its 2010 figures asserted a grip on 67 percent of QSR morning day-part traffic, compared with McDonald's 7 percent of restaurant coffee servings and 11 percent of morning day-part traffic. Tim's numbers formed a big, tasty target for competitors. And because Tim's has had the coffee market mostly to itself, its commanding position also means that when a QSR colossus like McDonald's decides it wants a much bigger piece of the Canadian coffee market, it only has to target one competitor, and fine-tune its product, its service and its marketing message accordingly. Like never before in its history, Tim Hortons is in the crosshairs of a multinational giant that wants as much of its market share as it can take.

"Until about five years ago," the Schulich School of Business's Alan Middleton noted for me, "Tim Horton's was in the 'all other' category of competitors for McDonald's. Then they realized Tim Hortons was bigger than they are."

Although it was true that QSRs across the board were getting into the premium coffee game, McDonald's was the one chain with the market presence, promotional budget and savvy to take a substantial piece of Tim Hortons' action. And McDonald's and Tim Hortons were moving almost in lockstep to expand beyond brewed coffee and adopt espresso-based products, even as their specialty sandwich menus were converging. Brewed coffee sales across the board were flatlining; specialty coffees held out the greatest promise of sales growth, but it was also possible they would cannibalize traditional brewed sales. Tim Hortons was already sending mixed financial signals about how it was doing. Its third-quarter 2011 results had shown impressive single-store sales growth: 4.7 percent in Canada and 6.3 percent in the U.S. But total transactions were down "moderately" in Canada, and it wasn't clear if this was because of price increases, persistent economic hard times or an erosion of the customer base, by McDonald's especially.

Analyst Kenric Tyghe thought McDonald's was posing a much more serious threat to Tim's dominant position in Canada than Tim's was ready to admit. "McDonald's is going to have 1,400 McCafé's in Canada by the end of the year," he reminded me in the fall of 2011. "That's a 50 percent overlap with Tim Hortons. Their new store designs feel like the new Tim Horton café and bake shop in the U.S." McDonald's, he said, "has done a much better job of refreshing."

Tim Hortons' fourth-quarter numbers for Canada were cause for investor relief. Despite the aggressive push by McDonald's with McCafé, Tim's reported 5.5 percent same-store sales growth over the same period in 2010, as well as "slightly positive same-store transactions growth." There was also an unspecified increase in the average cheque value. But it was too soon to say whether the performance indicated McDonald's was being held at bay, or Tim Hortons had benefited from factors other than customer loyalty to its coffee. As the company noted, milder weather had helped ordering. Pricing changes and the introduction of more expensive menu items like the beef lasagna casserole also contributed to the increased average cheque and revenues. And the sheer number of new products, including the lattes, probably contributed to the robust gains, as Timmy fans are renowned for trying at least once whatever the company introduces to the menu. The restaurant war was far from over.

*

THE MCDONALD'S AND TIM HORTONS remodellings are part of a renewed interest among QSRs in getting customers back into restaurants they had essentially pushed them out of with drive-through lanes and kiosks. By 2011, the North American industry was chock-full of restaurants—Burger King and White Castle, among others—trying to find a more grown-up, more welcoming interior ambiance.

While QSRs like Tim Hortons underwent a significant change in ambiance in moving from counter service to interior seating in the 1970s, the seismic shift came with the proliferation of drive-through windows. It is that shift from which QSRs like McDonald's and Tim Hortons are trying to recover with their recent interior reconceptions.

McDonald's opened its first drive-through restaurant in 1975, in Sierra Vista, California. The U.S. Army's Fort Huachuca is nearby, and McDonald's says the drive-through was created so military personnel would not have to leave their vehicles when ordering. It was the same year that the chain introduced the Egg McMuffin, starting decades of QSR migration toward the breakfast day part as other chains came around to recognizing the profit potential of opening early (if they weren't already, as in the case of round-the-clock Tim's) and selling an actual meal. No commuter meal is more hurried than breakfast, and the drive-through was the perfect delivery system. McDonald's did not invent the drive-through, but once the Golden Arches had combined it with a formidable menu of sandwiches and combos, eating on the fly was going to become normal behaviour for millions of North Americans.

When QSR was gripped by the profit possibilities of the drive-through window, the role of the restaurant as a provider of ambiance, as a gathering place and a point of interaction, was undermined, if not largely discarded. A drive-through is a much more efficient way to move product, and with innovations like kiosks, a chain like Tim Hortons could forgo providing the restaurant experience altogether where a location otherwise wouldn't permit one.

Tim's, of course, has never abandoned the traditional restaurant. At the same time that it was adopting drive-throughs, it was working ahead of the legislative curve in Canada to make interiors more welcoming by progressively eliminating smoking. The drive-through, in the meantime, allowed customers to get their Tim's fix without having to step inside a smoke-filled restaurant. But for QSRs in general, the rise of the drive-through meant years of diminished importance for interior space. In the café sector, it allowed independent operations and chain competitors like Starbucks and Canada's Second Cup to fill the ambiance/hospitality gap. These cafés became especially popular among a new generation of younger, urban customers who see a coffee break not as a Tim's run—a dash to and from a restaurant service counter—but rather as a respite from their hectic life, or a place of mellow atmosphere to connect with friends, co-workers and clients.

The most striking thing about Tim Hortons' television advertising in recent years is how the physical restaurant virtually disappeared. Actors have turned up in offices, in hotel lobbies, in cars, at cottages and on tennis courts consuming Tim Hortons' food and beverages; they've been shown on the way to or from a Tim Hortons hiding somewhere in the landscape. The actual restaurant has been rarely, if ever, seen, and the interior especially vanished. Tim Hortons, at least in its advertising message, had become a purveyor of specific foods that you ate elsewhere. This strategy was more akin to Subway and contrasted starkly with the consistent placement of actors inside restaurants by McDonald's and A&W of Canada. A new "Based on a True Story" television ad in October 2011, in which a young woman who has come to the big city meets with her parents inside an urban Tim Hortons, was notable for the use of a restaurant setting, which had gone missing but for a cameo appearance at the end of a summer ad for its Greek feta wrap, when the facade of an outlet was seen in the background in the closing moments.

Tim's was not selling its restaurants as a communal experience, a place of respite from the day's bustle. In Canada, Second Cup, Starbucks, Timothy's and independent cafés had been moved into that role with no television advertising at all. When Tim's began promoting its limited-offer $1 flavoured lattes in late January 2012, the actors were back to appearing everywhere but in a restaurant. But soon after that, a television ad promoting its specialty bagels sat the actors down in a restaurant booth in a way that immediately brought to mind the way McDonald's advertising has relentlessly focused on its interiors.

Given how central the automobile has become to Tim Hortons' marketing—far more cars have been seen in its recent advertising than restaurants—the company's original reluctance to embrace the drive-through is ironic, if understandable. The first outlet so equipped was a former Church's Chicken on Hamilton's East Mountain, at Fennell and Upper Gage. It already had a drive-through set-up when it was converted to a Tim's in 1985.

"We had trouble selling Mr. Joyce on it," franchisee Stew Galloway recalled for author Steve Penfold in *The Donut*. In *Always Fresh,* Joyce explained that he thought a drive-through was incompatible with the particular interactions between customer and product of a doughnut shop. "When customers entered our stores, the sights and smells of freshly made products was a sure trigger for impulse buying. A drive-thru window takes that away." He thought this was different with a doughnut shop than a burger or chicken restaurant. Paul House, Joyce wrote, was the one to argue strongly for drive-throughs, and Joyce was won over, to the point of becoming fascinated with their design and utility. Rather remarkably, House echoed the logic that Joyce had expressed some twenty-five years earlier when he explained in November 2011 why the chain was introducing more refined interiors to draw customers out of their cars into the restaurant: "A baked product is really, in some cases, an impulse buy, so if you're looking and you like what you see you're more likely to buy it."

Tim's was already strong in the breakfast day part because of its coffee and baked goods when it introduced drive-throughs, but it wouldn't have a breakfast sandwich until 2006, a menu feature that practically makes a drive-through lane a necessity in suburbia. What is noteworthy about the company's initial reaction to drive-throughs is that the issue was essentially transactional: Would customers still impulse buy if they didn't see the displays and smell the baked goods? It wasn't about customers walking in the door and *staying* in the restaurant to eat and drink whatever they bought. Yet diverting customers from the restaurant's seating areas has ultimately been the broad QSR impact of drive-throughs.

While much of Tim Hortons' sales growth and store-design diversification is due to the rise of the drive-through, it hollowed out Tim Hortons and many of its QSR competitors as customer experiences. If it's true that fewer and fewer people know who Tim Horton the individual was, it also may well be true that fewer and fewer Tim Horton's customers even know what the interior of a Tim Hortons looks like. The contemporary customer is orbiting what once was the central experience of a Tim's, drawn in by the gravitational field of its java, affordable quality meals and treats, only to be flung out of its orbit once the order had been made through the speaker and the quick exchange of goods for cash is concluded at the sliding window.

Where they predominate, drive-throughs have made the QSR hospitality experience either secondary or entirely dispensable. Customers have little interest in human interaction with staff, and complain mainly about staff not making change properly or getting their order right. This has left companies to duke it out on the basis of product offerings—constantly launching new products and seasonal specials—and pricing. And with products like arabica coffee becoming virtually indistinguishable in the struggle for market share, the differentiators are becoming very narrow indeed.

Tim's still holds an advantage among those who crave its signature baked goods, but McDonald's has an array of muffins and is offering comparable choices in breakfast sandwiches, wraps and specialty sandwiches. Subway too has gotten into the breakfast sandwich and coffee market, adding Seattle's Best from Starbucks. Country Style has repositioned itself as a café-bistro and introduced menu variety that rivals that of Tim Hortons. Montreal's La Prep has come along with a concept somewhere between Cultures and Tim's. Provided everyone serves decent food, choice comes down to brand loyalty, old habits, speed of service, store location and price. Once goods become undifferentiated commodities, the resulting price war in that struggle for market share becomes very nasty and unprofitable. Promotion becomes increasingly expensive, not only in absolute dollars but as a proportion of gross margins.

With McDonald's giving away coffee by the tanker truckload in promotional efforts to break Tim Hortons' stranglehold on the Canadian coffee market, the signature promotion of Roll Up the Rim to Win, which Tim's launched in 1986, has become increasingly expensive. In 2004, Tim's gave away 30 GMC Canyons, 100 Panasonic plasma TVs, 500 cash prizes of $1,000 and 7,600 Schwinn bicycles, above and beyond free coffee and muffins. In 2011, the twenty-fifth anniversary of the contest, Roll Up the Rim ran longer than it ever has, from late February through most of March, and the prize list had grown (in part commensurate with the growth of the chain) to include 40 Toyota Matrix XRSs, 100 Panasonic plasma TVs, 1,000 Napoleon Gourmet Grills, 5,000 Raleigh mountain bikes and 25,000 $100 Tim Cards (worth $2.5 million in restaurant offerings). McDonald's Canada tried interrupting the fun by giving away coffee for a week in the midst of it; the expense of the anniversary promotion was cited by Tim's as one of the reasons the company missed analysts' expectations in the first quarter, as it reduced same-store sales growth by one percent. And as noted, Canadian rivals like Country Style, Robin's and Coffee Time have been counter-programming with cup-based contests in the same contest period. In 2012, with McDonald's making its full-court press in coffee, Tim Hortons' contest became even more elaborate—the forty Toyotas, for one, were now Camry Hybrids—and included a new online and mobile-app roulette component.

The inside of the restaurant has emerged as a market differentiator that can challenge the expensive tyranny of constant product promotion and downward price pressure of commoditized offerings. In their redesigns of interiors, Tim's and McDonald's are striving not only to welcome the customer but also to not give them the bum's rush with unappealing institutional seating and signs telling them to move on after twenty minutes. They are realizing that the café rivals they now hope to emulate (and fend off) have been on to something in inviting their customers to hang around for pretty much as long as they like.

Among a new generation of coffee-loving consumers, ambiance is important. Seating and tables fixed to the floor on tubular steel frames have been giving way to the café model of tables with actual chairs. Interiors that seemed in the past to be braced for a prison riot, with everything bolted firmly in place, now accept responsible adults as clientele. When McDonald's launched the Forever Young renovations in 2007, the QSR giant signalled a massive change in attitude to its customer base. Restaurants that once appeared capable of being hosed down at the end of a day are beckoning adult customers to linger.

Tim Hortons didn't wait to announce new interior designs to begin refocusing on the customer's in-store experience, however absent that interior was from its television advertising. When I asked Cam MacDonald how he had managed to—and still expected to—compete in a restaurant-intensive neighbourhood like Greektown, and at the same time endure coffee wars with rival QSRs like Timothy's, Second Cup and Starbucks down the street, as well as the convergence in menu offerings across the QSR spectrum, he simply said, "Hospitality." The word had become the rallying cry of Tim Hortons' renewed determination to prioritize the customer experience within its outlets.

The Danforth and Logan store had none of the twenty-minute

table-limit signs that were once typical of Tim's outlets. "They're being phased out right across the chain," Cam MacDonald told me. "Five years ago, maybe, it was all about getting you served and getting you out, but that has changed." What once might have seemed a problem of loitering and table hogging has become a core value of hospitality. Tim Hortons' competitors have built ambiance around lollygagging. It doesn't matter if customers buy one coffee and nurse it for an hour at a table if their presence contributes to a sense of place, a point of gathering. The proliferation of free Wi-Fi had been part and parcel of the growing movement toward encouraging customers to linger, to use the restaurant as a place of study, of work, of meetings.

Free Wi-Fi has long been synonymous with the Starbucks experience, but in some urban areas it has proved to be a little too welcoming. Starbucks has been known to limit access to AC wall outlets for laptops, and went so far as to convert some of its Manhattan outlets' washrooms to employees-only. It's all part of an effort to stop abuse of what amounts to free office space as people settle in at a table all day in exchange for the purchase of a single cup of coffee. At Panera, such "computer parking" has been discouraged by informing patrons that Wi-Fi access can be cut off without warning.

I spoke with the Schulich School of Business's Alan Middleton only weeks before Tim Hortons announced it would be introducing more upscale interiors complete with free Wi-Fi in Canada. He wasn't persuaded that moving up-market was necessarily the right answer for the chain. "If Tim's gets any bigger and fancier," he warned me, "it will kill itself. It's not at all clear that Wi-Fi fits the profile of the Tim Hortons customer. They're always slightly ahead of the customer, and if they push it too far, they're spending money on one thing when they should be spending it elsewhere. They may also be providing something that only one-third of its customers want. Tim's has to skate down the middle. It wants to be moving over in a trend that appeals to half of its customers." Paul House, for his part, said that a new upscale interior concept might not be something the chain would necessarily introduce in rural Canada. "I don't know if they're going to want leather chairs. But in the city markets, especially in the downtown areas of Toronto and so forth, that's really what the market expects."

I had some inkling that free Wi-Fi was coming to Canada about two months before it was announced. I already had seen free Wi-Fi in Riese food courts featuring Tim's in New York City in mid-September. Later that month, I pulled into the parking lot of one of the Tim's run by Cam MacDonald's brothers-in-law on the south side of Barrie, Ontario. Checking my smartphone, I was surprised to see a free Wi-Fi hotspot pop up for Tim Hortons. A quick email from the parking lot to a corporate spokesperson confirmed an experiment was quietly under way: "Our Barrie restaurants are testing wi-fi. It's something we have in some US restaurants as well."

When analyst Kenric Tyghe bemoaned Tim's lack of Wi-Fi in a conversation with me in late October 2011, I mentioned to him my chance discovery of Wi-Fi radiating into the parking lot of one of the Barrie outlets. Free Wi-Fi was a given in café culture, he argued, and now that McDonald's had rolled it out in its redesigned and McCafé'd outlets, it seemed unavoidable for Tim's to make the simple technology upgrade as well.

He recounted visiting one of the new-format McDonald's in downtown Toronto and being impressed by the number of young people taking advantage of its upgraded interior and coffee bar. It was a generation that expected free Wi-Fi and plainly was lured there by it, along with the fireplace and flat-screen TV. As for coffee, Tyghe didn't think the average coffee drinker was enough of a connoisseur to favour one decent cup over another. "I saw a whole lot of people, students who would otherwise be in a Starbucks or a coffee shop. The youth demographic doesn't have that brand loyalty," he said, in a nod to Tim Hortons' supposed grip on the Canadian QSR habit. Without Wi-Fi and a more welcoming interior redesign, Tim's he felt was in danger of letting this new generation form its coffee, snack and meal habits in the Golden Arches.

The announcement of the new interiors and free Wi-Fi that soon followed our conversation made me recall how John Rothschild of Prime Restaurants had emphasized to me that summer the convergence of what were once considered to be firm divisions in restaurant sectors. "For us, there has traditionally been three very distinct forms of restaurant: QSR, casual dining and fine dining. There's no question that QSR has moved more upscale, offering more features and things that capture some of the business of casual diners. There's no question that casual dining has moved more upscale to invade, if you want, some of the territory of fine dining."

I proposed to Rothschild that the restaurant business is a bit like the automobile industry, in which models over time have tended to show "creep" in overall size, horsepower and features. He agreed that it was an apt analogy, then went on: "Customers are becoming more and more aware of food and of differences in food. They're much smarter clients, and we have more opportunities to offer greater variety to clientele. I know in our case, in that continuum of QSR, casual and fine dining, we're in the middle, and so we can enter, and have done so, on both sides. With East Side Mario's, our leading concept in a multi-concept company, we have something called East Side Mario's Pronto, which addresses those who don't want to have casual sit-down dining with table service, [but] who want a fast in-out experience.

"That edge or division between QSR and casual, and casual and fine dining, is becoming increasingly blurred, out of necessity. The number of meals being consumed outside the house is increasing dramatically. Though there are not that many new customers, there are many more opportunities for the restaurant trade in the different day parts."

I patronized an East Side Mario's Pronto that fall, at one of the new ONroute rest stops on Ontario's Highway 401 that was part of an ongoing introduction of twenty-three revamped facilities on the 401 and 400 highways. It shared the interior with a Tim Hortons, an Extreme Pita, a Burger King and a Starbucks. There was free Wi-Fi, and the central seating area featured faux-leather stuffed armchairs and coffee tables. Tim's is the dominant food franchise in this retooled rest-stop network of the provincial government, which are built and operated by the international firm Host Kilmer Service Centres. The roadside food court, in its ambiance, is converging with airport lounges and higher-end stadium and arena restaurants, which include a new-concept Tim's that opened in a 2,000-square-foot restaurant space in Nationwide Arena, home of the NHL's Columbus Blue Jackets, in the fall of 2011.

One reason these restaurant companies are rediscovering the importance of the interior is that ambiance is a differentiator at a time of increasing menu convergence. Tim's has also been expanding its menu with "cutlery meals" like the beef lasagna casserole it introduced to Canada in October 2011. Such meals are available for takeout, but many consumers would prefer to eat them in the restaurant, and the more appealing the restaurant interior can be made, the more likely consumers can be lured in to place their orders. In the third-quarter 2011 conference call, Tim Hortons CEO Paul House proposed that its new, higher-priced meal offerings "gets you to people trading down out of roadhouses." Tim's was thus taking aim at customer spending that was once considered the purview of casual dining, or of a fourth dining category some analysts call "family/midscale," which they wedge between QSR and casual dining. In Canada it's represented by value-conscious concepts like Swiss Chalet—quick service, but with table service. The higher-priced meal offerings are an effort by Tim's to get its own customers to stick around for a sit-down meal rather than head to an alternative in casual or family/midscale, while at the same time increase the average cheque price.

Yet another reason for this fresh emphasis on interior ambiance is that that QSRs have been meeting with increasing resistance, from municipal councils, local residents and advocacy groups, to new drive-throughs. If it is becoming harder to grow by building drive-through outlets, then chains have to rediscover and reinvent their interiors, to try once again to draw in customers they had trained to place and gather orders through a car window.

Tim Hortons once teamed up with other QSRs in Canada to commission a study that tried to refute the rap sheet slapped on the drive-through format, to little avail. Drive-throughs have become decried because of their impact on local traffic, the aesthetic and health consequences of long lines of idling cars, the greater issue of global warming as idling vehicles pump exhaust into the atmosphere, and a desire to preserve and promote the pedestrian-friendly nature of urban centres (while encouraging people to be more active).

Tim Hortons might be promising to lure customers inside with nicer interiors, but the customers themselves seem to be more enthusiastic than ever about drive-through purchasing, a trend to which the company is well attuned. In forecasting capital expenditures of $220 million to $260 million in 2012 for restaurant improvements, the company cited in part its "share of investments to increase restaurant drive-thru capacity in Canada, including initiatives such as selectively implementing order station relocations, double-order stations and double-lane drive-thrus." Creating double-lane drive-throughs is about the only way Tim's can assuage unhappy municipal planners when the queues of their single-line drive-throughs spill into adjoining roads. But doubling lanes at existing restaurants presumably will come at a price of parking spaces, and that would make sit-down visits even less of a priority.

Saskatoon's municipal staffers have become something of national experts in drive-throughs as they have tried to resolve headaches with Tim Hortons at its two dozen outlets where double lanes have been employed. The city's accommodations have included elimination of street parking to create a turning lane for drive-through customers and changing the timing of traffic lights. Saskatoon was prepared to add a concrete median to prevent right-hand turns into the popular outlet on Cumberland Avenue at Eighth Street—touted as the busiest drive-through anywhere in Canada—if Tim's couldn't relieve the traffic pressure on its own.

"Everyone is being faced with the type of demand Tim Hortons drive-thrus create," Angela Gardiner, the city's transportation manager, told the *Calgary Herald* in March 2012. She added, "It's a new phenomenon and it exceeds our traditional trip generation [models] for fast-food drive-thrus."

Local opposition to drive-throughs continues to pop up like wildfires. Toronto has imposed a moratorium on new drive-throughs, if not an outright ban. In July 2011 the Upper Mount Hope Neighborhood Association sued the city of Rochester, New York, over zoning changes that would allow Tim's to build a drive-through outlet on the doorstep of the University of Rochester's College Town development. In Halifax in September 2011, a motion was placed before council to ban drive-throughs downtown, where they hadn't yet taken root. The idea, said Councillor Dawn Sloane, was to ensure the city centre remained a "walkable, pedestrian-friendly" area. "If you go to any big city, in their downtown core, you don't see drive-thrus," she told *Metro Halifax*. "What you see is a lot of pedestrians walking and enjoying the feel and ambiance of the downtown." The ban went into effect in March 2012.

QSRs do have urban storefront outlets that rely on walk-in traffic, and nothing is better for such a Tim's than to have more people walking around. And as far as healthy food is concerned, independent purveyors are as capable as serving up high-calorie meals and treats as any QSR. Nevertheless, the drive-through debate is, at its core, one of lifestyle, a rejection of the anomie of suburban sprawl and the corporatization of food.

Drive-throughs have spread well beyond QSRs to include banks and dry cleaners, among other businesses, but they're seen mainly as a fast-food blight. Objections include not a little hostility to the creeping corporate QSR ubiquity that urbanists decry. Independent cafés and restaurants serving locally grown food don't have drive-throughs; national and international chains do. There is also an implied vector between people who don't get out of their cars when they want to eat and people who eat high-calorie QSR offerings and don't get enough exercise . . . from walking around downtown, for example, patronizing Wi-Fi-enabled restaurants as foot traffic.

It's no coincidence that the first place in Canada that Tim's has suffered a formal rebuke for the healthiness of some of its menu offerings is also where urban activists, sympathetic politicians and municipal planners decided there is no place for drive-throughs in a city centre: Halifax.

22

Weighty Matters: Counting Calories in an "Obesogenic Environment"

Dr. Sara Kirk arrived in Halifax from England in late 2006 to serve as the Canada Research Chair in Health Services Research at Dalhousie University's School of Health Administration. "I gained weight when I moved here," she recalls. It wasn't because she promptly developed an addiction to the menu offerings of Tim Hortons. For one thing, the nearest Tim's to the school's Applied Research Collaborations for Health (ARCH) office, which she leads, is a storefront outlet on Spring Garden Road, more than a kilometre away. For another thing, she has never really understood the chain's cult-like mass following in Canada.

Rather, urban sprawl caused her to walk less and drive more than she had in Leeds. And the food served in typical North American restaurants, she quickly found, comes in "huge proportions." Dr. Kirk became her own living proof of the consequences of an "obesogenic environment," which she defines as "an environment that promotes overconsumption." We eat too much because the environment wants us to.

"The health message says to eat less and move more, but the environment tells people to eat more and move less," Dr. Kirk explains.

"For an individual to change behaviour in this environment is really, really challenging. We also used to be physically active to get food. Now we need to be physically active to deal with the food we consume."

Dr. Kirk is one of a number of health-care professionals who have moved beyond the nitty-gritty of caloric intake and nutrition-consumption profiles for individual patients to also consider the overwhelming role played by society in determining our eating habits. "As a dietitian in England," Dr. Kirk says, "I spent a lot of time clinically with patients with eating disorders, dealing with bulimia, but I began to be referred women who were obese, who were engaging in binge eating and suffering from psychological stress. Opposite my door was a little cafeteria. After counselling these patients, I would watch them walk out my door into this environment."

She laughs, recalling the sense of helplessness engendered by turning patients loose in the world in which they had to function according to her best advice. "I began looking at the social/ecological approach to their eating problems, issues like who they lived with, where they lived, government policies on food, the ingredients in the kinds of foods they were eating."

When Kirk came to North America, the role of corporations (including restaurant chains) in consumption, and a belief in the unfettered rights of consumers, were particularly striking to her. "Governments here tend to be non-interventionist. They don't want to tell people what to do. Consumerism is rampant. That tends to be less so when children are involved, but there is a strong belief in freedom of choice. And the business model is to get people to consume for maximum profit. There is also agribusiness support," she adds, acknowledging the enduring controversies over the formulation of Canada's Food Guide. "They lobby and they're very powerful."

About one in four Canadian adults are thought to be obese, according to the World Health Organization. That's far fewer than the estimated one in three American adults, but disconcertingly high compared to countries like France (about one in six) or Japan (about one in thirty). Given how closely linked Canada and the United States are culturally, and how food and restaurant trends traditionally have a head start south of the border, there is good reason to fear that the catastrophic obesity figures of the U.S. (which are projected to reach one in two by 2030) are eventually bound for Canada.

Dr. Kirk joined the concerned health-care professionals and members of the public who appeared at public consultation hearings of Capital Health in 2011, urging that its hospitals start setting an example in healthy eating. Capital Health services 400,000 people at public hospitals and clinics in the greater Halifax area, and had been the first Canadian hospital organization to bring Tim Hortons onto the premises. Dr. Kirk and others weren't happy with the standard fare of a Tim's being served inside a health-care facility.

Health-care professionals like her had become increasingly queasy about the relationship between QSR and children's health, and the role their own institutions were playing. When kids visit friends and family in a large hospital, there's often a QSR ready to feed them in the food court. And the queasiness was not limited to Halifax. Following concerted lobbying, including by its own doctors, Toronto's Hospital for Sick Children (a.k.a. SickKids) in March 2011 terminated the lease of the Burger King outlet in its food court. Breaking with Burger King was not easy, as the QSR chain had a long-standing relationship with the hospital's fundraising arm, the SickKids Foundation.

In Halifax, Dr. Kirk advanced three options for food retailing in a hospital environment: "informed choices" for which retailers would offer healthy options but not change their menu, which she found undesirable; "informed choices" with some limitations on unhealthy options, which she found better, but not ideal; and finally, the removal of unhealthy options entirely from menus, which is what she favoured.

On May 20, 2011, Capital Health announced that it had gone with Dr. Kirk's third and most forthright option. Beginning in October 2011, "baked goods such as doughnuts and those muffins that do not meet Capital Health's healthy food guidelines will no longer be sold at Tim Hortons franchises operated by Compass group for Capital Health."*

Capital Health went on to note: "Tim Hortons is a part of the culture and the community in Nova Scotia. Capital Health was the first health-care organization in Canada to bring Tim Hortons franchises into hospitals and will also be the first to change the menu this way and continue the relationship with a focus on the healthiest choices. We have appreciated the support of Tim Hortons as we make this transition."

John Gillis, a media relations advisor at Capital Health, explained to me that the organization has dietary guidelines in place for its own restaurants that were applied to Tim Hortons. They're not hard and fast rules; as he noted, there's "some leeway" in certain factors, such as sodium and fat content. Though the original intent was to have a revised Tim Hortons menu in place by October 2011, it took until March 2012 to finalize the menu switch. Capital Health had helped to engineer a Tim's experience with the healthiest possible eating options.

The good news for Tim Hortons is how much of its menu has survived. The only full-service Tim Hortons in the Capital Health system, at the Cobequid Community Health Centre, has retained a considerable variety of soups, sandwiches and meals, including ham-only breakfast sandwiches (the sausage and bacon options had to go). The main change for all the outlets is in baked goods. Gone are the Timbits, doughnuts and goodies like eclairs. Muffins are down from about seventeen to four selections (cranberry-blueberry bran, blueberry, fruit explosion and low-fat double berry). One cookie, a trail mix variety with fruit and nuts, has made the grade. In March 2012,

* Compass Group PLC, headquartered in London, England, is a contract food-service company whose Canadian arm operates a number of Compass-owned brands, including Caffè Ritazza, On the Go, Coyote Jack's, The Big Pita and Upper Crust, while also acting as a franchisee of Tim Hortons, Second Cup, Starbucks, Yogen Früz, Bento Nouveau, Pizza Pizza and Mr.Sub.

Capital Health was working with Tim Hortons on the equipment to sell approved versions of its iced coffees and smoothies.

Tim Hortons must be at the heart of any discussion of the health of Canadians and their food consumption. It is not only the largest QSR business in the country in terms of outlets and gross revenue, its own menu has packed on the calories over time, and its widespread advertising promotes snacking—Iced Capps! Timbits!—for which there is no dietary need. It has also been a leading player in sponsorship of youth sports, which critics contend implicitly links the fun of exercise and play with the consumption of empty calories.

Ken Wong, the distinguished professor of marketing at Queen's School of Business, thinks the challenge that concerns about childhood obesity pose to QSRs are greatly underestimated. Those challenges are posed by proactive policymakers and activists who would like to ban all forms of fast-food advertising to children, which Wong says conceivably could extend to sponsorships of community sports programs, including Tim Hortons' high-profile Timbits Minor Sports, and even to the company's children's camp foundation. More broadly, public education on the link between empty-caloric treats and childhood obesity could significantly change consumer consumption patterns that have been essential to the popularity of Tim Hortons.

"The Tim Hortons ritual of parents going to the hockey rink with the kids and buying a Tim's coffee and box of Timbits is on shaky ground," he cautioned me.

In the interest of full disclosure, I really like what Tim Hortons serves where meals are concerned. On a road trip, I consult the company's TimmyMe smartphone app to find outlets, and will go out of my way to have one of its sandwiches, wraps, bowl meals or BELTs rather than have to settle for the standard QSR fare of burgers and fries. The food lives up to the promise of freshness, taste and good value. I don't know that you can do much better than Tim's in feeding yourself at a QSR when on the go. But from a strictly bottom-line point of view, one must ask if Tim Hortons can remain attractive to investors as it confronts what could become an increasingly difficult operating climate where the calories and nutrition of its drinks and treats are concerned. And can the rest of us figure out how to keep indulging in Tim Hortons' delectable offerings without surrendering in the battle of the waistline?

LINDA GILLIS, A RESEARCHER and registered dietitian at the Children's Exercise and Nutrition Centre at Hamilton Health Sciences, McMaster Children's Hospital, agrees with the idea that we suffer from an obesogenic environment. The food and beverage industries tell us incessantly that whether we're standing still, driving somewhere, taking a break from a home-handyman project or wrapping up a game of recreational tennis, we should be eating and/or drinking.

"We do not live in a society that is set up for a healthy weight," says Gillis. Socializing has become equated with consumption. When we are together, we need to eat something.

On September 28, 2006, Gillis appeared before the House of Commons Standing Committee on Health. It was the standing committee's third meeting devoted to childhood obesity. Just as Tim Hortons was going public and beginning a three-year process of returning to Canada as a corporation, the federal government was belatedly beginning to confront the issue of why so many Canadian kids were getting fat, and wondering what could be done about it. In an unfortunate coincidence of corporate promotion, the cover of Tim Hortons' 2006 annual report would feature a hockey dad sitting out front of a restaurant with three kids wearing Timbits jerseys. On the table were a fruit drink, cookies and a snack pack of twenty Timbits—a true extravaganza of largely empty, sugar-laden calories.

The day's testimony pitted the opinions of health-care professionals against spokespersons for the food and beverage industries. Industry representatives pledged their eagerness to work with government to find solutions, all the while finding problems with the solutions the health-care folks advocated—especially mandatory calorie counts on printed menus and menu boards. Although Tim Hortons was not in the committee hearing room, its products implicitly were, alongside those of every other QSR.

Gillis elegantly reduced the problem of childhood obesity for the benefit of the standing committee. Her research had shown that it wasn't fat, protein or carbohydrate intake that contributed most to childhood obesity; "it was actually the calories in the diet—the calories they were consuming and then the calories they were expending in energy out," she explained. Gillis had hit upon the essential role of what is routinely called "energy-in/energy-out," or the "energy balance." Obese kids consume more energy in food fuel than they burn through physical activity.

She followed up this study with one that was determined to identify which foods or food groups contributed most to obesity. The biggest difference turned out to be not so much what they were eating as *where* they were eating it. Obese families were "consuming more foods outside the home than the nonobese." The second biggest contributor to obesity was sweet drinks, which gave the obese a higher sugar intake. Gillis also found that "grains and meat group were significantly greater in the obese, and interestingly this was correlated with eating out."

Gillis offered two recommendations. Where dietary advice was concerned, "we should shift our focus right away from fat and carbohydrate to focus on total calories." And "we really need to stress the harm of eating out and of sweet drinks." She also wanted health advice "to target foods that are actually healthier" for when people are both eating out and shopping for groceries. "To give some examples, if we're going to provide apple slices but are going to put a caramel dip with it"—a shot at a McDonald's Happy Meal option—"then we're not decreasing the sugar intake. Or if we're going to recommend submarines, which are high in grain products, that's not going to help in reducing obesity."

Gillis's research supported the more provocative methodology of Morgan Spurlock's 2004 documentary *Super Size Me*: eating out all the time probably is not good for you. The fare offered by the QSR industry in particular tends to make it all too easy to exceed normal caloric intake as well as certain kinds of fattening calories, such as sugar and carbs.

The restaurant industry has routinely defended itself by saying consumers have choices on their menus that can be exercised responsibly. And it's true that McDonald's, for example, has long been offering "healthy choices." But "healthy" is as nebulous a concept as "green." Dr. Gillis, for example, was disappointed in Tim Hortons' "Real Fruit Smoothies." When the product was announced in March 2011, the company touted it as a "healthier, convenient and affordable snack." Its ten-ounce cup offered "a full serving of fruit." The company reiterated the smoothies were "bursting with a full serving of fruit" in promoting them that summer. But in the world of North American food guides, fruit *juice* constitutes a serving of fruit, and that's the basis of the "real fruit" in the company's smoothie.

Taking note of Tim Hortons' Strawberry Banana Real Fruit Smoothie, Dr. Gillis cited the company's own nutritional information in telling me, "It has no protein. They say it has fruit, but there's no fibre, so it's just fruit juice." It frustrated her that the company didn't create what she considered a truly healthy smoothie, with protein and fruit fibre. In contrast, Starbucks says its sixteen-ounce Strawberry Banana Vivanno Smoothie is made from a whole banana and a "natural strawberry puree," and delivers fifteen grams of protein and seven grams of fibre. But in the confusing world of consumer nutrition, the Tim Hortons Real Fruit Smoothie may strike many consumers as a "healthier" choice because it is fat-free and has fewer calories—180 in a fourteen-ounce serving, versus 280 in the sixteen-ounce Starbucks product. For that matter, Second Cup's sixteen-ounce Strawberry Fruit Smoothie has 380 calories, no protein and four grams of fibre. And while a sixteen-ounce McDonald's strawberry-banana smoothie is fat-free and delivers three grams of fibre and two grams of protein, it also delivers 260 calories.

Calories may not be the final arbiter of healthy choices, but they are in fact the central issue in the obesity crisis. There is no caloric info on display at most Canadian QSR drive-throughs or service counters, but change is being driven from south of the border. While in New York City in September 2011, I was impressed by the fact that restaurants included calories on menu boards, which local law has required since 2008. At Argo Tea, on the ground floor of the Flatiron Building in midtown Manhattan, the numbers listed beside different beverages on overhead displays were not prices, but calories. As multinational QSRs provide more easily accessed caloric information to avoid being regulated into mandatory disclosure on menu boards and the like, Canadian consumers have benefited. Starbucks includes caloric information in the menus within its smartphone store-finder app, and in 2011 McDonald's released a separate app dedicated to determining the nutritional details of any particular order. Tim Hortons followed suit, adding nutrition information to its store-finder app in December 2011. Meanwhile, like staff at other Canadian QSRs, Tim's employees continue to suggest add-ons—like a doughnut to a sandwich and coffee—in order to make a meal deal, which can virtually double the caloric intake.

Does more forthright disclosure of caloric information really make a difference in consumer consumption patterns? A Stanford University study published in January 2010 found that calories per purchase declined 6 percent at Starbucks outlets in New York after the mandatory menu-board-posting law went into effect, but the reduction was almost entirely in food, not beverages. The researchers said there was no impact on Starbucks' profit, which in fact increased in a subset of outlets located near Dunkin' stores. Dr. Yoni Freedhoff, an Ottawa specialist in bariatric medicine who regularly speaks out on obesity issues and the QSR industry, thinks that having caloric information more readily at hand can't hurt. Linda Gillis thinks that to be most beneficial, the calories need to be contextualized, by being shown as a percentage of a person's daily requirement.

Were customers of QSRs to understand one essential number, their snacking and eating habits might change significantly. The average adult only needs about 2,000 calories to power them through a routine day, one without any special exertion. With that knowledge in mind, they can begin to see how combo meals that exceed 1,000 calories, or muffin-and-café-mocha snack breaks that top 700, are helping nudge up the numbers on the bathroom scale—and are making it so hard to nudge them back down again.

The QSR industry has built a substantial part of its revenue stream on miscellaneous between-meal snacking, promoting the sort of drinks and goodies that can deliver more than one-third of a person's daily caloric requirements in a single delectable indulgence. Those indulgences are especially problematic: Dr. Gillis stresses that the *kind* of calories consumed are important to weight management.

"It's not as simple as energy in/energy out," she says, expanding on her original research findings. "For example, something that's straight sugar, like a soft drink or an iced capp, increases insulin levels, and that increases appetite. You'll just go eat something else." (The above-mentioned Tim Hortons Real Fruit Smoothie, for example, delivers forty-three grams—about eleven teaspoons—of sugar in a fourteen-ounce serving.) Overall consumption increases, she explains, and there's an even greater energy in/energy out imbalance. She also says new research is suggesting that some "bad" fats, the saturated and trans fats, may similarly induce a craving for more food and with them more calories. "If you consume higher amounts of protein per calorie, you are more likely to lose weight and to keep it off, and retain more muscle." In short, if you're prone to snacking on protein-deficient, sugar-laden treats, you can become juiced on empty calories and inclined to eat even more than you would have had there been some protein—something resembling a genuine meal—in that snack.

Tim Hortons' advertising has promoted the sugar-laden calories of Timbits, iced capps and smoothies as between-meal snacks. But its TV ads have also featured two couples leaving a wedding service and looking for something to tide them over to the reception—as one of the male actors puts it, an actual meal, rather than a snack. Ergo, they're off to the nearest Tim's for a soup or sandwich. Mind you, the ad doesn't say sugary snacks are bad, only that the actor is looking for something more filling.

Tim Hortons has done much to diversify its menu offerings into nutritious and well-priced meals, but it is still substantially, even overwhelmingly, in the snack business, selling "sweet treats" (as it calls them) that have little if any nutritional value and loads of calories. Doughnuts historically have been a high-calorie proposition; what has changed at Tim's (and its competitors) is the proliferation of high-calorie beverages, as the standard offer of a brewed coffee has been diversified by iced capps, lattes, mochas and smoothies.

Complaining that doughnuts have no nutritional value is to a large degree absurd: they're *doughnuts*. But in satisfying our cravings for sweet diversions at Tim's—as at a McDonald's McCafé, a Starbucks or any other QSR venue that sells coffee and baked goods—we can end up loading up on more calories than we ever have before. Concern has also been raised about kids drinking iced capps, although the issue has been more the intake of caffeine at a young age than the no less significant one of the caloric intake these drinks represent to small bodies.

The calories of a Tim's run used to be mainly in the baked goods, as a ten-ounce small cup of coffee (the old "medium" in Canada) with one cream and one sugar delivers 75 calories. Virtually all the calories are in the cream and sugar, which means the Canadian double-double habit is a 150-calorie hit in what is now a "small" serving. Opt instead for a small mocha latte, and the calories ring in at 190; an iced capp or a French Vanilla capp takes them to 250. Of course, if you order a larger size of drink, the calories balloon. Order a medium double double now, and the hit is 230 calories. The shift to larger cups in Canada in January 2012 carried the potential of calorie inflation. Someone who keeps routinely ordering a "medium" double double will now consume 40 percent more beverage—but because of the way Tim's dispenses cream and sugar by cup size, 53 percent more calories—than they did before.

There are ways to fight the calorie inflation in coffee-based drinks. Opting for milk instead of cream in a ten-ounce Tim Hortons iced capp slashes the calories from 250 to 150; opting for milk in a ten-ounce iced coffee similarly drops them from 110 to 70. You can really tame a double double with milk instead of cream, as the total calories in a medium drop from 230 to 130. Adding yoghurt to a smoothie will net a few grams of protein (while adding a bit of fat). And fitness-conscious lovers of Tim's coffee have figured out how to sidestep the more devastating caloric encounters in the side orders—opting for a bagel (260 to 330 calories) instead of a muffin (340 to 410 calories), or maple oatmeal (120 calories) instead of a sausage, egg and cheese breakfast wrap (420 calories). On its website, Tim Hortons has posted ordering strategies for customers on a "low-fat diet," and other basic dietary information. But apart from limiting consumption, it's pretty hard to dodge the calories in those sugary, compulsively edible depth charges known as Timbits.

In the summer of 2011, the company promoted the ten-pack as "road ready" snack food, and a television ad showed fit-looking, thirtysomething urban hetero couples bereft of children, en route to the cottage, engaging on this outing in hip-ironic CB lingo. The men and women were sharing a ten-pack; presumably they were consuming no more than five each. Bite-sized Timbits range from 50 to 90 calories each, and so the road-trip intake ranged from 250 to 450 calories per person. If an inspired consumer decided they needed to wash them down with a medium iced capp of about 360 calories, such an innocuous snack break would deliver a caloric punch of 600 to 800 calories. That snack break would represent a fourth meal for an average adult, with only about eight grams of protein besides. Still, it wouldn't be nearly as brutal as combining the iced capp with one of Tim's new Cinnamon Delights, which clock in at 600 calories. That snack combo would amount to almost half the daily-maintenance caloric intake of a lot of adults.

Tim Hortons is far from alone in retailing nutritionally challenged caloric hits. When my local McDonald's completed a renovation in the summer of 2011 with a new McCafé, a promotional sign appeared at the drive-through order station encouraging me to partake of a McCafé Mocha and a Double Chocolate with Oreo Crumble Muffin. I passed on the offer, and back home I consulted the online McDonald's calorie counter. The muffin was 450 calories, and a medium mocha was 280. I had dodged a 730-caloric hit on my daily energy-in tally, which would have made a serious deficit in my daily maintenance requirement of about 2,200 calories for a man of my height, weight and age.

It's the job of companies like Tim Hortons to convince consumers they deserve hi-cal snack breaks. Another ad in heavy rotation in the summer of 2011 had three fit-looking thirtysomething guys taking a snack break with a coffee and Timbits while building a deck. The implicit message is that such consumption is consistent with the physiognomy of the actors. But the caloric input of five Timbits alone is a significant energy infusion that pulling the trigger on a nail gun is not, in itself, likely to overcome.

Timbits seem to have become such a pervasive part of Canadian consumption that one has to wonder why consumers don't think of another popular baked good, cookies, in the same way. A single Decadent Chocolate Chunk Cookie by President's Choice contains

80 calories, which is comparable to a Timbit. Yet a President's Choice commercial showing a photogenic couple splitting ten cookies on a cottage drive would probably strike many viewers as absurd and not a little gluttonous. Cookies are something we eat one, maybe two, at a time; Timbits we just dive right into.

The day the federal government tries to legally limit Canadian consumption of Timbits is the day the Parliament Buildings are burned. So beyond increased public education on the hazards of gorging on QSR calories across the board, which could include stating the number of calories on menu boards, it's up to the average citizen to pay more attention to what they're eating, and when and why.

The consumer habit of "treating" is coming under increasing fire from health-care professionals. In a 2012 article in the *Canadian Journal of Cardiology*, three leading Alberta doctors in health-care academia proposed a new nomenclature for "junk" food. They argued it should be called "pathogenic," as they decried "government reluctance to respond meaningfully to the deaths and disability of tens of thousands of Canadians each year that can be attributed to our 'junk food' diets full of 'treats.'"*

Dr. Kirk points to two aspects of overconsumption, both tied to "treating." One is that we think we can routinely indulge in between-meal treats without consequence. "If you treat yourself every day," she cautions, "it's not a treat anymore." Our culture of work and play has inculcated a notion of regular snack breaks that QSRs are only too happy to encourage and fulfill. The office coffee break is as old as salaried drudgery, but today that has come to mean coffee (or a hi-cal alternative like a mocha or an iced capp) along with a muffin or a cookie that add up to several hundred calories. The caloric prognosis

---

* The article ("'Junk Foods,' 'Treats,' or 'Pathogenic Foods'? A Call for Changing Nomenclature to Fit the Risk of Today's Diets") was written by Norm R.C. Campbell of the University of Calgary and Kim D. Raine and Lindsay McLaren of the University of Alberta. It was awaiting publication as this book went to press.

is possibly direr at a Tim Hortons rival like Starbucks, where a single cookie can deliver 500 calories, as opposed to 220 to 280 at Tim's. The Tim's run is a treasured routine of many Canadian workers, but some of them need a fitness club membership to run off their casual QSR snacking.

The other "treating" aspect of overconsumption fingered by Dr. Kirk is the idea that physical activity should be rewarded with food. (This has been a theme in Tim's advertising, in the case of male tennis players handed fruit smoothies by their female other halves in a summer 2011 commercial.) She has seen the reward phenomenon in soccer games of her own children. In a ninety-minute game, she figures kids aged eight to ten might run around for sixty minutes and burn about 180 calories. She has been shocked when parent volunteers dole out treats as the kids come off the pitch—usually a sugar drink and a chocolate-covered cookie or Rice Krispie square. Treats adding up to 250 calories leave the kids with a 70-calorie surplus for an activity that was supposed to make them healthier.

Dr. Kirk made me guiltily recall the soccer games of my older son, now in his early twenties, when he was about ten years old. His community league was sponsored by the local Tim Hortons franchisee, and the kids wore shirts with the Tim Hortons logo. If they wore their shirts into Tim's after a match, they were treated to a free doughnut and drink, usually a bottled fruit juice. A Tim's doughnut ranges anywhere from 210 to 360 calories; a 300-millilitre bottle of juice contains 130 to 140 calories. (It is still Tim Hortons' corporate policy for locally sponsored minor sports activities to include giveaways such as Tim Cards, products like coffee and/or Timbits, and items for auction or raffle.) As parents, I now realized, we were voluntarily pumping more than 300 (and as many as 500) calories into our kids as a reward for burning likely fewer than 200. The cover of the 2006 annual report featuring kids in Timbits jerseys was a caloric blowout. The bottle of apple juice in front of one kid contained about 130 calories. A plate was stacked with cookies of about 230 calories each, and the box of twenty Timbits they were about to share, hopefully with Dad, totalled somewhere between 1,000 and 1,800 calories.

This brings us back to the essential dilemma for children and adults alike. There has been a misguided and unrealistic focus on energy out, rather than energy in, as a solution to the "energy balance" problem. The food industry, including the QSR sector, has found a rallying point that has been aided and abetted by governments, many health-care professionals, food industry members and the fitness biz.

The problem of people getting fat, according to this view, is not consumption of calories (or the kind of calories); it's being too lazy, too inactive, to burn off the calories consumed, wherever they came from. But, as health-care professionals have increasingly argued, without discouraging the idea of activity and its general benefits, stressing energy out is an unrealistic solution. Says Dr. Kirk, "You can't be physically active enough" to address the chronic additional calories many people consume, day in, day out. Consuming empty calories, which encourages overeating, has only exacerbated the problem, as has rewarding activity with treats.

"The public doesn't want to hear food is a problem," says Dr. Freedhoff. "They want to hear that fitness is a problem. That is a message that is actively spun by the QSR industry. What the industry is saying is, 'You can eat our stuff so long as you exercise.'"

The problem is, you have to burn 500 calories a day, above and beyond the calories you need to function, to eliminate one pound of unwanted weight over the course of one week. In other words, 3,500 calories of cumulative energy output is required to get rid of one excess pound of human being. A thirty-year-old man who is five foot ten and a fit 175 pounds, according to one calorie estimator, has to play a solid hour of singles tennis to burn 483 calories. That's not nearly enough to counteract the impact of an innocuous snack break of five Timbits and a medium iced capp.

In the discussion of "risk factors" in its financial statements, Tim Hortons makes no mention of the war on obesity. It does mention in its fiscal 2011 annual report the initiatives in various jurisdictions to put calories on menu boards, and says it will comply with whatever laws arise. Trans-fat concerns are raised, and it says that back in 2006, "significant progress was made to reduce trans fat in most of our products to at or below acceptable levels in Canada and the U.S." It also notes that it belongs to the Sodium Working Group, which is liaising with Canada's federal government. "We continue to work with suppliers to reduce the amount of sodium in our products. We have gradually reduced sodium by approximately 29% across our soup offerings." Tim's also voluntarily includes sodium information for its menu items. Consumers henceforth should probably be aware that a large turkey and bacon club sandwich on white bread packs 2,120 milligrams of sodium. In comparison, the notorious Double Down bacon and deep-fried chicken monstrosity from KFC returned to Canada in May 2011 with a tamed-down 1,580 milligrams of sodium. The Institute of Medicine in Washington, D.C., says 1,500 milligrams is an "adequate intake" for an entire day for people aged nine to fifty, with 2,300 milligrams being a "tolerable upper intake" for those aged fourteen and up.

Tim Hortons generally has been quick to respond whenever issues arise that could imperil the brand. It's a different company than it was back in 2006, when showing a bunch of kids gathered around an arsenal of largely empty calories on the cover of an annual report wasn't controversial. Society has changed, and the company has been changing with it. (Mind you, it is not a participant in the Canadian Children's Food and Beverage Advertising Initiative, an industry group formed in 2007 whose members pledge to "promote and support healthy dietary choices and healthy lifestyles to children under 12 years of age" and accept limits on how food is promoted to children under twelve. Its nineteen members include two QSR chains, Burger King and McDonald's.) While it lagged Starbucks and McDonald's in getting nutritional info into a mobile app, Tim Hortons does distribute nutritional information voluntarily, and it doesn't try to tell customers that the way to deal with the calories in its treats is to be more physically active. But it does associate itself through marketing with sports and recreation, and it also employs actors in commercials who are consuming sweet treats while looking fit and happy. And that has made the company the target of critics where healthy levels of consumption are concerned.

Mild treating, above and beyond regular meals, makes it easy to overshoot the daily basic energy-in budget and pick up an extra 500 calories a day—which add up to an extra fifty-two pounds a year. It is tough to figure out how to indulge occasionally in treats from the menu of even one QSR without blowing the personal calorie budget and ending up with an extra five or ten pounds in a year. The North American consumer is awash in offerings of surplus calories. And in Canada, a lot of those surplus calories are being proffered by Tim Hortons, its largest QSR chain.

"I really don't think Tim Hortons is doing anything wrong," says Dr. Freedhoff. The problem of overconsumption, he says, is societal, and the marketing activities of companies like Tim Hortons are the nature of the corporate beast. "The restaurant industry's job is to sell food, and it is good at that. Everything it does is geared to that," he emphasizes.

We can learn to curb our appetite for treating—by eating fruit instead of half a box of Timbits when driving somewhere, for example, or by "treating" our kids at sporting events with slices of watermelon or frozen yoghurt tubes, as Dr. Kirk advocates, which are refreshing and contain fewer than 100 calories. We can also eat and drink much less of what Tim Hortons and its competitors would like us to consider eating and drinking as a seeming matter of routine.

When I asked Tim Hortons franchisee Cam MacDonald what he thought of initiatives to restrict consumption of certain types of food and to limit food-associated sponsorship of children's sports programs, he simply wondered aloud, "Shouldn't people have choices?" Knowing the calories of my erstwhile popular menu choices made me choose to change my QSR habits over the course of writing this book. I no longer routinely eat blueberry fritters (330 calories) as part of a road refuelling, and if there are Timbits around, I limit myself to one or two. (Okay, three, but just this once.) I will not come within a mile of Tim Hortons' new Cinnamon Delight (600 calories), nor will I touch the McDonald's Angus Mushroom Swiss Burger combo (730 calories for the burger, 360 for the medium fries, never mind the beverage).

Which is all to the good, but I think posting calorie counts on menu boards in Canada would be a move in the right direction. In May 2012, the Ontario NDP's critic for health and long-term care, France Gélinas (who is a trained physiotherapist), introduced a private member's bill that enjoyed broad support among health-care groups. It called for chain restaurants with five or more locations in the province and earnings of at least $5 million a year to post the number of calories next to each menu item. Items containing high sodium levels would also be marked. Taking aim at Tim Hortons, without actually naming it, she posed, "Did you know the bran muffin has almost double the calories of the Boston cream–filled doughnut, at 410 calories for the muffin and 250 for the doughnut?" A raisin bran muffin at Tim Hortons does indeed contain 410 calories, and a Boston cream doughnut 250. Gélinas had previously tried and failed to get a similar bill through the legislature in 2009, when it was called "a step in the wrong direction" by the Canadian Restaurant and Foodservices Association.

Nutritional information may be out there on the backs of menus, on websites and in smartphone apps, yet I have found that friends are as oblivious as I had been to the calories they consume at QSRs. Food production at QSRs is so intensively standardized that it should not be a problem for them to start displaying caloric hits in the way I had seen in New York City. If the Stanford study of Starbucks outlets in New York is right, consumers are capable of using menu board information to reduce calories while still leaving the QSR as profitable as—if not more profitable than—it was before.

The debate over QSRs' responsibility for our growing girth problems also made me recall the ad-hoc snack pack that I secured from Ladan Pastry, the Iranian bakery that occupied the former site of Jim Charade's Tim Horton Do-Nut at Colony Plaza. Those heavenly pastries were saturated in honey. (They were also supposed to be consumed with tea, the national beverage of Iran.) I cannot even begin to imagine their individual calorie counts. I would never try to eat a half-dozen of them in a single sitting. And I never want the government to tell me I can't have them.

Dr. Sara Kirk is right in that Canadians don't want to be told forthrightly what they can and cannot eat. Unless, of course, the person doing the consuming is a politician running for office—in which case, heaven help them if they're spotted consuming anything other than a Tim's coffee and a Timbit or two while on the campaign trail. In the few years since Dr. Kirk arrived in Canada, the idea that being a loyal Tim's customer was synonymous with being a true-blue Canadian had reached the point of electoral mental gridlock.

23

The Donut Shop Gang: How Tim Hortons Came to Define the Canadian Political Landscape

Susan Delacourt, the *Toronto Star*'s senior writer in Ottawa, is not a fan of Tim Hortons coffee. She prefers Starbucks. This does not make her a bad person, but it did make her a little weary of the daily routine of the 2010 summer tour of federal Liberal leader Michael Ignatieff.

"I was complaining the first week of the tour how often we went to Tim Hortons," she recalled for me. Every day, it seemed, the bus made an obligatory refreshment stop at the double-oval sign. It wasn't because Ignatieff was hooked on Tim Hortons coffee; as she has reported, he doesn't even drink coffee; steeped tea is his hot beverage of choice. But under no circumstances was the Ignatieff bus going to be seen where Delacourt wanted to get her coffee fix.

During the summer tour of 2010, and the ensuing spring 2011 election that sealed Ignatieff's fate as the Liberal leader (and an elected politician), the most damning mistake he apparently was supposed to avoid making was *not* reviving the "green shift" carbon cap and trade system advanced by his predecessor, Stéphane Dion. Nor was it raising the spectre of a coalition between his Liberals, the NDP and the Bloc Québécois. The real danger to Ignatieff's electoral fortunes was that he would be photographed holding a Starbucks cup.

By the summer of 2010, Canadian political wisdom had reduced the broad mass of the middle-spectrum Canadian electorate to a quasi-mythical creature called the "Tim Hortons voter." To win power, federal parties had to curry favour with this Tim Hortons voter, who had become synonymous with another electoral trope: "working families." In the process of reducing the Canadian electorate to the customer of one particular QSR chain, political spin doctors and members of the media had also created a Tim Hortons/Starbucks polarity. If Joe or Joanne Average Canadian was a Tim's customer, then their antimatter nemesis was Richard or Rachelle Pretentious Internationalist, frequenter of Starbucks and espouser of non-working-family values.

As the 2010 Ignatieff summer tour wound down, the media on the Ignatieff bus began to thin out. Delacourt, however, stuck with it, and in the final days she spotted what previously had been unimaginable: a Starbucks cup, on a table in the bus, close at hand to Ignatieff as he conferred with staffers and his wife, Zsuzsanna Zsohar.

Delacourt snapped a picture with her BlackBerry and posted it as a Twitpic to Twitter: "Note #Starbucks cup on the table now that all the others are gone on #lpcx." As it turned out, the drink had been brought aboard by Ignatieff's wife, but when Conservatives who followed Delacourt's tweets caught wind of the photo, it was proof positive that Ignatieff was the faux-Canadian they'd been insisting all along. "The Conservative bloggers went wild," she recalled. "It was, 'The elite, latte-drinking Iggy is revealed.'" She thinks the image was retweeted more than 500 times.

The next day, the tour was back to the Tim Hortons routine. Delacourt snapped an image of a Tim Hortons takeout cup and a snack pack of Timbits on a counter in the bus. "Cue Jaws music," she tweeted. "Damn Timbits are back aboard #lpcx. #sugarshock #lifeonroad."

Ignatieff and the party he led could not shake the "Starbucks" pejorative. As Ignatieff's spring 2011 election campaign struggled through its final days, trailing badly in the polls, a story by Jennifer Ditchburn of the Canadian Press equated the Stephen Harper campaign, pressing for a majority government, with Tim Hortons, if only in its predictability: "Drive up to any Tim Horton's in Canada and the coffee will taste the same, the decor will be familiar and the menu largely identical—a comforting feeling of familiarity and consistency. Stephen Harper's Conservative team has run a Tim Horton's campaign: consistent in style, message and tone. No particular local flavour, nothing rough around the edges and no experimenting." Ditchburn never mentioned Starbucks, but the title a desk editor affixed to the story cruelly skewered Ignatieff and his Liberals with the politically poisonous polarity: "Harper's Tim Horton's campaign scours for Starbucks Liberals in its final hours."

The Starbucks Liberals were going down, crushed by one of the most remarkable branding exercises in Canadian political history. Somehow, being a true Canadian (in English Canada, at least) had become equated with being a Tim Hortons customer; being a Tim Hortons customer had become equated with being a Tim Hortons voter; a Tim Hortons voter had become equated with being a supporter of the Conservative party; and the leader of the country, Stephen Harper, was reaffirmed as the Tim Hortons prime minister.

How Tim Hortons had become an electioneering symbol, and the ardent consumption of its coffee an authenticity test for Canadian citizens, was a process both happenstance and calculated. Where the company and the mythologizing of middle-spectrum working families in the political arena are concerned, the initial nudge seems to have come not from incisive polling, but rather from a CBC television comedy.

Air Farce was a televised version of the long-running CBC Radio ensemble sketch comedy *Royal Canadian Air Farce.* The television series began running in October 1993; in Episode 9, which aired December 3, the cast made its first visit to "the doughnut shop," with a sketch called "You Got That Right," which became a standard tag line for the customer portrayed by Don Ferguson. The cast and writers didn't revisit the doughnut shop for another eight episodes, when the "donut shop gang" gathered on March 4, 1994, to discuss Canada's Olympic hockey team, which had to settle for silver in losing the deciding game to Sweden; they were back a week later to thrash out the takeover of media conglomerate Maclean Hunter by Rogers Communications.

Air Farce was on to something. A group of stolid working men and women gathered around a table in a doughnut shop, expressing almost idiot-savant perceptions of current affairs. The donut shop gang became a staple of the weekly show. Their recurring "A Canadian Moment" endured until the final episode on New Year's Eve 2008, when Dave Broadfoot made a guest appearance as the shop owner, kicked them out and closed the place.

The donut shop gang was never explicitly about Tim Hortons customers. When the sketches began running in late 1993, Tim Hortons was in the process of doubling its number of restaurants (between 1991 and 1995), but rivals like Country Style and Robin's were nevertheless quite strong, and Winnipeggers, for one, would have interpreted the setting as a Robin's. But by the end of the *Air Farce* show's regular run in 2008, a doughnut shop in Canada was pretty much considered to be a Tim's, and along the way, *Air Farce* had turned out explicit lampoons of Tim's beyond the donut shop gang. The show never parodied rivals like Country Style or Robin's because *Air Farce* was a national brand that needed a national brand to make fun of, and its Tim Hortons sketches were generally inspired by Tim Hortons' national television advertising.

Did the long-running donut-shop-gang "Canadian Moment" instill the idea that Tim Hortons customers are typical Canadian voters? At the least, the sketch reflected and perpetuated (and satirized) a notion that ordinary Canadians gathered in doughnut shops to hold forth on the issues of the day. A Tim Hortons, or a Country Style or a Robin's, was unquestionably a good place to meet and greet voters on any campaign, municipal, provincial or federal—outside Quebec at least. What changed dramatically, by the end of *Air Farce*'s television run, was that Tim Hortons had become identified in the wider culture as a baseline experience of Canadian life.

The image of the company (and its patrons), meanwhile, had been getting a pronounced boost from politicians who upheld the chain as both a beacon and a harbour of family and community values. No one did more to equate patronage of a local Tim's with values that had an equivalent champion in the political arena than the country's prime minister.

ON SEPTEMBER 23, 2009, Prime Minister Stephen Harper made one of the more intriguing and controversial public addresses of his political career. Tim Hortons was being repatriated as a Canadian corporation, and Harper turned up at the company's Oakville headquarters, along with Finance Minister Jim Flaherty and other party members, to formally welcome it back.

"This is obviously a big day for the Tim Hortons family, returning to your Canadian roots after fourteen years away," Harper began. In truth, the company had never really gone anywhere. The merger with Wendy's in 1995 had caused the company to register in Delaware, but the head office of Canadian operations had never left Oakville. What *was* returning to Canada was Tim Hortons' tax obligations as a corporation.

The prime minister's brief address, made in front of a service counter filled with doughnuts, was intended to showcase his government's economic policies, particularly reductions in corporate and personal tax rates. It might have been enough for him to welcome back the company, but Harper instead spun a web of warm associations between Tim Hortons and Canadian life.

"Now, if I were to look back to the early days, I think there were a couple of things about Tim Hortons that really connected with Canadians," he said. "First, of course, was the name and reputation of the co-founder, the great Toronto Maple Leafs defenceman Tim Horton. Baby boomers who grew up watching the Original Six remember him as one of the strongest and sturdiest blue liners ever to play the game. And of course, for millions of long-suffering Leafs fans across the country, the name Tim Horton conjures up their four Stanley Cups and the glory years of the 1960s.

"So the name was very important, but there is another thing even millions more know, millions more Canadian hockey parents like me know well, that when it is twenty degrees below zero and everyone is up for a 6 a.m. practice, nothing motivates the team more than a box of Timbits, and nothing warms the parents in the stands better than a hot double double."

The "hockey parents like me" reference, with the obligatory freezing temperature and practice at an ungodly hour, was met with subdued laughter. It seemed like a bit of folksiness that took the edge off the drier message of tax rates. Nevertheless, what the prime minister had just done in a carefully scripted address (which he delivered near verbatim) was place the company and its products—and himself—at the heart of a national family scenario, to the exclusion of every other coffee-and-doughnut chain and mom-and-pop business vying for the same consumer spending. He didn't quite say *only* Timbits can motivate a team and *only* a double double can warm the parents, but he had made the company's products the gold standard that was well known to himself and "millions more Canadian hockey parents."

It's highly doubtful Harper would have made a similar speech on the other side of Oakville, at the Ford assembly plant, and said nothing gets the family to the rink on a cold morning better than a fine Ford minivan—knowing that Chrysler, General Motors, Honda and Toyota were all building vehicles in southern Ontario. With Tim Hortons, it seemed safe and natural to elevate the corporation to an excellence acknowledged by virtually all ("millions" is quite a few) hockey parents, himself included. And hockey parents, as everyone should have known, were the heads of hard-working Canadian families who appreciated the prosperity the Conservatives were delivering to Canada. He went on to praise the Tim Hortons Children's Foundation camps and the Timbits minor sports program, which he reminded the audience had benefited hundreds of thousands of Canadian children.

Harper had covered the essential terrain of Tim Hortons' emotive connection to Canadian life. He had gotten in the moms, dads and kids at the 6 a.m. hockey practice, the nuclear family engaged in a national ritual of child rearing. That in itself is a bit of a national myth. In a country of 33 million, the total number of people involved in Hockey Canada—which includes everyone from minor-league kids to coaches to national-team talent—is 570,000. While my Hamilton childhood did in fact include cold, early-morning hockey practices, the majority of kids in Canada, whose population growth has relied on immigration from countries where the sport is unknown, don't ever play organized hockey. Harper himself never played organized hockey as a kid, although he had become a dedicated hockey dad with his own children. Nevertheless, the 6 a.m. practice is a sturdy notion of the quintessential Canadian family experience. We're kidding ourselves when we suggest that most families are ever subjected to it.

Harper's address at Tim Hortons was considered controversial not for what it said, but for where he had chosen not to be in order to deliver it. The United Nations General Assembly was in session, and Harper's political opponents accused him of skipping the opportunity to address the assembly in order to appear at a doughnut company when other world leaders were taking to the podium to address critical issues like climate change and nuclear proliferation. Harper's people said his UN speaking slot was actually the following day, and that he wouldn't have been able to address the assembly anyway because he was due in

Pittsburgh for a meeting of G20 leaders, and so had left it to the foreign affairs minister, Lawrence Cannon, to address the assembly.

The Liberals nevertheless seized on his Tim Hortons appearance, proposing it as yet another example of Harper's indifference to Canada's historic role in international affairs. "Mr. Harper does not believe in multilateral institutions . . . deep down he is an isolationist," said Liberal MP David McGuinty. Harper's no-show "betrays our modern history at the international level in a way like it has never been betrayed before."

"Look, I think that's an important forum and this is an important announcement for Canada," Harper responded. Harper's equivalency of a gathering of world leaders at the United Nations and what came across as an infomercial for Tim Hortons by the prime minister drove opposition politicians crazy. A year later, when Canada failed for the first time in sixty years to secure an available seat on the UN Security Council (after nine years of lobbying), the Conservatives' critics would point to the Tim Hortons episode as part of a pattern of Harper's indifference to the UN and internationalism.

But where his base was concerned, Harper probably got it right in choosing the Tim Hortons announcement over the UN session. To the average Canadian, the return of Tim Hortons to Canada (however much they actually understood that move) was probably a bigger deal than something going on at the UN. The Liberals championed the importance of that institution to Canada's standing in the world to a degree that many Canadians no longer believed.

As it happened, it was also during the address in Oakville in September 2009, in front of a counter of doughnuts, that Harper made the connection between his party and Canada's new, forthright role in global hotspots as a NATO combat partner, not as a UN peacekeeper, and he did it with the same double doubles and Timbits that he had made so central to families in their 6 a.m. rink routines.

Stephen Harper had not finished praising Tim Hortons role in Canadian life. "And I can tell you that Tim's is appreciated by all Canadians, none any less than by the brave men and women of the Canadian Forces. I know this well because I've served coffee and iced capps to our soldiers at the Tim Hortons at the Kandahar military base in Afghanistan."

Tim's had established an outlet at the Canadian Forces base in 2006 as part of the country's participation in the NATO mission. The restaurant on the base, operated as a corporate outlet and staffed by Canadian Forces personnel (as well as by Canadian civilians it recruited), had proved to be one of the most effective initiatives where branding Tim Hortons as a Canadian cultural icon was concerned.

The Kandahar outlet was not a one-off exercise, but rather an extension of Tim Hortons' ongoing efforts to tap the institutional opportunities of military bases. It was following the example of California's Green Beans Coffee Company, which was founded in 1996 initially to provide expatriate Americans with packaged coffee beans and began expanding into cafés on U.S. military bases in 1998. Green Beans now has more than thirty seven outlets on U.S. bases at home and around the world. (In Iraq, its twenty-four-ounce serving was dubbed the Mother of All Coffees.) Tim Hortons, for its part, now has franchises on Canadian Forces Bases Borden, Kingston, Trenton, Petawawa, Halifax and Edmonton. This effort hasn't been restricted to Canada: partnering with Kahala, franchisor of Cold Stone Creamery, has helped Tim's crack the U.S. military concession market dominated by Green Beans, as Kahala has some of its twelve different restaurant concepts on eighteen bases as well as at the Pentagon. Already at Fort Knox, Tim's opened an outlet at the U.S. naval station in Norfolk, Virginia, in January 2010 as part of a 4,500-square-foot restaurant facility that included a Cold Stone Creamery and another Kahala chain, Great Steak.

Green Beans had been in Kandahar since the NATO mission began in 2003. In a news release accompanying the official opening of the Tim's outlet in Kandahar in 2006, Tim Hortons said that the store (which served all NATO forces) was the result of a direct request from Canada's chief of the defence staff, General Rick Hillier, on behalf of his troops. The same release quoted Major General Doug Langton, chief executive officer of the Canadian Forces Personnel Support Agency, telling the assembled troops, "We hope this little piece of home will make your lives in Afghanistan just a little bit easier."

Although perhaps not quite as dangerous an initiative as Green Beans' Salerno outlet in Afghanistan, which was the first case of a food-service provider operating at a U.S. forward operating base, Tim Hortons' Kandahar store nevertheless was in an operations theatre freighted with genuine physical hazards (the Kandahar base was attacked several times by the Taliban) and potential negative associations. An Afghanistan presence was far riskier for the Tim Hortons brand than it was for that of Green Beans, as Tim's was a major consumer brand at home, whereas Green Beans was an embedded enterprise almost exclusively associated with the U.S. military. The NATO mission wasn't entirely popular with Canadians, who generally wanted the mission ended sooner rather than later, as caskets began bringing home troops killed mostly by roadside bombs. As Canadian deaths surpassed 100, as Afghanistan began to look like the same operational quagmire that had bogged down successive Western armies since the British in the 1840s and as the Conservative government appeared to be in danger of becoming bogged down itself in a scandal over the alleged torture of prisoners turned over by the Canadian Forces to Afghan authorities, Tim's risked suffering collateral damage as the concessionaire serving up double doubles, Timbits and other treats to soldiers being blown up by Taliban IEDs.

Instead, Tim Hortons came out of Afghanistan with its image as a Canadian icon only strengthened and broadened. Whatever the qualms about the actual mission, the Canadian public proved highly supportive of soldiers, their families at home and all who urged the country to "support our troops." Tim Hortons became part of the larger sentiment of troop support, delivering to men and women on a dangerous deployment a taste of what they had left behind at home, if not quite what they were literally fighting for. Troops were vocally delighted to be able to make a Tim's run so far from home. The Share a Cup with a Brave Canuck program, launched by Canadian paramedic services, which allowed Canadians to purchase $10 Tim Hortons gift cards for troops in Afghanistan, emulated the Green Beans program begun in 2005 that allows friends and family members (and corporate sponsors) to buy gift cards for U.S. troops stationed around the world. Whenever the media portrayed Canadian troops in Afghanistan beyond combat and foot patrols, the most consistent image it seemed to convey from the Kandahar base was that of typical Canadians on the other side of the world, relieving tension by playing road hockey and enjoying Tim Hortons coffee. And thanks to the special Roll Up the Rim contest, with camouflage cups and dedicated prizes that Tim Hortons ran at the Kandahar base, personnel could be seen sporting some of the thousands of baseball caps, in military-issue camouflage and bearing the Tim Hortons logo, that were among the prizes in the annual contest.

At Kandahar, Tim Hortons achieved through corporate goodwill a presence within a difficult and emotionally charged military mission that was without equal. No other Canadian corporate brand was so associated with this mission, which was itself part of a rebranding of the Canadian military, under General Rick Hillier, as a fighting force. That rebranding strove to put behind the Canadian military an image as a civil-service career option that could teach you how to be a truck mechanic as opposed to killing "scumbags" (as Hillier memorably branded the Taliban). It also emphasized Canada's dedication to combat operations within the purview of NATO, not to the sort of nightmarish, ineffectual United Nations peacekeeping role that had entrapped a Canadian contingent in the Rwandan genocide.

Afghanistan did not make Tim Hortons coffee the Red Bull of a new breed of Canadian warriors, but it did make the company a proud, apolitical supporter of those warriors, whose new, forthright and bloodied role in international trouble spots was in sharp contrast to the "peacekeeper" trope with which Molson tried to associate its flagship Canadian lager in its famous "rant" commercial of 2000. The actor playing Joe, the ideal young male target consumer, lectured Americans (while really lecturing Canadians, although the ad ran in both countries) on what a Canadian was. ("I'm not a lumberjack or a fur trader. And I don't live in an igloo or eat blubber or own a dog sled . . .") I suspect that a large part of Canadians' identity is wrapped up in a secret delight in outsiders miscasting them as hyper-outdoorsy woodspersons, just as there are times when they are happy to embrace their inner hoser and play along with being part of the great national donut shop gang. In any event, when Joe was finished telling the audience what he was not, he trotted out the shibboleth "I believe in peacekeeping, not policing."

With the hard-nosed agonies of Afghanistan, and with Highway 401 between Toronto and Trenton being renamed the Highway of Heroes in honour of the processions of military coffins bearing fallen soldiers, the idea that the Canadian military was on the world stage to wear blue UN helmets and watch impotently as genocides proceeded unabated was well past its best-before date among average Canadians. Those average Canadians, with remarkable spontaneity, began to gather on the 401 overpasses to salute the bodies of the fallen as the motorcades passed by on cold winter days. More than a few were clutching coffees to stay warm; more than a few of those coffees had been fetched from a Tim Hortons drive-through.

With the Kandahar mission, Tim Hortons was embedded in the narrative of sacrifice by ordinary Canadians who were supported by ordinary Canadian families, along with the schoolchildren whose classrooms contributed to Share a Cup with a Brave Canuck. Without having to forge any formal connection, Tim Hortons' central role in the Canadian identity was indirectly enhanced when Don Cherry emerged as a stalwart champion of the troops and made tearful and heartfelt tributes to every fallen soldier on his "Coach's Corner" segment on *Hockey Night in Canada*. The Share a Buck with a Brave Canuck program helped solidify the idea of troops as "heroes," a label that also began to be applied routinely to police officers, firefighters and the emergency-service workers that launched it. A cup of joe at Tim's became the point of convergence for a rapidly expanding sentiment that Canada was the home of the brave.

When Toronto Maple Leafs general manager Brian Burke visited Kandahar as part of a celebrity tour with the new chief of the defence staff, General Walt Natynczyk, as the Canadian mission approached its end in the summer of 2011, he handed $800 to the staff at the Tim's on the base and told them to keep the coffee coming. General Natynczyk put in a good word for Tim's with the media: "So popular is the Tim Hortons at Kandahar that Gen. Natynczyk says American and British soldiers have joked they wanted to immigrate to Canada," *The Globe and Mail's* Jane Taber reported in early July. "And with 3,000 of our troops all expected back in Canada by the end of July, Gen. Natynczyk says the Tim Hortons will remain open and operating until October, at least."

Canada by then had rewarded a Tim Hortons prime minister with a majority government.

24

Values Proposition: QSR Coffee as a Political Brand

The association between Stephen Harper and Tim Hortons goes back at least to 2006, when he secured his first minority government. In saluting his seeming ordinariness, his lack of membership in any Canadian elite, *Maclean's* magazine called him "the Tim Hortons Prime Minister." When he was spotted playing mini-golf in Buffalo, New York, on a short vacation in August 2011, the magazine's editors seized on it as proof positive that he truly was the average guy, the Tim Hortons prime minister he appeared to be: "The real Stephen Harper is identical to the packaged and scripted version. His ordinariness is no act."

The *Toronto Star*'s Susan Delacourt would beg to differ. The issues of branding, of Tim Hortons as a name on a sign and as a commercial personality, "so much fits Stephen Harper," she remarked as we discussed the restaurant, the Tim Hortons/Starbucks polarity, and Harper's September 2009 address welcoming Tim Hortons back to Canada as a corporate entity. "He bears no resemblance to the public figure people see. The public persona is not him."

Harper pauses in the video of that 2009 address to sip from a Tim Hortons mug, but Harper doesn't drink coffee; as she reported, he was actually drinking hot chocolate. The supreme irony of the Tim

Hortons/Starbucks polarity over coffee allegiance in Canadian culture during the 2011 federal election was that neither man cast in opposing roles, Harper and Ignatieff, would ever drink either company's java.

To some measure, the calculated branding of Tim Hortons customer values as their own values by Conservatives likely was an imported concept. Just as Jim Charade wanted to launch his own version of Mister Donut in Canada, the Conservatives seemed to have looked stateside and recognized a potent lesson from American politics: that who you are as a voter or a candidate is where you eat, because consumption speaks to values, and values, not narrow policy positions, are what drive voting behaviour.

Equating the Democratic left with Starbuckian drinking habits is not unknown in American politics. On February 29, 2012, Republican Utah senator Orrin Hatch said, "President Obama has traded in the hard hat and lunch bucket category of the Democratic Party for the hipster fedora and a double skim latte." But I could not think of an American example of electoral branding that came close to the Canadian phenomenon of the Tim Hortons voter. There were NASCAR dads and soccer moms, but these represented interest-group segments, not representatives of a broad electoral centre. Only Joe the Plumber of the 2008 presidential campaign came close, but he had no consumer brand association. Delacourt, however, directed me toward a book that created buzz in political and media circles in the U.S. when it was published in 2006—the same year that *Maclean's* proclaimed Harper the Tim Hortons prime minister. It was *Applebee's America: How Successful Political, Business, and Religious Leaders Connect with the New American Community.*

The authors, Ron Fournier, Douglas B. Sosnik and Matthew J. Dowd, examined how American politicians (especially Bill Clinton and George W. Bush), the casual-dining restaurant chain Applebee's and southern California evangelist Rick Warren had all found popular appeal through "gut values connections" with an American population rocked by change.

The authors sought out ordinary Americans like single mother Cindy Moran in an Applebee's restaurant in Howell, Michigan. "Buffeted by change, people like Moran crave the comfort of community. They want to know their neighbors and meet people like themselves no matter where they live. They want to help improve their neighborhoods and their country. They want to belong." One of the electoral myths the authors proposed to crush was: "The best indicator of how a person will vote is his voting history or views on abortion, taxes, and other issues." In reality, "the key to predicting how a person will vote (or shop and worship, for that matter) is his or her lifestyle choices."

One cannot help but suspect that more than one well-thumbed copy of *Applebee's America* rests in the bookshelves of Harper strategists. Its ideas are extrapolated to an extreme in the Tim Hortons model of the prime minister, his party and the electorate. Where Applebee's was proposed as an example of an enterprise that prospered by literally feeding a desire for comfort and community values, Tim Hortons in Canada became the defining brand of middle-class, working-family, middle-of-the-road values: the singular place where the donut-shop-gang voters congregated in a recognizable bloc of broad-based sentiment and carried its logo'd product into core-values activities like that most threadbare of supposed collective experiences, the 6 a.m. hockey practice. Tim Hortons became the commercial nexus of a nation's soul.

But as I have already argued, it is far from clear that Tim Hortons actually represents what politicians and members of the media have purported it does. In particular, the idea of a Tim Hortons/Starbucks polarity may be more myth (or wishful thinking) than reality. Tim Hortons' television advertising in its summer 2011 promotions had moved so far beyond the donut shop gang that only fit thirtysomethings needed to audition for the roles as childless hetero couples. The ideal Tim's customer was looking a lot like an ideal Starbucks customer. An actual family hadn't been seen since wraps were introduced over the winter of 2010/11, when several couples were shown chowing down on Tim's takeout in a hotel lobby, obviously at a hockey tournament, while their kids threatened to trash the place with boisterous stickwork.

At the same time, Conservative spin doctors wanted Liberals to come across as tedious urban creatures, disconnected from the real lives and real values of the donut shop gang. "Latte-sipping elites, ensconced in comfy chairs and typing away at laptops in their local Starbucks, are a fixture of Canadian politics today," Éric Grenier wrote in *The Globe and Mail* in November 2010 as he analyzed patterns of electoral results and the predominance of Starbucks outlets. "The stereotype is used—often scornfully—to describe Liberal voters, probably from downtown Toronto." It's an image that Conservative bloggers were eager to pin on Michael Ignatieff.

But as Grenier showed, the reality was that a resident of a riding full of Starbucks "is no more likely to vote Liberal than he or she is to vote New Democratic or even Conservative . . . In fact, there is very little difference between a typical Liberal or Conservative-held riding." What is more, he revealed, "Of the top 10 per cent of ridings in Canada with the highest Starbucks density, 17 are Conservative, nine are New Democratic and only five are Liberal." Grenier also found "almost no difference between the average number of Tim Hortons locations in each of the ridings currently held by the three national parties." Contrary to public perception, the Conservatives came out last among the three federal parties, with an average of about nine Tim Hortons shops per riding.

The most that Grenier could muster in support of the idea that Tim's customers favoured the Conservatives was that in the top 10 percent of ridings in terms of store density, the Conservatives held twelve, compared to ten by the Liberals and eight by the NDP. That was hardly a landslide vote for a Tim's-Conservative alignment. As Grenier further noted, a 2009 Harris/Decima poll showed "the proportion of Liberal,

New Democratic, and Conservative voters who preferred Tim Hortons to Starbucks were virtually identical for each party." The worst news for adherents of the Tim Hortons/Starbucks polarity theory was that Michael Ignatieff's riding of Etobicoke-Lakeshore had three times as many Tim's as the ridings of Harper and NDP leader Jack Layton.

If neither the latte-sipping Liberal at Starbucks nor the Conservative-allied, family-values donut shop gang really existed, that doesn't mean they weren't politically useful. The Conservatives, for one, tried to use the idea of the Tim Hortons voter to project themselves as a big-tent party for average Canadians, even though their use of "micro-targeting" in identifying discrete voter segments affirms that the Canadian electorate is far more diffuse and defiant of branding by a particular QSR habit than homilies about 6 a.m hockey practices, double doubles and snack packs of Timbits can uphold. The New Democrats have not shied from campaigning at Tim Hortons while avoiding Starbucks (especially given Starbucks' global corporatist taint); after all, if Tim Hortons is the true natural habitat of working families, the preferred New Democrat definition of a working family is one that has at least one breadwinner with a union card. The Liberals, meanwhile, have not so much campaigned as a party of the Tim Hortons voter as they have as a party that wants nothing to do with Starbucks.

Canadians like to make fun of Americans for their ignorance of their northern neighbours, although I think many Americans know a lot more about us than we care to admit. On his CBC show *Talking to Americans*, Rick Mercer got good-natured Main Street folks to agree that the name of Canada's prime minister was Tim Horton. But then, my own Member of Provincial Parliament, a PC backbencher named Garfield Dunlop, informed the Ontario legislature in May 2011, "A Tim Horton PC government will protect our communities." He meant Tim *Hudak*.

When confronted with the Tim Hortons/Starbucks polarity, Ignatieff tried to dismiss it. "It's something I actually don't like about the Conservative vision of the country," he told Delacourt in September 2010. "I don't think there's a division between a Tim Hortons nation and any other nation. I don't think there's a division between people who've lived outside the country and people who've lived inside. I don't think there's a division between people who go to Tim Hortons for their coffee and people who go to Starbucks for their coffee. I see one country, right?"

Ignatieff was absolutely right, on the coffee front at least, but the answer was assuredly absolutely wrong. A lot of Canadians believed in that polarity, and when Ignatieff said he didn't think buying coffee at Tim's or Starbucks indicated anything about who you are, many Canadians probably were inclined to believe the Conservative attack ads that said Iggy had been out of the country so long as an academic and journalist that he didn't understand Canada.

By the spring 2011 federal election, Tim Hortons had become a requisite campaign whistle stop for all parties outside Quebec. The reasons were twofold. First, candidates needed to be seen catering to and identifying with "working family" voters, and a Tim Hortons was supposed to be where they gathered. Second, candidates needed *not* to be seen looking for voters where "working families" weren't supposed to be—namely, at a Starbucks. Starbucks spoke of big-city urban. It was not where Mom and Dad stopped to buy Timbits and coffee that was simply called "coffee" while driving the kids to hockey practice. Nobody ever ordered a "double double" from Starbucks. They ordered an Espresso Con Panna or some other concoction that had no equivalent in the refreshment area of the local triple rink or curling club.

WHERE TIM HORTONS ITSELF stood in this political branding was the intriguing question. Ron Joyce had connections to Conservative politics, as did his cousin Archibald Jollymore, who had departed as a vice-president in 1994 to become a franchisee and is a prominent Conservative in Burlington, Ontario. Mike Harris, the Conservative premier from 1995 to 2002, sits on the board of the Tim Horton Children's Foundation, which Ron Joyce continues to chair. The new leader of Ontario's Progressive Conservatives, Tim Hudak, who was in danger of appearing to run as the leader of the Tim Hortons Party in the fall 2011 provincial election, had been a cabinet minister in the Harris government. But the company itself has been assiduously apolitical—for example, donating the maximum $9,300 permitted corporations in Ontario to both the provincial Liberals and Progressive Conservatives in 2011. Like most corporations, it gave the left-wing, labour-allied New Democrats a pass—additionally understandable, as efforts to organize Tim Hortons franchise employees failed in the 1990s.

Tim's did, by chance, prepare the ground for a voter brand association with its "Based on a True Story" television campaign, which successfully reinforced the idea that Tim Hortons was an elemental Canadian experience and indispensable to many of its citizens. It was a risky campaign in that consumers don't necessarily like to be told by a corporation that its business is so important to their humble lives, but for Tim's it worked. The company migrated the campaign to the Internet with its Every Cup Tells a Story promotion, in which customers create personal testimonials about the importance of Tim's and its products to their lives by uploading videos. As this promotion was the focus of a contest in 2011, it is difficult to judge how enthusiastic the average Tim's customer really is about voluntarily paying tribute to the company, but the company does seem to have been motivated to launch Every Cup Tells a Story by the sheer number of suggestions people were making for "Based on a True Story" ads after the campaign initially stopped running.

By and large, the idea that being an unpretentious, middle-spectrum, working-family Canadian also means being a Tim Hortons customer has been beyond the company's control or influence. Since launching the "Based on a True Story" campaign, Tim's has had to do little more than sit back and watch as the media (and politicians hypersensitive to the alternately beneficial and toxic messages of photo ops) ran with it and turned the idea into a national truth. It hasn't hurt the company's sales to have so many politicians, political operatives and journalists reinforcing the idea that being Canadian means patronizing Tim Hortons, however much that hurts innocent Canadian corporate bystanders like Second Cup, Robin's Donuts, Coffee Time and Country Style.

By the end of the 2011 federal election, the concept of the Tim Hortons voter was being dismissed as hackneyed by some political insiders. Once they had their majority government, the Conservatives moved on to a new branding exercise: elevating the role of the monarchy. As Jane Taber of *The Globe and Mail* reported on August 19, this royalty craze was part of an effort by Harper to "create a new frame" for the Canadian identity: "Dean Del Mastro, the Parliamentary Secretary to the Prime Minister, says this is about restoring Canada's national identity which has been 'lost.' Canada is more, he says, than hockey, 'saying "eh" a lot' and drinking Tim Hortons coffee."

Del Mastro's dismissal of Tim Hortons (along with hockey) as the most meaningful elements of the national identity showed how far the Conservatives had come from a minority-government prime minister embracing Tim Hortons as a central experience of Canadian life in September 2009. Tim Hortons as a Canadian symbol appeared to have become as disposable as a takeout cup as soon as Harper had his majority and Ignatieff's Liberals (and Ignatieff himself) were crushed.

But that cup turned out to be not so much disposable as it was recyclable. It was surprising that Tim Hortons made such a rebound in the ensuing Ontario election that autumn, which Tim Hudak's Conservatives began with a double-digit lead in the polls over Dalton

McGuinty's incumbent Liberals. Hudak wasn't the only party leader to work the Tim's angle. The premier made obligatory appearances at outlets. Andrea Horwath, a Hamiltonian who knows which cup her coffee is poured in, also turned up at outlets, choosing one in Oakville to announce her party's jobs platform, for example. The *Toronto Star*'s webzine *The Grid* subjected her to a "lightning round" of questions that included the predictable "Starbucks or Tim Hortons?" Horwath wisely replied, "Timmies."

Tim Hudak's performance was the most noteworthy where Tim's was concerned. Hudak spent a lot of time in all sorts of restaurants, both chains and independents, as if searching for the elusive Canadian version of the Applebee's voter, but he chose Tim's outlets especially for meet-and-greet photo ops and hit them hard in the final days of the campaign. Conservative leaders like Hudak have shown themselves eager to get behind the counter and serve customers. Harper did it during the spring 2011 election in Dieppe, New Brunswick, where he handed out coffees to customers (taking advantage of the heavy business of the Roll Up the Rim promotion). CBC reporter Susan Lunn noted that when she saw Ignatieff at a Tim Hortons in Halifax, he simply paid for the coffee his wife wanted and left.

When Hudak was interviewed by *Metro London* on October 2, he was videotaped in a conference room with a Tim Hortons cup in front of him. The editors asked, "Can you tell me how you deal with stress on the job?" Hudak joked, "Bourbon!" then added, "What helps me through the day, 'cause they are long days . . . a little bit of Tim Hortons, courtesy of *Metro* . . ." The next day, Hudak visited Tim Hortons outlets in London, Blenheim and Kitchener, and carried a cup of coffee to a local arena for another photo op. On the final day of campaigning, on October 6, he showed up serving customers at a Tim's drive-through window in Niagara Falls, in his home riding.

I asked the Schulich School of Business's Alan Middleton to comment on the brand alignment of Conservative politicians—Hudak in particular—with Tim Hortons. "It's a politician using the Tim Hortons brand just as filmmakers use products," he said. Even though filmmakers usually charge for product placement, they're nevertheless looking to access the connotations of particular brands. Whenever a politician aligns him- or herself with Tim Hortons, the goal is to reap the visual association the viewer makes with the values they assign to the brand.

It is tempting to interpret all the Tim's appearances by Hudak in the final days of the campaign, his commanding early lead in the polls having vaporized, as a reflexive if desperate attempt to connect with the average-Canadian, pseudo-Applebee's voters who were said to inhabit Tim's and were wont to identify with any politician seen drinking a Tim's coffee. If so, it didn't work. McGuinty's Liberals came within one seat of forming a third consecutive majority government.

I THOUGHT THE ONTARIO ELECTION of 2011 was the death knell of the Tim Hortons' voter. The restaurants would endure as places to meet and greet the electorate, but the idea that its customers form a voting bloc with shared values that can be drawn en masse to a particular political party likely had died. And with Tim Hortons having announced free Wi-Fi, more upscale interiors and a new line of espresso drinks only weeks after the Ontario election, I wondered if politicians and media members would still believe there is such a thing as a Tim Hortons voter the next time any part of this country goes to the polls.

Then the robocall scandal broke in February 2012. Bruce Anderson, a pollster with Harris/Decima and a CBC "At Issue" panellist, writing in *The Globe and Mail* on March 4, noted that if the allegations proved true, "experts will talk about how this is an affront to democracy, and use $5 terms like 'voter suppression.' But that's not what it will be called in your local Tim Hortons. To those non-partisans who decided to trust the Conservatives in 2006, and grew in number through 2011, this would feel like a slap in the face." In the same newspaper a day later, television critic John Doyle noted more generically the "disconnect between coffee-shop interviews and House of Commons barking" on the robocall issue.

The notion of the Tim Hortons voter was alive and well, the embodiment of what Bruce Anderson called "middle-class, mainstream Canada."

25

The End of the Road: Seeking the Legacy of Tim Horton

At around 4:30 in the morning on February 21, 1974, a white Ford DeTomaso Pantera left the passing lane of the eastbound Queen Elizabeth Way approaching the Lake Street overpass in St. Catharines, Ontario. The pavement was dry and clear; the grass median (which no longer exists, as the highway has been widened in both directions) was lightly dusted with snow. Reportedly travelling at more than 100 miles per hour, the gull-wing-door sports car plunged into the median, striking a storm sewer catchment 141 feet down the road. Becoming airborne, the car returned to earth 72 feet later, ploughed a gouge into the turf, became airborne again for another 62 feet, ploughed another gouge, and along the way lost the right rear wheel assembly, blew the other three tires and left behind the nameplate from its grill. The car began rolling, and 58 feet later, not far along from a shower of broken glass, the driver, who was not wearing a seatbelt, was flung through the passenger door. Crossing over into the westbound lanes, the tumbling and battered Pantera, its hood all but torn off, came to a halt, upside down in the centre of the roadway, more than 400 feet from where it had first left the eastbound lanes.

An Ontario Provincial Police constable, M.W. (Michael) Gula, and an ambulance were on the scene almost immediately. No one else was in the car. The driver was rushed to St. Catharines General, a trip of less than two miles, where he was pronounced dead on arrival at 4:50. He had massive skull fractures, a fractured and dislocated neck and four broken left ribs. He was dressed nattily in a brown-checked overcoat, a yellow sports jacket over a yellow shirt, brown pants and brown boots. He was forty-four years old, a solid, muscular man, five feet, nine inches and 210 pounds. His driver's licence said he was Miles Gilbert Horton and that he lived on Bannatyne Drive in Willowdale, Ontario. The registration of the Pantera was in the name of Timothy Horton, who lived in suite 14K at the Statler Hotel in Buffalo, New York.

The driver and the owner were one and the same person. As the coroner noted, he was "the famous hockey player" on the roster of the Buffalo Sabres.

Tim Horton's violent death ended a career in professional hockey a quarter-century long. It also emphatically ended his association with his chain of coffee-and-doughnut shops, about forty of which were either open or in development. Only days earlier, Gary O'Neill had entered the picture as the franchisee who would begin building the chain's presence in Atlantic Canada. Horton's death had come soon after a late-night—make that early-morning—session of conversation and alcohol with his partner, Ron Joyce, at the restaurant chain's headquarters in Oakville, which had been flecked with a moment of tension over which of them was actually in charge. The consequences of that death cascaded through the company's history, affecting the trajectory of its ownership and the marketing options of its brand. Tim Hortons today possesses a widely admired brand name whose promotional possibilities nevertheless have been severely limited by the legacy of its namesake. With more than twice the legal limit of alcohol in his blood as well as traces of barbiturate, Horton's violent departure from life left his personal and corporate legacy decidedly in limbo.

I discussed with Ken Wong of Queen's University Tim Hortons' predilection to associate itself with hockey in the U.S. market, through promotional partnerships with the NHL's New York Islanders, Pittsburgh Penguins and Columbus Blue Jackets. Tim's had also sponsored the Winter Classic outdoor games, and would be lead sponsor of the 2012 NHL All-Star Game. Here was a company, I remarked, seeking to build a brand affiliation with NHL teams, and which was named for a celebrated NHL All-Star, Stanley Cup winner and Hall of Famer, and yet Tim Horton, as an individual that could be resurrected as a brand persona, remained largely out of sight. Wong told me that employing Horton's persona in a prominent way is highly unlikely: "He did not lead a lifestyle that would be conducive to this."

It bothered me, with all I had learned about Tim Horton when I wrote his biography, that the end of the road had to come for him on a highway straightaway in St. Catharines, that a horrific wreck snuffed out his life and to a substantial degree his good reputation, as so many people had told me how much they had admired him and now missed him. I wanted to see what lay at the end of another road where his legacy was concerned, if something more about him had been left behind than a damning coroner's report and a stylized script on a restaurant sign.

HIGHWAY 400/69, on the east side of Georgian Bay, linking Sudbury in the north with the metropolitan sprawl of Greater Toronto farther to the south, was an undivided two-lane ribbon of pavement when Tim Horton was alive, wending its way through blasted rock cuts, First Nations reserves and blink-of-an-eye vacation hamlets. With the extension of the multilane Highway 400 north from Barrie, 400/69 is now twinned as a multilane divided expressway as far as the north side of Parry Sound, making the drive largely bereft of the sometimes-harrowing intersections and unforgiving narrows through the dynamited rock of the Canadian Shield that haunted the route only a few years ago. Tim Horton had known the road well. It linked his home in Sudbury and his junior hockey team in Copper Cliff with his professional destiny in Toronto. He liked to drive like hell, and he survived the original highway's multiple hazards, only to end up losing his life on a die-straight stretch of the multilane QEW.

As the 400/69 highway has been civilized and gentrified, so has the vacation country through which it snakes. There is still plenty that is wild along eastern Georgian Bay, but as the highway passes through the district of Muskoka, it has gathered up the monetary momentum of one of Canada's pricier vacation destinations and distributed the cash deeper into erstwhile hinterland. Modest cabins have given way to four-season homes; glorified logging roads have been paved and are ploughed all winter long. Parry Sound is still a modest centre of 6,000, but a far cry from the late-nineteenth-century lumber town that, even in its earliest days, serviced sportsmen and families from southern Ontario and the eastern United States seeking a recreational respite.

At the Bowes Street exit, an infestation of QSR franchises has taken hold amid the greater commercial bustle. On the north side, a Starbucks drive-through beckons urbanites from its location in a Canadian Tire gas bar. To the east of it is a McDonald's, and beyond to the west a Pizza Hut and a KFC. Across the road from the Pizza Hut is a tight franchise cluster: a Harvey's and Swiss Chalet share a development with Richard's Coffee, and immediately to their west is a standard Tim Hortons store with a drive-through.

I once interviewed a subject for a magazine article at the Richard's. My interviewee chose the location as the rendezvous because it would be easy for me to find from the highway, but there was also something of an anti-corporate sentiment in the determination to meet there, and not at the Tim's (an 80/20 outlet) right next door. It didn't much matter that the Richard's menu of coffee, baked goods, soups and sandwiches mirrored that of the Tim Hortons. One can forget how the purported Canadian obsession with all things Timmy is not necessarily embraced in every community.

In mid-August 2011, I pulled into that Tim Hortons drive-through. Given my destination, it seemed like the right thing to do. It was mid-afternoon on a Saturday, and a healthy parade of vehicles snaked around the building in the drive-through lane. I ordered a small coffee (cream only) and an apple fritter. As I was still trying to shave away a few pounds, I had no business indulging in 300 calories of sugary baked confection. The fritter was warm, doughy and sweet. It mattered to me not at all that it had been parbaked in a factory in Brantford and finished off in a microwave-convection oven in the back of the store. The fritter was gone before I was on the northbound ramp to the 400/69, looking for the exit to Highway 124 that would take me east to Lorimer Lake, to the legacy of the restaurant's namesake that has come to matter more than doughnuts and coffee to many Canadians.

THE ONLY SIGN along the entire route from Parry Sound indicating the direction to the Tim Horton Memorial Camp is at a Y-junction where Lorimer Lake Road splits with Bunny Trail. A post there is plastered with the handmade signage of vacation country that helps cottage guests stay on the not-so-straight and narrow route to their destination. Below an inscribed paddle indicating the direction to a private paradise called Breezy Bay Isle, and above a simple lettered board indicating that Awana Landing is twenty-one kilometres farther down Bunny Trail is a rectangular sign labelled TIM HORTON MEMORIAL CAMP, with its logo and a red arrow telling the driver to bear right.

That modest nudge at the fork in the road is more than enough to deliver a steady stream of visitors to the camp, about six kilometres farther north. "We're a pretty big tourist attraction," the camp's general manager, Shannon Benner, told me as we toured its 100 acres of facilities. "And they want a coffee. Everybody is welcome, but we're pretty protective of the kids." Newly arrived kids, for their part, sometimes wonder when the Timbits feast is going to start.

The Tim Horton Memorial Camp does not look like a Tim Hortons, does not have a Tim Hortons outlet and does not serve the Tim Hortons menu to guests, staff or campers (although some of the food, such as sandwich buns, are from the company, and the large kitchen that services the dining room in the main building, Ontario House, does have an Always Fresh parbaking oven). The storage area beneath the main lodge is full of food donated by suppliers to the restaurant chain, so full that the camp has no food budget. No corporate signage or logos suggest Tim Hortons in any way, shape or form. The camp logo—stylized hands cupping a child—looks nothing like the company logo. While the camp is closely affiliated with the restaurant chain, and could not exist without it, this retreat at Lorimer Lake—and the other five camps that now form the foundation's system—are their own world.

The idea of establishing a camp for underprivileged children to honour Tim Horton's life and memory came together with remarkable speed. His friend, the Reverend Gordon Griggs, announced the intention to establish the Tim Horton Memorial Camp at Horton's funeral. That Horton's charitable memorial would have something to do with children scarcely required any thought. Tim Horton came from fairly modest (but hardly impoverished) means, but a camp for economically needy children surely struck a particular chord with Ron Joyce, who had been raised by a single mother on a widow's allowance and would recall in his memoir the astonishing words a teacher wrote in an autograph book at the end of junior school: "Rich boys have many faults, poor boys have but two:/Nothing is any good they say and nothing is any good they do."

Griggs announced at the funeral that the camp would be built on 150 acres near Orangeville, Ontario, that were co-owned by Horton, Joyce and their lawyer, Ken Gariepy. However, at the last minute Gariepy withdrew his support, as he could not afford the donation. That sent Joyce and his late partner's widow in search of an alternate property. They found it on the shore of Lorimer Lake, an old fishing camp they picked up for $75,000. Lori at least had been through this sort of acquisition recently; about sixty-five kilometres to the east, Tim had bought a former fishing camp, a four-acre property with five guest cabins on Peninsula Lake, just east of Huntsville, when he came to the Buffalo Sabres in 1972. A contractor was hired to extensively renovate it while Horton was playing the 1972–73 season, and he enjoyed his one and only summer at this lake retreat in 1973. The charitable foundation was created in June 1974, and a flying squad of family, friends and store franchisees descended on the Lorimer Lake fishing camp, whipping it into sufficient shape to welcome the first campers the following summer. Joyce told me, fondly if ruefully, that in the beginning it was "an underprivileged camp for underprivileged kids."

Old-time cottagers on the lake have told the staff which of the present-day camp's numerous buildings is built on the original modest fishing camp. The camp otherwise is unrecognizable from its original configuration. About $6 million was spent on a major renovation and the construction of two new accommodation lodges in 2009. Nearing the end of the third season for the overhauled facility, the operation sparkled. The buildings had the same candy-apple-red metal roofing and light grey wood stain. The grounds were impeccably neat—one of the few clues that the camp had anything to do with the restaurant chain was the presence of one of the signature waste bins from the restaurant, with different receptacles for trash and various recyclables. The lodges are heated and air-conditioned. The rooms, with four kids in two bunk beds, share a washroom and shower area, and the ones I was able to poke my head into while touring the facility were unnervingly tidy for the age of the children and the fact that they had been at camp for nine days. Most middle-class Canadian families would be thrilled to stay at the Lorimer Lake camp if it happened to be a resort. Instead, it is a once-in-a-lifetime opportunity for the kids who do come here.

THE CAMP BEGAN WITH LITTLE MORE than a wish to give disadvantaged kids an opportunity to experience something remarkable. Having them fly to the camp was one of the early characteristics, and some camp goers still travel that way, between major airports, as part of the experience. But by the 1980s the foundation realized it needed to offer more than a brief getaway for poor children, that it needed to effect lasting change in young lives. It began to develop a signature program that is built around setting and meeting challenges.

The Tim Hortons camps are widely admired for their professionalism and programming. Shannon Benner had been Lorimer Lake's general manager for four years when I met her. She grew up just south of Vancouver in Tsawwassen, and had worked for Outward Bound, leading sea kayaking tours. Moving to Princeton, New Jersey, she designed a program for former youth gang members. "We rode the Underground Railroad route on bikes, all the way from the South to Niagara Falls," she recalled for me. After ten years away, she wanted to come back to Canada, and brought with her an American husband and their two small boys, to take charge of the Memorial Camp.

The camp is highly structured. For ten days, counsellors lead kids aged nine to twelve through activities built around a GREAT beads system. These multicoloured beads create a bracelet that symbolizes their accomplishments at the end of their stay. Blue is for G—Goal Setting (setting goals and learning how to achieve them). Yellow is for

R—Responsible Leadership (setting a good example for others, having a positive influence on those around them and helping solve problems). Green is for E—Environmental Awareness (respecting the environment and learning the importance of conservation). Orange is for A—Adventure and Creativity (discovering new things and participating in challenging activities). Red is for T—Teamwork and Friendship (accepting people's differences, making new friends and working together in a positive and friendly environment). Along the way, the kids participate in obstacle courses, rock-wall climbs, zip-lining and crafts, and canoeing, kayaking, sailing and tubing on the lake.

Kids can attend only once, although they are eligible to return for the leadership program for teens, who can participate for five years. Years two through four are spent at the camp; the first and last years are dedicated to wilderness outings. At the Memorial Camp, leadership teens venture to Killarney Provincial Park, on the north shore of Georgian Bay, working with Friends of Killarney Park on projects such as portage maintenance. At the completion of the leadership program, the participants received a bursary toward their postsecondary education.

The key drivers of the foundation's camps are the franchisees. They raise funds through Send a Kid to Camp Day, when proceeds of the day's coffee sales are donated to the foundation. The franchisees are also responsible for how kids are chosen to participate. Every franchise outlet (both owner and 80/20) sends two kids per summer. "We connect restaurant owners with the community," Benner explained. "Sometimes teachers, sometimes Big Brothers and Big Sisters, sometimes [Children and Youth] Services recommends the kids." The applications must then be reviewed and approved by the foundation's office at another one of its camps, Onondaga Farms. A nominee needs to meet the current Canada Revenue Agency definition of low income for a given size of family, but the application also must indicate why a particular child would benefit from the camp experience. Where possible, the foundation tries to accommodate children with disabilities, and will send them to a camp with a program most appropriate to them.

From this original camp at Lorimer Lake, the foundation has grown to a network that includes five other facilities: Onondaga Farms at St. George, Ontario; the Children's Ranch at Kananaskis, Alberta; the Children's Camp at Tatamagouche, Nova Scotia; Camp des Voyageurs at Quyon, Quebec; and Camp Kentahten in Campbellsville, Kentucky. Each has its own character. Where the Memorial Camp at Lorimer Lake, for example, is very much an Ontario summer camp on a northern lake, Onondaga Farms features a working farm with cattle, horses and sheep, and Kananaskis is an equestrian ranch that also offers white-water rafting.

Although the camp system initially expanded to Tatamagouche at the urging of Moncton franchisee Gary O'Neill so that children in Atlantic Canada could have a camp as well, the current system is not organized regionally. Kids are sent around the country (and to and from the United States), regardless of the camp nearest to their homes. It gives them the experience of new places, new people, and in some cases, a first ride on a commercial aircraft.

Two nurses are on staff at Lorimer Lake, and they assess the campers at a wellness centre as they arrive. They do more than check for the typical head-lice issues of school-age kids. Children from disadvantaged backgrounds can show up with a host of physical needs, ranging from malnourishment to bad teeth, and the camp arranges for treatment.

During the summer camp sessions, 148 children and 70 staff are on the 100-acre property at Lorimer Lake; the camp also owns an island at the north end of the lake that is used for overnight canoe trips. Less well known is the fact that the camp operates year-round. "On any given day, there will be forty to sixty kids here, for three- to four-day experiences, " Shannon said of the off-season. "They've come with church groups, Toronto [Children's] Services, Manitoulin Secondary

School . . ." When she learned that my wife works in the public school system, she gave me a brochure and urged me to make sure that the teachers at my wife's school (who already are involved in nominating kids for the camp) knew about the year-round opportunities.

Back in the early 1990s, when Lori Horton began objecting to both the camp system and the fundraising poster using her late husband's image, the association with Tim Horton was downplayed, with the annual fundraising drive at franchises called Camp Day. Ron Joyce told me then that the foundation had considered removing Tim Horton's name altogether, but the franchisees, he said, would never support that.

Still, there's almost nothing at Tim Horton Memorial Camp that resembles a memorial to Tim Horton. On the lower right corner of the stone entrance gate is the bronze plaque from the camp's opening in 1975. Beneath the Tim Horton Children's Foundation logo is a simple inscription:

M.G. (Tim) Horton
1930–1974
This camp is dedicated in memory of Tim,
a loving husband and father,
an outstanding athlete and businessman,
and a wonderful person friend to so many of us.
Always remembered.
Founders: Lori Horton, Ron Joyce

No statue of Horton graces the grounds; no memorabilia is enshrined in a display case. Nowhere did I see the camp foundation fundraising poster portraying Horton, created by the artist Ken Danby, that caused such a legal kerfuffle with Lori Horton in the 1990s. The only portrait I saw of Horton anywhere that I wandered, indoors and out, was a drawing on a commemorative plate (salad size) hanging on the wall of Shannon Benner's office. Labelled TIM HORTON CAMP DEDICATION, JULY 6, 1984, it honoured the tenth anniversary of the creation of the Lorimer Lake camp.

I asked Shannon Benner, as we watched youth leaders tackle the climbing tower and the children practise archery, what might be imparted to the campers about the man in whose memory this first camp was opened.

"They're certainly told who he was," she said, but there is no activity that invokes Horton as a person or an inspiration. Where individuals are concerned, the emphasis, she says, is on the restaurant franchisees.

The children cannot help but be mindful of the fact that the chain's franchisees are responsible for creating and maintaining the camp, and for personally sending them for ten days at no cost. Some of the buildings are named after franchisees, and on the soaring interior wall of Ontario House, where the campers gather to dine, is a roll call of names with an explanatory sign: "This honorary role [*sic*] recognizes the unselfish efforts and generous contributions by the Store Operators of Ontario in funding the total cost of Ontario House."

When their session is over, each camper writes a personal letter of thanks to the "store owner" who is said to have sent them. At the banquet that ends the session, one child is selected from every cabin group to read aloud their letter. I listened to the kids from the sixth of seven sessions of the summer of 2011 read their letters. Nine-to-twelve-year-olds are not necessarily the most expressive and introspective people when it comes to written prose, and for the most part they appreciatively listed their activities: the tubing, archery, kayaking and overnight camping. Some praised the food, others the friends they'd made and the coolness of their counsellors.

The counsellors, male and female, *were* pretty cool. They did a great job praising the kids at this ceremony, of recounting how they not only met their goals but "smashed" them. I doubt these boys and girls had ever experienced so much positive and practical influence in one sustained period in their lives. Two declared they had just had the best week of their life, and given the disadvantages that merited their participation, and the gleaming facilities and professional programming, there was no reason to doubt their sincerity.

A cynic might view the letter-writing exercise as part of a marketing scheme to turn underprivileged kids and their families into lifelong devotees of Tim Hortons restaurants. I think the company and its franchisees have less elaborate and far more inexpensive ways to inculcate a following. If this letter-writing exercise had any marketing target, it was the franchisee. The foundation ensured that every franchisee who sent kids to camp, by whatever selection method employed, heard directly from those kids, and was made to understand what a difference the camp experience could make for a single life.

Cam MacDonald confessed to me that when he became a franchisee, he didn't really understand the point of the camps. His late father had been instrumental in raising funds for hospital projects in Hamilton. If the company and its franchisees wanted to make a difference in kids' lives, why didn't they just raise money for a hospital cause? (The company does that as well, through the Smile Cookie program.) Then he attended a police safety function at a local school, handing out free Cold Stone Creamery treats. (The participation of QSRs in school functions like this angers bariatric medicine specialist and anti-obesity crusader Dr. Yoni Freedhoff, but never mind for now.) A girl came up to him and said, "Cam and Karen MacDonald." She had once been sent to camp by one of his outlets and had written one of those obligatory letters. Now, meeting Cam face to face, she said, "You changed my life."

"I get it now," Cam said of the camps. "I do."

*

ABOUT THREE KILOMETRES SOUTH of the Memorial Camp at Lorimer Lake, on the west side of the road, is a small pioneer cemetery. I stopped there to look at the tombstones, a ragtag assortment of memorials. One of them above all impressed me—a weathered slab with a simple inscription:

Wife.
As a Wife devoted.
As a Mother affectionate.
As a friend ever kind and true.

That was all. Beneath my feet lay a woman bereft of mortal identity: the Tomb of the Unknown Spouse. I could not explain how she had come to be interred this way, grieved yet shorn of her own name and the basic milestone dates of birth and death. I also wondered how much further ahead Tim Horton was, with a Memorial Camp in his name, a place in the Hockey Hall of Fame, his name inscribed four times on the Stanley Cup and his stylized signature on coffee cups and thousands of restaurant signs. We can ladle on all the details we want and still have precious little sense of who we are remembering. But I imagine that, for a man who was profoundly uncomfortable playing the role of a celebrity, the legacy of the camps and what they represented—a dedication to improving the lives of disadvantaged children, and not to raising statues and drawing ham-fisted lessons from his own uneven trajectory through life—would sit very well with him indeed.

Years ago, a fellow writer suggested to me that a coffee and Timbits were a form of sacrament, the wine and host of a particularly Canadian secular religion that worshipped Tim Horton's memory. I was mulling over the nature of memorial—of the camp, of the strange tombstone, of the ghost inside the restaurant machine—as I wrote this chapter, when I learned that the son of friends had just died.

Stuart was thirty-four, and after a courageous battle that had lasted six years, he had been claimed by a recurring brain tumour. A memorial celebration of his life was being held at the Royal Hamilton Yacht Club, and on a cool and occasionally rainy October day shortly before Halloween, I drove there—back to the city where I had grown up, to the place where the Tim Hortons chain started, to the sailing club where I had first met Cam MacDonald, who in his outlet at Danforth and Logan had started recounting for me the story of how he got involved as a franchisee by recalling the funeral in Hamilton of his sister Nancy.

The first appearance of the tumour had cost Stuart the sight in one eye, and with it his career as a pilot, but with forthright pragmatism he retrained as an aircraft structural technician. The return of the tumour had left him paralyzed on one side. Stuart had spent his last summer rediscovering a love of sailing in a Martin 16 designed for the physically disabled. With special controls, he had been able to sail with the use of one hand and one foot. He even managed to compete in the Mobility Cup, mere weeks before he passed. A memorial plaque had been prepared for the club's Able Sail dock, which was to be renamed in Stuart's memory.

On top of all of the other challenges Stuart and his family were facing, it was only in the last year of his life that a formal diagnosis indicated that, like my younger son, Stuart was autistic, although in Stuart's case he was placed in the high-functioning category of Asperger syndrome. The main reason I am so familiar with the offerings (and the drive-through lanes) of McDonald's and Tim Hortons is that if it were left up to my son Drew, he would probably subsist on McDonald's hamburgers and french fries, Tim Hortons Timbits and chocolate-dip doughnuts, and chocolate milk from either place. I don't need a smartphone app from either chain to find an outlet within an hour's drive of the house. Drew has visited them all in Google Street View, and has helpfully entered their locations in the GPS device in my car.

As Stuart's conditioned worsened, and the end of his life's journey approached, his language was reduced to single words. At the memorial celebration, his mother, Za, recounted how, one day while out in the car together, Stuart said, "Timbits."

Za told him he couldn't have Timbits because he couldn't swallow them. Stuart replied, "Blender."

So Za placed an order at a Tim Hortons drive-through and took it home. She poured a double double in the blender, tossed in a dozen Timbits and pushed the button. The result was a smoothie that is unlikely to enter market testing any time soon, but Stuart got the Tim's run he wanted.

"It made us all laugh at the time, including Stuart," his dad, Rob, later told me, when I asked for his and Za's approval to tell the story of Stuart's Timbits smoothie, "at a time when we needed something to laugh about."

When I got home from the memorial for Stuart, a box of Timbits was sitting on my kitchen counter, evidence of at least part of the day's activities of my wife and our younger son, Drew.

True story.

26

Defending the Brand: Tim Hortons Goes "Expresso" and Faces Down the Golden Arches

Canadians worry about Tim Hortons a lot. Devoted customers and media pundits seem to fear for its existence—or at least for its continued authenticity, regardless of growth and profitability. An innocuous menu introduction like the beef lasagna casserole becomes an issue for radio and television news and the subject of bounteous column inches for newspapers and bloggers. A decision to change the Canadian coffee cup sizes in January 2012—adding a twenty-four-ounce extra large and renaming the existing cups one size smaller by making the old extra large the new large, and so forth, which CBC's *This Hour Has 22 Minutes* lampooned when the change was being trialled—is regarded as one more sign of creeping Americanization. The introduction of espresso is supposed to mark the end of the world as Tim's devotees and Canadian culture critics know it. For a company that has been doing so well, it perpetually seems, in the eyes of critics and devotees alike, to be on the verge of blowing it.

If you have read the rest of this book, you know that the challenges facing Tim Hortons are not illusory. One of its greatest challenges is its own phenomenal success as an iconic Canadian brand. It has reached the point where, like other celebrated brands in the world, "Tim Hortons" belongs to the consumer as much as it does to the company that holds its trademarks. Canadian customers have delivered Tim Hortons its success, and many seem to feel that Tim's belongs to them. They view present management as mere custodians of a national treasure, and its moves to update the restaurants and expand the menu offerings sometimes are greeted suspiciously, and not a little hysterically.

When Tim Hortons announced its decision to start selling espressos as well as espresso-based lattes and cappuccinos in its Canadian outlets after releasing its third-quarter 2011 results, CBC pundit Rex Murphy went verbosely postal in his November 7 segment at the close of *The National*. "It may be the wildest flouting of doctrine since the Reformation," began his "Cuppa Woe" rant. He cast the move as a sign that Tim Hortons was morphing into Starbucks.

"Look, Starbucks is Noam Chomsky and Seattle," he disdainfully lectured. "Tim Hortons is Don Cherry and Sault Ste. Marie." He declared that both companies were trying to become more like each other, an existential impossibility. "Timmy's and Starbucks are polarities, shadow and light that cannot mingle, lest the earth and all who sip upon it should be let fall from orbit and the Great Barista have us plunge into the espresso machine of the sun."

Murphy kept calling espresso "expresso," a determined mispronunciation of a foreign word reminiscent of the indifferent butchering of names of eastern European hockey players by that other iconoclastic CBC defender of hearty Canadian values, Don Cherry. Murphy revealed some of the cold judgmental fury Michael Ignatieff had tried to avoid on the hustings as he insisted Starbucks was a place apart from the true-Canadian Tim's, or at least Tim's as it was before fancy hot beverages and lasagna showed up. "People go to Starbucks to show off their Lexus or their Apple iPad," Murphy sneered. The Occupy movement, he urged, should occupy Tim Hortons in order to save it from itself.

At times like this, I want to tell the Murphys of the Canadian cultural landscape: "For heaven's sake, *relax*—it's all just hot bean juice." Tim Hortons managed to popularize drip-brew coffee in Canada and to introduce new Canadians to this far-from-universal caffeine habit. Many immigrants come from countries where, if coffee is consumed at all, it is not primarily as a double-double shock of sugar and cream in a cup of drip-brewed java. Espresso-based drinks, created and popularized in Italy in the 1980s, helped give rise to a global coffee-bar culture that goes far beyond anything attributable to Starbucks, Noam Chomsky and iPad snobs.

Tim Hortons in 2011 had two choices. It could stake its hot-coffee future solely on a drip-brewed product that was under increasing competition from other North American QSRs, a category that was also flatlining in sales growth. Or it could diversify into a sector of coffee consumption that is growing in North America and not wait until it had to play catch-up with a rival like McDonald's. Whatever connoisseurs think of Tim Hortons' new offerings, the company did the right thing. But most of the North American coffee business remains a straight brew, and Tim's has to maintain its grip on the majority of that sector, which is its cash cow.

Certainly, Tim Hortons' stranglehold on almost 80 percent of coffee transactions in Canadian restaurants has at least as much to do with old habits and ubiquity of outlets than any hands-down superiority of its brewed coffee. McDonald's isn't the only QSR to have upped its brewed-coffee game lately in a quest to steal away some of Tim Hortons' market share. The coffee-buying habit has been key to Tim's getting its customers to try other parts of the menu, especially the meal offerings. If competitors can break Canadians of their predilection for Timmy coffee runs, then maybe they can wrest away (or wrest back) some of the meal spending as well.

In a blind taste test of brewed offerings from QSRs organized by *The Globe and Mail* and published November 8, 2011—the morning after the Rex Murphy "expresso" rant—the panel of connoisseurs preferred the new Redhead Roasters from Wendy's, followed by McDonald's, followed by Tim Hortons, followed by Starbucks house blend. Lest one think that coffee tasting is any more objective than wine tasting, in December 2011 Starbucks house blend topped a *Consumer Reports* test of thirty-six different blend coffees for home brewing.

On November 17, 2011, Victoria, B.C., coffee blogger and media go-to guy Colin Newell did a series of CBC radio interviews coast to coast on the Tim Hortons espresso launch and the aggressive move by McDonald's into coffee. In a recap of his CBC interviews on his coffee blog, Newell criticized Tim Hortons' drip-brew method as "1950's old school miserable; poorly blended arabica coffee brewed in old school gravity brewers into glass urns where bitterness is given an open invitation to the caffeine party within minutes of the pots being put out on the hot plates!" Even McDonald's, he said, "has joined us in the 21st Century with sealed air pots and professionally sourced 100% arabica blends that taste, well, like coffee . . . and often good coffee at that." Newell praised the Franke machines McDonald's had introduced to its McCafés: "more reliable than gravity and unflinching in their coffee brewing precision." They also cost more than $30,000. "Tim's coffee needs work," Newell wrote. "And it is a simple fix."

I spoke with Newell in January 2012 about Tim's and the coffee sector in general. "They don't seem to be interested in changing their technology," he said of Tim Hortons' old-school drip brew. When I asked him what the "simple fix" was, he replied, "They need to follow McCafé and Starbucks and install super-expensive machines, and train their staff to use them." Tim's he felt also needed fresh talent in sourcing beans, especially for espresso. "It's not just a coffee blend to pour through a drip machine."

Of the McDonald's McCafé product, Newell said, "It's not bad. It's vastly superior to the average coffee being served, but the average is moving up very quickly." The challenge he felt Tim Hortons faced was one it shared with Starbucks. "The quality of Starbucks has gone down because it's so large." It's becoming harder for big chains to source quality beans in batches large enough to meet their consistency promises. And consistency without variety is counter to the trend in coffee consumption. "There's a renaissance of delivering locally purchased coffee," he said. When I mentioned I had been making my morning coffee lately with an Ethiopian bean (the Caribou Coffee gift from an American friend), he replied, "It's nice, isn't it? Ethiopian is what I offer people when I want them to experience something different."

I dislike cold coffees and coffee concoctions adulterated with sugar, chocolate, whipped milk and whatnot, so I'm useless as a judge of iced capps and the various competing lattes out there. My coffee tastes run to something a little stronger and earthier than the QSR norm, with cream only, black if necessary. I can't tell enough of a difference between a coffee from Tim Hortons or McDonald's to prefer one of them. To some aficionados, tossing two helpings of cream and sugar into a coffee suggests Timmy's double-doublers don't even know what good coffee is supposed to taste like. But if, in the judgment of the average consumer, Tim Hortons' staple brewed coffee really does need fixing, we'll have to see whether the company and franchisees are willing to spend the money and change the way the coffee is sourced and roasted by Tim's itself and then brewed in the outlets.

Tim Hortons' new line of espresso drinks has received middling to poor marks from connoisseurs, but that may not matter to the average value-conscious Tim's customer. "Don't underestimate customer loyalty," Newell said to me, which went for Starbucks as much as for Tim's. "Whatever Tim Hortons puts on the menu, people will try. The key is to keep them coming back to have it." And that's the trick for Tim's: to convert some of its customer base of drip-brew double-doublers into regular espresso drinkers, and not have the espresso roll-out prove to have been a one-time taste test.

Meanwhile, Tim's was arousing concerns among some analysts for lagging in developing a strategy for the way coffee increasingly is being prepared at home and in businesses: with single-cup technology.

Single-cup premium brewing, dominated in North America by the Keurig system's K-Cup format owned by Green Mountain Coffee Roasters of Vermont, is promising a revolution in coffee consumption. Companies are installing single-cup systems of quality coffee for employees and customers, which can only impact the number of people wandering to the nearest QSR for a takeout cup. I saw such a K-Cup machine at my local Honda dealer in November 2011 while getting snow tires installed. A decent cup of free coffee (Timothy's) on the premises was reason enough for me not to walk to the nearby Tim's as I waited for my car. Single-cup systems (including France's Tassimo, which can also make hot chocolate, latte and tea) are making tremendous inroads into consumers' homes, thus changing the way specialty-brand coffees are being sold through retail channels like grocery stores.

One of analyst Kenric Tyghe's harshest criticisms of Tim's to me was that, based on its brand identity, revenues and profits, it is fundamentally a coffee company (a point essentially made by the judge in the Fairview suit), and as such it has badly trailed competitors in getting into the single-cup market. Tim's sells cans and packets of ground coffee for home consumption at its restaurants as well as through grocery stores and TimShop, an online e-commerce presence. These sales are so negligible that the company doesn't even break them out in its financial statements. Tim's, Tyghe argued when we spoke in the fall of 2011, is "three years behind the market leaders in K-Cup." Dunkin' Donuts followed the example of Caribou Coffee and moved into K-Cups in February 2011; Starbucks followed in turn in March. These American chains were adapting to the rise of the home and office single-cup market by having their outlets sell their K-Cup brands as well as the machines.

When Starbucks made its K-Cup partnership deal in March 2011, every major coffee producer in the United States except Folgers was on board with Green Mountain's Keurig technology. (In addition to Timothy's, Green Mountain owns the Seattle-based Tully's chain. It also bought LJVH Holdings, owner of Montreal's Van Houtte specialty coffee brands, in December 2010. All of their coffees naturally are available in K-Cup.) Analyst Scott Van Winkle of Canaccord Genuity predicted at that point that K-Cup machines would be in 30 percent of American homes within three and a half years. Seven months later, in October 2011, analysts at Canaccord Genuity released a more bullish note, proposing: "The world of coffee brewing is changing at home and we believe the penetration won't be a modest 20% or 25% of homes, as some assert, but 40% or 50% at a minimum."

At an investor conference in January 2012, Caribou Coffee estimated that the U.S. home-market penetration of K-Cup was already at 7 to 10 percent. Caribou had seen 52 percent revenue growth (and 65 percent earnings growth) in its commercial sales operations, which include K-Cup, in fiscal 2010. To appreciate how rapidly U.S. consumer coffee consumption (which represents 25 percent of the global market) is changing, consider that commercial sales at Caribou went from less than 5 percent of net sales in the third quarter of 2007 to 24 percent in the third quarter of 2011, even while the rest of the company grew. The increasing sophistication of the home coffee market was underlined by the decision of *Consumer Reports* to compare in its December 2011 issue seventy-five products in five categories: blends, Colombian, Kenyan, Sumatran and Ethiopian. A few K-Cups were included. Nothing produced by Tim Hortons was assessed, which tells you that, as a home-consumption product, Tim's doesn't register a blip on the U.S. consumer radar.

Tim's was still missing in action when its president and CEO, Paul House, was asked about the single-cup market during the analyst conference call for its third-quarter 2011 results.

"Well, yes, we're still looking at the market," he replied. "As you know, and as we've talked about on the call, I mean, espresso lattes has taken our attention and we're rolling that out. [The] single-serve market is still a relatively small market in Canada. We still enjoy a wonderful takeout business in cans and pouches and so forth, in supermarkets, in our stores and so forth. Quite frankly, we are not happy with anything that we've looked at to date that satisfies our quality and price point that we want to deliver that single cup. It is in our future plans, but until it reaches certain criteria, we will not come out with it. And, we have not satisfied our criteria at this point in time. And so, all I can say at this point is stay tuned."

In the conference call that followed the release of fourth-quarter 2011 results on February 23, 2012, there was surprisingly little interest from analysts about Tim Hortons' lack of movement on entering the single-cup business. Only Michael Kelter of Goldman Sachs (who would slap the stock with a "sell" rating in July 2012) asked for an update. "Well, we continue to look at the market, and we're working on some opportunities, but we don't have anything to announce at this point in time," House tersely replied. In April 2012 the company introduced TimmyRun, a web-based tool that allows up to twenty people to combine a beverage order. Tims's remained committed to takeout coffee.

With Tim Hortons so conscious of its "value" positioning, price point is an arguable issue with single-cup systems, as a single serving can be about five times as expensive as that from a regular drip maker. Analysts, however, are seeing consumers adopt the system because it can brew a single premium cup quickly, saving them the bother of brewing up a carafe or grinding a few beans. Consumers also enjoy the varietal selection, much like choosing premium tea bags for single servings (a market Tim Hortons is already in). Above all, they are willing to spend money to get what they want in a quality coffee at home. Yes, single-cup is more expensive than a drip brew made from a can of ground coffee, but the difference is minuscule in an overall household budget and a relatively cheap form of pampering. Many households can afford to indulge in coffee. The more refined consumers' tastes become, the less concerned they are with the value proposition of the regular grinds.

"Commercial" sales, as driven increasingly by single-cup product, are considered where the real money awaits in the coffee biz, as consumer-product profit margins are generally much higher than those of restaurant sales. Starbucks' adoption of K-Cup and the introduction of the mellower "blonde" roast have both been hailed as moves to make even more money through grocery-store sales. Tim Hortons may be resistant to the idea of plunging into home- and business-based single-cup sales because the revenues could be seen as counter to the interests of franchise restaurants, whereas Starbucks doesn't have franchises and so is more at liberty to pursue different sales opportunities. But single-cup systems also may prove to be an important way for any chain to expand a restaurant brand in the U.S., prepping consumer interest through the supermarket before brick and mortar outlets arrive. Caribou Coffee, for one, has extended its brand recognition far beyond the reaches of its coffee houses. The company's outlets are in twenty states, but its coffee products, particularly K-Cup, are sold in at least forty states and more than 7,500 stores. Caribou believes that its K-Cups are being retailed in an *additional* 17,000 stores in all fifty states. Without a single-cup program, Tim Hortons' growth is overwhelming skewed to developing more restaurants and squeezing more same-store sales increases out of them. Putting more effort into commercial sales through single-cup product, as its coffee-shop competitors have, would open up fresh revenue and profit streams and relieve pressure on constant geographic growth in brick-and-mortar outlets.

I suspect that with the K-Cup format at least, the lack of progress by Tim's might have had something to do with the fact that Keurig, which held an estimated 70 percent of the single-cup market in 2011, is owned by Green Mountain, which in November 2009 bought Timothy's, the Toronto-based chain and coffee producer founded in 1975. Timothy's had partnered with K-Cup in 2003 as it targeted the home and office market for growth. Tim Hortons may have been finding it hard to stomach partnering with a direct rival (there are more than 100 Timothy's outlets in Canada) that is also a source of long-standing brand confusion. More than one person has voiced to me the impression that Timothy's is an up-market café division of Tim Hortons.

Tim Hortons' decision to use the term "Timmy's" in recent marketing has perhaps perpetuated the confusion with Timothy's. But then, people inside Tim Hortons have long felt that the confusion started with Timothy's. Back in March 2000, at the hearings into Ontario's Wishart Act, a member of the legislature in questioning Tim Hortons exec Nick Javor asked if Timothy's is a division of his company. Javor disabused the MPP of that notion, and also quipped, "They were clever enough to name themselves after us to a point."

Single-cup technology is very much in flux. Starbucks had previously offered product for Tassimo machines, but had discontinued the relationship, and in November 2011 began retailing its K-Cup product in Canada and the U.S. Analysts were already concerned that when key K-Cup patents expired in September 2012, Green Mountain would see its Keurig technology commodified by low-cost imitators. The company responded by launching an additional Keurig single-cup system, called Vue, in February 2012. To enliven matters, Starbucks then announced in March that, while it would continue to produce product for Keurig's K-Cup format, it would be introducing a single-cup system of its own, the Verismo, developed with Germany's Krueger. Its high-pressure system would be able to make both espresso and standard brewed coffee. Green Mountain followed with an announcement that it was working on its own high-pressure espresso machine with Italy's Luigi Lavazza that would complement its low-pressure Keurig K-Cup and Vue machines.

Tim's was seriously behind the single-cup curve entering 2012, yet that may have been a calculated risk it had taken so as to avoid dealing with Green Mountain, hoping that the single-cup market would not be too advanced before it finally, belatedly, entered the market, even with a machine of its own that franchisees could retail along with the cups, as it already sells house-brand drip-brew machines. Tim's so dominates restaurant coffee sales that its mere entry into the single-cup market could drive consumer adoption in Canada. Tim's has to hope that the consumer coffee experience—and brand loyalty, especially of new, young consumers—hasn't changed radically by the time it adopts a single-cup product for home and office.

THE INCREMENTAL SHIFT in coffee tastes toward espresso-based drinks means that all mass-market QSRs have a relatively level playing field on which to start developing a customer base for this category. Tim's can enjoy some knock on effect from its commanding presence in brewed coffee, but if Rex Murphy is right, and the core Timmy's customer is not an "expresso" drinker, then it is going to be a challenge to shift the company's direction into an aren't-we-fancy beverage category served in more upscale interiors without alienating the substantial and loyal customer base.

Persuading loyal customers to try a $2 cappuccino (or a limited-offer $1 small flavoured espresso latte) for a change in routine may not prove to be the greatest challenge Tim Hortons faces. Rather, the challenge may lie in those loyal customers believing the culture critics like Murphy who argue that Tim Hortons selling cappuccinos and lattes with bistro interiors and free Wi-Fi represents a betrayal of a brand that many consumers believe belongs to them. The moment Canadians start thinking that patronizing Tim's is no longer a desirable way to brand *themselves* is the moment the chain jumps the shark as a national icon. Canadians might decide Tim's no longer triangulates with Don Cherry and Sault Ste. Marie, and go looking for a consumer experience that does. Or they might decide *they* no longer triangulate with Don Cherry and Sault Ste. Marie, and so have no further use for a personal brand alliance with Tim's.

Tim Hortons' dilemma is a familiar one for all great brands, which face challenges in undergoing necessary evolutions, in attracting new customers without driving off the old ones. "It's a delicate balance, keeping your brand relevant," John Rothschild of Prime Restaurants observed when we spoke in the summer of 2011. "You don't want to alienate the customers that you do have, but you certainly want to bring in new customers. The customers you do have, they're getting older. Customer taste profiles are changing. Some of the experiences and the taste profiles of the public have changed greatly. If we had our original Casey's today, we would be out of business. As our customer base matures and also becomes different, we have to do the same."

Tim Hortons cannot afford to grow old with the donut shop gang. The company and its franchisees also need to avoid the pitfall of believing too earnestly that Canada truly is one big donut shop gang, with unswerving loyalties to the Tim Hortons brand. The idea that Tim Hortons is an institution at the heart of Canadian life may find some positive reinforcement if the company is successful in pursuing its final phase of Canadian expansion into small Canadian towns in rural areas. Meanwhile, there may be fences to mend with the customer base.

The television ads in high rotation in the summer of 2011, plugging smoothies and Timbits, overshot the broad customer base by narrowcasting the typical patron into that thirtysomething-childless-hetero-couple mould and ignoring entirely the in-store experience. These on-the-go, pseudo-Starbuckers contrasted sharply with the customer profile championed by McDonald's, whose ads place teens to seniors of all shapes and sizes inside its restaurants. In the short term, Tim's sold a lot of Timbits and smoothies. In the long term, it may have yielded critical terrain to McDonald's in defining itself as the QSR of choice for average Canadians.

Advertising for McCafé in Canada in the fall of 2011 also took direct aim at Tim Hortons' dominance of the national caffeine habit, not to mention activities like hockey and curling. It recruited younger *Hockey Night in Canada* personalities P.J. Stock and Kelly Hrudey for ads (again, inside a restaurant) in which they drink McCafé product at a booth while bantering about the greatest hockey moment with a retirement-age couple or restaurant staff in a promotional tie-in with *HNiC*. Another McDonald's ad featuring salt-of-the-earth Canadians argued with good humour that they could be loyal to a curling rink or friends for decades, and still be capable of changing where they got their takeout coffee. The message was that you didn't have to source your coffee from Timmy's to be a true Canadian. Canadian values of loyalty were rooted in friends and community, not in a particular hot beverage.

Judging brand value is less of an exact science than even economics, but Tim Hortons had been riding a crest of accolades among firms that make it their business to put numbers on the ephemeral. The consulting firm Interbrand issues a brand valuation ranking every two years, and in 2010 ranked Tim Hortons sixth among Canadian companies with public financial data, up from tenth in 2008 (which had been a drop from sixth in 2006).

At the height of the controversy over espressos, Tim Hortons' reputation appeared to be hanging in with consumers. From November 23 to 30, polling and market research firm Ipsos Reid interviewed 1,013 Canadians to determine its 2012 list of the country's "most influential brands." The brand rankings included both domestic and international labels, putting Tim Hortons up against global heavyweights like Microsoft (#1), Google (#2), Apple (#4), Walmart (#5), Facebook (#7) and YouTube (#8). Timmy's ranked #15, one behind BlackBerry—

which was en route to a comeuppance verging on free-fall—and ahead of Canadian Tire (#23), but most important ahead of McDonald's (#30) and Starbucks (#48). No restaurant business ranked ahead of it.

Still, a bit of panic within the company over its grip on an iconic role in Canadian life wouldn't hurt. Tim's and its franchisees do not need to believe that the brand is unassailable.

While the Tim Hortons name and logo are instantly recognizable in Canada, the brand cannot afford to take its reputation for granted. In Judge Tingley's 2012 decision against Dunkin' Donuts' Canadian operation, in which he agreed with plaintiff franchisees that Dunkin' had "abandoned" the Quebec market by 2003, he called Dunkin's regional implosion "a case study of how industry leaders can become followers in free market economies." And the restaurant industry is full of cautionary tales of once-dominant chains that lost their way. The chain of tea/bake shops J. Lyons & Co., founded in the late nineteenth century, dominated the British scene for decades as part of an integrated food and hospitality conglomerate. The parent company failed to reinvest adequately in the chain in the years following the Second World War, and a misguided effort to modernize the outlets along an American cafeteria/automat model spelled its doom in the 1970s. In the late 1960s, the only North American QSR chain larger than Burger Chef was McDonald's. Acquired by General Foods in 1968, Burger Chef promptly made an aggressive move into Canada, opening five outlets in British Columbia and twenty-four in Ontario, while parent General Foods snapped up a number of B.C. restaurants, including the White Spot chain. General Foods also initiated and abandoned a bid to acquire Harvey's in 1969. Burger Chef had been an innovator in menu items (which were aped by McDonald's) and in bringing interior seating to the drive-in format, but the chain stumbled throughout North America in the 1970s and ended up being sold to Imasco in 1982, at which point most of the surviving stores were converted to Hardee's outlets.

Queen's University's Ken Wong worries that since the 2006 IPO, Tim's has coasted on the goodwill that the brand had accumulated over decades in Canada. He thinks the time may be at hand when it has to get back to brand basics, the way another respected domestic brand, Canadian Tire, recently has with a renewed focus on its automotive and tire services designed to appeal to men and women.

According to Alan Middleton of York University's Schulich School of Business, Tim Hortons is abundantly aware of the danger of complacency. The company hired him to speak to its franchisees at their annual symposium in Banff in 2009. "My job was simple. It was to shake up the franchisees." His presentation, "The Good, Bad and Ugly of Branding," presented a PowerPoint slide called "The Ugly Brandscape." It showed the logos of Massey Ferguson, Eaton's, Powerstore, Dominion Stores, Simpsons, Salon Selectives, Woolworths, Pontiac and Studebaker. His message: These were all iconic brands in their day, and they all had disappeared.

"Tim's is very aware of what happens to older franchise systems," he assured me in late 2011. "The franchisees become used to the revenue stream, and become unwilling to take risks. There is absolutely the danger of complacency." Tim Hortons can keep moving the brand forward only if its franchisees don't dig in their heels. I would add that the parent company also has to ensure these franchisees don't politicize their brand and alienate about 60 percent of Canadian voters by allowing it to become known as the local host of choice for campaigning Conservative politicians.

I was also reminded, after the 2011 provincial election in which clutching cups of Tim Hortons coffee failed to secure Tim Hudak the premiership when it had seemed easily within his grasp, the words of Prime Restaurants' John Rothschild: "A brand has to be meaningful. If you're not meaningful or relevant to your customers, you're a dying brand."

Rothschild cited McDonald's as a company that had met the task of being flexible yet recognizable across different markets. "Once upon a time, all McDonald's had to be exactly alike. Now, there are urban and suburban types, and their designs are different, yet they have mastered the idea that although they're different, you know that you are in a McDonald's." As Tim Hortons announced the introduction of Wi-Fi and more up-market interiors in November 2011, it was plain from the comments of CEO Paul House that the chain was coming to grips with the McDonald's-like idea that what urban centres now demand in amenities and ambiance might not play in suburbia or a small Saskatchewan town. I thought Tim's had muddied its brand image in New York City and sacrificed core values beloved by New Yorkers who already knew the chain from elsewhere. It remains to be seen whether Tim's can manage to be different-but-the-same for diverse markets within Canada.

I was reminded in turn of how impressed analyst Kenric Tyghe had been with the crowds of young people he had seen frequenting the new McDonald's concepts with their fireplaces, flat-screen televisions and free Wi-Fi. The allegiance to Tim's that is assumed to be innate in Canadians didn't seem to be holding them back from enjoying the coffee and ambiance of the McCafé. Equally important, old or even parallel associations of McDonald's with Ronald McDonald and moulded-fibreglass benches weren't discouraging them from frequenting the new McDonald's store concepts.

Tim's as a brand is anything but dying, but the QSR market is changing—in its customer profiles, the strategies and growth ambitions of established competitors, and the arrival of new concepts. For example, Panera Bread, the café-bakery concept that has won so many admirers in the U.S., is training its sights on Tim Hortons' backyard. It had opened the first of three outlets in suburban Toronto in 2008, and unveiled its first downtown Toronto location, on Yonge at Edward near Ryerson University, in January 2012. Domestically, the Montreal-based franchise chain La Prep now has more than fifty outlets, mainly in Montreal, Greater Toronto, Edmonton and Calgary, chasing the same light-meal and quality-coffee consumer. With more than 3,000 names on Tim Hortons' franchisee waiting list, there are sure to be wannabe restaurateurs who realize the cause of securing a Tim's is hopeless and are willing to help its competitors expand in Canada. Tim's is also striving to defend a leadership position in Canada against daunting opponents like McDonald's while making fresh inroads into the difficult U.S. market as a self-described "challenger brand." The company managed to outlive the death of its namesake co-founder in 1974. Now it must outlive its reputation as an unassailable Canadian institution.

If McDonald's, for one, can decouple Canadian identity from consumption of Tim Hortons coffee, it may be on to something truly game-changing in QSR. But that may be a taller order than a twenty-ounce Venti Caramel Macchiato from Starbucks. Tim Hortons remains a celebrated made-in-Canada success story with a tremendous reservoir of home-team consumer goodwill and a knack for introducing products that its considerable following gobbles up. And it still has that ghost in the brand machine, Tim Horton himself, to call off the bench and anchor the power play, should this company need to mount a late-game rally.

Acknowledgments

IN ADDITION TO THE DOZENS OF PEOPLE I interviewed in the course of writing Tim Horton's biography *Open Ice,* almost twenty years ago (many of whom are no longer alive), and above and beyond the many people I idly chatted up or checked facts with while working on this project, I must acknowledge the following for sharing their time and insights:

A special thanks goes to Cam MacDonald, for allowing me inside his franchise world on the Danforth. Ken Wong of Queen's University and Alan Middleton of York University's Schulich School of Business entertained my questions about the Tim Hortons brand. Analyst Kenric Tyghe let me pick his brains about Tim Hortons' market challenges in both Canada and the United States. Dr. Sara Kirk, Linda Gillis and Dr. Yoni Freedhoff all chipped in on my exploration of QSR food and public health. John Rothschild of Prime Restaurants held forth articulately on the nature of the Canadian restaurant industry, the meaning of a restaurant's brand, his personal childhood experiences with the hockey star Tim Horton and his Stanley Cup–winning Uncle Sam, the Hunk of Ham. Shannon Benner squired me around the Tim Horton Memorial Camp at Lorimer Lake and answered every question I pitched at her. Susan Delacourt chatted about her experiences covering the Starbucks-crossed Michael Ignatieff and the idea of the Tim Hortons voter. In addition to directing me to the book *Applebee's America*, she provided me with a copy of the speech Prime Minister Stephen Harper gave at Tim Hortons headquarters in 2009, which I was able to compare with a video of his actual delivery (almost spot on).

Glen McGregor of the *Ottawa Citizen* was generous enough to post online a scan of Tim Horton's autopsy report after securing it in 2005 through Ontario's Freedom of Information Act, once Horton had been dead for thirty years. "If you're a journalist and use this document for a story, please credit me and/or the *Ottawa Citizen*," McGregor wrote when he made it public. "It was a huge pain in the ass to get." Duly noted. Touran (she would not divulge her last name and I am too accommodating to bother hunting it down) of Ladan Pastry and Bakery graciously answered my questions and arranged my blissful acquaintance with Iranian pastry. My dad reached into his memory vaults to recall the original Tim Hortons outlet and my brother's hockey practices at nearby Scott Park. A tip o' the hat goes to Stacy Nation-Knapper, the "American friend" who brought me Ethiopian beans from Caribou Coffee in Minnesota and praised that chain's ambiance. Coffee blogger Colin Newell ably riffed on Franke machines and the quest to make a better corporate cup of coffee. Rob and Za Mazza were kind enough to allow me to recount the story of the Timbits smoothie that Za told at the memorial celebration for the life of their son Stuart.

On other fronts, my agent, Jeff Gerecke, held a chair for me at Junior's as I raced from one Tim Hortons outlet to the next in mid-town Manhattan. He also helped me fulfill my long-standing ambition to write this book by finding it a welcoming home at HarperCollins Canada. My editor, Jim Gifford, gave crisp and helpful direction while bantering about all things Tim Hortons. Finally, my wife, Deb, kept me motivated but never overcaffeinated. My thanks to all.

Bibliography

Books, Reports and Publications

Bird, Peter. *The First Food Empire: A History of J. Lyons & Co.* Chichester, U.K.: Philmore & Co., 2000.

Canadian Franchise Association. *Franchise Canada Directory 2011.*

Filey, Mike. "Harvey's Began a Beautiful Thing." In *Toronto Sketches 7: The Way We Were,* 52–54. Toronto: Dundurn Press, 2003.

Heimann, Jim. *Car Hops and Curb Service: A History of American Drive-In Restaurants 1920–1960.* San Francisco: Chronicle Books, 1996.

Horton, Lori, and Tim Griggs. *In Loving Memory: A Tribute to Tim Horton.* Toronto: ECW Press, 1997.

Hunter, Douglas. *Open Ice: The Tim Horton Story.* Toronto: Penguin Canada, 1994.

Joyce, Ron, with Robert Thompson. *Always Fresh: The Untold Story of Tim Hortons, by the Man Who Created a Canadian Empire.* Toronto: HarperCollins, 2006.

Manitoba Law Reform Commission. "Franchise Law." May 2008.

Penfold, Steve. *The Donut: A Canadian History.* Toronto: University of Toronto Press, 2008.

Research Strategy Group for Gowling Lafleur Henderson. "Franchising & Distribution: What Motivates a Franchisee to Invest?" December 2008.

INTERNET RESOURCES

Brown, Kyle. *Burger Chef Memories.* http://www.freewebs.com/burgerchef.

Dillon, Peter Macrae. *Good Faith—The Shelanu Decision.* http://www.franchiselaw.ca/pdf/Good%20Faith%20The%20Shelanu%20Decision.pdf.

Hoffman, Jeffrey P. *A Recent Developments of Importance in Franchise Law.* http://m.gowlings.com/KnowledgeCentre/article.asp?pubID=1156&lang=0.

Jones, Paul. *Recent Franchise Decisions: Good Faith and Fair Dealing.* http://www.cba.org/OBA/en/pdf/GoodFaithcases.pdf.

Lawrence, David. *An Electronic History of J. Lyons & Co.* http://www.kzwp.com/lyons/index.htm.

Sterns, David. *The Fiduciary Relationship in Franchising: Jirna Reconsidered.* http://www.sotosllp.com/2000/01/the-fiduciary-relationship-in-franchising-jirna-reconsidered.

World Health Organization. "Global Database on Body Mass Index." http://apps.who.int/bmi/index.jsp.

CORPORATE ONLINE RESOURCES

Argo Tea Café. http://www.argotea.com.

Burger King. http://www.bk.com.

Caribou Coffee. https://www.cariboucoffee.com.

The Coffee Bean & Tea Leaf. http://coffeebean.com/index.aspx.

Coffee Time. http://www.coffeetime.ca.

Cold Stone Creamery. http://www.coldstonecreamery.com.

Corey Craig Group. http://coreycraig.ca/index.php.

Country Style. http://www.countrystyle.com.

Don Cherry's Sports Grill. http://www.doncherrysgrill.ca.

Dunkin' Brands. http://www.dunkinbrands.com.

Green Beans Coffee. http://greenbeanscoffee.com.

Green Mountain Coffee. http://www.greenmountaincoffee.com.

McDonald's. http://www.aboutmcdonalds.com/mcd.html.

Pret A Manger. http://www.pret.com/us/.

Prime Restaurants. http://primerestaurants.com.
Riese Restaurants. http://rieserestaurants.com.
Robin's Donuts. http://www.robinsdonuts.com.
Second Cup. http://www.secondcup.com.
Starbucks Coffee Company. http://www.starbucks.com.
Tim Hortons. http://www.timhortons.com.
Timothy's Coffees of the World. http://www.timothys.ca.
Wendel Clark's Classic Grill and Sports Lounge. http://www.wendelclarks.com.

JOURNAL ARTICLES AND SCHOLARLY STUDIES

Bollinger, Bryan, Phillip Leslie and Alan Sorensen. "Calorie Posting in Chain Restaurants." Working Paper 15648, National Bureau of Economic Research, Cambridge, Mass., January 2010.

Campbell, Norm R.C., Kim D. Raine and Lindsay McLaren. "'Junk Foods,' 'Treats,' or 'Pathogenic Foods'? A Call for Changing Nomenclature to Fit the Risk of Today's Diets." *Canadian Journal of Cardiology* 28:4 (July 2012), 403–04. Published online February 13, 2012.

Haight, Colleen. "The Problem with Fair Trade Coffee." *Stanford Social Innovation Review* 9:3 (Summer 2011). http://www.ssireview.org/articles/entry/the_problem_with_fair_trade_coffee.

MEDIA (PRINT AND ELECTRONIC EDITIONS; BLOGS)

Anderson, Bruce. "Lacking 'Hand' in Robo-Call Debate, Tories Ought to Try Humility." *The Globe and Mail,* March 4, 2012.

Associated Press. "Chain's Troubled Story Not Over." *Sun Journal,* April 26, 2004.

———. "Franchisees Make Bid on Bess Eaton." *Sun Journal,* April 22, 2004.

Avery, Simon. "Green Mountain, Starbucks Get Jolt from Coffee Deal." *The Globe and Mail,* March 10, 2011.

Bloomberg News. "Dunkin' Donuts Parent Fights Bess Eaton Offer." *The Boston Globe*, March 17, 2004.

Bolger, Timothy. "Watch Out Dunkin' Donuts: The Canadians Are Coming." *Long Island News*, November 19, 2010.

Brethour, Patrick. "Esso to Serve Up Tim Hortons." *The Globe and Mail*, March 22, 2002.

Brooks, Zach. "Blockbuster: Tim Hortons Set to Invade New York City." Midtown Lunch, July 9, 2009. http://midtownlunch.com/2009/07/09/blockbuster-tim-hortons-to-invade-new-york-city.

Campion-Smith, Bruce. "Doughnuts over Diplomacy." *Toronto Star*, September 24, 2009.

Canadian Franchise News. "Chairman's Brand Grows on Spending Spree." October 4, 2006.

Canadian Press. "Afton Food Seeks Protection under Bankruptcy Act after Lenders Seek Repayment." *National Post*, July 13, 2003.

———. "Leather Chairs, Soft Lighting, Wi-Fi: Welcome to the New Tim Hortons." *Toronto Star*, November 11, 2011.

———. "NDP Critic Wants Ontario Menus to List Calories." CBC News, Toronto, May 8, 2012.

———. "Tim Hortons Aims for 'Ambience' with Store Redesigns." *Marketing*, November 11, 2011.

Caplinger, Dan. "How the Wrong Stocks Can Get You in Trouble." *The Motley Fool*, September 13, 2011. http://www.fool.com/retirement/general/2011/09/13/how-the-wrong-stocks-can-get-you-in-trouble.aspx.

CBC News. "Coffee Time Hit with High Number of Health Violations: CBC *Marketplace* Probe." Toronto, February 21, 2007.

———. "EI Changes' Effect on Foreign Workers Unclear." Nova Scotia, May 28, 2012.

———. "McDonalds Bars Reusable Coffee Mugs." Charlottetown, January 13, 2012.

———. "Tim Hortons Bringing In Philippine Workers to Staff Manitoba Store." Winnipeg, March 24, 2009.

———. "Tim Hortons Launches Anti-Litter Campaign." Nova Scotia, July 6, 2005.

Center for an Urban Future. "Return of the Chains: This Year's Borough-by-Borough Analysis of New York City's Largest Retailers." *New York by the Numbers* 2:4 (August 2009).

CityNews. "Toronto Ponders Drive-Thru Ban to Help Environment." Toronto, December 17, 2007.

The Columbus Dispatch. "Tim Hortons Readies Doughnut Shop Downtown in Former Dunkins Location." May 11, 2011.

CP24 News. "McDonald's Spending $1B to Renovate Stores." Toronto, September 7, 2011. http://www.cp24.com/mcdonald-s-canada-adds-plasma-tvs-fireplaces-1.693725

CTV News. "Donut Shop Owner Sold Drugs to Customers: Police." August 28, 2011.

———. "Tim Hortons Gives Afghan Troops Taste of Home." June 29, 2006.

Cuff, Daniel F. "Dunkin' Donuts Suitor Has Takeover History." *The New York Times,* May 18, 1989.

Cuozzo, Steve. "Yecchh! Flunkin' Donuts." *New York Post,* July 14, 2009.

Delacourt, Susan. "How Voters Became Political Consumers." *Toronto Star,* September 11, 2010.

———. "Is the U.S. Tea Party Movement Seeping into Tim Horton's Territory, Canada?" *Toronto Star,* September 10, 2010.

Ditchburn, Jennifer. "Harper's Tim Horton's Campaign Scours for Starbucks Liberals in Its Final Hours." Canadian Press, May 1, 2011.

Dobson, Sarah. "Aboriginal Inclusion Focus of Training." *Canadian HR Reporter,* March 12, 2012, 3.

Donoghue, Kimberley. "Even More Dunkin' Donuts to Open in R.I." *Providence Business News,* September 8, 2011.

Dow Jones Newswires. "Green Mountain Looks to Differentiate from Starbucks Verismo." WSJ.com, March 9, 2012. http://online.wsj.com/article/BT-CO-20120309–706039.html.

Doyle, John. "Robo-Call Scandal Makes for Terrible TV." *The Globe and Mail,* March 5, 2012.

Eaton, Dan. "Dunkin' Donuts out at Casto Complex." *Business First,* March 23, 2011.

———. "Tim Hortons Skating into Cotters' Former Nationwide Arena Space." *Business First,* August 5, 2011.

Elan, Elissa. "Tim Hortons Operator Hands Out 7,000 Gift Cards in NYC." *Nation's Restaurant News,* September 7, 2009.

———. "Tim Hortons to Revamp US Units." *Nation's Restaurant News,* June 21, 2010.

Ferguson, Rob. "Calorie-Count Bill Clears Hurdle." *Toronto Star,* April 10, 2009.

Fickenscher, Lisa. "Riese, Dunkin' Divorce Long Time Coming." *Crain's New York Business,* July 10, 2009.

———. "13 Dunkin' Donuts Try Fresh Approach." *Crain's New York Business,* July 9, 2009.

Fien, Christine Carrie. "Neighbors Fight to Preserve Collegetown Vision." *City Newspaper* (Rochester, N.Y.), August 31, 2011.

Financial Post Business. "Getting a Piece of Tim Hortons." March 6, 2006.

Findlay, Stephanie. "Protest a Boost for Starbucks and Timmy's." *Toronto Star,* November 18, 2011.

Flavelle, Dana. "Food Court King Buys Country Style." *Toronto Star,* April 14, 2009.

Fontevecchia, Agustino. "Mounting Competition for Green Mountain and K-Cup Actually a Bullish Signal." *Forbes Online,* October 24, 2011. http://www.forbes.com/sites/afontevecchia/2011/10/24/mounting-competition-for-green-mountain-and-keurig-actually-a-bullish-signal/.

Forbes, Paula. "NY Starbucks Covering Outlets, Cutting Off Laptop Squatters." *Eater* ('bucks Wire), August 3, 2011. http://eater.com/archives/2011/08/03/ny-starbucks-covers-outlets-cuts-off-wifi-squatters.php.

Freedhoff, Yoni. "Tim Hortons Junkie? Prepare to Gain Weight." *Weighty Matters* blog, August 30, 2011. http://www.weightymatters.ca/2011/08/tim-hortons-junkie-prepare-to-gain.html.

Gallagher, Danny. "The 'Idea Guy' behind Tim Hortons Saw Others Get

Rich while He Went Bankrupt." *The Globe and Mail,* August 13, 2009.

Garcia, Krista. "Fast Food International: Tim Hortons." *Serious Eats,* July 13, 2010. http://newyork.seriouseats.com/2010/07/fast-food-international-tim-hortons.html.

The Globe and Mail. "Cost of Humphrey's Gave Canada Harvey's." January 9, 1969.

Grenier, Éric. "Does Easy Access to Starbucks Latte Really Make You Vote Liberal?" *The Globe and Mail,* November 14, 2010.

———. "Does the Tim Hortons Crowd Really Vote Tory?" *The Globe and Mail,* November 22, 2010.

Griffiths, Alison. "This Tim Hortons Franchise Hired 82 Disabled Workers." *The Hamilton Spectator*, June 11, 2012.

Ha, Tu Thanh. "Nova Scotia Hospitals Ban Tim Hortons Doughnuts." *Globe and Mail* Update, May 20, 2011.

Helliker, Kevin. "Dunkin' Donuts Heads Back to Russia." *Wall Street Journal,* April 27, 2010.

Hughes, Tracy. "A Simple Way to Shop Local." *Salmon Arm Observer,* October 12, 2011.

Hutton, David. "Tim Hortons Drive-Thru Jams Trouble Saskatoon." *Calgary Herald,* March 9, 2012.

Kelly, Kaitlin. "Tim Hortons Wins Fans in Big Apple." *Toronto Star,* July 14, 2009.

Kelso, Alicia. "Coffee Chains Ramp Up Cup Recycling Efforts." QSRweb.com, September 21, 2011. http://www.qsrweb.com/article/184847/Coffee-chains-ramp-up-cup-recycling-efforts.

———. "Survey: Dunkin' Donuts Coffee Fans Are the Most Loyal." QSRweb.com, February 10, 2012. http://www.qsrweb.com/article/190303/Survey-Dunkin-Donuts-coffee-fans-are-the-most-loyal.

Kosman, Josh. "Just a 'Wee' Change: 'Bucks Shuts Loos." *New York Post,* November 16, 2011.

Kosman, Josh, and Holly Sanders Ware. "Dunkin's Brouhaha: Donut Shop Franchisees Frying over Lost Dough." *New York Post,* July 23, 2009.

Kramer, Louise. "Wendy's Importing Tim Hortons to U.S.: Canadian Baked-Goods Chain Needs to Build Identity Here." *Advertising Age,* September 29, 1997.

Lee, Lisa, and Timothy Sifert. "Dunkin's Financial Story Still Has Holes." Reuters Breakingviews, November 16, 2010.

Leung, Wency. "Avoid the Venti: Some Starbucks Closing Toilets to Customers." *Globe and Mail* blog, November 16, 2011.

Libin, Kevin, and David Menzies. "In the Hole: AR Plan at Country Style Doughnuts Has Some Feeling Fried." *Canadian Business* 75:6 (April 1, 2002): 58–64.

Lieber, Ron. "Tim Hortons Arrives in Bits and Pieces." *The New York Times,* July 14, 2009.

Los Angeles Times. "Possible Bid for Dunkin' Donuts." May 12, 1989.

Lunn, Susan. "A Tale of Two Timmies." *Inside Politics* (CBC), April 4, 2011.

Maclean's. "A 'Tim Hortons Prime Minister' Hits the Golf Course." August 8, 2011. http://www2.macleans.ca/2011/08/08/a-tim-hortons-prime-minister-hits-the-golf-course.

McGeehan, Patrick. "The Morning Doughnut? The Choices Are Getting Complicated." *The New York Times,* July 9, 2009.

McGinn, Dave. "Goodbye, Timbits: Should Junk Food Be Banned in Hospitals?" *Globe and Mail* Update, May 20, 2011.

McNeil, Mark. "Flashback: Nov. 25, 1985. The First Tim Hortons Drive-Thru Opened, at Upper Gage and Fennell in Hamilton, on This Day 26 Years Ago." *The Hamilton Spectator,* November 25, 2011.

Metro. "Decision Ontario (Video): *Metro* Speaks with the Conservatives' Tim Hudak." October 2, 2011. http://metronews.ca/news/219570/decision-ontario-video-metro-speaks-with-the-conservatives-tim-hudak/.

Miller, Talea. "Obesity Rates Rising Worldwide, Half of U.S. Could Be Obese by 2030." *The Rundown News* blog, *PBS NewsHour,* August 25, 2011.

Milstead, David. "Dunkin' for Dollars in a Red-Hot Java Market." *The Globe and Mail,* July 25, 2011.

Moore, Michael. "Fast Food's Industry 50% Growth Rate Expected to Level at 12%." *The Globe and Mail,* February 24, 1970.

———. "Pace Slowing As Fast Food Meets Snags." *The Globe and Mail,* August 5, 1970.

———. "Supermarkets Can Be Major Factor As Burger Giants Battle to Keep Growing." *The Globe and Mail,* August 6, 1970.

Nation's Restaurant News. "Dunkin' Sues Riese Org. in Bid to End Franchise." June 2, 2003.

Nuttall-Smith, Chris. "McDonald's? Tim Hortons? Who Makes the Best Brew?" *The Globe and Mail,* November 8, 2011.

Powell, Betsy. "Man Says He Sold Coffee, Not Crack." *Toronto Star,* January 12, 2008.

Pompeo, Joe. "Food Court Press." *New York Observer,* September 15, 2009.

Pugh, Terry. "Business Booming As Tim Hortons Franchise Opens in Warman." *Clark's Crossing Gazette,* September 7, 2011.

Olive, David. "A Legend Grows Stale." *Toronto Star,* August 20, 2004.

Olshan, Jeremy. "Doughnut Wars! Hortons Horns In on NYC Dunkin's." *New York Post,* July 10, 2009.

Osoyoos Times. "Offshore Labour Being Used to Fill Empty Shifts." October 14, 2011.

Ransom, Jan. "Dunkin' Donuts Officially Departs Penn Station to Make Way for Canadian Chain Tim Hortons." *New York Daily News,* July 11, 2009.

Robertson, Grant. "Meet John Bitove." *The Globe and Mail,* March 28, 2008.

Romaniuk, Ross. "Rejig at Robin's Donuts." *Winnipeg Sun*, August 17, 2004.

Rose, Marla Matzer. "New Tim Hortons to Open at Nationwide." *The Columbus Dispatch*, August 6, 2011.

Ross, Jim. "Let the Doughnut Wars Begin." *The New York Times,* July 9, 2009.

Rubin, Josh. "Tim Hortons Brews Up Deal with Jays." *Toronto Star,* August 23, 2011.

Sain, Andrew. "Third Tim Horton's Location Opens in Engineering Building." *The Manitoban* 93:15 (November 30, 2005).

Shaw, Hollie. "Latte Wars Steaming Up." *Financial Post,* November 25, 2011.

Shea, Courtney. "Andrea Horwath: The Anti-Hudak." *The Grid TO,* September 21, 2011. http://www.thegridto.com/city/people/andrea-horwath-the-anti-hudak.

Simpson, Jeffrey. "Tim Hortons Signs Beckoning Fans in Jolly Old England." *Toronto Star,* March 7, 2011.

Smith, Michelle (Associated Press). "Tim Hortons Closes All Southern New England Stores." *The Herald News,* November 11, 2010.

Starbucks Gossip. "Should Starbucks Cover Power Outlets When 'Computer-Parking' Gets Out of Hand?" August 3, 2011. http://starbucksgossip.typepad.com/_/2011/08/should-starbucks-stores-cover-power-outlets-when-computer-parking-gets-out-of-hand.html.

Strauss, Marina. "Future of Tim Hortons' Baking System Uncertain." *Globe and Mail* Update, May 20, 2010.

Sun Journal. "L-A Tim Hortons Locations Will Stay Open As Chain Closing 36 Stores in NE." November 12, 2010.

Taber, Jane. "A Double-Double, Compliments of the Maple Leafs." *The Globe and Mail,* July 5, 2011.

———. "Harper Spins a New Brand of Patriotism." *The Globe and Mail,* August 19, 2011.

Thomson, Aly. "Drive-Thru Ban Considered." *Metro Halifax,* September 22, 2011.

Time. "Advertising: Dollars for Doughnuts." November 11, 1940.

WBNS-10TV. "Popular Coffee Shop Hires Ex-Cons." Columbus, Ohio, May 2, 2012.

Weiser, Benjamin. "Dunkin' Donuts Sues Shop Owner over Mice." *The New York Times,* January 5, 1999.

Willis, Andrew. "Trouble in the Kitchen at Tim Hortons." *Globe and Mail* Update, May 14, 2010.

Willis, Donna. "Dunkin Donuts Evicted from Broad & High Building." nbc4i.com, Columbus, Ohio, August 6, 2011.

Wolf, Barney. "Rolling in Dough." *QSR*, September 2010. http://www.qsrmagazine.com/menu-innovations/rolling-dough.

York, Emily Bryson. "Rivals Try to Loosen Keurig's Grip on Single-Serve Coffee Market." *Chicago Tribune,* February 26, 2011.

Legal Cases

Bertico Inc. et al v. Dunkin' Brands Canada Ltd., 2012 CanLII 2809 (QCCS)

Fairview Donut Inc. v. The TDL Group Corp., 2012 ONSC 1252

Horton v. Joyce (February 1, 1993), Toronto Court File No. 24555/87 (Ont. C.J. (Gen. Div))

Horton v. Joyce, 1994 CanLII 1373 (ON CA)

Horton v. Ronald Joyce, 1994 CanLII 2545 (ON CA)

Horton v. Tim Donut Ltd., 1997 CanLII 12372 (ON SC)

Jirna v. Mister Donut of Canada, [1975] 1 S.C.R. 2 1973–10–29

Murray v. TDL Group Ltd., 2002 CanLII 23609 (ON SC)

TDL Group (The) v. Zabco Holdings Inc. et al, 2007 MBQB 303 (CanLII)

Legislative Proceedings

House of Commons Canada, Standing Committee on Health. HESA, Number 017, 1st Session, 39th Parliament. Evidence, Thursday, September 28, 2006.

Legislative Assembly of Ontario. Committee Transcripts: Standing Committee on Regulations and Private Bills. Bill 33, Franchise Disclosure Act, 1999.

Index